D0630665

JOURNAL FOR THE STUDY OF THE OLD TESTAMENT SUPPLEMENT SERIES
101

Editors
David J A Clines
Philip R Davies

JSOT Press
Sheffield

The
CHRONICLER
in
HIS AGE

Peter R. Ackroyd

Journal for the Study of the Old Testament
Supplement Series 101

Copyright © 1991 Sheffield Academic Press

Published by JSOT Press
JSOT Press is an imprint of
Sheffield Academic Press Ltd
The University of Sheffield
343 Fulwood Road
Sheffield S10 3BP
England

Typeset by Sheffield Academic Press
and
Printed on acid-free paper in Great Britain
by Billing & Sons Ltd
Worcester

British Library Cataloguing in Publication Data

Ackroyd, Peter R. (Peter Runham) *1917–*
    The Chronicler in his age.
    1. Bible. O.T. Chronicles - Critical studies
    I. Title   II. Series
    222.606

    ISSN 0309-0787
    ISBN 1-85075-254-0

CONTENTS

PREFACE

The first volume of my essays, conveniently gathered under the title *Studies in the Religious Tradition of the Old Testament*, was published by the SCM Press in 1987. This second collection, anticipated in some measure in the earlier one, concentrates attention on the post-exilic period, and it gathers conveniently around 'the Chronicler', a title used for the figure or figures lying behind both the books of Chronicles and the books of Ezra and Nehemiah. Opinions differ about matters of authorship, and my own position has become much less certain than it once was. The essays on these various but interrelated subjects are printed as they were first published, or, in certain cases, since they have not been previously set in print, as they were written, with varying amounts of reference and bibliographical accompaniment. The reader who wishes to, will know where to find more recent discussions, especially in the main Journals and the book lists of the Society for Old Testament Study.

I am grateful to Professor David Clines for his willingness to publish these studies at the Sheffield Academic Press, and to the staff of the Press for their patience and help. I must also express my thanks to Dr Robert Carroll of the University of Glasgow for his continual encouragement.

Peter R. Ackroyd
November 1990

Chapter 1

THE AGE OF THE CHRONICLER[1]

1. *Political and Social Aspects*
of the Life of the Jewish Community

The title 'The Age of the Chronicler' is designed to offer a convenient but not too strict designation of that period—from the rebuilding of the temple c. 515 BCE to the time of Alexander the Great—for which our primary biblical source is to be found in the last part of the Chronicler's work, viz. Ezra 7–10 and Nehemiah. The precise date of his activity is uncertain, and it must also be in some measure an open question whether we are concerned with a coherent work or one which has come into being as a result of a gradual process of revision and extension of earlier forms of the material now to be found in 1–2 Chronicles and Ezra–Nehemiah. Clearly one earlier form is known to us in Samuel–Kings. The possibility that the revision which is found in the work of the Chronicler depends upon a text different from that which we have as the Masoretic Text for those books is strongly suggested both from Septuagint and Qumran evidence. The possibility that the Chronicler's work represents a selection from earlier forms of the material—a selection with concentration upon the true community centred upon Jerusalem and Judah, its nature and composition—must certainly be entertained, especially if we observe that we have yet another such selection in 1 Esdras which is probably better so described than as a mere fragment of the longer work. (A quite different selection is to be found in the Samaritan text, Samaritan Chronicle II.) The selection

---

1. Reprinted from the author's essay *The Age of the Chronicler.* Supplement to *Colloquium—The Australian and New Zealand Theological Review* (Auckland, N.Z., 1970).

found in the Chronicler's work has been given a larger setting by the use of a mass of genealogical material as preface and for expansion purposes, material which itself clearly has a long pre-history.

The earlier Deuteronomic History offered a presentation and interpretation of the experience of the community leading up to the exile, and, probably from a vantage point within the exilic age, envisaged only with the utmost tentativeness the possibilities of restoration (cf. Ackroyd 1968a, ch. 5). The Chronicler was also deeply concerned with a theology of the exile—a matter to which we shall return; but he was able to view it from a longer perspective. The final stages of this work may well belong to a much later age, perhaps even to the second century BCE; but it is clear that the major stage in its evolution belongs to that moment after the activity of Nehemiah and Ezra when reflection on their achievements was possible. The consideration of their chronology has been largely left on one side, not because the issues are unimportant but because the ground has been so often covered that it appears more profitable here to consider other matters. Nehemiah is assumed to belong to the mid-fifth century; Ezra to belong to the opening of the fourth century. Much of what is said would apply equally if other dates were regarded as more satisfactorily demonstrated, though the relationship between the two men would need to be differently defined. If this now widely accepted date of 398 BCE is assumed for Ezra, who then follows Nehemiah at a distance of about four decades, the writing up of the account is likely to follow long enough after for there to be time for reflection and an interpretation which places materials in theological rather than merely chronological order. But since it is not possible to see any reflection of the fall of the Persian power to Alexander the Great, we may suppose that the date lies before, say, 335 BCE.

A caution must, however, be entered in regard to this point. The fact that we are unable to detect any indication in the writings of the Chronicler of the change of rule brought about by the conquests of Alexander the Great is one of those pieces of negative evidence which so often fail to satisfy. One may argue that the Chronicler's favourable comments on the activities of Persian rulers would make it all the more strange that he should have failed to indicate that all this lay in the past if in fact he was working after 330 BCE. But the argument is not entirely convincing. He could be interpreting a now complete stage of the community's experience with a view to offering encouragement or warning to a later generation which viewed its own situation in too gloomy a light, which was without that faith which is here traced, under Persian rule, as enabling the re-establishment of community life. The negative is, after all, only one example of an almost total non-relationship between the biblical evidence and the precise historical information available for the whole period of Persian rule.

In using the designation of 'the Chronicler' as one for the whole period, a certain assumption of his centrality is being made, and this must be corrected in so far as we can detect something of the wider range and variety of thought and of interpretation in the literature which may reasonably, even if not certainly, be assigned to this period. Yet there is some validity in giving him the central place. Other materials can only tentatively be dated in the period; in a number of cases there is a very wide divergence of opinion about them. Ruth and Jonah, probably; Zechariah 9–14, perhaps; the book of Job, surely, unless we are persuaded of a closer literary and theological affinity with the Second Isaiah and take its date back to the sixth century; Joel, a case for virtually unending debate; the Priestly Work, very likely; Malachi, to the earlier end, but with a recognition of the indeterminate nature of the evidence. And to these we may add, with considerable hesitation, Esther and Judith and perhaps elements in the Daniel tradition; and more surely Samaritan origins, and the sidelights into the Jewish military post at Elephantine.

But none of these is an attempt at a coherent statement about the total position of the Jewish community in these years. Without the interpretation offered by the Chronicler, we should have even less evidence with which to engage in the task of dating writings which offer no precise indications of the moment to which they belong.

To anyone who comes over from the study of the classical world into that of Palestine, the virtually complete lack of correlation between biblical evidence and the tremendous series of events which took place during Persian rule must be astonishing. How could the Jewish community have lived through a period when the conflict between Persia and Greece was at its height and have produced a biblical literature which so completely ignores what was happening? It need not surprise us that there have been biblical scholars who have sought to remedy the deficiency. Morgenstern, in a series of articles, built up a complete picture of the impact upon biblical writings of an unattested revolt and destruction of Jerusalem in 485 BCE—a moment of tension, as Xerxes I began to establish himself on the throne. Upheavals in the mid-fourth century BCE attracted Oesterley as an occasion for explaining particular texts. The advance and victories of Alexander have been sought in obscure prophetic oracles such as are to be found in Zechariah 9–14 and in Ezekiel. At another extreme, Buttenweiser was able to write quite a considerable history of the period by dating in it psalms which could then be used to provide information about otherwise unattested events.

That these attempts are largely discounted should not conceal the dilemma which they reflect. From this so important period of Jewish development, a period to which Jewish tradition assigns the evolution of its scriptures in their more definitive form, and the origin of that style of interpretation of the law which was to be so determinative; a period which begins with the vital moment of the rededicated temple, and then, after obscurity for two centuries or more, re-emerges as the period of party strife, religious tension, persecution, of the second century—surely something must remain to show the impact of major events?

The problem is not solved, but it is somewhat illuminated, by the recognition that by this time the degree of stylization in presenting events and their interpretation is such that relatively straight narrative accounts and direct historical allusions have tended to become very much rarer. The patterning of events to conform them to known experience is a marked feature of Old Testament literature. The experience of the Exodus tends to dominate many passages which describe events which can be seen to conform to that pattern. The captivity of exile is to become an equally potent expression of an experience which is not just that of a historic moment, but of a continuing state; this is of particular importance for the post-exilic period. The more elaborate symbolism of later apocalyptic is itself an expression of stylizing of events; they are often no longer described, but only alluded to in such ways as suggest their relationship to larger patterns of thought. The heroes of the Maccabaean age are not given a simple factual description; they are portrayed in part at least in accordance with a tradition. Both 1 and 2 Maccabees subordinate events to interpretation. Such stylizing is of particular interest and importance in the complex presentation of Nehemiah and Ezra. An age which had inherited a great wealth of psalmody and prophecy was able to project its experience into the use of this, in part no doubt by actual modification and reapplication— and sometimes this may be detected, though with caution. Even more, it was able to read the older material in the light of its own experience and needs; what it used was illuminated by the contemporary scene. The older stories, the already existing longer narrative and legal documents, which in their earlier use had been given a strongly theological turn, could now be read as wise tales, didactic narratives, parables for the times, examples for the edification of the faithful. The emphasis was moving from 'This is what happened and it demonstrates—as homily can show—the working of the divine will' to 'These things happened to them as a warning, but they were written down for our instruction' (1 Cor. 10.11).

The effect of these considerations upon our study of the Persian period is to make us realize that we must be very cautious of trying to indicate a direct cross-reference from extra-biblical events to those which can be detected or described within the biblical record. But on the more positive side, it demands two things: (i) We must, by a sufficient knowledge of the wider background, be sensitive to the kind of needs which are likely to have been felt by the Jewish community. Granted such a political and social situation as we can discern, we can properly ask how the life of one particular community, centred on Jerusalem and Judah but belonging also to many other areas, would appear to itself, what problems it would face, what pressures it would be bearing. (ii) We may also, where the biblical evidence provides a sufficiently clear indication of chronology, ask whether it is possible for us to detect, in what is known to us of the wider setting, some features which help to explain aspects of the behaviour and thought of the Jewish community. This latter must quite evidently be very tentative. Thus, when it can be shown, after a sufficient consideration of the biblical and extra-biblical evidence, that the dating of Nehemiah to the mid-fifth century BCE is secure—reign of Artaxerxes I, period of Sanballat as governor of Samaria—then we may ask whether, in the political history of that moment, there is anything which would shed light on the appointment of this man to take action in Jerusalem and Judah.

The larger aspect of this can be expressed quite simply in terms of the question: What must the community be if it is to be true to its ancestral faith and tradition when it finds itself quite evidently on a more permanent basis under the aegis of an imperial power? How can a subject people be the people of God? To this type of question, there may be two main types of answer. Some may immediately resist the premise of 'being a subject people', and so we may expect to find indications of nationalist pressure, movements to rebellion, claims for independence. It was not in a political vacuum that the enemies of Nehemiah could suggest that he was perhaps thinking of setting himself up as a king (Neh. 6.6-7) The subsequent history of Judah under Greek and Roman rule is shot through with attempts expressive of this view, and it would be absurd to suppose that it was not attractive to some in the Persian period. Others in the community, accepting the political position, or regarding it as essentially irrelevant, will be concerned rather with the problems of conflict between political demand and religious faithfulness. The effecting of a compromise—not necessarily to be seen as a bad word—demands a continuous sensitivity to what is right and proper, as well as to what is possible. If, from our vantage point, we may be inclined to view the Chronicler as too complacent, too quietistic, too conscious of the benevolence of Persian rule, we should recognize the difficulty of equating one situation with another, and ask whether, given the situation of the reign of Antiochus IV Epiphanes, the Chronicler would—in the light of his particular presuppositions—have stood with the resistance movement or with the apostates, or whether perhaps he would have been with neither but rather more closely with those who, like the author of the book of Daniel, saw no great promise in the activities of a resistance movement, but great hope in the reality of faith and obedience expressed in martyrdom. It is not my purpose to try to answer this particular question, though it is my hope that what is said in these studies about the theology of the Chronicler will enable us to approach a judgment of the kind of stand this particular man and his circle were prepared to make.

What has already been said makes it clear that if we cannot enter upon a full account of the political and international history of the Persian period, this is not entirely a loss. The detail of Persian politics, the complexity of the international situation, are matters which can at some points be traced in great detail; they belong to a necessary background knowledge, but neither can nor need be taken up fully in this context. What is important is some general comment upon the situation, as it fluctuated during nearly two centuries of Persian rule.

On the one hand there is the long-drawn-out struggle between Persia and Greece, beginning with the campaigns of Darius I, followed up by Xerxes' disastrous expedition across the Hellespont and his defeat at Salamis. The problem of the Greek cities in Asia remained a source of conflict through succeeding years. Greek mercenaries were concerned with the establishment of Artaxerxes II on the throne. The final climax came in Alexander the Great's reversal of the campaign of Xerxes, and in his series of rapid advances in which he overthrew the whole Persian empire and established the Greek rule which, in divided form, was to last for about two centuries and was to have considerable influence on Jewish history. The biblical record does not refer to these struggles directly at all, but that they had an influence on Jewish life must be evident from the indications of the burden of taxation which was inevitable with such long-drawn-out and substantial military campaigns.

On the other hand there was the continual Persian concern with Egypt. Conquest in the period of Cambyses and Darius I was followed in the fifth century by rebellion at the beginning of the reign of Xerxes. The fact that Xerxes' Greek campaign followed so soon after shows how speedily it was dealt with, for security in this area would be essential to so major a campaign into Europe. Rebellions in various areas in the early years of Artaxerxes I involved Egypt, with an attempt at a take-over from Libya. Greek support made this seem a possible manoeuvre, but the Egyptians themselves appear not to have welcomed it, and in due course order was restored. A major collapse of Persian rule in Egypt came at the end of the fifth century, when a rebel Amyrtaeus established himself for five years in the Delta region (405–400; cf. the Elephantine papyri for dating by this ruler), and from then on Egypt became independent until just before the final conquest of Persia by Alexander the Great when first Artaxerxes III Ochus and then Darius III were able to regain control briefly. Again, no direct indication appears in the biblical material.

These larger political insecurities provide a general background. More specific relationship with the biblical history ought surely to be discoverable in regard to the events which took place within the area of the satrapy Beyond the River, that to which the whole of Palestine belonged. The rebellion of the satrap Megabyzus c. 450 BCE was much nearer home; it appears to have ended in reconciliation and the re-establishment of the satrap in his position, but the situation must have been one of great delicacy in the western part of the empire. Where did the Jewish community stand in this? Can we trace some relationship between these events and those which led up to the commissioning of Nehemiah who is to be placed, as we have noted, in the following years? To what moment and to what political necessity does Ezra belong? Is he, placed at 458 BCE, to be understood in relation to the insecurities of the early years of the reign of Artaxerxes I? Does he perhaps belong towards the end of that reign, at a time when perhaps power was weakening, as it was to be found weak when Darius II came to the throne in 424? Or does he, as so many have concluded, and I believe rightly, belong to an attempt at improving security in the early years of Artaxerxes II, shortly after 400 BCE when that ruler had at last succeeded in establishing himself more firmly but Egypt was lost? These are questions in which the biblical evidence provides us only with certain aspects of the whole picture; the interpretation of biblical evidence in terms which are relevant to the understanding of Persian politics must be undertaken with great caution, though it is proper to recognize that such an interpretation is *prima facie* likely.

Beyond the likely dates for biblical events known to us are the upheavals of the mid-fourth century BCE, though here is a point which may be relevant to the consideration of the Chronicler's position. In the reign of Artaxerxes III Ochus (359–339) there was rebellion in the Palestinian area and campaigns to subdue the rebels. Action again Phoenicia in 346 is attested. An examination of archaeological evidence at various Palestinian sites has suggested the possibility that destruction indications at these could belong to about the same period. Diodorus Siculus (first century BCE) has information about some of the detail of this period; later traditions, found for example in Eusebius, know of an exiling of Jews to the region of the Caspian Sea, but the evidence both there and elsewhere is by no means clear. The assigning of particular biblical passages to this situation has been attempted; but it must be acknowledged that the evidence is very slender. If, on other grounds, it is thought right to assign the main composition of the Chronicler's work to such a period of emergency, then his quietism could be seen to stand out in even stronger contrast to probable encouragements to insurgence among his contemporaries. But the supposition can be no more than that, and it is unsatisfactory to base conclusions on so slender a foundation.

The general and more specific indications of political insecurity provide a background to any attempt at interpreting the internal history of the Jewish community in this period. At certain points—in particular in regard to the activity of Nehemiah and Ezra—we may reasonably look for more precise background, by way of understanding both the reasons for Persian policy and the needs of the Jewish community. It must, of course, be recognized that the possibility of purely chance factors in the situation cannot be excluded; Nehemiah may have been sent to Jerusalem because he was a royal favourite, or for any number of other hypothetical personal reasons. It is, however, much more likely that the Persian king's action was in some measure connected with the general lines of government policy. The provision of military support and of instructions to Persian administrators in the Palestinian area argues for a more deliberate working out of policy than merely arbitrary action; even if it began in a show of personal favour, we may see it as being carried through in an atmosphere of political calculation.

The more general indications of the political situation need to be further supported by a consideration of the organizational side of Persian rule. Allusion has already been made to the burden of imperial taxation. Neh. 5.4 points to the mortgaging of property by some members of the Jewish community to raise the necessary money for the royal taxes. This incidental reference, part of a more general reflection on the economic problems of the people in the period of Nehemiah—and used to show the justice and probity of Nehemiah's own conduct—suggests what otherwise appears in the indications of the level of taxation imposed. Imperial taxes and external burdens, in addition to the more immediate demands and on top of an inevitably somewhat precarious economy, were to provide a cause of discontent and of rebellion through the Greek and Roman periods. To have this kind of burden, in addition to being a subject people with all that involved of emotional distress, could not fail to produce a situation of continuing tension. It is true that for the average Judaean peasant a life which was always relatively hard could barely seem more so; but urban life, close as it was to the land, would feel the stresses more considerably. For the imperial authorities, the keeping of control, the exercising of a duly balanced policy of conciliation and subjection, was always a delicate matter. There must always have been sufficient of local discontent for any more major upheaval to find repercussions in many parts of the empire. For the Jewish community, being a subject people—as again we may detect when we consider the comparable situation in the New Testament era—was equally a matter of delicacy. Changes of policy, the advent of a new governor, personal and political involvements, must make for a continually fluid situation. To the opponents of Nehemiah and of Ezra—the latter much less attested than the former—the concerns were real and the dangers evident.

a. *A Subject People*
The more general effects of being under the control of the imperial power of Persia have been briefly indicated. Some

further comments need to be made upon more particular aspects of the Judaean situation, in so far as this can be detected in the available evidence.

Here one of the major questions concerns the status of the various known officials who were involved in the life of Judah during the years of Persian rule, and their relationship, if it can be established, to their neighbours. Albrecht Alt argued some years ago (1934), in an essay on 'The Role of Samaria in the Establishment of Judaism', that many of the problems of understanding the Judaean situation could be resolved if it were assumed that both Babylonian and Persian authorities established the governor at Samaria as controller of the larger area including the main part of what had been the kingdom of Judah. After the fall of the city in 587 BCE, the position of Gedaliah could be interpreted either as that of a governor directly under Babylon or as that of a commissioner whose function was to carry out Babylonian policy for the rehabilitation of the Judaean community and its control under the aegis of the authorities in Samaria. Certainly after the assassination of Gedaliah there is no indication of another governor or officer acting in this capacity, and the assumption of control from Samaria is at this point at least very reasonable. It must be recognized that the argument is from silence. But when we move on into the post-exilic period, while again much of the argument is from silence, the position becomes more readily understandable on the assumption that Samaria was the centre of control. The non-mention of governors in Judah, while it could be due to the particular tendencies of the Chronicler in his account of the period, is more natural if we may assume that they did not exist. Furthermore, the difficulties met with at various points by the Judaean community find a ready explanation—in part at least—on the assumption that the governor in Samaria had no desire to see his authority threatened by the redevelopment of the economically important but rivalling position of Jerusalem and Judah. The relative ineffectiveness of Sheshbazzar, the difficulties confronting the community at the time of the rebuilding of the temple under Zerubbabel and Joshua, the disappearance of Zerubbabel before the completion of the temple (though this may have a more simple explanation in the expiry of the term of years for which he was appointed as commissioner), would all find reasonable explanation on the assumption that at such a distance from the centre of government control, the governor in Samaria could act with some freedom. Only when a specific directive from Darius I supported the activities at Jerusalem was the work there completed without further opposition. There are many obscurities and uncertainties in this period; some of them are discussed in the relevant sections of my *Exile and Restoration*.

For the years following on this, the evidence is again lacking in clarity but capable of explanation on a similar basis. Malachi 1.8 refers to the consequences of treating the 'governor' (*peḥâ*) in the way that worshippers are treating God; if he is offered poor-quality gifts, will those who approach him—presumably in the endeavour to obtain satisfactory results to legal cases—find that he is inclined to 'accept them' or to show them partiality? But the term *peḥâ* is used so loosely that we cannot definitely conclude that this indicates the actual presence in Judah of a governor in charge of Judah as a separate administrative area; at the same time this cannot be ruled out. If we knew for certain to what date the Malachi passage is to be assigned, we should be better able to make some statement about the position at a given moment; but even so, we could not rule out the possibility that the reference is either to a special commissioner or to the governor in Samaria. The absence of mention of a governor in Jerusalem at the time of Nehemiah's arrival is another example of argument from silence. Neh. 5.14-15 makes important reference to the normal dues appropriate to the governor's position and thus indicates a well-established procedure; Nehemiah claims that he and his associates have not made use of this privilege. It also contrasts the practice of Nehemiah with that of previous governors who acted in such a way as to be a burden to the community, and whose subordinates had acted tyrannically. How much can we deduce from this? Granted the propagandist tendency of the Nehemiah material (cf. §2b below), can we be sure that it is right to deduce so sharp a contrast? The modern analogy of political life in which those in power contrast their own moderation with the excesses of their predecessors should warn us against accepting everything that is said here at its face value.

But clearly the passage indicates the existence of previous governors. Again the use of the word *peḥâ* leaves the question in some measure open, and it does not exclude the possibility that there is a reference to the governors in Samaria rather than to such officers in Judah. The issue is at this point further complicated by the references to the governors of other neighbouring areas; the opponents of Nehemiah are indicated not simply as the governor in Samaria, Sanballat, but also the royal officer (*'ebed* used quite properly in its technical sense but no doubt intended to carry the overtone of 'slave') Tobiah in Ammon, and Geshem the Arab. Were these two, as seems very likely, the governors of two other neighbouring administrative areas, controllers respectively of the two adjacent to Judah, and is it possible to suppose that in the years prior to this the area which was eventually to be defined more strictly as the administrative area of Yehud had been divided up for control between these neighbouring sub-sections of the satrapy Beyond the River? (It is worth observing that although only these three are mentioned, there is particular reference also to Ashdod, the remaining area contiguous with Judah on the west, in the material against foreign marriages in Neh. 13.23-24. The mention there also of Moab is perhaps best to be understood as coming in alongside Ammon in view of the dependence of Neh. 13.1-3 on Deut. 23.3ff.)

The evidence at this point is far from clear. The appointment of Nehemiah for a term of years where, so far as we may judge, Sanballat in Samaria was governor by family inheritance and was subsequently to be succeeded by his sons and then by the continuing family line suggested by the evidence of the Samaria papyri, would seem to imply that even now the position of Judah had not been fully resolved. At the end of the fifth century, the Elephantine papyri provide evidence of a governor Bagoas (Bigvai) in Judah to whom appeal is made alongside that to Samaria. The coinage evidence from the fourth century—coins with the title Yehud indicating the grant of a right to mint coins for the area—now shows the measure of independent action accorded to Judah. Still later evidence shows that Judah was treated as a separate entity. But we are left with the marginal period, during the fifth century, in which the changeover was evidently made. Alt was persuaded that the change was made with Nehemiah; but this is by no means certain, and the terminal limitation of his office suggests rather that the problem was not resolved so neatly. Should we perhaps see here an example of a politician's process of *solvitur ambulando*? The authority of the governor of Samaria (and of other neighbouring governors) could hardly be whittled down without some risk of repercussions. The need for the re-establishment of Jerusalem and Judah was, however, important—and the personal factors in Nehemiah's appointment must not be overlooked here; a contented Judaean community could be a valuable asset to Persia in the west. The wording of the protest to Artaxerxes preserved in Ezra 4.11-16 is relevant here; the protest appeals to the history of Jerusalem, well known to be a rebellious city which had to be destroyed because of its activities; in that particular instance the protest was effective, but its emphasis could very easily operate in a reverse direction. For if Jerusalem was potentially so dangerous, it could equally be argued that it was potentially of special importance, that its tendency to rebellion should be met with conciliation. The relationship between the curious fragment of Ezra 4.7-23 and the commissioning of Nehemiah is not clear, but it has often been supposed that the record of an attempt at building the walls and its forcible interruption by the government authorities in Samaria would provide a very appropriate moment for an appeal to be sent to Nehemiah to see whether some more favourable action could be taken. Nehemiah's appeal on the basis of the distressed condition of Jerusalem would provide the obverse of the complainants' protest at its rebellious proclivities.

The situation—from the Persian point of view—was a delicate one. As we have seen, the Egyptian uncertainty was virtually always with the Persians. Security and contentment in Palestine were a matter of importance. In the mid-fourth century, it was to be an area of major upheaval; in the mid-fifth century the satrapy Beyond the River had already been a centre of rebellion for a short period. In such a situation, the direct action of separating the area of Judah and making it a separate administrative unit could provoke undesirable results; on the other hand, failure to do anything about Judah could equally prove unfortunate. Samaria, as Alt points out, could claim a historical precedent for continuing control over Judah; Judah equally, looking back to Josiah and to David, could claim rights over the whole area. What better than to compromise, to leave the political situation nominally the same, but by the appointment of Nehemiah for a term of years to effect a measure of conciliation with the Jewish community? Provided this worked—and on the whole, in spite of the difficulties it raised, it seems to have done so—the final solution of the administrative questions could wait. If we had more information, we might know precisely how this was done. A possible answer might be that the more definitive division of Judah into a separate area took place as Sanballat reached old age and was at first virtually and then fully replaced by his sons. But other factors could have intervened, and it could be that Artaxerxes I's successor, Darius II, was prepared to take more direct action than his father had done.

The absence of any reference to a governor in the Ezra narrative poses further problems. The conventional dating of Ezra has here some support in that such a non-mention could fit well with the situation before Nehemiah when there was as yet no thought of an independent governor of Judah. But more important would seem to be the consideration of the whole attitude of the Chronicler to the development of the history. He is writing a religious history, not a political. The position of Ezra is his central interest in the development of the religious community. One of the objections often raised to the dating of Ezra in 398 BCE is that he appears to be closely associated with John (Jehohanan), son or grandson of Eliashib, and probably though not certainly to be identified with the chief priest of whom Josephus tells a story of how he murdered his brother in the temple (*Ant.* 11.7.1). The appearance here of one Bagoses, 'general in Artaxerxes' army', suggests an immediate association with the evidence of the Elephantine letters. But Josephus's story in fact lays the real responsibility on the murdered man, who was conspiring to get the high priesthood, and further indicates the imposition of a period of seven years of punishment of the Jews for the murder. Even if we were to give complete credence to Josephus's story—and there must be some considerable doubt about its reliability in view of the way in which Josephus handles this period of history—the position of Ezra is intelligible. That nothing of this appears in the biblical record could imply that there was something to cover up; more probably we should simply recognize that to the Chronicler it was irrelevant.

The precise position of Judah politically thus remains uncertain, though we may trace a development from a position of probable subordination to the governor of Samaria to one of much greater independence of action in the fourth century. The possibility exists that the commissioning of Ezra is an important stage in this development; the nature of his commission, the extent of his powers to regard as members of the Jewish community all within the satrapy Beyond the River who accepted the law, must be subjects of later comment. This could fit in well with the decision to make Judah into a more definitively separate administrative area and the granting of certain rights such as that of issuing coinage.

But what of the internal attitudes of a subject people? How far can we detect these in the literature of the period and in the traditions concerning this period which have come down to us in other places? There are some general points to be made, and some specific passages of biblical material which provide clues, sometimes more directly, but more often by presenting a picture of how the period was viewed by those who described it.

A general point can be made in regard to the Psalter. The process of its formation is obscure; the recognition that probably most of its contents belong in origin to the pre-exilic period does not preclude the probability of adaptation and re-interpretation (with or without adaptation) in the post-exilic period. The long-established description of the Psalter as the hymn book of the Second Temple is misleading, but nevertheless contains at least the truth that it was in association with the actual liturgical practice, and in reflection of the liturgical needs, of the post-exilic community, that the Psalter was shaped. By the second century BCE, its main form is likely to have been determined. At the earlier period of the Chronicler we have evidence in his use of psalm material—particularly in 1 Chronicles 16—of both a free handling of the psalms as reflected in current liturgical use and of the actual existence and use of particular psalms. In very general terms we may reflect that a community which in the process of time selected a psalter in which lamentations are particularly dominant is in a sense thereby proclaiming its recognition of its own condition of need; the fact that large place is also given to hymns and psalms of thanksgiving provides a measure of balance to this and reflects the confident faith of those who know that distress lies within the larger purpose of God. To look for precision of evidence here is unsatisfactory; to see something of the community's mood is possible.

We may go a stage further in the related preservation in narrative material of psalm and prayer forms. A particular example here is the prayer put into the mouth of Nehemiah in Neh. 1.5-11. It is more of a homily than either a psalm or a prayer, though the homiletic element is a not uncommon feature of prayer forms, providing a mechanism by which the offering of reflections upon the community's historic experience is both an extension of the motifs of appeal to God to act in accordance with the established patterns of his grace and a reminder to the congregation of what they ought to believe about a God who so acts and how they ought to respond in obedience to his demands. Prayer-forms in all ages, whether set or extempore, tend to contain these two elements. (The minister who illustrated an obscure point in his prayer: 'Lest this point should seem too obscure, O Lord, permit thy servant to illustrate it with an anecdote'—was, after all, only stepping over the boundary between homily and prayer in a somewhat more blatant form than is commonly done.) The prayer of Nehemiah 1 is concerned with present distress and its relationship to past failure; it is a reminder of divine warning of exile and of divine promise of restoration to Jerusalem. It conveys exactly the concern which we may observe generally in so many of the writings of the period, and most of all in the Chronicler. The exile is the right outcome of the people's failure; restoration depends on acceptance and response, but basically upon divine promise and grace.

Two prayers belonging to the Ezra tradition offer some further evidence. Of these the first, Ezra 9.6-15, provides a close parallel to the Nehemiah passage. It reflects on the disastrous situation through which the community has gone in exile and humiliation. It speaks of the momentary revelation of divine grace in the preservation and restoration of a remnant. The possibility of rehabilitation of the shrine, of protection for the holy community, is emphasized. This moment of grace has been answered by apostasy in the disobedience of the people to the Deuteronomic command to preserve itself free from pollution. It anticipates the possibility of inescapable and final wrath, the wiping out of the whole community in its sin. It asks for divine regard as it confesses guilt. But at two points the prayer—and whatever its origin or date it here purports to convey the community's sense of its own condition—appears to allude directly to the contemporary dilemma. 9.7 speaks of the disasters and humiliations—death, captivity, despoiling and 'shameful humiliation as at this present moment'. The sufferings are not simply those of the past; they reflect the contemporary sense of still being humiliated by foreign rule. It is only a hint, but it is followed up by the further emphasis in 9.9: 'We are slaves, but even in this condition of slavery our God has not abandoned us'—and the confidence is illustrated by a reference to the benevolence of the Persian ruler who has permitted restoration. It is as well to emphasize that, whether or not this prayer is an original part of the narrative—and it is so evidently apposite to its context that there seems no good reason to excise it or to attribute it to a later author—it reflects a view of the condition of Judah under Persia. With all that the Chronicler has to say about the benevolence of Persian rulers, and by implication about the propriety of submission to authority, he is under no illusions about the realities of contemporary humiliation, of its being a condition of slavery. It is a community in this state which is called upon to be obedient and responsive, sensitive to the reality of its position.

The other prayer is found in Nehemiah 9. MT ascribes the prayer to the Levites whose names are listed in vv. 4-5. The LXX adds an ascription of the prayer to Ezra at v. 6, thus subordinating the loud cry of appeal in v. 4 and the ascription of praise in v. 5 to the actual prayer associated with Ezra. In the context of the reading of the law in Nehemiah 8, such an ascription to Ezra is entirely natural. It does not in fact in any way affect the sense, since what Ezra the scribe, the exponent of law, says may be regarded as echoed and supported by the whole Levitical group. The main part of the prayer follows a familiar pattern, that of the historical review, directed primarily towards the praise of God and in this towards a reminder to him of the nature of his acts of deliverance of his people in the past. In itself, it is of considerable interest as reflecting a selection of motifs. Its concern with the Exodus in particular provides a complement to the main writings of the Chronicler for whom the Exodus is not emphasized as a primary moment, but whose work nevertheless carries the implication that this was one of the great stages of Israel's religious experience. The climax of the survey is found, after a stylized picturing of the period of settlement and monarchy, in the disaster of exile and the graciousness of God in his not rejecting them finally.

For our immediate purpose, however, the interest lies in the concluding verses of the prayer, vv. 32-37. It recalls the faithfulness of the covenant God, and appeals to him not to minimize the degree of the people's distress from Assyrian times 'even to the present moment' (v. 32). It acknowledges the rightness of divine judgment and the wrong action of the people and their refusal to heed divine warning. Even in the time of independence under the monarchy, they were unfaithful (vv. 34-35). And then the comment on the contemporary situation: 'Today, here we are as slaves; as for the land which you gave to our ancestors so that they could eat its fruits and its produce, here we are slaves in it. Most of its produce is for the kings whom you have set over us in our sins; they rule over our bodies, act as they please in regard to our beasts, and we are in great distress' (vv. 36-37). This is in the moment of Persian rule; this is under the rule of the king who has sent Ezra to establish the law. The prayer or psalm—for it is something of both—may or may not be original to its context; but it is doubtful if we have sufficient grounds for denying that this is how Persian rule looked to the members of the Jewish community. It was a moment of slavery; a moment of arbitrary action by their overlords; a moment of the burdens of taxation. Above all, the free occupation of the land of promise was no longer to be enjoyed; they were slaves in the land of freedom and deliverance. There is a poignancy in this statement which must not be overlooked.

Other possible sources of information are much less precise. Two narratives, that of Esther and that of Judith, are ostensibly set in the period of Persian rule. The date of origin of both these books is very much open to question. It is natural enough to see them, as some scholars would do, as reflections of the period of intense pressure on the Jewish community in the second century BCE. But, as with the narratives of the book of Daniel, the possibility (or, as with Daniel, the certainty) of a second-century date for the final presentation of the material does not alter the fact that these narratives are more likely to rest upon older traditions than to be pure invention; and if they do thus rest upon older traditions, then we must ask what kind of situation produced traditions which could be so rehandled in the second century. The narratives of Daniel do not describe the conditions of the Jewish community in Babylon in the sixth century BCE, but they do indicate that, in the centuries that followed, the view of Babylon as the great persecutor was becoming strongly felt. Daniel 6 has a historically confused tradition concerning Darius; that he has now been placed before Cyrus and has become the ruler of a supposed empire of the Medes between those of Babylon and Persia is of less consequence than that it associates with a Persian ruler an act of hostility to the Jewish community. As such it may be placed side by side with the tradition, also associated with the reign of Darius and found in 1 Esdras, by which Zerubbabel was appointed as royal commissioner to Judah as a result of a contest of wits at the imperial court. Here in these two narratives, we have two aspects of the tradition concerning Persia. On the one hand, there is the hostile aspect, the king who can be moved by his courtiers to take action against the faithful and pious Daniel. A historical parallel appears in the action of Artaxerxes against the rebuilding of Jerusalem when he is appealed to from Samaria, as this is indicated in Ezra 4.7-23. On the other hand, there is the benevolent aspect, the king who is moved to take action to re-establish Jerusalem and to send a favourite courtier to act as his deputy. The analogy with the Nehemiah tradition is very close; there are points of contact also with the Ezra tradition. This then is another aspect of the Persian period, as it has come down in the tradition.

In each case here, it is possible to show that there is resemblance between the portrayal of Persian policy in these probably relatively late traditions and those which may be regarded as deriving from a period closer to the actual events. We may also consider the evidence of Esther and Judith as shedding some light on the way the Persian period was regarded. In the former we have a court narrative—having some points of resemblance with the Nehemiah tradition—of how a member of the Jewish community who had come to be in a position of influence (and in the case of Esther an elaborate narrative demonstrates how this had come about), was able, at personal risk, to influence the Persian ruler to protect his Jewish subjects from unwarranted attack. In the third and second centuries BCE, there were occasions of attack of this kind in both Palestine and Egypt; in the fifth century, we have from the Elephantine papyri a picture of a small Jewish community under attack—for various reasons—from its Egyptian neighbour. This evidence of the book of Esther could suggest that eastern Jewry too was subject to pressures from the local population. That this has in Esther been magnified into a major onslaught is intelligible; it does not, however, affect the main point, which is that the Persian period may be here detected to be one in which the life and faith of Jews in the empire was not by any means one of security; it could be threatened by government action, by local jealousies, by personal rivalries and the like.

The book of Judith is, it is clear, primarily a combining of various tradition motifs—a major assault on the Jewish community in spite of the warnings given to Holofernes of the risks of attacking a people whose whole history testifies to the protecting power of its deity (Jdt. 5), the contrast between the immensity of the onslaught and the tiny, apparently powerless, Jewish people, the heroism of Judith who, like Jael, undertakes an act of heroism to deliver her people and who, like Esther, takes her life (and also her morals) in her hands, and, putting her trust in God, is able to bring about deliverance for her people. Attempts at finding some precise historical situation from which the tradition derives would appear to be less relevant than recognizing that here is a portrayal—probably from a later period—of how it felt to live under the alien rule of Persia. The passages from the prayers of Ezra 9 and Nehemiah 9 discussed earlier confirm the impression that being a subject people created many difficulties, both political and religious, for those among the Jews who saw in their ancestral faith and in the history of their people's life a testimony to the activity of God who could save. One might well imagine that such among the faithful could echo the words of Gideon: 'if the LORD really is with us, why has all this happened to us?' (Judg. 6.13).

b. *The Reactions to the Situation*
Ideally we should be able to distinguish between the situation of members of the Jewish community in Jerusalem and Judah and those in other areas. We have some first-hand knowledge of a particular Jewish group in Egypt, and some inferential information, both from the earlier record of Jeremiah 44 and from the later development of the important Jewish community in Alexandria. The impetus to renewal and reform which is indicated as coming from Babylonia at various points in the history of this period provides us with some indication of the vitality and thought of particular groups there. How far we may generalize is doubtful. The fact that a Nehemiah could rise to a position of particular influence and privilege, and that tradition tells of the similar fortunes of a Mordecai or a Daniel, and of the even higher status of Esther, points to the possibility that Jewish affairs, minor though they must have been in the total political picture of Persian life, were not entirely insignificant (though the paradigm of Joseph in Egypt may suggest a typical motif). The strategic position of Jerusalem and Judah would, in any case, ensure that they could not be overlooked, and would provide a lever for urging the Persian authorities to take appropriate conciliatory action. The conflicting interests of Jews in Babylonia and in Palestine and other political groups such as the authorities in Samaria and in other contiguous administrative areas, reveal themselves in the various traditions of conflict, of suspicion, of attempts at sabotage, of tendentious reporting to the central administration.

But all this tends, inevitably, to be generalized. It is what we might expect from our more detailed knowledge of the succeeding period of Greek rule, and of the many and varied attempts made by Roman generals and procurators at solving 'the Jewish problem'. It is in part a political matter, the problem of dealing with the aspirations and needs of any subject people. That we know more about the internal life and thought of the Jewish community should not obscure the recognition that other groups too—the Phoenicians for example, in rebellion against Persia in the mid-fourth century BCE—had their own view of Persian authority and its undesirable pressures. It is also a religious question, and here too it is over-easy to assume that the religious susceptibilities of the Jewish community, known to us because of their subsequent history of faithful adherence to their ancestral traditions, are to be regarded as unique simply because we can attest that survival and see the way in which the element of uncompromising loyalty to the faith also becomes an essential part of the Christian tradition. It is all too easy to assume that other religious communities found no difficulty in accommodating the demands of imperial overlords; to assert, as Jewish propaganda does, that the Samaritans happily accepted religious syncretism in the time of Antiochus IV Ephiphanes, and to assume that because there is no clear continuity of religious faith from ancient Moab or ancient Phoenicia that the willingness to compromise was, in the end, bound to lead to dissolution. Before we draw such conclusions we should recall that in the history of Christianity there have been areas which, once strong in the faith, have in the course of time succumbed to superior forces, as in North Africa and most of the Near East and Asia Minor. It is easy to assume that the decline was due to the adulteration and weakening of the faith; less certain that this is really a sufficient explanation of the historical facts. In one of those areas in which we can define, that of the development of the Samaritan community, we can with confidence affirm that the allegation of religious syncretism is in very large measure a piece of hostile propaganda; for whatever else is uncertain, it does at least appear most proper to see the Samaritans as primarily religious conservatives rather than as religious decadents. Furthermore, a dispassionate examination of the evolution of both Judaism and Christianity strongly suggests that the religions with which they came in contact, and which have subsequently disappeared, have at least in some measure survived in the process by which both Judaism and Christianity have shown themselves to be adept at absorbing and integrating into themselves elements which could be regarded as alien. The relationship between Israel's faith and that of Canaan—to take the most obvious and clearly attested example—is much more subtle than the oversimplified statement of utter contrast and repudiation would suggest.

The relevance of this to the life of the Persian period is to be seen in the recognition of the variety of ways in which the community, or particular groups or individuals within it, could react to the political and religious stresses of the time. The urge to discover a single supposedly orthodox line of development is understandable. But Judaism in the New Testament period can clearly be shown to be much more diverse than was at one time supposed. The Judaism of the second century BCE is shot through with differences, all too easily and wrongly dismissed as being simple contrasts between true piety and apostasy. Virtually all our sources are propagandist in some degree, and for that period we can see the contrast between the pious and faithful adherents of the Maccabaean family, who saw there the true hope of resistance and recovery, and the other pious and faithful who either for a time—as is said of the Asidaeans—joined the armed revolt and then withdrew or—as seems to be the case with the writer of Daniel—saw in the armed movement only a minimal degree of assistance to those whose faith must rest in the reality of a direct divine intervention. And while religious compromise may be seen to have made too many concessions in certain circles labeled apostate, it is not proper to assume that the only motives of those involved were what their opponents claimed. To preserve the community would, to some, appear to be the first essential in preserving the faith.

For the Persian period, we must make similar assumptions. Orthodoxy is a later and in large measure an artificial concept. The prominence which has to be given in the discussion of the period to that presentation of events which is found in the Chronicler is an inevitable result of the sources available to us being limited. If we wish to assess the full range of reactions to

the particular situations of the Persian period, then we have to
look not only at such works as this but also at those indications
of other ways of thinking which appear either possibly at the
time or in subsequent writings reflecting other ways of thinking. The Elephantine community is important, in spite of its
disappearance from history about 400 BCE, because it shows us
something of the way such a small isolated group could actually live. The history of Samaritan developments, in so far as
we can trace them back into this period, shows another way in
which there could be response to the particular tensions. The
appearance in the later years of new and more precise forms
of messianic thought, the apocalyptic strands with all their
variety, the quietism—if that is the right term—of the later
developments of the wisdom writings—all these provide some
suggestions of currents of thought which must have existed at
the earlier time.

The discussion which follows is concentrated in the first
place upon the two great moments of religious revival and
reform for which we have significant evidence in the biblical
sources: the work of the great reformers, Nehemiah and Ezra.
The sequel to the consideration of the great reformers must be
a discussion of some of the main elements in the theology of
the Chronicler to whose work we owe their presentation, as it
now stands; and a look at some of those other ways of thinking
which reflect alternative lines of approach to the problems of
the period. It opens a prospect of wide variety and richness of
theological thinking.

2. *The Great Reformers*

The first section has attempted to set the scene both for the
theological evaluation of the situation which is the subject of
the third section and for the consideration of the two great
reformers, Ezra and Nehemiah, who stand out in the tradition
as the leading named figures in the life of the Jewish community in the fifth and fourth centuries. The qualifying
'named' is deliberate, for it would at least be arguable that the
theologian whom we designate the 'Chronicler' or the author
of the book of Job—if it is assigned to this period—could be
considered even more influential than these two men whose

names we know. It is in any case clear that were it not for the Chronicler's work, we should know very much less about either of them, though we may certainly recognize that other traditions have been preserved for both—by Jesus ben Sira, by the author of 2 Maccabees, by the author of 2 Esdras, by Josephus, by later Jewish writings—which indicate that their memory is not entirely, even if it is chiefly, dependent upon the one primary biblical document and its part-parallel in the apocryphal 1 Esdras.

The point is also important for another reason. From very early times, the urge to identify and name the authors of sacred writings has been strong. It has been supposed that the Chronicler was Ezra; it has been thought that Moses wrote the book of Job. The maintenance of the ancient, but in some measure traceable, traditions of the authorship of the Pentateuch, of the books associated with Isaiah, of Daniel, and the like, carries with it a concern for authority and authenticity. The writers of pseudepigraphical works such as *Enoch* were in part at least anxious for the authority of their writings. A book without an author, a hero without a name, carries less weight than one who can be thought to have a greater measure of historical viability by having at least that amount of precision. The use of the cumbersome 'Second Isaiah' must always be somewhat of a hindrance to the full appreciation of the unnamed prophet of the exile. The circumlocution 'the author of Job', and the artificial shorthand term 'the Chronicler', carry less immediate conviction than the names Ezra and Nehemiah.

But the tendency toward naming, understandable as it is, and the appearance of names attached to certain personages in the tradition, do not of themselves carry historical weight. The impression of historicity created by their occurrence is not infrequently belied by the problems which are raised by a detailed consideration of the available evidence. It has been suggested that Ezra was a fiction of the Chronicler's creation, though it is difficult to see what precisely would have been achieved by such a piece of gratuitous invention—unless it were based upon a real figure, in which case we are confronted with a partly imaginative, or partly theological, interpretation of the life and work of a real person. Similarly, if we were to go by some of the later elements in the Nehemiah tradition—particularly those in 2 Maccabees—we might wonder whether he was a real person; the existence of such obviously unhistorical material in the tradition raises for us questions about the nature and so about the historicity of the at first sight virtually straight Nehemiah 'Memorial'. There is more to the accounts of these men than a simple historical record; from the very earliest point, such was their impact, there were attempts at assessing what place they occupied, and they are depicted in some measure at least in typical or traditional roles.

This point is brought out by the fact that they appear now—in the main sources of our information—as a pair. A closer analysis of the material reveals that they do not really belong together quite so nearly as the narratives at first suggest. The awareness of this has led to the discussion of the chronological problems, and to the various solutions to them—with the advantage of placing them under different rulers of the same name appearing to outweigh alternatives which demand either somewhat arbitrary textual emendation or somewhat artificial argumentation to persuade us that events could have happened in precise biblical order and in accordance with precise biblical chronology. We must disentangle them and view their achievements separately; but we cannot so disentangle them that we can suppose the traditions regarding them to be completely separable. Both Ezra and Nehemiah stand for certain types of development in religious thought. Whoever placed them together in the Chronicler's work— whether it was the Chronicler himself, or, as seems in many ways more probable, a successor—was not undertaking a piece of arbitrary historical jigsaw work. He was clearly aware that, by the time of the combining, the functions and outlooks of the two men had been sufficiently drawn together for them to be supposed to have been co-operators in a single operation. If we still come down on the side of following the biblical record in its precise order, we should be bold enough to recognize the possibility that Jerusalem and the Judaean community, small as it was, could conceivably have contained two such men at one and the same time, though on the whole the arguments for separation are strong enough. The force of this is clear if we consider that Ezra and Nehemiah as a linked pair of leaders may be compared with other notable pairs in the biblical tradition.

That two personages appear together and act together or in close association is a common enough feature of the biblical record. (Whether it is a feature of other historical or religious traditions, I am not sure.) Perhaps it is characteristic of the human spirit to set one man over against another, either in rivalry and opposition or in co-operation and complement. The result is a portrayal of both which is more complex, in which elements belonging to the one pass over to the other, and the problem of sorting out what belongs where is the more difficult since in most cases we have no independent evidence for making the analysis and checking the distinction.

We may observe this in the Old Testament in a number of important instances, and there are others where the 'pairing' is less obvious but nevertheless similarly relevant to the discussion. Moses and Aaron provide an example; the much more prominent Moses at certain points appears to overlap with the much more problematic Aaron. In the process of the combining of the diverse traditions, some measure of assimilation has taken place. We may note here that the one is leader and/or prophet and the other is priest. Elijah and Elisha provide a different kind of overlap and interrelationship, and one which is chronologically not altogether unlike the Ezra/ Nehemiah pairing. As the narratives now stand, Elisha has become the successor of Elijah; but the narrating of similar stories about both, and the ascription to both of the same political intent in relation to both Jehu and Hazael, strongly suggest that traditions concerning two distinct figures are now in part conflated and in part resolved into a relationship of master/ disciple. Some parts of each tradition stand out clearly as not associated with the other, but a complete distinguishing of the two is no longer possible.

Nearer to the Ezra–Nehemiah situation is another prophetic pairing, that of Haggai–Zechariah 1–8. The association of them in the traditions utilized in Ezra 1–6 is such as to provide no distinguishing of their message. The presentation of the two prophets in the collections associated with their names provides at a number of points—notably in Zechariah 7–8—a measure of overlap which suggests that the eventual presentation is allied to that utilized by the Chronicler and that it saw in the period of these two a moment of great renewal, an example to later generations, and perhaps even more than this a token of the coming new age which is still not fully experienced in the time of the Chronicler.

With Ezra and Nehemiah, the relationship is very complex, but we may observe that the tradition has preserved both certain clearly distinguishing features which enable us to see a measure of difference of emphasis in their policies and at the same time a sufficient indication of assimilation to suggest that what was to be said of the one must also be said of the other. These aspects will need to be investigated if we are to make an adequate assessment of the two.

We may at the outset observe—having in mind both the Moses/Aaron pair, and also the expression of that relationship to be found in Ezekiel (the prince alongside the priestly order) and in Haggai and Zechariah (the governor or commissioner Zerubbabel alongside the high priest Joshua)—that Ezra, the priest, the scribe, is paired with Nehemiah, the governor, the political leader, but one who is also presented in terms which touch on both royal and prophetic features. This concept of dual leadership, itself perhaps in part the outcome of a particular form of presenting historical narrative, is observable in a clear prophetic statement, of relatively late date, in 1 Sam. 2.27-36, where the relationship of priestly order to monarchical is made part of the future establishment; and indeed, this relationship of true priesthood and true kingship (and true shrine) is an underlying one of the whole sequence of the books at least from Samuel to Kings, and is of importance also for our understanding of the theology of the Chronicler.

It is always a temptation when evidence is discovered of a pattern to see it in every other instance. That is not the intention of this survey. But sufficient has been said to suggest that, whatever our solution of the literary and chronological relationships between Ezra and Nehemiah, we cannot neatly separate the two, even if we can at most points distinguish what parts of the material belong to each. (Neh. 10 forms the one very difficult borderline case, and it is therefore particularly important as providing possible evidence within the biblical narrative of the conflating and harmonizing tendency.) We have to recognize that the tradition, rightly or wrongly, has drawn them together. The community in which the traditions were shaped contributed its own patterns, its own assessment, to the presentation of two men who may, in the upshot, prove to have been very different in outlook and emphasis. Here we need to be aware of the already present tendency to move towards the view—even within the Old Testament framework—that there is one orthodox position, one true tradition, one valid theology. The urge to standardize, to systematize, is very strong; the result is that the markedly diverse personalities of the tradition come gradually to exhibit plainly only their common features and disclose their distinctive elements only to very close scrutiny.

One aspect of the assimilating of the various traditions to one another is the imposition of patterns upon them, patterns which may be discernible also in other contexts. The Chronicler, in his description of the re-establishment of the post-exilic community in the books of Ezra–Nehemiah, shows a repeated pattern of action. This may be seen as consisting of a royal command (from the Persian ruler), the story of the carrying out of that command, and the culminating religious celebration. The pattern may be seen in Ezra 1–6; the various sources are in a measure subjected to this, though there is much more than a straight sequence. It may be seen further in Ezra 7–10 and Nehemiah 8–10, taken together as the two parts of the Ezra narrative; the order has here been achieved by a dislocation of the materials in such a way as to place the action in regard to foreign marriages before the reading of the law and the celebration. It may also be seen in the shaping of the Nehemiah material, but here we may observe that the result is again achieved by the chronological dislocation of the material—and so the dedication of the walls forms the climax to the group of stories concerned not only with this theme but with others such as the repopulation of the city. This pattern is, however, then broken by the appending of the narratives associated with the second period of Nehemiah's administration, which do not fit in with the structure. (We may observe the same pattern, with some modifications, in Esther, and in 1 and 2 Maccabees.)

The very fact that such patterns are observable—and patterns of similar kinds may be detected in other parts of the Chronicler's work—indicates how much of caution is necessary in any attempt at extracting precise history from these sources. The recognition that at some points—e.g. at the end of the Nehemiah traditions—the material breaks a pattern is important in that it suggests a limitation to the imposition of patterns on the information handed down. The richness and variety of the tradition, both biblical and non-biblical, concerning Ezra and Nehemiah, make it proper that we should, however, be concerned with much more than the mere detection of historical and non-historical elements. We are concerned with adducing the evidence on the basis of which we can usefully ask the question: What kind of a man was this, what kind of function did he perform, if he was able to leave this kind of impression on his successors, this variety of tradition about him and his work? What follows in the discussion of the two reformers is therefore directed only modestly towards pointing out some aspects of the material, some features of its form, some indications of the ways in which it reveals the growth of traditions concerning two influential personages.

a. *Nehemiah*
There has been much discussion of the character of the Nehemiah narrative, often described as his 'Memoirs' or more recently his 'Memorial'. The occurrence in these chapters of a repeated—though varying—refrain, appealing to God to have in mind the achievements of Nehemiah and also not to overlook the offences of his opponents, has suggested a contact with various types of writing, and in particular with votive inscriptions of a well-attested kind in the ancient Near East. The typical formula,

> May N.N. be remembered for ever for good and prosperity

set out by an ordinary person, is close to the formula used in the Nehemiah narrative:

> Remember for good, O my God, all that I have done for this people (5.19).

The form is used four times in ch. 13, at vv. 14, 22, 29 and 31. Its use here is remarkable first for its frequency, four times in one relatively short section as against twice only (5.19 and 6.14) in the whole of the remainder. Two observations may be made on this: (i) we may suspect that this repeated use could be due to the desire of the compiler of 13.4-29 (31) to conform this passage to what precedes. We have noted already that this account of the second period of Nehemiah's activity cuts across the pattern of the narratives in Ezra–Nehemiah. Is there here an indication that the whole section is a later addition, consisting possibly of several small sections, now integrated into one account, but marked by this repeated use of the refrain as part of the compiler's endeavour to show its relationship? Is it an indication of an early stage in the evolution of the Nehemiah tradition, by which the major account of his activity is being supplemented, not without a quite possible historical basis, with further indications of his piety and reforming achievements? (ii) The close occurrence of the refrain in vv. 29 and 31 is at first sight even more remarkable, but we may observe that the second of these is a very simple formula (on the simple and complex forms, cf. below), and that vv. 30-31 look very much like a concluding summary, perhaps really to be regarded as the original conclusion of the Nehemiah narratives and properly to be regarded as the direct sequel to 13.3. There the theme of separation from foreigners is made clear; it would be well rounded off with the two verses 13.30-31, and the book provided with an appropriate ending. The relationship between this last section and the work of Ezra falls to be considered subsequently. We are then left with a clearer structure, but one in which the three times repeated formula is still remarkable enough.

The second noteworthy feature about the formulae in ch. 13—apart from that in v. 31—is the much greater detail which they contain. 5.19, already cited, is a brief general comment; so too is 13.31. 6.14 is, in a sense, the obverse of these; it is longer and more elaborate because it specifies by name the opponents of Nehemiah on whom an evil memory is invoked:

> Remember, O my God, Tobiah and Sanballat according to these evil deeds of theirs, and so too Noadiah the prophetess and the rest of the prophets who were in awe of me.

13.14 follows the positive pattern, but adds detail:

> Remember me, O my God, for this, nor let my loyal actions perish which I have performed in the temple of my God and in the ordering of his worship.

13.22 similarly:

> For this too, remember me, O my God, and spare me in the greatness of your mercy.

13.29 follows the negative pattern:

> Remember them, O my God, for their defilings of the priesthood, and the priestly covenant and the Levites [or, the priestly and the Levitical covenant].

This greater measure of specification in the three passages in ch. 13 which appear to belong to the supplement again suggests that we have the use of an already familiar formula, but with an attempt at making it fit more exactly the particular narrative to which it is attached. By contrast the 'original' use in 5.19 and 13.31, and its obverse in 6.14, would seem to be closer to the votive inscription pattern, and perhaps therefore earlier and simpler.

The votive inscription pattern itself would seem to be connected with royal inscription forms in which the heroic deeds of kings are set up—by themselves or their successors—partly at least to serve as reminders before the deity of their actions, with particular emphasis upon their obedience to divine commands and their attribution to the deity of their great achievements. The inscription of Mesha of Moab is of this kind, and whatever other purpose such stelae might be intended to express, this religious aspect would seem to be the primary one. Reminding posterity of the king's deeds is in this context part of that process by which the king's memory is kept alive, and hence kept before the deity to whom the attribution is made.

This whole aspect of the Nehemiah material suggests that we are dealing with an assimilation of Nehemiah, the governor, to royal traditions, and we shall have occasion to see certain other points in which such traditions appear to be continued. There is here a link with that aspect of the problematic social development of the post-exilic age by which the older institution of monarchy, seen to be both under judgment and also a sign of divine purpose, was carried over into the newer organization. The 'prince' of Ezekiel provides us with one potential line of development; Davidic messianic ideas point to another. The subsequent variety of endeavours at political organization in the second century BCE—where the picture of Judah's internal life again becomes clear, if complex—show how the position of the political leader needed to be clarified, and in particular his position vis-à-vis the religious head, the high priest. The history of the last two centuries BCE shows something of the variety of ways in which the offices could be combined or could exist side by side, and the repercussions which these various methods produced in the evolution of a variety of groups within the community favouring or reacting sharply against particular rulers or particular procedures.

But the votive inscription is not the only background to the Nehemiah refrains. We may observe the closeness of the formula to prayer forms in both the psalms and in narratives; the call to God to 'remember' is, in the end, a basic religious form. In particular we may observe a link with psalmody and prophecy, and notably here with Jeremiah. Such an appeal to be remembered is a characteristic of prayer forms, as, for example, in the prayer of Hezekiah briefly given at 2 Kgs 20.3 and implied in that of Hannah in 1 Sam. 1.11. It is developed, particularly with an emphasis on the retribution to be brought on opponents, in a number of passages in Jeremiah, e.g. 15.18-20; 17.18; 18.19-23; and a counterpart to these may be seen in the psalms, as, for example in Ps. 109.14 where God is asked to remember and not to blot out the evil deeds of the father and mother of the psalmist's enemy.

The comparison with the situation of the psalmist and his opponent is clearly related to the Jeremiah passages, for in these the language and style of lamentation psalms is employed, and the position of the prophet is envisaged in terms of the innocent faithful adherent contrasted with the wicked opponents. The relevance of this to Nehemiah may then be seen in the fact that the narratives concerning him are in some measure stylized as prophetic narratives. First-person narratives (alongside third-person forms) are well known from the prophetic books; the distinction between these in prophecy appears to be minimal. (The presence of the same double form in the Ezra material is a reminder that here, too, we are possibly dealing with alternative methods of presentation but not with sources which are autobiographical in the strict sense by the side of others which are merely biographical.) The narrator may speak in the prophet's (or other leader's) person, or may describe him obliquely. The opening words of the book of Nehemiah, as this is now marked off from its predecessor Ezra, 'the words of Nehemiah ben Hacaliah' could be an editorial addition designed to ease the transition from the Ezra narratives which now stand immediately before, divided from the Nehemiah material only by a minimal textual break. They could equally well be the title of the Nehemiah memorial, which otherwise begins abruptly: 'Now in the month Kislev of the twentieth year, I was at Shushan...' —an opening which seems to demand some introduction, perhaps even some link to a preceding narrative. But in either case, although *dibrê* can certainly here be rendered 'acts' rather than 'words', there is a relation to the style of presenting the prophetic message. For this is exactly the mode of opening in the books of Jeremiah and of Amos.

What follows is not a prophetic call such as to be found in the opening of Jeremiah 1; but it is a narrative equivalent of such a call. The presentation, with its chronological data, is like that of the later prophets—from Jeremiah onwards, in which precise dates become increasingly common. The occasion of an experience of divine command and commission is obliquely indicated, for distress is brought about by the description of Jerusalem's continuing destroyed condition, and this leads into a prayer which indirectly approaches the question of what Nehemiah is to be commanded to undertake. The narrator does not—as we might have expected in a prophetic narrative—show God as speaking directly to Nehemiah, but the implication is present that a command has been given, the fulfilment of which will depend upon the working of the divine purpose through the favour which Nehemiah enjoys in the presence of the Persian ruler. The precise nature of the commission is described as being worked out between Nehemiah and the ruler, but the very possibility of it is clearly linked to the divine will.

The prophetic features in the presentation of Nehemiah in the opening section of the narrative find their counterpart in subsequent material. We may note briefly three points at which this may be clearly seen: (i) in 3.33-37 (EVV 4.1-5), we find the mockery of the opponents of the builders answered by a passage invoking judgment upon them. The phraseology used is like that of psalms such as 109.6-19; it may be compared with the direct attack upon an opponent found in Amos 7. The enemies of the people of God are to be taken away captive, to suffer exile such as the true Israel has suffered. The succeeding narratives, while primarily concentrated upon the practical measures undertaken to ensure that the rebuilding could continue, also contain what may be regarded as essentially a prophetic word: 'Do not be afraid of them; remember the great and terrible LORD, and fight...' (4.8 [EVV 4.14]). This stands in a line with Hag. 2.5, and further back with the words of Moses in Exod. 14.13. (ii) More precise prophetic elements appear in ch. 5. Implicit in the judgment upon those who oppress their fellow-Jews is the recognition that prophetic condemnation fell upon such practice. The words attributed to Nehemiah are appropriate to a politician rather than to a prophet. But the judgment of the offenders culminates in the performance by Nehemiah of a prophetic symbolic action; those who default are thereby under judgment. (iii) 6.10ff. show Nehemiah in conflict with the false prophets. It is a situation comparable to that in which we find the prophets Micah and Jeremiah, confronted by those who purport to speak the true word of God. Here we find Nehemiah able to discern that 'God had not sent him' (cf. Jer. 23.21).

None of these passages suggests that Nehemiah was a prophet; what they indicate is the way in which prophetic modes of conduct, prophetic types of action, prophetic words, are being attributed to the political leader. The fact that we are unable to find clear indications of continuing prophetic tradition in these years in the prophetic books themselves—though some part of the present material shows that prophecy was not dead—may in part account for the attribution to Nehemiah of such functioning. Prophecy in the more formal sense is receding; the spirit of prophecy and the succession to the prophetic tradition are to be found in men of God such as this.

The other main element in the presentation of Nehemiah is the royal. We have already seen that there are links with votive and royal inscription forms. But more than this, there is a natural transference to Nehemiah of features which belong to the activity of kings. His position is that of a royal commissioner, a governor under Persian authority. In such a position, he does, of course, represent royal authority, a sort of extension of Persian royal power into the Judaean context. This is one reason why he is so dangerous to his opponents, as well as showing why devious action is taken to bring him down. But more important are the indications of his engaging in royal activities, activities of a kind associated with the earlier kings; he becomes a successor to the now lost line of the monarchy. Here again we may note a number of features.

(i) The very function of rebuilding is closely linked with royalty. That kings 'built'—that is to say 'rebuilt'—cities and temples is often recorded both in the biblical and extra-biblical records. It is a straight statement of policy and at the same time an indication of royal position. Nehemiah as the rebuilder of the ruined city of Jerusalem appears, in fact, to be only the rebuilder of the walls; but this one main activity is linked in the opening chapter with the ruined state of Jerusalem (cf. 2.3, 5). The repopulation of the city may be seen as a further development of this theme, for while it clearly has a quite simple sociological explanation, it may also be seen as a recognition that a restored city involves a restored people.

(ii) The king in ancient Israel was the upholder and promulgator of the law. It is in this aspect that Moses has royal features, though there may well be others too. David is described as upholder of law, and the king is seen as the final court of appeal. Legal reform, in the narrower sense, has been seen to underlie such covenantal procedures as are described for Josiah. The Chronicler has extended this principle somewhat more broadly. So for Nehemiah the upholding of right legal practice in ch. 5 provides a good example. A public reading of the law is associated with him in 13.1-3. The laws of Levitical life and of the sabbath and concerning intermarriage are all reaffirmed or restated by Nehemiah.

(iii) Closely related to this—and indeed considerably overlapping it—is the picture of the king as religious reformer.

The matters just mentioned provide an immediate parallel with the activities associated with Josiah, and by the Chronicler much more prominently with Hezekiah, who in this respect occupies a lesser place in the older traditions. Much of the detail of ch. 13 is concentrated upon matters which can be most conveniently summed up as 'religious reformation'. Naturally enough, the attempt has been made to discover what particular compilation of laws underlies the actions of Nehemiah. The point is at its clearest in 13.1-3 where the prohibition of Ammonites and Moabites clearly points to Deut. 23.3-6, and it actually quotes the basis for the hostility in the reference to Balaam.

If, turning from questions which are partly those of form and presentation, we ask what aims are attributed to Nehemiah, then we may say that all that is said of him is concerned ultimately with the protection of the community and its restoration. It is to be a rebuilt, repopulated community. It is to be circumscribed by the prohibition of alien marriage bonds. It is to be one in which the protection of its members from oppression is clear. It is to be rightly ordered according to the prescriptions of the law. And here we may note that the subsequent Nehemiah traditions continue this kind of emphasis, but with greater precision. That Nehemiah was the rebuilder of the ruined city becomes for the compiler of 2 Maccabees the even fuller tradition that he was the restorer of city and temple at the end of the exile. With a total disregard of chronology, the narrator tells us that it was Nehemiah who was sent back by the Persian king (2 Macc. 1.20); it was he who rediscovered the sacred fire 'after he had built the temple and the altar' (1.18). There is no room here for Sheshbazzar or Zerubbabel; history has been telescoped to attribute to Nehemiah the major moment of restoration. Similarly too, we note that in the same source another aspect of the restoration of the community is associated with him. In a period during which the gradual fixation of a canon of sacred writings was taking place, reaching its culmination only rather later, but nevertheless moving considerably towards the concept of a fixed canon, it was possible for there to be associated with Nehemiah a major part in the collecting and preserving of ancient writings; Judas the Maccabee is seen as his counterpart. The list of what Nehemiah gathered and preserved is impressive, for it would appear to cover the historical books, the prophetic books, the psalms and 'royal letters about sacred offerings', the kind of material which is traceable in Ezra 1 and Ezra 7, but perhaps implicit in other parts of the record. It is also noteworthy that 2 Maccabees gives a description of Nehemiah's activity which is strongly reminiscent of that of Elijah on Carmel. The prophetic element is being developed, and, in view of the place which the figure of Elijah came to occupy—cf. Malachi and the New Testament, and cf. also Ecclus 48.10-11—the measure of identification sheds an interesting sidelight on the way in which Nehemiah was coming to be viewed in certain circles. 2 Maccabees has moved a lot further in the glorification of Nehemiah than the Memorial itself, and certainly further than Jesus ben Sira, whose brief mention reflects only the rebuilding of walls and gates, and—an important addition— 'he rebuilt our ruins' (Ecclus 49.13). It is possible that his placing of Nehemiah beside Zerubbabel and Joshua indicates that he believed them all to be contemporaries. 1 Esdras 5 also seems to take this view (cf. v. 40), though otherwise this work has no concern with Nehemiah; it does, in fact, present a glorification of Zerubbabel comparable with that offered in Nehemiah 1–2 for Nehemiah (1 Esd. 3–5).

I have here indicated only some aspects of the developing Nehemiah tradition (fuller discussion may be found in Kellermann 1967). The importance of this subsequent growth lies in the way in which it enables us to see already in the biblical material the beginnings of the process. We are already confronted not with historical narrative, but with a particular kind of interpretation, and one which has to be considered in any attempt at assessing the place of Ezra alongside Nehemiah.

b. *Ezra*
The structure of the Ezra narratives presents very considerable problems, quite apart from the basic questions of the relationship chronologically of Ezra to Nehemiah, and the present partial interweaving of the traditions concerning the two. The order of the material—Ezra 7–10 + Neh. 8–9 (10)—is perfectly intelligible; it is this order which stands as a consecutive

narrative in 1 Esdras 8–9, breaking off (perhaps because it is a fragment) at the point corresponding to Nehemiah 8–13. This order leads through from the royal commission to Ezra to the celebration of a festival and a covenantal ceremonial which form a climax, one comparable to that discernible in Ezra 1–6 (see above). But even within this order there are problems of chronology. The dates which run through the chapters present a curious picture if they are read in this order: Ezra 7.7ff. the journey 7th year, months 1–5, arrival in Jerusalem on the first day of the 5th month. The events of Ezra 7–8 fit well into this, and 8.33-36 refers to the immediate handing over of silver and gold and temple vessels, and a sacrificial procedure, associated also with the delivering of the royal commission. But Ezra 9–10, the foreign marriage section, implies a gap of time till the ninth month, and the carrying through of the investigations from the tenth month to the first month of the next year. Did nothing happen in the intervening months?

Nehemiah 8 however, provides us with material which can fill this gap, for here the events associated with the reading of the law are dated appropriately in the seventh month; the feast of tabernacles is celebrated, and this is continued on the twenty-fourth day of the month (9.1; no month number is given) by the fast associated with separation from foreigners. The covenant ceremonial which is indicated by Nehemiah 10 includes a prominent section on foreign marriages. Quite apart from the chronology, it is difficult to see how Ezra 9–10 can have preceded this. It is much more natural to suppose that the original order placed the reading of the law at the first appropriate date—the practice appears to be closely associated with that reflected in Deuteronomy 31—namely at the autumnal feast. The reading of the law is indicated as disclosing the requirement of purity for the community, and a more detailed account of this is given in Ezra 9–10. This does not, however, solve the literary problems. We have to observe the occurrence of both first- and third-person forms of the material. Ezra 7.27–9.15 either clearly or implicitly uses first-person forms. The remainder is in the third person. As so often seems to happen with this kind of division of material, the breaks are not satisfactorily linked with any obvious analysis of sources. The first section in 7.27ff. clearly presupposes some

account of the commissioning of Ezra. Chapter 9 (first person)
and ch. 10 (third person) are clearly closely related, and the
narrative of ch. 9 is clearly incomplete without ch. 10. To build
an analysis on the divergence of forms is evidently unsatisfactory. That there is, however, some evidence of duplication in
the source material must also be noted: the foreign marriage
action in Ezra 9–10 forms in some measure a duplication of
the indications of this briefly at the opening of Nehemiah 9. To
attempt a complete integration of the material as it now
stands would require a certain measure of wresting it out of
context. It is better simply to acknowledge more than one
tradition; to recognize that some parts of the material were in
first-person and some in third-person form; and most important of all, to see that the eventual compilation represents a use
of this varied material ordered within a theological conception
of the meaning of the events being described.

It is clear that there are three aspects of Ezra's activity as it
is now set out; they are closely interrelated. The first concerns
the commission and its nature; the second the reform; the
third the action to protect the community. The precise interrelationship of these is less important than the consideration of
the nature of the activity as it is understood in the present
form of the material.

(i) *The Commission.* The opening brief narrative summarizes
the commissioning of Ezra and his journey to Jerusalem. In
some measure therefore, it anticipates what follows and
overlaps with it. It is divided from the sequel by the Aramaic
document, introduced in 7.11 with a Hebrew description,
which in part duplicates the statements of the preceding
verses. The document is followed by an ascription of praise put
into the mouth of Ezra for the divine action which disposed the
Persian king to be favourable to Ezra's wishes. The fact that
7.28b and ch. 8 clearly form a first-person section, suggests
that vv. 27-28a could in fact be part of the same material. The
Hebrew text lacks any introductory formula, though this may
be supplied from 1 Esd. 8.25; but we might more properly prefer to put the formula in the first person, and thus suggest that
this word of praise is part of a narrative which—perhaps in a
style not unlike that of Nehemiah 1–2 and of Esther—told of

the way in which the request for permission to return was put before the king. The whole passage would seem to demand some such introduction, and this could have simply been replaced by part of another account (7.1-10) and the commission which would appear to be separate. There may be a hint here of a similarity in the Ezra and Nehemiah traditions which is otherwise obscured.

The commission itself is concentrated on the imposition of the law and instruction in it. The emphasis rests on Ezra as expert in the law, and in this the commission echoes the opening narrative section (esp. chs. 7–10). 7.25-26 requires the appointment of legal officers, the strict control of all within the province who accept the law, and the instruction of those who do not. The implication of the passage could be that the whole population of the province is to be subject to Jewish law, but it is more natural to suppose that the word 'am is used to denote not the whole population but the 'people of God', the true community; its renegade members are to be brought to a true sense of their responsibilities, and this is set here under the authority of Persian government order. We may note, however, that the commission contains a number of other elements. There is the provision of support in money and kind for the temple, and the taking of temple vessels; no explanation is given of the latter, and it may be regarded as expressive of piety on the part of the Persian ruler who wishes to avoid possible disaster at the hands of the deity of the Jerusalem shrine. It provides a base from which the tradition can grow—again like that in the Nehemiah material—that Ezra was ultimately responsible for the restoration of the temple; in the bringing of vessels, he is placed alongside Sheshbazzar, the first post-exilic royal commissioner. Ezra too is to become the true rebuilder after the exile. Furthermore we note an example of special favour in the exemption from taxation of all the temple officiants, at whatever level. This may be seen as related both to other Persian examples of proper regard for the religious susceptibilities of subject peoples (and the nearest parallel is to be found in the inscription concerning the 'holy gardeners of Apollo' from whom tribute had been wrongfully required (the text is in Olmstead, 1965 [1931]: 571), and to later policy—under Greek and Roman rulers—which was directed in part

to the conciliation of subjects and in part to the concern for
religious difficulties raised for members of such a community
by government policy in which religion was not infrequently
bound up with military or fiscal matters.

It is not so difficult to see the present intention of the commission as it is set out. The following up of this in the reading
and acceptance of the law and in the foreign marriage action
shows the carrying out of the legal aspect of it. It is less certain
how far we have here an original document, and how far an
elaboration of an original commission. At certain points it lays
down precise financial limits of support (v. 22); at other points
(vv. 20, 23) it is without limitation. The understanding of the
applicability of the law as relevant only to the Jewish community can perhaps be considered to be in some measure
contradicted by the extension to the whole province of this
requirement; is there perhaps some implication that the
province, Beyond the River, which could be regarded as coin-
ciding more or less with the ideal extent of Davidic rule, was
again to be regarded as coming under the control of the true
people? Is the quotation of a document in Aramaic, the imperial diplomatic language for the west, designed to indicate the
authority of the claims made, just as the narrative in Ezra 5–6
similarly finds in direct citation of the authority a support for
the actual existence of the temple at Jerusalem? The use of
Aramaic seems to suggest originality; but the occurrence of
Aramaic sections in chs. 4–6, and the double language of
Daniel, and the use of Aramaic for some other books associated
with the community (*Enoch*, Tobit, etc., among the Qumran
materials), indicates a quite wide possibility of having materials available in that language, here perhaps skilfully used to
suggest authority. The problems of origin, authenticity and
interpretation are very delicate.

The interpretation of the commission in terms of law will be
seen again in the sequel, but it envisages a conception of membership of the community which is clearly of fundamental
importance. There is here a carrying forward of the educa-
tional procedures envisaged in Deuteronomy 31, where the
seven year reading of the law to a community including its
younger members suggests a procedure by which at regular
intervals there are incorporated into the community those

who on a previous occasion were not in a position to give adherence to the law. All members of the Jewish people within the province are known and included (or excluded) on the basis of adherence to the law; the potential extension, in possibly political terms, to all people within the province would indicate both a political ideal of occupation and also a recognition that membership of the community is not simply to be restricted to the one people but can include all who accept. The subsequent action against foreign marriages is not necessarily a contradiction of this, but may be seen as a logical exclusion of those who by contamination have themselves shown their unfitness.

(ii) *The Reform.* The account of the reading of the law is now the climax of the Ezra story, the sequels being only the carrying out of what it involves. We may note two points towards the elucidation of this narrative. (a) It is clearly in a line with already existing practice, or should we perhaps say, it is narrated with a consciousness that it belongs in existing practice. There is behind it the seven-year practice of Deuteronomy 31, and the reform of Josiah. The stress here on Tabernacles as the occasion makes the link with Deuteronomy 31; the relation of law-reading and exposition and religious festival allies it with the Passover celebration of Josiah. That the Josiah reform, so-called, is itself in some degree a stylized presentation of a normal practice, is a view that can, I believe, be argued. That Ezra's reform is something more than a particular single occasion is perhaps to be read in this relationship to other occasions. There may well, it is true, be some features of the narration which are specific, or which are related rather to contemporary practice known to the Chronicler (or his source): the wooden pulpit, the Levitical expositors, the particular forms—these are perhaps best seen as reflections of what was normal at the time. But the more this is emphasized, the more it becomes likely that the Chronicler has here utilized a familiar procedure for the presentation of what he regarded as being a particular, and indeed, unique moment. (b) We may observe, cautiously, that although it can be argued that such a reading and acceptance of the law was a proper element in the procedure envisaged in the commission of

Ezra, it does not precisely correspond to that commission. The most obvious omission is any reference to the province Beyond the River. If Ezra's commission was to impose a single law on the Jewish community throughout the province, then we might have expected some mention of this in the carrying through of his work. What is here undertaken is much more restricted and narrow. It does not—at least as it is described—form either the first stage in such a wider activity, or the climax and epitomizing of it. What is the relationship of the 'reform' here described to that other conception of his commission?

Clearly, unless we are simply to dismiss the problem as characteristic of the carping mind of an analytic critic, or to suppose that, since we have only a partial record of Ezra's work, the rest of what he did is not mentioned here but must be assumed, some explanation must be offered. If that latter supposition is proper, then we must surely ask why the Chronicler, having recorded the commission, chose to omit its fulfilment? And then we are coming near to supposing that in reality the lack of relationship is due on the one hand to the stubbornness of the tradition, which does not quite fit neatly together and on the other hand to the presuppositions of a theologian who is much more concerned with Truth than with mere history.

We could envisage the discrepancy as due to one of two alternatives. On the one hand, we could suppose that the Nehemiah 8ff. narrative is basic, describing the actual achievement of Ezra, and that the commission, as set out in Ezra 7 in its statutory form, is really a piece of idealization, an element in the growth of the Ezra tradition. We have seen that such a growth, even within the biblical records themselves, is likely in the case of Nehemiah. On the other hand, we could argue that in reality the commission was basic and historical, and that its too political emphasis—its links with the religio-political complex of Persian diplomatic activity—was uncongenial to a theologian of the Chronicler's stamp, and that he retold the story of Ezra so as to present him as the ideal of what he thought should have taken place. The politician becomes the religious reformer.

We could also—and perhaps more satisfactorily—envisage the process as due to something of each of these apparent alternatives. We may see the 'political' Ezra, the man who under Persian aegis was fostering Persian aims in the west, as also one for whom the care and nurture of his own community was a paramount political necessity; the function of this political leader has been given an enlargement, a wider significance not only in the politics but also in the religious development of the whole area. We may see the theologian, the Chronicler, picking up one element in a whole series of actions undertaken by Ezra, his engagement in the reading and exposition of the law—which was perhaps more probably a series of actions rather than a single one—and seeing in this the epitomizing of the way in which the need of the community for religious stability was met, the theological elucidation of its positions declared.

The reading of the law, the celebration of the festival, the prayer with its exposition of faith in historical terms and its expression of contemporary distress, attributed to the Levites or to Ezra in Nehemiah 9, and the making of the covenant in Nehemiah 10, represent the central element in the Chronicler's exposition of the meaning of the work of Ezra; it is linked to the position of Ezra as 'scribe' or 'secretary'; it is linked to the commission with its evidently political aspect, an aspect which was to have further repercussions in the succeeding centuries when the problem of who should control the mixed communities of Palestine was much to the fore. It is linked also to the moves to purify and so to consolidate the religious life of the community by the exclusion of alien elements. For this, one element in the celebration of the fast (Neh. 9.2), and one element in the covenant as it is now set out in Neh. 10.30, is given a fuller exposition in the narrative and comments of Ezra 9–10.

(iii) *The protection of the community*. This is the part of the narrative which is to most of us the least sympathetic. The concern expressed in various parts of the Old Testament about the problem of purity and non-contamination with alien life, is one which we may recognize as having consequences in subsequent Jewish and Christian history. On the Jewish side, we may see it in relation to the resistance to assimilation, in the understandable belief that that can so readily mean the loss of Jewish values and faith. On the Christian side, it is seen in the exclusiveness which belongs to a greater or lesser degree to Christian groups and which has been expressed particularly strongly in those extreme areas in which 'not being yoked with an unbeliever' has been applied with an absurd rigidity. The problem of faith and unfaith and the relationship between different communities and different religions, have always created difficulties of adjustment. The Old Testament offers us no one picture of the problem, but a tension between the stress on absolute purity of race, absolute exclusiveness—expressed most clearly in the Deuteronomic injunctions to destroy the inhabitants of the land and in the Joshua descriptions of the application of the ban (*ḥerem*)—and an awareness of the universal reign of God which, if sometimes expressed in narrow terms, nevertheless implies the holding together of all peoples and along with this a sober recognition that the Jewish people was never of pure descent, but numbered among its ancestors and among its member groups those, like the Gibeonites, who were not really part of some supposed strict ancestral line.

The Chronicler—and this is an important feature of his theology—stands rather more on the side of the former line than of the latter, though not absolutely so. But our understanding of the general situation in the fifth and fourth centuries BCE, and our recognition of the intensification of these same problems in the centuries which followed under Greek and Roman rule, should make us sympathetic to the problems which the community was seeking to meet when it laid its emphasis on exclusion.

The Ezra narrative, at first sight, reads like a simple narration of a rather narrow policy being carried out with rigidity and lack of feeling. It is often thought that the Nehemiah policy was less rigid, being concerned only to avoid such intermarriage in the future and not to break up already existing marriages. It may be questioned whether the evidence is really sufficient for such a view. Nehemiah's laying of an oath upon the members of the community not to permit intermarriage for their sons and daughters certainly looks to the future; it is the strict application of Deuteronomic law. But his action, engaging in legal contention (*rîb*—rather stronger then NEB 'arguing'), cursing and beating and tearing out of hair, implies very strong moves to bring doom upon those who have committed the offence. We are not told what it involved for those who were cursed; could the curse be evaded if the wrong action was not persisted in? The verses following take the point a little further: the son-in-law of Sanballat is driven out (v. 28), the community is purified of everything foreign (v. 30). May this not imply a root and branch policy?

Whatever the explanation of this Nehemiah passage, it is evident that the greater detail of the Ezra narrative makes the action appear much more ruthless and inhuman. But here too we need to examine carefully what appears. The narrative begins in Ezra 9 with a statement which is strongly related to the stylized presentation of the whole intermarriage question in Deuteronomy. The list of the peoples of the land which belongs to the tradition is here used as if in the time of Ezra it were still these peoples which existed; but of those mentioned, it would seem doubtful if any other than the Ammonites and Moabites could be held to have contemporary validity—for the mention of Egyptians is clearly linked back to the Exodus events. And even these two peoples represent a stylized presentation, as we may see from the Nehemiah law reading in Neh. 13.1-3 which more or less directly quotes Deuteronomy, and the Neh. 13.23 passage which again has these two, though it adds Ashdod, presumably as a representative of Philistia, another ancient and symbolic name. What kind of presentation is this, so stylized that no really contemporary reference is made? The sequel is a prayer which rehearses recent events and bases its confession of failure on a wealth of Deuteronomic phraseology. The undertaking of the people to remove the foreign women moves over into a less obviously stylized presentation, and the mention of the dissent of a small minority from the rigid policy points to a much greater degree of verisimilitude. The problem here is in part to decide how much of historical fact there is in the account, and in part to consider what purpose the material is designed to serve. The genealogical aspect of the Chronicler's theological presentation must concern us subsequently; it is clearly relevant here, for it involves the question of the nature of the community and

membership of it. For the moment, we must look simply at
that aspect of it which is expressed in later discussions about
the degrees of membership of the community. Joachim
Jeremias in *Jerusalem in the time of Jesus* (ET; London 1969),
has a whole section on the maintenance of racial purity, and in
particular cites the relevant rabbinic statements. The complexities of the later situation do not necessarily apply in the
period of Ezra or of the Chronicler; in any case, we must in
some measure see in the later developments the exegesis of
just such passages as the one under discussion. But what we
need to observe here is that the three groups of the list in Ezra
10—priests, Levites, and Israel (i.e. full Israelites)—correspond to that top stratum of the pure society in the later organization which specifies that only those who could prove pure
descent in one of these groups could marry into priestly families. Below this, was a second stratum in which there was a
slight blemish: marriage with priestly families was forbidden,
but not with Levites or legitimate Israelites; and there was yet
a third stratum of families with grave blemishes of ancestry.
Now the various documents are in agreement about the first
stratum, but show some differences in regard to the lower
ones. In particular they appear to reflect a changed view
towards proselytes, who at an earlier stage may have been
accepted in the second grade, while later they were perhaps
relegated to the third. The importance for our understanding
of the Ezra 9–10 passage is the recognition that here we have
one approach to the whole problem of legitimacy for the life of
the community. The very centre of that community—the
authentic priests, Levites and true Israelites—is to be preserved strictly from contaminating contacts. That all manner
of relationships were engaged in which contravened this
would appear—from the later information—to be a matter of
experience. But the endeavour to keep the community right at
the centre is one way of ensuring that there is no total dissipa-
tion of the pure and faithful line. We may note that the same
concern, limited to the status of the priesthood, is to be found in
the name lists of Ezra 2 = Nehemiah 7, where a note is made
of those who could not determine their descent and therefore
could not be regarded as qualified for priestly status. The situation was one of 'not proven', since it appears to have been a

deficiency in genealogical information; but, pending a divine decision through the sacred lot, they must not engage in the full priestly duties.

In our, properly, humanitarian concern, our anxiety for the unfortunate dismissed wives and children, we may overlook the central problem here. Since no information is given about the way in which the social problems were handled, we have no right to suppose that there was not at least the possibility of a concern for the needy who could perhaps be regarded as having some status. But this is not the Chronicler's concern. To him, it is the question of clarifying what the true Israel really is; unless it has at its very centre a pure faith, expressed in a pure community, it cannot truly be the people of God. The sociological questions are subordinated to the theological motif.

The presentation of Ezra is unlike that of Nehemiah, in spite of the measure of overlap to which further reference will be made. The links—made explicit by the genealogy of ch. 7 and by the description of his qualifications as scribe, learned in the Law of Moses—are with Aaron on the one hand and Moses on the other. The genealogy makes the priestly link the dominant one, and this is also implicit in the function of Ezra as mediator and interpreter of the law; the priestly relation to law, the priestly reading of the law (cf. Deut. 31), and the levitical exposition of law are all clearly attested here. But the more evident concern is with the giving of law, and the nature of law, as these are related to the figure of Moses; it is in this latter capacity in particular that the figure of Ezra may be seen to evolve in later tradition. His function as the restorer of the lost law in the exilic age is brought out both in 2 Esdras 14 and in rabbinic tradition. The restoration of the law is also associated with the giving—or re-giving—of the square script. The later development of the position of Ezra as responsible for the canon is comparable to the more modest attribution of scriptures to Nehemiah. Ezra eventually was to overtake Nehemiah completely in this respect, and to become the one who maintained the community's life through the post-exilic period. It is in a line with this that one tradition (cf. 2 Esd. 3.14) associates him with the actual restoration after the exile—thus making him, as 2 Maccabees does Nehemiah—a contemporary of Zerubbabel and Joshua. It is yet another example of the process—which is so evident already in the Chronicler and subsequently in Daniel—by which the exile is held to endure until a new point of full restoration is reached (cf. *Exile and Restoration*, ch. 13).

What has been said has already indicated that there is some measure of overlap between the two figures of Nehemiah and Ezra. What was said about the pairing of figures in the tradition is particularly evident here; whether it is after they come to be associated closely, or as part of the process by which they come to be associated, is difficult to say. We may see the evolution of the Nehemiah and Ezra traditions as showing the way in which two originally quite distinct figures have come to be regarded as epitomizing the concern with restoration and reform and the law which form the centre around which the life of the community is held to turn, according to some groups within it. The final section of this discussion will in part be concerned with looking more fully at the nature of this type of tradition and at other alternative lines which co-exist with it.

At certain points the overlap is such as to raise questions about the way in which the one figure may have influenced the other. The reading of the law is clearly a case of this; the elaborate description of Nehemiah 8 and the association with it of a major account of festal celebration and fasting completely overshadows the brief and rather second-hand reference of Neh. 13.1-3. If it is right—as we have suggested—to consider whether 13.4-29 may not be an addition to the Nehemiah narrative, then 13.1-3 forms virtually the end of the basic narrative, rounded off only with the brief summarizing statement of 13.30-31. It is not possible to ascertain from the text precisely to what moment the reading of the law is attributed; the completion of the wall in the sixth month (Neh. 6.15) would not inappropriately suggest that the dedication could have been made to coincide with tabernacles in the seventh, but there is no date in 12.27-43, nor any precise mention of a festival. To it is appended the imprecisely attached ('on that day') description of enactment of levitical and other matters (12.44-47) and equally imprecisely this reading of the law (13.1-3). The fact that the latter is so abbreviated and merely a reference to the exclusion of Moabites and Ammonites makes it appear even more artificial. Is it perhaps a growth of the Nehemiah tradition giving him a law-reading comparable to that of Ezra? If so, what should we make of certain other points of overlap?

The problem of Nehemiah 10 has already been indicated. As it stands, it appears to offer the covenantal ceremonial appropriate to the events of Nehemiah 8–9. The presence of Nehemiah's name at 10.2 (EVV 10.1) could, of course, be a mark of editorial shaping. But the coincidence of much in the detail of the reforms of the covenant with those described in Nehemiah 13 has suggested that the original Nehemiah covenant has been utilized here by the Chronicler and so has replaced the version—whatever it was—associated with Ezra. But the coincidence could have an alternative explanation. It could be that the Ezra tradition had its covenant; the terms set out here accord well with the Ezra material in Ezra 9–10; 10.35 has the same grouping 'priests, Levites, people', which can be seen in Ezra 10 in the analysis of the culprits. Could the extra material of the Nehemiah narrative in ch. 13 represent a filling out of the tradition of the second period of governorship—not mentioned in ch. 5—on the basis of the kind of traditions which were growing up associated with the figure of Ezra? Though such a suggestion can probably be little more than speculation, it is at least worth bearing in mind the way in which transfers of material can take place between figures whose traditions are growing up, and that the fusion of Ezra and Nehemiah into contemporaries could in the end be due to more than the mere supposition that they belonged in the reign of the same king; it could derive rather from the increasing recognition that they were cast in similar roles, in some degree overlapping, in some degree complementary.

It will have become clear in this exposition that I see greater interest in studying the way in which the traditions and interpretations develop than merely in trying to define what is and what is not historical. Against the general background of the complex political, social and religious issues of these centuries, these two men stand out, as the named heroes of a wealth of tradition. It is not proper to dismiss them as having no historical status because we cannot precisely define when they lived and how they operated—though the ultimate chronology is sufficiently establishable at least for Nehemiah and probably

also for Ezra. But it is also quite inappropriate to suppose that
we have a merely historical tradition, and so to take no adequate account of the richness of that growth of interpretation
which placed these two men in so central a position.

3. *Theological Strands in the Age of the Chronicler*

What has already been said about the variety of thought, and
of the need for avoiding the concept of orthodoxy as a central
line from which other ways of thought may be said to deviate,
makes it important that this third section, in which primary
place is given to the writings of the Chronicler and an exposition of his theological approach, should be seen as indicating
only some of the areas which need to be discussed. The uncertainties about the dating of biblical writings, the problems of
the formation of the literature and the evidence within virtually all the writings of stages of development, internal exegesis, re-presentation in the light of new needs and problems,
make it inevitably open to question whether this particular
writing should be included or that should be excluded. A good
case could be made out for maintaining that whether or not
particular writings are assigned to this period, they all need to
be examined to see how far they may have undergone adaptation or reinterpretation even without adaptation; the textual
changes—such as may be detected where we have parallel
texts—made in reference to some particular situation ought,
ideally, to provide us with some further insight. But, regrettably, it remains clear that there is too great a measure of
uncertainty for redaction history to be undertaken except in
rather general terms. Hypotheses designed to explain the origins of particular glosses or reapplications can be nothing
more. General outlines rather than specific details are all that
can be achieved. And it is clear that to venture to examine all
biblical material would be to draw out the present discussion to
inordinate length. That the Persian period was one in which
there were moves towards what was to be eventually the full
canonical concept is clear; what the law of Josiah typifies for
the immediate pre-exilic period—a measuring of standards by
an accepted written document—is paralleled in our period by
Ezra's reading of the law, which may be viewed as the

Chronicler's counterpart to the work of Josiah. Both events are significant in that they show us glimpses of a community in which judgments are made and reforms are undertaken in the light of an accepted norm, a canon of scripture. That this canon is not yet fixed, that its text can be further modified and reapplied, that it does not in any way represent a designation of an agreed collection of writings, does not alter the fact that the canonical or scriptural principle is here expressed. There is no adequate reason for supposing that the Jewish community was unique in such an acceptance of writings as authoritative; the eventual position of the canonical scriptures in both Judaism and Christianity was to be the result of a much longer and more complex process in which scriptures and community were to be in a mutual relationship, each exercising an influence on the other. To that process, the community of the Persian period contributed its part. We may sometimes detect where they saw authority to lie, and we may, as particularly in the writings of the Chronicler, see that the acceptance of writings as having some measure of authority did not preclude the possibility of a substantial measure of rewriting and interpretation. It is not the scriptures themselves that provide the authority; it is the particular interpretation offered of them. This is a distinction not always observed, and indeed one that is often implicit rather than explicit in the recognition of the existence of a canon.

a. *The Chronicler*

In an article published in the *Concordia Theological Monthly* (38 [Sept. 1967], pp. 501-15), entitled 'History and Theology in the Writings of the Chronicler' (see Chapter 10, pp. 257-75), I outlined my approach to the literary and historical problems of this comprehensive survey of Israel's life and experience. What has already been said here has indicated that in my view the writings now described as Chronicles–Ezra–Nehemiah have undergone several stages of development, possibly from a first revision and concentration of attention on Jerusalem and Judah, as a development of the approach of the Deuteronomic historian in the books of Samuel and Kings, to later stages, in the addition of further genealogical and other material, and in particular, very probably, the Nehemiah narratives: I have been concerned to indicate here that the addition of the Nehemiah material is not to be regarded as an arbitrary piece of editing but rather as an understanding of the relationship between two reformers for whom the growing traditions made similar though not identical claims. In the study mentioned above, I was concerned with trying to arrive at a sound evaluation of the Chronicler's work—viewed as a whole, independently of the literary development—since it seems so easily to suffer from wrong understanding. At one level, it is simply used to supplement gaps in the Samuel–Kings narrative, as if the Septuagint title 'The things omitted' were to be accepted as a correct description; as a result, the Chronicler's own theological approach may be overlooked and undervalued. At another level, claims have been made for the sound historical value of the Chronicler's 'special' material; while this is not necessarily to be dismissed as invention, since there is no good reason why passages which appear only in a late work should not be based on ancient and reliable information, the way in which the Chronicler handles his material strongly suggests that whatever of historical value is to be found has to be very carefully disentangled from the complicating interpretative additions and arrangements. The resultant judgments on the Chronicler have either been derogatory—he is a writer whose sense of history is minimal and whose arrangement of the material inspires no confidence— or extravagant—he is a writer whose preservation of ancient material marks him out as very perspicacious. In either case, the judgment—like those often made on other parts of the Old Testament—appears to be based upon an unexamined assumption that a good historian is what we are looking for in a biblical writer. Yet, our judgment of the Chronicler, like our judgment of other biblical authors, must ultimately rest not upon the verifiability of their statements about what happened, but upon our appreciation of the soundness of their theological insights. Assessment of the Chronicler's theology has in some measure suffered from the assessment of his qualities as a historian; it has been wondered how a man who could describe battles with such a lack of awareness of how battles are fought could possibly have any real theological understanding. Or again, his apparent concern with ecclesiastical detail and his lack of prophetic, let alone apocalyptic, hope have made him seem to belong in the choir or the pulpit rather than in the real world in which men of faith find themselves confronted with political and social and moral dilemmas. To arrive at a more adequate assessment of his theological position and contribution, we need to look at the nature of the work and at the method of presentation, as well as endeavouring to see the possible relationship between his interpretations and the situation in which he and the Jewish community found themselves, probably in about the mid-fourth century. In general terms at least, we may discern how he viewed his community's problems and where he saw the right understanding of the contemporary situation to lie.

In the earlier Deuteronomistic History there is clear evidence of a patterning of narratives; this is particularly clear in the first half of Joshua, in the stylizing of the judge stories, and in the stereotyped presentation of the kings. It is the last of these which is specially relevant to our consideration of the Chronicler's patterning of history, since at certain points we may see how an alternating pattern of good and bad kings over-simplifies the account. While it is possible to relate the estimates of Ahaz and Manasseh as bad kings, and Hezekiah and Josiah as good kings in some measure to the external political situation—Assyrian pressure making for subservience, Assyrian weakness allowing for independence and reform— this really represents too easy an explanation of an account which has to a considerable extent drawn in Manasseh especially the picture of a king responsible ultimately for the total downfall of Judah. A full discussion of this would be out of place here, but we may observe that this alternation is particularly developed by the Chronicler who sees (sometimes in terms of contrasting rulers but more often in terms of changes of heart in the lives of particular kings) the evidence for the working out of a divine purpose which is expressed in grace and judgment. So stylized does the narrative become that for the modern reader it has a certain monotony; it is rather like a musical theme with variations of which the composer has written so many that the audience begins to count to see how far off the end is. But here we need to allow both for the effect of repetition in driving home the teaching and also for the pos-

sibility that while the work may well have been read continu-
ously, it could also have been utilized section by section as a
series of connected homilies. (A suggestion of this kind has
recently been developed by M.D. Goulder in his Speaker's
Lectures at Oxford in an interesting thesis connected with a
view of lectionary practice reflected in the Gospel of Matthew
[Goulder 1974]. While it inevitably, like other lectionary theories, tends to suffer from attempts at over-precision, it does
offer an opening towards an understanding of the kind of situation in which such a re-presentation of the older traditions
could have been undertaken in the post-exilic period. Exposition of the earlier narratives, known from a later period to
have been marked off into lectionary sections, would provide a
basis for the Chronicler's activity. Since Goulder's discussion
has been seen by me only in a preliminary form, it would not
be fair to comment on it more fully until it appears as part of
the larger study in which it is only a preliminary.) Such
homiletical use might tend—at least in the mind of a modern
congregation—to invite the comment that the preacher
always preaches the same sermon; but if the sermon is on
divine grace and human response, we might not unreasonably
recognize that at least the preacher is not speaking on the
fringe of doctrine but at its very centre!

From 2 Chronicles 10, where the breaking away of the
apostate north is described, the pattern is developed. The
period of Rehoboam's obedience, in which he is supported by
the faithful Levites and people from the north, is one of
strength and well-being (2 Chron. 11.17); but in this position of
security, Rehoboam becomes faithless and retribution follows
in the form of Egyptian attack (12.1-4). Prophetic comment is
followed by the submission of king and leaders. The punishment is lightened, divine wrath averted, and prosperity
returns (12.5-12). A comparison with the narrative in 1 Kings
shows how the Chronicler, building upon the tradition of
Rehoboam's evil ways (to which he makes brief allusion in his
concluding summary, 12.14), has, in fact, developed both the
theme of disobedience and that of loyalty. The theme of faithfulness is expressed in fuller form in the account of the reign of
Abijah, and particularly expounded in his sermonic address to
the north (ch. 13). The contrasting themes are drawn out in

accounts of other kings, some of whom, like Asa, show right response to the injunction to have faith and loyalty. But although he is described as remaining religiously faithful (15.17), in contrast with the Great Lady, Maacah, he is shown as lacking trust when he forms an alliance with the alien power of Aram; so he comes to final disaster (ch. 16). Even Jehoshaphat, reformer of justice and encourager of faith in his people, is castigated for his alliance with faithless Israel (17.20), and similar patterns are developed for the reigns that follow. The major reform, as the Chronicler has it, is undertaken by Hezekiah; yet even he does not escape a note of warning. The Chronicler, somewhat elliptically, alludes to the illness and recovery of Hezekiah, but indicates that his lack of gratitude brought disaster upon Judah and Jerusalem until Hezekiah submitted in his pride (chs. 28–32). Manasseh provides a balancing example, that of the wicked king who is brought into captivity in Babylon—thereby anticipating the doom of the whole people—but in repentance finds the help of God, and restoration and reform are undertaken in Jerusalem (ch. 33). Josiah, though a reformer, had come to a doubtful end; the Chronicler is explicit in showing that this disaster was due to his refusal to hear the word of God, spoken to him though it was through the strange agency of the Egyptian Pharaoh (chs. 34–35). Disobedience is summed up in the final comments on the downfall of the kingdom of Judah, whose leaders and people refused to hear the repeated warnings of the prophets, and so disaster was inescapable (36.14-16).

What is demonstrated in this repeated pattern then becomes the climax. The disaster of exile is the final statement of judgment upon a disloyal people, and we may see here a possible line of approach to that curious problem of the Chronicler's writings—his lack of concern with the Exodus. It is true that much of the homiletic material which is quoted by the Chronicler, the prayers and psalms which are included, assume the Exodus theme, so prominent in the older traditions. But with the Chronicler, there is a new historical perspective; the Exodus is no longer in the same way the determinative event, the pattern to which subsequent occurrences may be moulded. The Deuteronomic historians, writing from the exilic situation, could not yet see that period in perspective, but saw it rather as a word of divine judgment to be accepted as right, and found in acceptance the possible basis for a new and better understanding. The Chronicler, two centuries on, was able to see in the exile the central moment of the history, the moment upon which earlier events could be patterned, becoming in a measure anticipations of the major disaster. At the same time, the message of faith and of divine grace could find here its ampler justification.

This is a point to which I want to return, but before it is further developed, there is another aspect of the Chronicler's presentation which needs to be set out. It involves the recognition that he is in reality very much less concerned with history and historical events than the presentation of this story might suggest. History is for him very much dehistoricized. Not that we should suppose that there is any doubt in his mind that experiences took place; they were part of the real tradition of the community in which he belonged, but his patterning of them to an even greater extent than by his predecessors shows how relatively free he was in the handling of historical tradition. Narratives are for him much more evidently the basis for instruction than they were to his predecessors, though we should beware of making too simple a contrast. The older narratives show a variety of methods of making theological points. Sometimes, as, for example, in the story of the death of Saul, the narrator is content to tell the story, leaving it to the reader to draw out the theological consequences of what is told. No one can read through the series of narratives built together to lead up to that final disaster without being aware that in a sense Saul has been as good as dead from the moment of his rejection for disobedience. At other times, as for example, in the homiletical introduction to the judge narratives in Judg. 2.6–3.6 and in the punctuating sermons which appear here and there in what follows, the theological motifs are brought out explicitly, and the stories, presented in their traditional, localized dress, are given a significance which depends upon their position and their reinterpretation as pictures of all Israel's disobedience, penitence, restoration and faith. The dehistoricizing process is illustrated perhaps most clearly in the older narratives in the opening chapters of Joshua, where the highly stylized picture of conquest, concentrated almost entirely on Jericho and Ai, takes the community through the whole range of themes found in the Exodus–wilderness narratives, and brings them to a climax of victory as a result of solely divine action at Jericho, and through disobedience and disaster at Ai to purification and victory in the sequel. The task of rediscovering history in such narratives is made all the more difficult in that to the narrator and interpreter what counts is meaning rather than event.

The Chronicler has presented events in an even more stylized form, though the line of his thinking may be traced back both to the homiletic style and to the theologized history of Joshua. So too, he has presented in schematic form the whole history from creation to the post-exilic restoration, summing up the course of events not in narration but in names, names which reflect both the outline of the tradition and the concern with the nature of the community's life which so mark his work (1 Chron. 1–9). Central to his statement is the very lengthy section which is devoted to David and Jerusalem and the temple (1 Chron. 10–2 Chron. 9); and this is balanced at the end by the section devoted to the restoration and re-establishment of the temple and the people in Ezra–Nehemiah, into which the Nehemiah narratives fit as an appropriate extension of the basic theme. History moves from creation to its first climax in David and the temple; it moves again through judgment to its second climax, reached in the interrelated work of rebuilding and of Ezra. (We may incidentally observe—in the light of what appears in later forms of the tradition where Nehemiah becomes contemporary with Zerubbabel, and Ezra bridges the exile, that it could be argued that the Chronicler had so little concern with true chronology, and so little historical sense—as we understand it—that he viewed the work of Ezra as following virtually directly upon the rebuilding and rededication of the temple. Ezra 6.15 speaks of the sixth year of Darius; 7.7 of the seventh year of Artaxerxes. In view of the chronological to and fro in ch. 4 [Cyrus, Darius, Ahasuerus, Artaxerxes, Darius]—if that was due to the Chronicler and not to another hand—it would not be impossible to suppose that he was more interested in pointing out how one event led on into another than with—from his viewpoint—relatively minor matters such as changes of reigns. To him the Persian ruler, whatever his name, was a mediator of divine favour, protector under God of a people re-learning obedience.)

A closer look shows how exile and restoration form the recurring theme. First, in 1 Chronicles 1–9, the genealogies trace the history of the people of God, from its beginnings at creation, through the descendants of the tribes. We shall return to the genealogies, both here and elsewhere. The greater degree of concentration upon Judah and upon the Davidic house—though the latter may be the result of some expansion—points to the south, with Benjamin included as the seat of Jerusalem, as the focal point. The survey leads into the brief statement of Judah's exile for its sin, and so the re-occupation of the land, beginning with Jerusalem as the centre of restoration, and listing the lay families, the priests, Levites and temple-servants (so 1 Chron. 9 where vv. 35-44, repeating 8.29-38, should probably be regarded as deliberately reintroduced to provide an opening to Saul's downfall in ch. 10). The first account thus leads through the establishment of the people to its exile and its restoration.

Second, in 1 Chronicles 10, the theme of loss is picked up, for the people of God is found to be living and suffering disaster under a faithless ruler, Saul. We might have expected the Chronicler, to whom clearly the kingship of David was the only valid kingship, to omit any mention of Saul. He could leave unmentioned most of the kings of the north—they appear only as opponents of Judah or as involving Judah in sin. He could equally have ignored Saul and passed straight to the anointing of David. But the theme of restoration, of the rebuilding of Jerusalem and its temple, of the establishment in security of the people of God, is presented rather in terms of contrast. It is out of the moment of disaster, the consequence of the unfaithfulness of Saul, that David is brought to the throne. It is, of course, the first true kingship; yet it was by transfer from the failed Saul. It is only at this moment that Jerusalem is occupied; but it is the occupation of the city which now shows that a new age has begun. Only now can the true and full life begin for the people, but it can nevertheless be pictured as restoration, since it is in a sense the rehabilitation of the true people. The Chronicler does not utilize the traditions of slavery in Egypt and deliverance, nor those of disobedience and faith in the wilderness period, nor yet those of conquest and settlement in which the same themes were elaborated in the earlier history; but he is just as conscious as were the earlier writers that the establishment of Jerusalem and the building of the temple, the dynasty and the priesthood side by side, mark a climax which both follows an earlier pattern and sets a new tone. The immense elaboration in 1 Chronicles 11 to 2 Chronicles 9—which must be seen as one, since it is around David as founder of the dynasty, taker of Jerusalem, planner of the temple, that everything revolves—shows the full and obedient life of the faithful people. Yet even here, the Chronicler does not shrink from using an incident discreditable to David—that of the census and plague (1 Chron. 21)—because it both emphasizes the nature of human frailty and ushers in the temple site as itself the outcome of a moment of disaster. (It is often claimed that the Chronicler simply left out everything that could cast a shadow on his idealized David, and the particular instance of the Bathsheba incident is highlighted as an example. We may, however, observe that this incident had no relevance when the succession of Solomon could be seen to be obligatory; none but the temple builder, the completer of David's work, could come to the throne. An alternative explanation is also possible of this 'omission'. The story of Solomon's birth and succession is no doubt a somewhat sordid one, but it is already used by the Deuteronomic historians to demonstrate the working of divine grace; even the failure of David is brought to fruition by God's direct action. Since the Chronicler could build the census story directly into the temple theme, he could presumably have done the same with this. Did he perhaps not do so because the particular form of the tradition known to him did not include this incident, but related the Ammonite war alone without the Uriah–Bathsheba narrative which has been woven into it in the 2 Samuel form of the text?)

No failure mars the reign of Solomon, but with him the ideal moment passes. The third stage is reached with the accelerating pattern of faith and unfaith through the reigns of the kings until the exile marks the inevitable doom and at the same time provides the moment for sabbath rest, for rehabilitation for the land, and so paves the way for the final restoration, that which through its various stages leads to the law-reading and covenant of Ezra. The final picture is of a renewed and purified people, with city and temple restored—a theme to which the Nehemiah narratives add a further facet—accepting the law as the one criterion of membership of the people, one aspect of which is the establishment of purity, the link back to the past in acceptable ancestry.

The interpretation of exile and restoration in the Chronicler's theology is linked to a number of points. First, it is through this judgment and purification that the people comes to recovery; there is no way into the future except this. Hence the restored community—so in the opening of 1 Chronicles 9 and again in the description of the restoration in Ezra 1–6—consists of those who have returned from exile, with the concession—a concession like that allowed in the reform of Hezekiah—that those who separate themselves from impurity may be regarded as having undertaken the purification embodied in the exile experience (so Ezra 6.16 [Aramaic] for the stress on only those who had returned, followed by 6.21 [Hebrew], which appears to represent the Chronicler's own reinterpretation of his sources, where the emphasis rests upon purity of the returned exiles and separation of those who joined them from the peoples of the land. The same point is made by the present intention of 4.1-5, whatever its original import may have been). The genealogy of 1 Chronicles 9 which sums up the first part of the whole work makes this point abundantly clear; these are the families with whom the pure community will have to be connected. The genealogies elsewhere are linked to this need. The Chronicler in this emphasis on 'through the exile' develops themes already found in earlier material—the good figs of Jeremiah 24, the judgment on Jerusalem in Jeremiah 29 and the hope in Babylon, the emphasis of Ezekiel, the possible eventual understanding of the end of 2 Kings (for these points, cf. my *Exile and Restoration,* p. 244 and elsewhere).

Second, the high point of the Chronicler's picture in the establishment of David, Jerusalem and the temple, is balanced in the final stage of the work by a reinterpretation of this, a reinterpretation which is read back into the earlier stages, too.

Jerusalem and the temple are re-established; the stress which rests upon this in Ezra 1–6 is clear. The religious celebrations in the Ezra narrative, together with the bringing to Jerusalem of contributions and vessels for the temple, mark an embellishment of the temple, a further stage in its rehabilitation. The whole ordering of worship, essential to the restored temple, is seen in the light of regulations laid down by David at the outset; everything which belongs to the normal practice of the later Jewish community is regarded as having derived from this original ordaining by David. In this, the hand of David rests upon the later situation. The Chronicler makes no attempt at finding a successor to David in the post-exilic period. Zerubbabel, of the Davidic line, is for a time the royal commissioner, charged with the rebuilding of the temple. He disappears from the story, and this disappearance has given rise to much speculation. It may be that we should see in the relevant passages in Haggai and Zechariah 1–8 some reflection of a royalist revival movement. I am myself more inclined to believe that the prophets, too, while seeing in Zerubbabel a sign of divine favour, were cautious in their statements about him; but it is possible that there has been a toning down of the 'messianic' elements in the final presentation of their words. The disappearance of Zerubbabel from the scene—he is not mentioned at the rededication of the temple—is less likely to be due to his deliberate removal by the Persians for rebellious activities, which would surely have carried with it action against the temple builders and the whole community; it is more probably due simply to the termination of his appointed period of office. But if this latter is so, then it may be that the Chronicler allows him to disappear without comment, because no weight is to be laid upon the position of the Davidic descendant. It is not a Davidic monarchy which the Chronicler hopes to see restored; it is the expression in the life of the community, particularly in its being gathered around the temple and its worship, of what David had established. The organizer and controller of worship, the provider of the plan and materials of the temple, the one who committed to Solomon and to his people their task, it is this David whose spirit lives on into the life of the post-exilic community and ensures the embodiment in them of the values which are really lasting and effective. The presence in 1 Chronicles 3 of substantial Davidic genealogical material may be seen as expressive of the same intention. The reality of the succession of David is there expressed; but no weight is laid upon any suggestion that here might be a line of hope for the future. If, as has been supposed, some part of this Davidic material is of later origin, it may be that we should see in this the continuing interest in the Davidic line, a pointer to that other way of thinking about David which is to be found in later more strongly political Davidic thought. The repercussions of this are observable in the New Testament. But so far as the Chronicler is concerned, any political emphasis appears to be lacking.

Third, we may see in the genealogical emphasis in the Chronicler's writings the concern with the nature of the community and its true ancestry. The detailed discussion of the structure and use of these genealogies cannot be undertaken here. An important recent study is that of M.D. Johnson, *The Purpose of the Biblical Genealogies* (Johnson 1969), which, though primarily concerned with the New Testament material, devotes its first part to the Old Testament, and in particular to the Chronicler. He has claimed that the concern for legitimation is more characteristic of the material found in the books of Ezra and Nehemiah than in the opening chapters of 1 Chronicles. But in particular, he stresses that there is in this work a concern with continuity, and although this is not the same as legitimation, it is difficult not to see a close link. For the post-exilic community, living as it did as a subject people under alien rule and therefore unable to exercise the kind of control over its own life that it would ideally have, the question of continuity with the pre-exilic Israel (that is, the pure community of Judah–Benjamin, the Israel of the Chronicler with which others from other tribes are associated, provided they accept the hegemony of the south) was clearly of fundamental importance. What the Chronicler expresses in his stress on David and the ordering of the worship of Jerusalem—and hence the legitimacy of those who stand within that succession—is expressed further in the genealogical links provided by the lists. That the same lists may be used in more than one context simply indicates the somewhat arti-

ficial use being made of material which may have come originally from a variety of sources. Our concern now is not with
origins but with use, a use directed towards continuity and
towards legitimation and purity. For it must be noted that the
clearest indications of the purpose of the genealogies are to be
found (a) in the verses of Ezra 2 = Nehemiah 7 which speak of
priests who could not establish the legitimacy of their line and
therefore could not for the moment function, and (b) in the
association of genealogical interest with alien marriage
alliances in Ezra 9–10. The listing of those who there dismissed foreign wives established the point that, though
charges might have been brought against these families of
impurity and therefore of unfitness to be members of the
community, the charges are hereby shown to have been met
and the problem dealt with by the resolute action of Ezra and
his associates. Johnson goes on in his study to point to the narrowing of interest towards the question of purity or towards
the ancestry of the Messiah. (In the latter it is of interest, in
view of the previous point in this discussion, that where the
Old Testament assumes Davidic ancestry for the Messiah,
later Judaism has a wider range of concepts.) This narrowing
is already in some measure prepared for by the concerns to be
found in the writings of the Chronicler.

The various points which have been made suggest the measure of concern which the Chronicler felt about the nature of
the community of his own day. The question of his attitude
towards the contemporary situation and its relation to past
and future has been much discussed. There is a sense in which
his presentation is anachronistic, a picturing in the past of
what he regarded as the realities of his own time, or the ideals
of his own time. It may be held that he is so concentrated upon
the expression of those ideals in the contemporary situation,
particularly as he sees this in Ezra, that he needs no outlook
towards the future; his is a realized eschatology. But it is probably unfair to be as rigid as this in our appraisal of his thinking. It is characteristic of much Old Testament material to
make little explicit reference to the future; the future—as that
which lies 'behind one's back'—is inevitably the unknown.
The Deuteronomic history, for example, voices no clear indication of what will come after the disaster now experienced,

though implicit in Deuteronomy is the recognition that the possession of the land, the gift to be bestowed by God, still depends upon the response of the people in obedience or disobedience. So too with the Chronicler; he has portrayed the whole history in terms of obedience and disobedience, in terms of disaster and restoration, exile and return. He is concerned to show in the final return of the post-exilic age, that age to which he and his contemporaries belong, the victory of faith and the working of divine grace. Already, as he writes, he is looking back from some distance and in theological perspective, at the moment of Ezra. It is of one piece for him with the whole restoration, an age of faith, an age which sought to re-establish continuity with the past—by its temple, by its priesthood, by its ancestry, by its embodiment of ancient promise. To his immediate contemporaries, the message was one of encouragement, perhaps a corrective to too low a level of faith, an urge to believe that when God acts and man responds, the life of the people of God is secure and will be secure.

b. *Other Strands of Thought*
The danger of concentrating so large a measure of attention on the Chronicler has already been indicated; but the risk of getting the discussion out of proportion has to be taken, if only because the Chronicler's work is the only full-scale and coherent document we have which enables light to be shed on the Persian period. Because of this, it is tempting to view the Chronicler's viewpoints as standing somewhere centrally in the life of the community, and to assess other lines of approach as being off-centre. Not that this is by any means an invariable approach to the study of this period. In fact, all too many studies of the Old Testament make a jump from the immediate post-exilic period to that of the Greek pressures in the second century BCE, with only a brief reference to Malachi and Job and to the activities of Nehemiah and Ezra considered without there always being an assessment of the literary work in which their figures appear. By handling the Chronicler first, we have a base from which to operate, even though the problems of interpretation are inevitably considerable. A man who writes his theology in the form of narrative and comment is

less easy to interpret than one who expounds directly with reference to his own situation.

We have seen—particularly in the prayer of Nehemiah 9— that the view that the Chronicler was complacent, content with the political and social situation as he saw it, is hardly borne out. The very choice of the particular prayer form there utilized is indicative of his concern; so too is the frequency of his stress upon faith and obedience. That he sees the community of his own time as the inheritor of the promise of the past does not blind him to the need for a wholeness of faith and a ready response in life and worship if the relationship between community and deity is to be real.

The final compilers of the prophetic books of Haggai and Zechariah 1–8 appear to have had very similar concerns. That the final presentation is related to the work of the Chronicler is suggested first by their appearance in the narratives of Ezra 1–6; it is clear that they stood prominently in his tradition and his sources for the restoration period. The chronological structures of these two books provide points of contact with the Chronicler's own styling of his account of the restoration. W.A.M. Beuken has developed considerably further the close analysis of the material, drawing attention to some stylistic difference between this editorial activity and the Chronicler's method, and suggesting that, while there may be seen to be a close relationship, this could not be claimed as pointing to an identity of literary activity. Alongside the Chronicler and his circle—perhaps a group of Levites, active in association with the temple worship—there appears a group in which the words of these two prophets were cherished and reapplied. If, for a moment leaving aside the importance of these two prophetic books for their own day, we try to read them as they might appear to one who lived a century or a century and a half later, then we can appreciate the note of appeal and warning, and in particular the note of faith. This is at its clearest in Zech. 8.9: 'Take courage, you who in these days hear these words from the prophets who were present when the foundations were laid for the temple of Yahweh of hosts; the temple is to be rebuilt'. What was experienced by the people of that time, the enabling of those who had faith to rebuild at a moment when, as both the prophecies and the narratives suggest, there were difficulties of many kinds to overcome, is now an encouragement and a warning to those who come after. In particular, the series of oracles of promise and hope in Zechariah 8, coming as they do after visions with a message of encouragement, of divine power to act, of the divine will to restore, and the symbols and utterances which point to the earlier consequences of disobedience (and by implication the risks that attend the contemporary situation) are set out so as to provide both warning and encouragement. Where the Chronicler provides an overall pattern, culminating in his understanding of exile and restoration, this presentation of prophetic teaching brings the matter more closely to the consideration of how what has once taken place in the events of the rebuilding period can take place again in the contemporary experience of distress and uncertainty.

We may sense something of this same concern with the need for faith and a right response in the prophecies gathered in the so-called book of Malachi. Targumic tradition associates the unnamed messenger with Ezra; the placing of the material as one of three appendices to the Book of the Twelve (along with Zechariah 9–11, 12–14) suggests that a relationship was seen between this and what precedes, for just as Zechariah 9–14 can in some measure be seen to represent a further development of the Zechariah tradition, with many points of linkage, so the Malachi chapters may be seen to pick up the concern with obedience and faith. The commonly accepted dating of Malachi in the period just before Nehemiah has, in fact, very little assured basis; the supposed historical references to an Edomite disaster are difficult to assign and could well be more stylized than actual, for Edom has become a symbol of the non-chosen outside world. The presumed allusion to alien marriage (2.11-12) appears more probably to refer to religious apostasy. Lack of response, which derives from lack of faith, expressed in unbelief in the reality of the divine election love, is stressed as the human side of a contemporary condition of distress. The apparent injustices of the situation which trouble the pious are met with an outlook towards the future divine intervention in which the true state of affairs will appear, and the God-fearing will triumph. The book contains both an appeal for a rectifying of contemporary failure and for a whole-heartedness of faith in a perplexing situation, and a confidence of outlook resting in the reality of divine intervention. The concept of the day of Yahweh, seen in some exilic thought as being in some measure incarnated in the disasters of that time and seen, in its more hopeful aspects, as expressed in the realities of the restoration, still remains an active one. There is an element of 'not yet' in the prophetic teaching, an outlook which enjoins faith in the reality of God's action.

What is expressed here, in the development of ideas about coming intervention in some ways reminiscent of the Second Isaiah, is presented somewhat differently and in symbolic form in the book of Jonah. I have commented elsewhere on the possible relationship of its symbolism to the understanding of the exile as the people's experience (*Exile and Restoration*, pp. 244-45), suggesting that while too rigid an interpretation would over-confine the teaching of the book, some element of this particular part of the historic experience may well have influenced in particular the use of the psalm in Jonah 2. But this psalm, with its highly stylized presentation of human distress, in mythological language, does not exhaust its application in such a supposed reference; it continues as a valid expression of contemporary distress. We may picture the writer of Jonah as urging his readers to recognize that distress and discontent may be due to their failure to accept the full demands which rest upon them as the people of God. Their distress can be read as a summoning back to their true vocation, the recognition of what, as a community, they are commissioned to be.

The concern with the function and nature of the people of God—a theme to which the Chronicler contributes—is here very evident. The book of Jonah makes clear its understanding of the people's position as comparable to that of the prophet; the mediation of the divine will to bless, expressed in the pronouncement of judgment which invites and invokes response, is that function for which the special relationship exists. The expression of the consciousness that God's concern is with all peoples, even with the symbolic centre of a hostile world-power, is seen in the prophet's utterance of his knowledge that God is a God of mercy and forgiveness (4.2). We may see here, too, how the people's own experience, set out in the

historical surveys and in comparable material in psalmody
and prophecy, is that of a God who, though he judges, is ready
to forgive and to restore. Again, if there is oblique reference in
the book to the exilic experience, it is seen as an experience
which testifies to the restoration of a penitent community. But
more than this, the book takes up a theme found in Second
Isaiah, the theme that restoration is not for Israel alone, but is
related to the wider purposes of God for the nations. It is the
theme which in Ezekiel is expressed in terms of the nations as
witnesses of the divine action in saving Israel. The people is
restored, as the prophet Jonah is restored, by being brought
back to a starting point, the point from which the fulfilment of
the divine commission is to be undertaken. Just as the prophet
is shown as endeavouring to escape from his true mission, so
the people through historic experience is brought to a deepened understanding of its mediating role to the nations.

The same climax is reached at the end of Zechariah 8. Whoever was responsible for the present order of the material
clearly saw here the ultimate significance of what was to be
said about the post-exilic community. With so much of concern for the nature and position of the people, there is here
drawn out the full measure of its responsibility. The passage
(8.20-23) echoes the prophetic words of 2.15 (EVV 2.11), which
speak of the coming of the nations to be bound to Yahweh and
to be for him a people. It is the theme also of some words in
Malachi—less certain of interpretation—in which the
glorification of the name of Yahweh among the nations is
contrasted with the failure of his people (2.11, 14). (What is not
certain here is whether this glorification is seen as the
response of scattered members of the Jewish community—in
the diaspora—or as a recognition that he is recognized as
supreme universally. 2.11 is ambiguous; 2.14 appears to come
down more firmly on the side of the nations offering their
acknowledgment of the supremacy and glory of Yahweh, and
it is possible from this to read 2.11 in the same terms.)

The other aspect of concern is with the nature of the people
of God. The presence of this is clear in the writings of the
Chronicler, and it has sometimes been thought that the book of
Ruth is designed to provide a polemical statement against the
narrow exclusivism especially associated with Ezra. That

exclusivism, as we have seen, is the expression of a concern that the people should be the true people, faithful to its ancestral position, uncontaminated by the kind of alien connections which, as Deuteronomy insists, constitute the major threat to the faith. But in reality, we should see Ruth rather as a presentation of a concern with the nature of the community. It shows how the adherence of a faithful person, who undertakes total acceptance of obligation and protection, brings that person into the community. Ruth has 'taken refuge under the wings of the God of Israel' (2.12) and her reward is full participation in the people. If there is polemic, it could be more strictly against a too literal interpretation of Deuteronomy 23 (picked out for mention in the law-reading associated with Nehemiah in Neh. 13.1-3) which makes a particular point of the exclusion of the Moabites. In many ways, a much deeper concern of the book—though this is not unrelated to the question of the nature of the people—is with the problem of its preservation. The laws which govern redemption and the levirate marriage, around which the story turns, are not simply family laws, concerned with the preservation of the whole complement of Israel which would be incomplete if one of its families were missing. (We may compare the story of Abel-beth-maacah in 2 Sam. 20 where the wise woman claims that the destruction of a city is the destruction of Yahweh's own possession.) The preservation of the people and its life and faith may be looked at from two angles. It may be seen as a question of preserving purity, the removal of contaminating influences, the consideration of true descent. Or it may be seen as a matter of preserving the whole people, the recognition that Israel consists of tribal and family groups. This latter theme is also expressed in the genealogies of 1 Chronicles; it is a concern comparable to that of the Priestly writers who depict Israel on the threshold of the promised land (so especially in the book of Numbers), and of the final chapters of Ezekiel, with the vision of a new geography of the land and a new layout of the tribes. It is expressed in later emphasis on the twelve tribes, as for example in the twelve thousand from each tribe in the final age as the book of the Revelation depicts it (Rev. 7.1-8) and in the concept of God 'making up the full number of the elect'. These are two approaches to the same concern, a concern ultimately with the being of the people, its relationship to God, and its function.

So far, we have observed various lines of approach which are either directly or by implication connected with the community focused on Judah and Jerusalem. It is true that Jonah makes no mention of this, and Ruth only in so far as the story is located in Bethlehem and has an application to the Davidic line. But the concern for the community which these writings express, and the endeavours to meet the situation with a call to faith and obedience, represent only one group of ways in which the problems of the post-exilic community could express themselves. Because of the particular forms in which the traditions have come down to us, the centrality of Jerusalem is assumed. But not all those who claimed the ancestral faith took this view, and because they have come to be regarded as off-centre, their claim to make a contribution tends to be underestimated or treated as only a side issue.

In one area, the claims of particular groups of Jews clearly need to be heard. That is in the diaspora. From this period we are able to observe the impact on Judaean life from the diaspora. We are able, by inference, to see there a live community, concerned with the affairs of the homeland, particularly as this may be seen expressed in the undertakings of Nehemiah and Ezra. We have the traditions handed down in books such as Esther and Daniel, to provide us with a picture of Jewish life as it was subsequently believed to have existed. But these indications, useful though they are, leave us without any direct information. Our speculations about the position and activity of the character involved remain unconfirmed. The more literary work we assign to the exiled Jews in Babylonia and to that community that emerges into a clearer light centuries later, the more we have to postulate active religious life. But the decisions remain uncertain, and the picture inevitably sketchy.

For one such diaspora community, that of Elephantine, we have some direct information, but we need to be cautious before we assume that it is to be regarded as typical. It has, so far as we know, no successor, though the precise fate of those who composed it at the end of the fifth century remains uncertain. For here was a small Jewish military garrison, employed over more than a century by the Persian (Egyptian) authorities in the protection of the southern frontier and the control of an important trading centre. For a considerable period it had its own shrine, and it is because of this and the correspondence which resulted from its destruction and rebuilding that the documents which portray certain aspects of its life have been seen to have special importance in the understanding of the development of Jewish religious life.

The interpretation of the evidence from Elephantine is not easy. We have no clear information about the origin of the military colony, other than that its members claimed that its temple had been in existence already in the reign of Cambyses (529–522 BCE) and that he had respected its existence and not permitted it to be destroyed. (We cannot necessarily accept this statement at its face value, since we must recognize that it is made in a polemical setting.) No indication appears of any link with the Jewish refugees of Jeremiah 44, though it seems not impossible that the military colony originated in the period after the fall of Jerusalem in 587 BCE, and that its members to some extent preserved the ways of thought characteristic of the Judaean community then. What is quite evident is that the primary religious allegiance of this community was to Yahweh (Yhw); the preponderance of theophorous names compounded with Yhw makes this abundantly clear, and the temple was dedicated to him. When the temple was destroyed, the appeal for help was made to Jerusalem, and subsequently the appeal was renewed and an accompanying appeal made to Delaiah and Shelemaiah the sons of Sanballat, governor of Samaria. The fact that the appeal was made shows quite clearly that this Jewish community considered itself to have close affinity with that in Jerusalem and Judah. It is doubtful if the appeal can be interpreted as indicating that the authorization of the Jerusalem authorities was considered necessary, but rather that the support of the authorities—and perhaps particularly the governor—would be of assistance in encouraging the Persian governor in Egypt to take action. The implication would then be that it was in Jerusalem that the primary seat of the God Yahweh was to be found; but no necessary implication that it exercised some kind of 'pontifical' control.

Much discussion had centred around the problem of names which include other theophorous elements, though these are in a small minority; and also the difficulties raised by the evidence of a document listing contributions for the temple of Yhw, a large part of which appears to have been allocated to other deities. While the names can in some measure be explained as due to the use of divine titles applied to Yahweh— just as *ba'al* and *melek* can be so used—the occurrence of the female deity Anath creates greater difficulty. The legal documents of the community also provide some points of question in this respect, for they include oaths taken in the names of other deities, particularly Egyptian, by members of the Jewish community. The supposition that the divine names used in proper names can be regarded as evidence of a description of the deity by his attributes does not satisfactorily fit the temple contribution problem. The use of oaths in the names of other deities also points in the direction of some element of syncretistic practice. But perhaps our approach to these questions should be basically the pragmatic one. Here we have some insight into the daily life and social intercourse of a small Jewish community. We observe that it does not live in total isolation from its non-Jewish neighbours; there is clear evidence of intermarriage, and there are many indications of contractual undertakings between Jews and non-Jews. There are various ways in which a community may resolve the problems of preserving its own identity in an alien setting. One is to enjoin total separation, as is attempted by some extremist Christian groups today; this introduces a situation of some unreality. In a real situation intermarriage and other types of social and legal relationship are inevitable. There is a measure of compromise. It may, as in the case of members of the Elephantine community, involve the drawing up of a contract or a letter in which the forms of speech used imply the acceptance of the reality of other deities. By contrast with the firm denials of such reality in various Old Testament passages, this looks like an act of apostasy. But is it really as simple as that? Is it not in some measure an acceptance of the forms of social intercourse, a realistic handling of practical, day-to-day problems? The question of contributions to the temple may provide a corresponding case. The logic of a particular situation may demand the refusal to pay any taxes because some part of them is devoted to purposes of which one does not approve; but to contract out is also to avoid rightful responsibility. Since we do not know the precise situation in which the temple contributions were made, and the document in question is fragmentary, there may be some quite straightforward explanation. One might suppose a situation in which not only the temple of Yahweh but other temples too were maintained.

When the allowances have been made, and the situation of such a community imaginatively appraised, it is only proper to recognize too that prophetic diatribe and priestly legislation make clear that in biblical times apostasy was a real threat. The appurtenances of the temple in the time of Josiah include some which point to a clear infiltration—perhaps even a long-standing acceptance—of a female consort for Yahweh and rituals associated with this situation. The full range of religious opinion, from the severity of the extreme puritan wing to the easy-going compromise, can be detected in biblical material. So too in Elephantine. No community consists of people entirely of one mind; some who worshipped Anath as consort of Yahweh were no doubt just as sincere in their belief and practice as the refugees of Jeremiah 44. The ultimate working out of the religious tradition of the Old Testament excluded this particular area, but in the process of making this exclusion, it went through various stages and included various compromises. For compromise in this area is not simply a poor expedient; it may well represent the willingness to appropriate new elements of thought and to incorporate older ideas within a new complex of religious belief. It is not for nothing that Old Testament prophecy includes Hosea as the exponent of marriage symbolism in religious thinking, or that the Song of Songs stands among the writings of the eventual canon. And one could well draw more modern parallels.

The very existence of a temple at Elephantine appears to run contrary to biblical precept, but here again we must beware of judgment from a supposedly already existing central orthodox norm. The supposition that the Josianic reform excluded all other sanctuaries is easily made. Such other shrines as we know of—Leontopolis in the second century BCE, that at 'Araq el-Emir also in the Hellenistic age, that at

Gerizim—may have particular political background or derive from particular moments of religious strife. Others—such as Arad and Tell Deir 'Alla—existed over longer periods. But the very fact that they could exist poses problems for the supposed uniqueness of Jerusalem.

Recently, J.G. Vink in a monograph on the *Priestly Code* (Vink 1969) has raised questions about the nature and purpose of that code and has seen in some elements within it, and in some materials in Joshua which he believes should be associated with it, reflections of the work of Ezra and of the religious problems of the dispersion. Whether or not the detail of his argument is accepted, he has drawn attention again to the practical questions which needed to be resolved as between the claims of the Jerusalem community and those of Jewish groups elsewhere, whether in remote areas of Palestine or further afield.

It is probably also in this area of practical problems that we need to look for a right approach to the difficult evidence for the Samaritan community. The uncertainties about the period of origin of this community are well known. That there is no indication of such a division in the fifth century is clear; yet we may perhaps detect some of the factors which led eventually to the sharp schism which we know from later times. The destruction of the Gerizim shrine by John Hyrcanus in the second century was as much part of a politico-religious movement as was Josiah's action at Bethel in the seventh. The claim of the Samaritans, expressed particularly in their own name for themselves of *šōmᵉrîm*, the keepers, the guardians (of the law? of the tradition?), perhaps just 'the obedient', to be the true inheritors of the ancient ways, has at least as much justification as Jewish claims for Jerusalem. Where, in the end, it may have had cause for failure was in its backward-looking, perhaps even in what could in some respects be described as its uncompromising ways. For the Judaism which emerged in the later period, however much it claimed to be ancient and traditional and conservative, was in fact the product of a much more varied and much less hide-bound tradition, one that was both conscious of the past and acutely aware of the needs of the contemporary situation.

The tentative and incomplete nature of so much that has been said in these studies will be evident. To attempt to draw some precise conclusions would therefore be premature. What needs rather to be said is that we have seen some of the evidence from this period which points to the varieties of ways of thinking, and the approaches which can be made to some of the practical problems of being the Jewish community—a subject people centred in the tiny area of Jerusalem and Judah, a scattered people spread through the Near East, a people conscious of its past and aware of demands upon its life in religious terms. There are quietist elements here and stronger and more nationalistic; there are practical concerns with the day-to-day problems of living and negotiating in a delicate political situation. There is a sense of distress, and a summons therefore to faith and hope. There is an attempt at interpreting experience.

We may see this as an age of consolidation. It attempts interpretation of historic experience, particularly that of exile and restoration, seeing in the acceptance of judgment and the purification by exile a way through to the future, or seeing in the continuous character of ancient tradition a link with the past and a way of life for the present. It is a period of interpretation, particularly of the older, and in many cases, already written traditions; of the understanding and application of law, the reading of ancient narrative, the appropriation of the values of history as a story that has meaning. The ascription to the period—in more than one form—of the evolution of the sacred canon of scripture cannot be demonstrated historically; but it was with a right instinct that later tradition placed it here. The work of the Chronicler is one attestation of the way in which older material was being re-presented; the exegetical elements which may be detected within prophetic and psalm material is another. Jonah and Ruth and Job may all be described as offering the reapplication to this period of older story and tradition, a way of viewing what were evidently regarded as historical traditions as being meaningful to a later generation.

It is the development of the understanding of law which has come to be seen as the central characteristic, and so as the main feature of later Judaism. But in fact the matter is to be more broadly based, in the recognition that Judaism, like Christianity, has had the advantage—and also the disadvantage—of being in large measure attached to a written canon, a canon continually reinterpreted but nevertheless always in danger of becoming a static and stultifying factor in religious development. In this, the Persian period is not unlike other periods of Old Testament thought: it marks a development within the tensions which are inevitable in a community which both holds to the past—the tradition, the scriptures— and seeks to be itself in a contemporary situation.

This last, which finds an immediate echo in our own position, may offer a further reason for reckoning the fuller discussion of this period to be one that is not without its relevance to modern Christians and Jews.

Chapter 2

ARCHAEOLOGY, POLITICS AND RELIGION
IN THE PERSIAN PERIOD[1]

The prospect of the appearance this year (1982) of the English
version of Ephraim Stern's study of the archaeological evidence for the Persian period makes it appropriate to offer
here, not a review of that volume, but some comment on ways
in which in recent years various attempts have been made at
clarifying the life and thought of that still so obscure episode in
the life of the biblical community. Stern's volume is devoted, as
its title indicates, to Palestine: he writes on *The Material Culture of the Land of the Bible in the Persian Period*. The special
concern of this volume is to draw together, and to attempt a
synthetic treatment of, the significant range of evidence for
that period, deriving from archaeological work within the
Palestinian area. The questions on which I propose to comment will, naturally enough, concern that area primarily; but
we cannot expect to understand the Jewish community in
Palestine, its development and its thought, without taking
some account of two facts. (1) Jewish life in this period, even
more clearly than in the immediately preceding Babylonian
period and in the pre-exilic age, belongs to a wider stage than
that limited area. Here, for the first time, with rather minimal
exceptions, we become aware of Jews in Egypt and Babylonia.
We are also aware of relationships within Palestine outside
the narrow administrative unit of Judah (Yehud). Jewry is
larger than Judah. (2) The control of political life by an alien

---

1. This essay represents the text of the author's Inaugural Lecture
of the Walter G. Williams Lectureship in Old Testament, delivered in
May 1982 at the Iliff School of Theology, Denver, Colorado, and published in the *Iliff Review* 39 (1982): 5-24.

power—in this case the empire of the Persians, successors to Assyrians and Babylonians and predecessors of Greeks and Romans—inevitably means that domestic concerns, however central to the lives of the majority of the community, are in some measure overruled by international power politics; for the majority most obviously expressed in imperial military activity and taxation. The importance of this last is clear, but its intangibility is underlined when we recognize that we have little direct information about such matters in relation to the Jewish community. We have to infer what kind of effects were produced by Persian fiscal policies from our broader understanding of what Persian rulers were doing, and endeavouring to apply that to the interpretation of the particular problems of Jewish life (Stern 1982: 234-35).

The inclusion of the word 'archaeology' in the title of this chapter is an indication of the importance of interpreting the biblical text in relation to all the evidence which may appropriately be adduced for its understanding. One area in relation to the Persian period is our knowledge, extensive but with its own problems of understanding, of the classical world. The conflicts between Greece and Persia, and the involvement of Egypt in these conflicts, are an important background element to the understanding of Jewish life. The term 'archaeology' might not normally be applied to such evidence, yet it is important not to separate textual from archaeological evidence, especially since there are so many points at which the elucidation of Greek and Egyptian history, as well as Persian, depends on the right assessment of more narrowly 'dirt' archaeology (for references cf. Widengren 1977: 95-99; Sancisi-Weerdenburg 1980).

But while this broader background is clearly important, we have to recognize the extreme difficulty of correlating the external information with what we know from the biblical texts of the internal history of the Jewish community. Largely this is because of the nature of the texts, and this is a problem which we meet at almost every point in the assessment of biblical history. Narrative texts, such as we have for the Persian period in the two books of Ezra and Nehemiah, lack precision at the very points at which we should most expect them. While reference to Cyrus the Persian at the beginning of Ezra (Ezra

1.1; cf. 2 Chron. 36.22) gives us a precise link, subsequent references to Persian rulers are almost invariably less than clear. The most problematic of these is the reference to the 'seventh year of Artaxerxes' in Ezra 7.7, where no agreement exists as to which ruler of that name is meant. The similar allusion to a ruler Artaxerxes in Neh. 2.1 is generally assumed to be more precise, and reference to Artaxerxes I thought to be virtually certain, giving a date for Nehemiah's first period of activity as beginning in 445 BCE; even this is not in fact absolutely sure, and arguments can be adduced for placing Nehemiah under Artaxerxes II (404–358). We may observe that Josephus places Nehemiah after Ezra, indeed after Ezra's death (*Ant.* 11.158); we also now have fairly clear information which shows the existence of at least two and probably three governors of Samaria named Sanballat (Cross 1975, p. 5 [188] and references there), so that identification of Sanballat I as contemporary with Nehemiah, as is normally done, cannot be regarded as absolutely proved. Strong probability is not the same as certainty, and there must be caution in making clear just what is being built on the assumptions of identification or dating where the evidence is not fully assured.

Indeed, in many respects, historically and archaeologically, the Persian period represents a sort of interregnum. Knowledge both of historical sequences and of archaeological material is much more abundant for the Hellenistic and Roman periods. In part this is a question of available external witnesses in texts; in part it is the consequence of a greater interest until recent years in the archaeology of earlier and later periods. This also follows from the degree to which later building radically disturbed what may have existed from the Persian period. Recent work, and especially that of Ephraim Stern, provides the basis for advance; but it must still be observed that the total amount of evidence is relatively small and conclusions are still modest (see Stern 1982: ch. 9).

It is therefore with caution that the study of the period must be approached. The difficulties and limitations imposed on our knowledge of it must be fully recognized, but must not be allowed to discourage the attempt. And here we may observe a shift of emphasis in recent years which enables a more satisfactory approach to be made. There is today a much greater willingness to recognize the significance of a period during which so much must have happened internally to the Jewish community, and so much effect must have been produced on the formation of the biblical writings. When we emerge from its obscurities into the often better-known Hellenistic period, we observe how far the biblical writings have been given a form which must be very close to what we now know. Manuscript evidence from Qumran, some of which goes back in all probability to the early Hellenistic period, and all of which belongs before the destruction of Jerusalem in 70 CE, shows the degree of textual fixation which has been reached. The writings of Jesus ben Sira (Ecclesiasticus) show the existence of something not far removed from the three-part canon of Jewish tradition (Prologue and chs. 44–49). That both textual and canonical questions were still in some measure open is clear, but the situation is very different from what it must have been in the sixth century BCE. It is clear that the effect of the disasters of that period and the demand for rethinking which they occasioned in the rehabilitation under the Persians had as one of its results a much greater degree of formalizing of the already existing writings. In the years of Persian rule, much must have taken place. To understand the nature of the community in which that was happening is vital to the appreciation of the final form of the writings themselves.

It is also of enormous importance for the understanding of the Jewish and Christian communities which were eventually to emerge from the biblical context. Jewish tradition has always given a much greater place to the developments during the Persian period, attributing to Ezra and to his successors in the 'men of the Great Synagogue' (cf. Barth 1976, for references) both the preservation of the ancient scriptures (cf. e.g. 2 Esd. 14) and of the continuing tradition. The understanding of the past is in terms which, even if too rigid, are nevertheless significant for what they say about the importance of religious continuity. Christian scholarship has often looked more to the earlier period, partly because of an overemphasis on the prophets dictated by a too narrow view of New Testament understanding of scripture and its significance; partly because of a misunderstanding of the contrast between law and gospel which has often formed a convenient but less than satisfactory basis for distinction between Christian and Jewish thinking. A better appraisal of Christian origins and of the nature of the Christian movement follows from a clearer appreciation of the post-exilic period. I make no apologies therefore for choosing the Persian period as the one to which I devote my attention. It is in any case the area in which much of my own thinking has been concentrated over the past twenty years and that to which I hope to devote further time in the next few years in the hope of clarifying some of its problems. (See also Ackroyd 1984.)

I propose to consider a small group of questions in which consideration of archaeological and textual evidence offers the opportunity for making some comments on problems of interpretation.

1. *The Political Organization of Judah*

a. *The exilic period and its consequences*
We shall need first to move a little further back into the period of the exile and ask what kind of political situation existed after the second fall of Jerusalem in 587 BCE. At this point the Babylonians appointed one Gedaliah son of Ahikam son of Shaphan, a member of a prominent Jerusalem family in this period. Identifications are always open to some question, since our records, biblical and non-biblical, show the degree to which the identical names appear in the same period. But it seems most probable that Gedaliah's father and grandfather are the same as the Ahikam and his father Shaphan who appear prominently in the reign of Josiah, the latter as 'secretary', a high office of state (2 Kgs 22.8, 12). Another of his sons, Gemariah, and his son Micaiah, appear in Jeremiah 36 as part of the royal entourage; yet another son, Elasah, in Jer. 29.3 as one of Zedekiah's envoys to Babylon.

Gedaliah was appointed by the Babylonians, but we do not know precisely to what office; no title is ever given him, and the verb denoting his appointment (*pqd* hiph.) leaves the matter open. There is a question here which we cannot answer. Is the silence deliberate and is Gedaliah's true position thus concealed? There is no hesitation in describing Zedekiah, the Davidide, as king (2 Kgs 24.18), though alongside this we find that the tablets discovered in Babylon—the so-called Weidner tablets (*ANET*, 308)—in indicating Jehoiachin as 'son of the king of Judah', may be understood to be stating his legitimate royal status, which could suggest that for the Babylonians he remained king, even in captivity, and Zedekiah was a substitute. Gedaliah was not of the royal family. Is it for this reason that he was not designated king? Yet evidence in the narratives in Jeremiah 40–41 could suggest that he had some kind of royal status, for we find that he had charge of 'the king's daughters' (Jer. 41.10) and we observe that Ishmael of the Davidic house, who assassinated Gedaliah, took these royal women with him. May we see these royal women as the royal harem whose possession is part of the rights of a royal successor, or can be regarded as constituting a claim to the throne? (For indications, see the narrative of Absalom in 2 Sam. 16.20-22 and of Adonijah in 1 Kgs 2.) Was Gedaliah appointed as king by the Babylonians, who thus quite skilfully reduced the claims of the Davidic house and put in control a man whose reputation and that of his family could be regarded as pro-Babylonian, and whose standing in Judah was evidently high (cf. Jer. 41.11ff.)?

But then nothing. After the assassination of Gedaliah and the escape of the assassin to the protection of the Ammonites (and what were they up to?), we have no internal information about the Judaean community at all. Was another official appointed by the Babylonians? Was some other administrative organization imposed? (We shall return to this question.) Is the silence in our sources a result of ignorance, or of indifference, or of a deliberate passing over of the period in the interests of a later situation?

The clue may lie in the account at the end of 2 Kings (25.27-30) of the release from captivity of King Jehoiachin (he is specifically given his title 'king of Judah') and his restoration to a position of honour in the royal Babylonian household. We may note the degree of honour—'his throne exalted above the thrones of the kings who were with him in Babylon'—allow something for the writer's patriotic feelings, but still recognize that this is evidently a significant event in Jewish tradition. We may note that, as it is presented in 2 Kings, it provides a positive counter to the negative detail about Gedaliah. (The

Gedaliah material in Jeremiah 41f. is also negative, but not in quite the same way.) We may note also that in the parallel text in Jeremiah 52, which follows closely, though with important differences, the final part of 2 Kings, the Gedaliah material is absent: we move from the details of the three stages of exile (Jer. 52.28-30) to the release of Jehoiachin (52.31-34).

We may, I believe, legitimately suppose that, in the view of some members of the Jewish community, this event marked the restoration of the Davidic monarchy. It was to be of no lasting significance for Jehoiachin, though we do not know how long he survived. 2 Kings 25 shows him restored to favour 'for the rest of his life', which may imply a slightly more positive note than 'to the day of his death' in Jeremiah 52. But either expression can readily imply a restoration without reservation. His restoration to favour was a royal act in the accession year of Nebuchadnezzar's successor. Since that successor was to be murdered only two years later, we may ask— but we cannot answer the question—whether his downfall was accompanied by ill fortune for his protégé at the court. But this does not affect the way in which the event was evidently regarded, and the restoration thus effected, however token, could be significant for the sequel.

The next information we have about a Davidide concerns Zerubbabel, grandson of Jehoiachin, whose position under the Persian authorities in the early years of Persian rule is also unclear. He is described as 'governor' (*peḥâ*) in Haggai, though not in Ezra 3 nor in the Aramaic material in Ezra 5.2. He is claimed as 'my servant' (*'abdî*) and as appointed 'like a seal' or 'signet ring' (*ḥātôm*) and as 'chosen' (*bāḥar*) in Hag. 2.23; if, though not named, he is intended in Zech. 3.8-10, he is there designated as 'my servant "branch"' (*'abdî ṣemaḥ*). These are royal titles; they are perhaps echoed in the problematic passage Zech. 4.6b-10a where he is named (the passage is intrusive and perhaps does not even belong to Zechariah); and in the equally problematic Zech. 6.9-15, where, however, he is again not named. What kind of claim is being made for Zerubbabel? How far should we link that claim to the Jehoiachin material? Is the stress on the status of Jehoiachin and the silence about the status of Gedaliah and about any successors directed to the complex political situation in the

early years of Persian rule? (A fuller discussion of some of
these issues and their sequels is in preparation and to appear
in *Cambridge History of Judaism* I.)

b. *The Judaean restoration under Persian rule*
We have already stepped over the boundary between the
Babylonian and Persian periods with these comments on
Zerubbabel. Now we must put him in context so far as we
may.

The literary evidence is complex. Ezra 1–6 is closely linked,
as it now stands, with the final verses of 2 Chronicles. Whatever may be said about unity or diversity of authorship for the
two works, Chronicles and Ezra–Nehemiah—and the issue is
a very difficult one to resolve—we certainly encounter in Ezra
1–6 problems of historical reconstruction as great as or
greater than those we should face if we only had 2 Chronicles
as an account of the period of the Israelite and Judaean
monarchies. The narrative is disjointed; characters appear
and disappear; chronology is piecemeal or nonexistent. The
narratives are interrupted by ch. 2 which consists largely of
lists. The narratives of chs. 1, 3 and 5–6, which belong to the
period of the first Persian rulers, Cyrus and Darius, are interrupted in parts of ch. 4 by material which is set in the reigns of
Xerxes I (486–465 BCE) and Artaxerxes I (465–424 BCE, if we
assume the first ruler of that name), without any explanation.

If we concentrate on what appears to belong to the immediate restoration period, we find a prominent personage Sheshbazzar in ch. 1. He is 'prince' or 'leader' (*nāśî'*); he has no
genealogy, and his title is certainly not necessarily suggestive
of the royal house. The supposition that he is to be identified
with a Davidide is without foundation (Ackroyd 1979: 331). He
reappears in 5.14 in the Aramaic text as governor (*pehâ*); the
sequel in the text describes Sheshbazzar as beginning the
temple rebuilding and indicates that the rebuilding is not yet
complete. The absence of Sheshbazzar's name earlier in this
Aramaic narrative implies that he himself was no longer
active, and when a further reference to a governor appears in
6.7, no name is given. We may assume that this is not Sheshbazzar. Zerubbabel appears in 5.2, but not described as a governor; he does not reappear, and neither does Joshua, the

priest named with him. I suspect that both names are here intrusive, and belong to an editor who was attempting to integrate the apparently conflicting material of the whole section. According to this Aramaic narrative, then, Sheshbazzar was governor under Cyrus; a further governor, direct successor or not, was operating under Darius.

The intervening narrative of ch. 3—with which we may associate the final Hebrew section in 6.19-22—refers in its first part to Zerubbabel and Joshua; the latter is indicated as priest, the former by his father's name and with reference to his brothers, to be understood more broadly as his kinsmen. But, as we have noted, Zerubbabel is not here given a title.

It is not possible to resolve the administrative questions here. Sheshbazzar is not described as governor in one passage, but as prince or leader; in another and clearly separate section, he is described as governor. Zerubbabel is not described as governor in Ezra; he is so described in Haggai, but not in the only passage in Zechariah which names him. He is given implied royal status in Haggai, and possibly also, without being named, in Zechariah 3 and 6; but nowhere else. It has been argued that both Sheshbazzar and Zerubbabel were special commissioners rather than governors. The title *peḥâ*, governor, is used very broadly, for different levels of officials. Nehemiah, we are told, was appointed governor (though the title is used only in Neh. 5.14, 18 and 12.26), and this was for a fixed term. Perhaps we are making unreal distinctions if we talk of 'special commissioners' and 'governors' as if they were quite different. We do not know whether the Persians appointed such officers regularly for specific periods. In the case of Samaria, the office appears to have remained in a family, perhaps over as many as five generations.

The gap between the period of restoration and that of Nehemiah, the next named governor in the biblical text, is bridged only by the allusion in Neh. 5.15 to governors who have preceded Nehemiah. It is a somewhat intangible comment, since it belongs within the whole context of the Nehemiah presentation which is quite evidently a glorification of him. To contrast him favourably with his predecessors could be a device directed towards such praise, rather than necessarily a piece of valid historical information. This is possibly underlined by what seems to be the clear intention of the opening verses of the Nehemiah narrative which in effect presents him as the rebuilder of Jerusalem, ruined at the exile: Nehemiah is already here on the way to becoming the complete restorer of city and cult as which he is presented in the opening chapters of 2 Maccabees (Ackroyd 1970a: 32-33; 1973: 266). We have to be cautious how much history we endeavour to reconstruct from this kind of evidence.

Another possible bridge is in Malachi where 1.8 refers to a governor. The natural inference is that this is a governor of Judah, though it is not so stated. Its usefulness as evidence depends on the dating of Malachi, for which there is very little clear information; the conventional date in the period before Nehemiah is little more than a guess, partly at least based on the evidence of the Nehemiah material. Such a writing can hardly be used in reconstructing the historical sequence; its date must first be established independently.

There are references which use another title, *tiršātā'* 'excellency', for Nehemiah in Neh. 10.2; for an unnamed personage in Ezra 2.63 = Neh. 7.65 and also Neh. 7.69; and a problematic reference to Nehemiah with this title in the Ezra material of Ezra 8.9, probably a harmonizing addition (cf. 1 Esd. 9.49 where the name Nehemiah is not found). But this adds little that can be satisfactorily used.

When we move out of the biblical text, we find other evidence. There is reference in the Elephantine papyri (30.1) to *bgwhy* (Bigvai, Bagoas) *pḥt yhwd*, datable to 408 BCE (Cowley 1923: 108-19). The same name appears as Bigvai in post-exilic lists (Ezra 2.14; Neh. 7.19; sons of Bigvai, Ezra 2.2; Neh. 7.7; associated with Ezra, Ezra 8.14; cf. also Neh. 10.16 [MT 17]).

Over recent years bullae (small lumps of clay used to seal letters or documents, pressed on the string and stamped), seals, and also jar impressions have been discovered bringing new, but still problematic, evidence. The full account of these does not belong here (see Avigad 1976; Stern 1982: ch. 6); we may simply extract the relevant evidence. This amounts to a governor named Elnathan (*'lntn*); another named Yeho'ezer (*yhw'zr*); another named Ahzai (*'ḥzy*). From a coin comes another name Yehezkiya (*yḥzkyh*). All are described as *pḥw'*, i.e. *peḥâ*.

The addition of four names to the meagre evidence for governors is of clear importance. But unfortunately substantial problems remain. The dating proposed for the bullae and seals, which lack archaeological contexts, varies from the sixth to the fourth century (for a survey see Stern 1982: 203 and notes. Stern himself [1982: 21] promises a fuller discussion). Avigad provides a chronology (1976: 35):

> Sheshbazzar, c. 538
> Zerubbabel, c. 515
> Elnathan, late sixth century
> Yeho'ezer, early fifth century
> Aḥzai, early fifth century
> Nehemiah 445–433 (to which would be added his second
> period of office, Neh. 13)
> Bagoas, 408
> Yeḥezqiyah, c. 330

The evidence for this is partly epigraphic, placing Elnathan ahead of the other two names, but this is very dubious; for the last name, the coin points to the end of the Persian period, and it is noted that there was a chief priest Ezekias (not, it appears, 'the high priest') in the period of Ptolemy I, from about 301 BCE (Stern 1982: 223; cf. Josephus, *Contra Ap.* 1.187). Identifying this priest with a governor in the late Persian period appears to me very questionable; chronologically it is possible since he is said to be sixty-six years old under Ptolemy I, but too much rests on the similarity or identity of name which must be insufficient evidence unless otherwise supported.

Talmon (1976: 325) presses the evidence further. One of the seals is inscribed 'Belonging to Shelomith maidservant of Elnathan the governor' (Avigad 1976: 11: *lšlmyt 'mt 'lntn p[ḥ ..]*). Talmon interprets the word *'ammâ*, 'maidservant', as a term denoting 'wife'; 1 Chron. 3.19 names a daughter of Zerubbabel as Shelomith and he considers this to be evidence that Elnathan was successor and son-in-law to Zerubbabel; he also identifies the name *ḥnnh* on a storage jar as that of a son of Zerubbabel, Hananiah; and a *brwk bn sm'y* as that of a nephew of Zerubbabel, son of his brother Shimei. Such a conjunction of names looks persuasive, but is highly conjectural. Before it could be accepted, the dates of the archaeological evidence would need to be much firmer. Until such time as that is clear, deductions of this sort are not satisfying (Stern 1981: 21 n. 25. Stern himself dates these governors on the bullae to the period after Nehemiah).

Thus a consideration of this evidence leaves us with a series of as yet unresolved problems. Can we arrive at a more satisfactory order for the indications we have of new governors' names? Can we develop a clearer chronology? Along with this go problems of status for the officers about whom we have some detail, Sheshbazzar, Zerubbabel and Nehemiah. Can we find clearer evidence to date the material of Malachi, so that its statements can contribute to this discussion? What literary and hence historical assessment should we accord to the Nehemiah memorial? Most of these questions are long familiar; they remain still as important as in the past, and discussion of them must, we may hope, continue to be lively.

2. *Samaria and Judah—Another Aspect of Administrative Status*

It will be clear from the preceding discussion that we still know much less about the organization of the Judaean area in the Persian period than we could wish. The new pieces of information are clearly important, but their correlation with our existing knowledge remains less than certain.

But there is another aspect to this problem which needs attention. This concerns a view which was first put forward by Albrecht Alt (1934) as part of a fuller study of the interrelationships between Samaria and the formation of post-exilic Judaism. He maintained that Judah had been placed under the control of Samaria. The proposal has been influential and has found numerous supporters. In recent years, partly as a result of a very critical appraisal by Morton Smith (1971: 193-201), and partly now with the discovery of further names of governors, it has come to be treated with more caution. I do not propose here to go over the debate in detail; much of Alt's thesis and much of Morton Smith's criticism are concerned with wider issues, and in so far as the former's views concern the origin and development of Samaritanism, they have been overtaken by more recent work. Morton Smith's comments are largely concerned with these wider issues, but quite prop-

erly he stresses that Alt's was a hypothesis. By repeatedly ital-
icizing the word *perhaps* and with much use of 'hypothecate'
in his strictures on Alt, he underlines this point. It would be
possible to go through his own comments and indeed his whole
volume and introduce the same kind of emphasis to describe
many of his statements. But hypothesis is an essential tool of
scholarship: the reconstruction of this period invites hypothesis for the simple reason that we have so few hard facts.

I wish only to draw out what appear to me to be the issues to
which answers are still needed if we are to get an adequate
explanation of the Persian period, so far as Judah and
Samaria are concerned. I would suggest that there are three
main areas which demand discussion; to these may be added
the general point that the hypothesis that, after the death of
Gedaliah, Judah was placed under the administration of the
governor in Samaria, is an attempt to fill a gap in our information. If in due course we are able to identify governors for
that period, then the hypothesis either becomes unnecessary
or would be applicable only in a rather different form. The
three main problem areas would still need elucidation.

(a) We need to ask what is the basis for the opposition of
Samaria to the restoration of Jerusalem. We may observe
such opposition at two distinct points, though the chronological
relation between them is not clear. The more precise moment
is that of Nehemiah's activity. In the narratives there, we find
the opposition of Sanballat, governor of Samaria. He appears
in Neh. 2.10, together with Tobiah the servant, the Ammonite;
and again in 2.19 with the further addition of Geshem the
Arab (cf. Cross 1975: 7 [190]) for what appear to be too simple
identifications. Subsequently, in 4.1-6 (MT 3.33-38), Sanballat
appears, with Tobiah in an apparently subordinate position
(v. 3; MT 3.35); and in 4.7ff. (MT 4.1ff.) we find Sanballat and
Tobiah and the Arabs and the Ammonites and the Ashdodites.
In ch. 6, Sanballat appears with Tobiah and Geshem in v. 1,
and with Geshem alone in v. 2; then Sanballat appears separately in v. 5, with Geshem very oddly appended in v. 6. In the
immediately following passage, 6.10-19, Sanballat does
appear, but in second place to Tobiah. This detail is needed for
the discussion, since it is evident that if Nehemiah was dealing
with three opponents all of equal or more or less equal status,

then arguments about the reasons for opposition from
Samaria become part of a general appraisal of the political situation. But a close consideration of the evidence strongly suggests that for the main narrative in ch. 4 and the first part of
ch. 6, Sanballat really stands alone. The second part of ch. 6 is
a Tobiah narrative, and the basis of Tobiah's conflict with
Nehemiah is very differently indicated. Do we here have indications that a main opposition theme has been extended by the
incorporation into it of separate and perhaps less important
opposition themes? If so, we may justify the consideration of
Sanballat and Samaria separately, and recognize the degree to
which the Nehemiah story has been extended—as we have
already seen—in the interests of glorifying him and his status.

Why then the opposition? It could be economic, and there
might be some clue to this in Nehemiah 13 in the action taken
against foreign merchants who broke the sabbath; but nothing
in the narrative really suggests that foreign trade came to an
end, only that entry on the sabbath was precluded; violent
action was threatened to prevent the merchants setting up
their stalls outside the wall, with a view to encouraging the
inhabitants to ignore the sabbath and come out to them. If economic questions were the root issue, there seems no special
reason for associating this with Samaria. More generally, we
can suppose that Samaria would not welcome revival in
Jerusalem, and part of the reason for that could be economic,
but nowhere in the text is this suggested. (See below on Ezra 4
for a possible allusion to such a motif.)

A second possibility would be religious, and this is clearly a
delicate question. But we may observe that there is no indication of any religious grounds for Sanballat's opposition. What
we do find, both in Nehemiah 6 and in Nehemiah 13, are indications of close relationships between Sanballat (in the latter
case by marriage) and Nehemiah's opponents within Judah.
This could suggest personal reasons for antagonism, which
might be a contributory factor. We have clues here to internal
troubles in Jerusalem and Judah, in which Sanballat was
apparently involved, but religious grounds are not really
adduced except in the pious comment of 13.29. Nor can we
deduce any indications of fundamental religious distinction,
since Sanballat's sons bore Yahwistic names, Delaiah and

Shelemaiah (so the Elephantine Papyri, 30.29); the religious schism between Jerusalem and Samaria belongs to a later date than this, though it is conceivable that there has been some influence on the narrative from subsequent events. What does appear, in Neh. 2.20, is a refutation of claims which are evidently made by the opponents; it is clear that they—and we may perhaps deduce primarily or even solely Sanballat—are making certain precise claims to rights in Jerusalem. Nehemiah denies to the opponents three particular rights: *ḥēleq, ṣedāqâ* and *zikkārôn*. The precise meaning is not easy to determine, but we need not doubt that something quite specific is intended. *Ḥēleq* suggests 'territorial rights' in the sense of ownership of or control over some piece of land in Jerusalem; perhaps we should compare the trading rights in Samaria for Aramaeans and in Damascus for Israelites in the period of the conflicts between Aram and Israel (1 Kgs 21.34). *Ṣedāqâ* perhaps implies legal rights; and *zikkārôn* closely related traditional rights, customary rights. But even though certainty about these is not possible, it would seem clear that the three terms together effectively deny any kind of rights in Jerusalem; such a denial presupposes that there were grounds for the claim being made to possess such rights, and the nature of the relationship between Samaria and Jerusalem must presumably have included the recognition of such rights. This could suggest that Nehemiah is here being described as claiming a degree of independence not previously possessed by Jerusalem. The evidence is insufficient to build a firm case, but it points in the direction at least of some degree of external control.

The other opposition passage in Ezra 4—consisting in reality of more than one element—is much more difficult to assess. First, we have no adequate basis for fixing its date: one piece (4.6) is set early in the reign of Xerxes (486–465 BCE); one (4.7) in the reign of Artaxerxes; the third (4.8-23) also in the reign of Artaxerxes. Which Artaxerxes is meant is not stated; it is usually assumed to be Artaxerxes I (465–424 BCE). The latter two complaints can hardly be one and the same, though the text seems to imply that the latter is an Aramaic version of the former; the names of the people involved are quite different. It is this last and fuller passage which includes reference to Samaria, in the context of the other areas of the province Beyond the River. The fact that Samaria alone of the separate areas is mentioned by name suggests either that Samaria was the prime mover, and that we may therefore see this as evidence of opposition to Jerusalem from there; or that the passage has subsequently been modified as part of anti-Samaritan polemic (for comments see Coggins 1975: 66ff.). We again have the problem that the present form of the material in this passage is clearly designed to glorify Jerusalem and its ancient history, and historical reconstruction is made all the more difficult because of this. The chronological uncertainty too makes it difficult to use the material in any satisfactory way.

There is in this material some indication of claims made over Jerusalem by Samaria which need an explanation. One possible explanation is that at some point Judah was controlled from Samaria; that is not necessarily the only possibility.

(b) The second point takes further the question of the relationship by considering how it came about that the Elephantine community appealed in 408 BCE (Papyrus 30) to both Samaria and Jerusalem. We can appreciate that an appeal to Persian authorities could be assisted by support from other governors. Clearly such support would more readily be given by governors who had some interest or concern in the fortunes of the Jewish community in Elephantine. That it was Jewish, Judaean, is clear from the name which it uses to describe itself—the Jewish force (*ḥyl' yhwdy'*). Appeal to Jerusalem is therefore natural. But why appeal to Samaria unless there was some special reason for this? Is that reason religious? We have observed the Yahwistic names of Sanballat's sons, and other Yahwistic names appear in the later indications of the line of governors in Samaria (Cross 1975: 17 [203]). Or is there here a reflection of a particular kind of administrative link between Samaria and Jerusalem?

(c) The third point is evidence to suggest an administrative change in Judah towards the end of the fifth century. Stern (1971; 1982: 211) points to the replacement in that period of Achaemenian motifs on seals by *yehud* stamps; and to the granting of the right to mint coins which is revealed by the appearance of *yehud* coins from about the same period. He considers that this change could come from after or at the time of Nehemiah. Does this suggest that the administrative position before this period was different, and if so what kind of position existed? Does the appeal from Elephantine to both Samaria and Jerusalem argue for some degree of uncertainty about the position at the time of the appeal? If the change to greater independence for Judah was relatively recent, perhaps even as yet insufficiently formalized, such a double appeal would be intelligible.

To these points we may add one further reflection. As things stand at present, we have no established sequence of governors for Judah. We have a much clearer picture of a family succession in Samaria, though our precise evidence here covers only the period from the mid-fifth century towards the end of Persian rule. Why did this administrative difference exist?

It is perhaps appropriate here to make a more general comment on Persian policy. Attempts are frequently made at determining the precise nature of Persian policy at any given moment. The discussions of the Cyrus cylinder in relation to the decree of Cyrus given in two forms in Ezra 1 and 6, and the relating of this to other indications of Persian action in regard to religious establishments have involved attempts at finding some kind of consistency in Persian policy. In the discussions of the commissioning of various officers—Sheshbazzar, Zerubbabel, Nehemiah, Ezra—attempts have been made at correlating the moments of their appointment with the broader political situation (cf. e.g. Ackroyd 1970a: 15ff.; Ackroyd 1970b: 174ff.; Schultz 1980: [esp. 233-34]).

This is entirely proper, but it must not be carried too far. Imperial policy is not necessarily always consistent. Pragmatic decisions may be at different levels, responding to different needs as they are perceived. Politicians, as we all know, can make mistakes of judgment, and they can show themselves to be inept. Often—and we may suppose this for the Persian rulers as for more modern politicians—what they do depends on the quality of the advice given to them. In addition, as we may see from the Nehemiah story, a personal act of favouritism could result in political action. It seems to me to be worth considering—since so much of our evidence is inconclusive—whether the precise administrative situation between Samaria and Jerusalem was in some degree undermined by the commissioning of Nehemiah; and that the Persian policy associated with this and the subsequent apparent emergence of a greater degree of autonomy for Judah could be partly explained by spasmodic and inconsistent action, and also by that great expedient of politicians faced with intractable problems, that of 'wait and see', in the hope that perhaps the problem will go away. We must not look for a greater coherence and intelligibility in political action in the past than we should expect to find in our own time.

3. *Religious Levels and Differences*

The unravelling of the religious situation in the Persian period is as difficult as the recovery of historical sequences. There are obvious reasons for this. We may appreciate the concern of a later time to establish a coherent and continuous line of tradition which would show the direct link between the religion which was re-established after the Babylonian exile and what had preceded. An idealized picture of a single religious tradition traceable back to Moses and beyond him to the patriarchs was an important element in the maintaining of religion and in the stresses and pressures of the Hellenistic and Roman periods and beyond. To some extent that idealism was already present at an earlier stage. So we may see the importance for the immediate restoration period itself of showing such direct links with the past, and within the writings of the period we may detect various ways in which such a continuity was presented. (For elements in such preservation of continuity, see Ackroyd 1972, 1977, 1980.)

An emphasis on continuity with the past and on unity of tradition inevitably obscures the diversity which in fact is likely to have existed and which can be partially demonstrated by a close examination of the material. A comparable situation exists in both Jewish and Christian theological development. Thus, diversity in the New Testament, strongly emphasized in much contemporary scholarship, is observable in spite of the strong pressures in the early post-New Testament period to present a picture of uniformity. An analogy may, with suitable caution, be drawn between the sharp divisions of the Hellenistic period in the second century BCE, the period from which we may clearly trace the development of the sharply divided groups known to us from the New Testament and from Qumran, and a comparable situation in the sixth and fifth centuries BCE. The whole question of what constituted continuity is inevitably raised as a result of the political uncertainties of the preceding period of Babylonian conquest, destruction and control; we should expect differences of view on this, in addition to the survival of elements of an earlier diversity.

It is convenient to begin here by going back to a point raised earlier in connection with the problems of the administration of Judah. This is the Davidic theme. We have seen evidence for the continuing emphasis on Davidic claims, expressed particularly in the figure of Zerubbabel. But we observe a number of problems which arise here. One of these concerns the precise status of Zerubbabel under Persian authority; another the uncertainty which surrounds this Davidic figure. Later legend was to be quite explicit. 1 Esdras 3.1–5.3 tells a story, set at the court of Darius, of a contest of wits between three young guardsmen concerning what is strongest (cf. also Josephus, *Ant.* 11.33-58). The third of these appears to have described women as strongest; but an addendum mentions Truth (3.12). When he comes to speak, he is quite unexpectedly identified as Zerubbabel (4.13), and when he has won the contest, he is able to get from the king permission to carry out the king's own vow to rebuild Jerusalem and restore the temple. It is clear that here a story of quite independent origin (see Sancisi-Weerdenburg 1980: ch. 7) has been used to provide an explanation, not provided by the biblical texts, of how Zerubbabel came to be appointed and what his precise commission was. Furthermore, the narrative of his appointment in 1 Esdras leads on into the list of returned exiles which we have in Ezra 2 (= Neh. 7), but does so with a short passage (1 Esd. 5.4-6) emphasizing the Davidic descent of Zerubbabel, indicated only by means of a patronymic in Ezra 3 and Haggai. There would appear to be evidence in 1 Esdras of some development in the Davidic emphasis, though even here the Davidic theme follows the priestly; it is of interest in relation to the rather different situation which we find in the Chronicles–Ezra–Nehemiah complex.

The other aspect of uncertainty regarding Zerubbabel is one of which much has been made and it need not detain us here. It is the supposition that he was removed from office because of royal aspirations which amounted to something like claims to independence. Now we have a somewhat similar situation in the Nehemiah material, especially in Nehemiah 6, where accusations against Nehemiah run along these lines. We may naturally suppose that opponents of Nehemiah used such evidence as there was, or as they could concoct, to discredit him with the Persian authorities. Whatever they did, Nehemiah remained in office, apparently for the whole of the period for which he had been appointed, twelve years (Neh. 5.14). He was subsequently reappointed (13.6), and this shows that he was still acceptable to the authorities. The second period of office has no terminus, and in effect Nehemiah disappears from the narrative just as much as Zerubbabel does; at least the narrator has no interest in telling us, for example, that he served for so many years in his second term, or that he died in office, or whatever else might mark a fitting conclusion. (Equally, of course, there is no terminus to the activity of Ezra, though Josephus does mention his death.) Indeed, this is not uncharacteristic of biblical narrative; there are numerous instances of 'disappearance' which simply mark the narrative as having other concerns. The status of Zerubbabel and his activity are more important than what subsequently happened; and there is no indication in the narrative that action against him could have been taken by the Persians.

We can observe what may be three levels of estimate of Zerubbabel, in addition to the later 1 Esdras evidence. In Hag. 2.20-23, he is given titles, as we have seen, which are royal, expressive of the hope of a new and idealized Davidic ruler. In addition, we note that Zerubbabel in Haggai always precedes Joshua the priest. In Ezra 3 he appears as a Davidide, but no emphasis rests upon his Davidic descent; it is indicated, but not drawn out. This is on a par with what we may observe elsewhere in the Ezra material, for in Ezra 8, in the list of those who accompanied Ezra, arranged according to their 'fathers' houses', we note in v. 2 that priority is given to the two priestly lines, those of Phinehas and Ithamar, in that order (cf. 1 Chron. 24 for a fuller statement of this). Following them is the mention of a Davidic descendant, Hattush. (The genealogy of 1 Chron. 3 notes Hattush as eldest of the six sons of Shemaiah [v. 22—only five are in fact listed], but continues the genealogy not from him but from the next youngest, Neariah. This does not suggest that Hattush has any continuing significance as a member of the Davidic family.) Thus the narratives in the book of Ezra could be said to play down the Davidic element, and to emphasize the priestly. (When Zerubbabel is first mentioned, in Ezra 3.2, he follows Jeshua the priest; subsequently, in 3.8, 4.3 and 5.2—this last probably intrusive—he appears first. This latter order [see above] is the one always used in Haggai.)

Thus we may draw some contrast between the Haggai emphasis and that of Ezra. The position in the Zechariah material is more complex, partly at least because of the absence of names where we might expect them. In Zechariah 3, prominence is given to the rehabilitation of Joshua the High Priest, and to his function, with his associates, in relation to the coming 'messianic' figure, the Branch (3.8). Haggai 2 does not use this term. A similar absence of name in Zechariah 6 has more difficult problems since the text appears to imply that two personages ought to be named; we expect Joshua and Zerubbabel, but the latter is not named. It has often seemed most probable that the text in these two Zechariah passages has been modified by the removal of the name of Zerubbabel; and on the basis of this it is supposed either that he had fallen from favour with the Persians (see above) or that, at a later date when the position of Zerubbabel was no longer relevant, the theme of the priestly line was linked with a future expectation of a Davidic figure. The Qumran material has something comparable in its two messiahs, the messiah of Aaron and messiah of Israel (cf. 1QS.9), where an element of subordination of the latter is perhaps also implied.

The only direct reference to Zerubbabel in Zechariah is in 4.6b-10a, which, as already indicated, is clearly intrusive. It includes an emphasis which is similar to that of 6.12 where the Branch is identified as the temple builder; but it does not use the same language, and it would seem to belong to a separate piece of tradition. We may note also that the two passages which have cryptic allusion to a Davidic figure, 3.8-10 and 6.9-

15, are not actually part of the vision material, but belong with the oracular, supplementary material. If we are trying to trace the stance of Zechariah himself, we must start from the visions, recognizing the degree to which there has been extension in the present form of the text (cf. Beuken 1967). From this we get the impression that the concerns of Zechariah are really rather different from those of his contemporary, Haggai. The appearance of two mysterious figures together in the vision in ch. 4 may, as has normally been supposed, point to Joshua and Zerubbabel; but we are faced with a lack of identification which is puzzling. Should we perhaps suppose a different theological level in Zechariah from that which we find in his contemporary?

These differences in Davidic emphasis clearly have a religious dimension in view of the close links of the pre-exilic king with the religion of the community. They provide pointers forward to an eventual development of messianic thinking, to be so significant in the New Testament period but also present in a variety of oracular passages in the prophetic books—and particularly those in Jeremiah and Ezekiel are here relevant as being so very evidently out of step with the general lines of thought which we may attribute to those prophets (cf. Jer. 23.5f.; 33.21-26; Ezek. 37.24f.). But the very modest and indeed almost negative handling of the Davidic theme in the book of Ezra suggests an area of thought in which this particular motif was not a central one at all. A counterpart to this may be seen in the very limited Davidic reference within the later parts of the book of Isaiah (Isa. 55.3), though this is in some measure to be balanced by a group of passages, particularly in chs. 9, 11 and 32, in which that theme is dominant, passages which have some similarities with those just mentioned in Jeremiah and Ezekiel. This suggests that the 'Isaiah tradition', however precisely we describe it, preserved some more positive appraisal of this theme, perhaps incorporating also a transformation of it in the use of the royal 'servant' motif in passages in Isaiah 40ff.

A contrast is possible between these indications and the books of Chronicles, and it is one of the bases on which separation of Chronicles from Ezra–Nehemiah is proposed (cf. Braun 1979: 60-62 and references). The enormous concentration on David and with him on Solomon in 1–2 Chronicles, and the deep concern with the Davidic monarchy during the whole survey of the pre-exilic period suggests that for the 'Chronicler' this was a primary and positive theme. That it certainly is, but it must be observed that the primary emphasis in this presentation is much less on monarchy as such and much more on the relationship between monarchy and religious life and practice. David is repeatedly presented as the originator and organizer of temple worship, priesthood, Levitical functions and the like. His successor Solomon becomes the fulfiller of the temple-building part of this, providing therefore for the adequate carrying out of David's plans. Later rulers, particularly Hezekiah, Manasseh and Josiah, are concerned with the purification and preservation of this tradition. If the work ended with 2 Chronicles, then nothing appears to suggest any Davidic restoration. There is no mention of the release of Jehoiachin from captivity, and hence no pointer to hope there. Restoration, in the final verses, is of the temple at Jerusalem, not of its royal house. I find it difficult to believe that the work does really stop at that point; at least the opening of the book of Ezra is necessary for the rebuilding of the temple to be effected; and it is not entirely satisfactory to stop even then, since the links into the Ezra narrative are close, particularly the chronological link between Ezra 6 and 7, and the priestly genealogy of Ezra which links him back directly with the priest taken into exile (Ezra 7.1 where he appears as 'son of Seraiah'; cf. Koch 1974: 190). This would make it possible to view the Chronicler's own presentation as a middle position, its succession found in temple and priesthood rather than in political Davidic hope.

This Davidic concern provides a convenient pointer to the variety of thinking in the restoration period. It strongly suggests that the attempt at simplifying that period into two main lines of thought does not do justice to the evidence. Hanson (1975) with his emphasis on 'establishment' and 'visionary' parties does not take sufficient account of the variety, and indeed it may be questioned whether either of his categories is satisfactory (cf. also Plöger 1968). The establishment with which he associates Haggai and Zechariah is certainly not uniform. The attempt of Morton Smith (Smith 1971: chs. 4

and 5) is similarly too simple. He sees a 'Yahweh-alone' party, in contrast with syncretistic groups continuing from the pre-exilic period, and a third group consisting of priests whose interest lay in the restoration of temple and cult, but who were not 'Yahweh-alone' men in view of their foreign marriages. I suspect that the truth is much more complex than this.

There are numerous hints of differences of view, but little precision. It has been argued that Isa. 66.1f. presents a view of the temple in direct contradiction to that of Haggai (e.g. Smart 1965: 281ff.; see my comments, Ackroyd 1968a: 156 n. 15 and 229 n. 44). It is more probably that we have both in that passage and also in Haggai an awareness of a kind also present in 1 Kgs 8.27 that the deity's relationship to a shrine cannot be determined by the shrine or its builders but only by the deity himself. But these passages do indicate the presence within Judah—assuming that Isaiah 66 belongs to a Palestinian context, its date being a matter of debate—of differing understandings of temple and deity.

Similarly, in the fifth century we may detect, both in the Nehemiah narratives and in those of Ezra, sharp conflicts in which, inevitably, our presentation is one-sided. The opponents of Nehemiah included Tobiah who appears in Nehemiah 6 to enjoy considerable support in Jerusalem; it would be naive to suppose that he is to be regarded in purely negative terms. Indeed Neh. 6.19 notes that his associates 'were relating his good deeds in my [Nehemiah's] presence'. Similarly, we observe differences of view in regard to Ezra's action on foreign marriages (Ezra 10.15 where the opposition is minimized). Without our being able to determine with precision just how and when the division between the Jerusalem and Samaritan communities took place, there are clear indications in Samaritan conservatism that a cause of the break could have been a reaction against a too liberal attitude, as it was seen, in Jerusalem. It is only in the second century—not so very much later and possibly the period in which with the destruction of the Samaritan shrine on Mount Gerizim by John Hyrcanus that division was hardened—that we find the Qumran community representing perhaps another conservative breakaway. But that takes us beyond our chosen period.

The Persian period is still too little known to us for entirely satisfying judgments to be made on it. The possibility of quite different constructions is indicated by the variety of approaches in recent years; the work of Hanson, Plöger and Morton Smith, among others, shows how the same evidence may be differently used in the attempt at providing coherence of presentation. The endeavour of this discussion has been to open up some of the questions, both political and religious, which confront us. The limited textual evidence in the biblical writings, augmented in some measure by non-biblical texts and illuminated in a degree by archaeological information and by knowledge of the wider international background, still leaves us with alternative options. It is a case where repeated re-examination of the material and judicious use of analogy may help us to ask new questions and hence to penetrate a little further. We may always hope for new discoveries which will clarify the political scene and hence provide a clearer background for our interpretation of the religious thinking of the community, though new discoveries have a way of posing new problems too.

But if the results sometimes seem meagre, we may console ourselves with the thought that, in spite of what appears to be a much larger range of evidence both biblical and non-biblical for the pre-exilic period, there too as many unsolved problems of history and interpretation remain. In part, indeed, the apparent clarity of some of the information may easily suggest a greater certainty than we really have. At least so far as the Persian period is concerned we can know our own ignorance, and in some respects a clear recognition of where we stand may provide a better basis for posing questions.

Chapter 3

PROBLEMS IN THE INTERPRETATION OF
HEBREW LITERATURE:
THE HISTORY AND LITERATURE OF THE PERSIAN PERIOD[1]

1. *Chronology*

The outline chronology of the Persian period is available to us
only from non-biblical sources: these provide sufficient evidence for the order and dates of rulers with a high degree of
exactness. The biblical documents provide only a limited note
of precise dates: Cyrus year 1, Darius years 2, 4 and 6 (Ezra
1.1 = 2 Chron. 36.22; Ezra 5.13; 6.3; Ezra 4.24; Hag. 1.1; Zech.
1.1; 7.1; Ezra 6.15) and Artaxerxes 7, 20 and 32 (Ezra 7.7; Neh.
1.1; 2.1; 13.6); these last present the problem of identifying the
ruler of that name. There are in addition undefined Artaxerxes dates in Ezra 4. The sequence of rulers known to us
from non-biblical sources is only partly represented in the biblical material: Cambyses is not mentioned here at all, Xerxes
in Ezra 4.6 and in Esther, with no chronology in the former,
years 3, 7 and 12 in the latter (1.3; 2.16; 3.7). Daniel offers the
muddle of placing a Darius before Cyrus, making Darius the
Mede take over from Belshazzar (5.31): Darius year 1 is
named in 9.1, Cyrus year 3 in 10.1. (So Darius the Mede in
5.31; Cyrus follows Darius in 6.28; Darius year 1 in 9.1; Cyrus
year 3 in 10.1—this order may, of course, not be intended to
convey a historical sequence.)

1. This essay, to accompany one offered by Professor Sara Japhet,
was presented as part of a discussion session at the Annual Meeting of
the Society of Biblical Literature in Atlanta, Georgia in November 1986.
It was published in a collected volume presented to Professor Kent
Richards (privately printed).

In the present discussion, the Esther dates must be regarded as marginal; the evidently fictional nature of the narrative does, however, point to a use of dates, not having any likely archival basis, as part of the verisimilitude of a story, and this may be relevant elsewhere. The Daniel dates belong to legend rather than to history. The problem of identifying Artaxerxes in the Ezra and Nehemiah narratives, and the considerable lacunae in the biblical material regarding the whole period, leave open the question as to how far the narrators either knew or cared about aspects of the history which did not impinge on the particular matters with which they were concerned.

I wish to consider two aspects of the question of dates: (a) can they be regarded as reliable, based on precise historical information? (b) whether reliable or not, what function do they perform within the narratives? The relationship between precise history and symbolic use needs to be borne in mind.

The first year of Cyrus, a date normally accepted as reliable and used in statements which are made about the recovery of the Jewish community in Palestine, appears both in the general material of Ezra 1 and precisely in the report to Darius and in the quotation of Cyrus's edict in Ezra 5–6. If the edict is taken to be a copy of a historical document, actually available in the Persian archives, then some historical credence would need to be given to it. But the questions which have been raised about the precise wording of both forms of the material must leave the matter open to some doubt. If we suppose that the documents are constructions based on an actual or supposed written edict, it still does not follow that such a detail as the date is actually historical. There is a degree of parallel here with the Cyrus cylinder, clearly a propaganda document directed to the claim to legitimacy of Cyrus as royal successor in Babylon: the biblical material could be related to a similar presentation of Cyrus as successor in Jerusalem, the restoration of the temple of its deity paralleling the cylinder's references to the restoration of deities to their places and of the Babylonian temple to Marduk. The cylinder associates the whole of this activity in Babylon with the year of Cyrus's entry into the city; since it hardly seems probably that so much could in fact have been carried out in so short a time, it is legitimate to ask whether the intention is to make the claim, an obvious propaganda item, that he saw it as a prime responsibility, and therefore one for this initial year, that he should carry through the building and other tasks at once. On that basis, the biblical material could reflect a presentation which, from the Persian side, constituted the royal claim; the legitimacy of rule is naturally and properly associated with the beginning of the reign, at whatever point in actuality the question of Jerusalem was dealt with. From the Jewish side, the designation of the first year would serve to underline that priority of the claims of Jerusalem, its temple and its deity, which the community would wish to stress. This would argue for a symbolic use of the date both by the Persians and by the Jews: in each case a proper and significant statement is being made. (The fact that 2 Chron. 29.3-4 indicated the very first year of Hezekiah's reign as the moment at which he began reform [a point not in 2 Kgs 18] shows a similar technique.)

There is a further point here. In spite of the narrative of Ezra 1, and the more elaborate account incorporated in the Aramaic material of 5.1-18, the activity of Sheshbazzar remains very shadowy. This may be set against the evolution of the pictures of the Persian rulers which appear in non-biblical sources. The two rulers, Cyrus and Darius, both emerge with very large-scale claims made for them. The latter, whose claim to the succession remains very unclear, can be seen to make great efforts to establish his legitimacy. There are indications that the figure of Cyrus has been idealized as the traditions develop. We may legitimately ask (the question is not new), whether, in view of the strong evidence in Haggai and Zechariah, as also in the narrative of Ezra 3, it was actually in the reign of Darius that the restoration of the temple took place. The two stories of Sheshbazzar would be examples of projection back, both making particular claims about the nature of that restoration: the first concentrates on a legitimacy and continuity for the restored temple based on the theme of the temple vessels, the second offers a much fuller account which in the process presents an uninterrupted rebuilding from the time of Cyrus to that of Darius. Such a claim for continuity does not accord with the alternative offered by Ezra 3 and 4, which, on the one hand, stresses continuity with the past by drawing parallels with the Solomonic building, and, on the other hand, utilizes quite independent material to explain why what it assumes to be a beginning under Cyrus (unnamed) could only be completed under Darius. In all this material, the themes of continuity and legitimacy are elaborated; but chronology is notoriously thinly based.

The Darius sixth-year date in Ezra 6.15 also presents problems. While it is possible that it is simply an accurate date preserved in the temple records (the day of the month is differently given in 1 Esd. 7.5), we may note first that it presents the completion as falling immediately in advance of the Passover celebration in 6.19 (in the Hebrew narrative), where no year is mentioned. Furthermore, analogies with the Solomonic building in Ezra 3 raise the question whether that date is connected with the seven-year period given for that (1 Kgs 6.28). Josephus (*Ant.* 11.4.106-107) is explicit, by making the completion come in the ninth year, counting seven years from the second year previously mentioned (Ezra 4.24). Does the biblical text invite us to count seven years, one of Cyrus, six of Darius? In addition, but hesitantly, we may ask whether the date of completion is linked with the 70-year theme, utilized in various ways in the biblical material (notably in 2 Chron. 36.21, Zech. 1.12 and Dan. 9). Is the period from 587 to 516 determined by such a calculation? If we have confidence in the chronological knowledge of the writers (as for example Williamson 1982: 417-18), then the date is real; but it would seem possible to consider that the fixing of the date is part of an endeavour to fit history to prophecy, and to use as part of an exact scheme a figure which we know to have been widely used as symbolic in biblical and non-biblical material.

The dates in Haggai and Zechariah 1–8 present a different kind of question. On the one hand, it is proper to assume that each date originally belonged with a specific oracle: such dates are to be found to a limited degree in Ezekiel, and assignments of a more general kind are common in other prophetic collections. There is no obviously discernible significance in the dates as such, which makes arguments for their being invented less persuasive. However, as they are at present used—in Haggai to cover each stage of a sequence of messages and actions, in

Zechariah to mark off the three divisions of the material—
introductory, visions and interpretations, prophetic messages
associated with the restored temple—they appear to serve the
purpose of presenting a wholeness and coherence for the
activity of the two prophets which is not entirely borne out by
the detailed examination of the material. If it is not easy to see
why such dates should be invented, and it is therefore most
readily argued that they must have been available in the
prophetic material as it came to its final shapers, the example
of Esther, and the fact that it is of the nature of fictional material to offer precision, must warn us of the possibility that here
too we may be dealing with a construction. Uncertainties
about the precision of the statements do not undermine the
significance of the presentation: these two now united
prophetic collections offer an interpretation of the restoration
period which appears to be directed to a later audience, just as
the presentation now brought together in Ezra 1–6 makes
related but in some respects dissimilar claims. The questions
just raised do at any rate put into doubt some of the attempts
which have been made at writing a detailed sequence of events
for the period covered by the activity of the two prophets.

Whatever the individual judgments on particular dates, it
must be clear that the relationship between these literary texts
and the history of the period is a much more subtle and complex one than that of providing direct evidence of what actually happened. Interpretation is of more importance than
events.

2. *History and Fiction*

The use of such a word pair may suggest a contrast greater
than is my intention. There are, of course, historical data
which can be demonstrated to be unassailable; particularly for
modern times, many details can be precisely fixed. But for both
ancient and modern periods, the range of interpretation of historical data and of the handling of those data, whether close to
the events or further from them, shows the extreme difficulty
of defining with assurance many of the aspects of events
which are likely to be of greater interest than the mere ascer-
taining of 'this is how it was'. Nor is the term fiction without its

difficulties, if it is held to imply that the fictional is the purely invented. For the writer of fiction, even if setting the story in an imagined world, is in fact projecting aspects of experience through the interpretative and selective processes of the mind; the claims made by novelists that their characters are not based on actual persons are likely to be true only in the specific sense that they may not be portraits of individuals, not in the broader sense of being derivative.

The failure to make this distinction is particularly acute for the world of biblical history, since so often the assumption is made that the narrator of a biblical story is either telling the truth, that is, telling us how things happened, or that he is inventing the story, and, in some circles at least, that means lying. Such an alternative lacks reality; though whether in a particular instance we are justified in supposing that the narrator has used what he believed to be reliable sources, or has constructed the story out of materials available to him but which belong in reality to another context, or is using the story method to present an interpretation, will depend, in some measure at least, on the bent of the biblical reader's or scholar's mind.

By taking a particular example, we may see some of the problems which attend both the interpretation of a story and the use in historical reconstruction which can be properly postulated. The example I propose to consider is the account of the reign of Ahaz in 2 Chronicles 28.

We are immediately confronted with a problem which is present virtually throughout the books of Chronicles: the story purports to relate what happened in the eighth century BCE, and one level of study is the attempt at discovering how much of historical reality may be postulated. This is done in part by assessing the differences between the Chronicles narrative and that of Kings (2 Kgs 16). Often the discussion turns on how far it is proper to assume the existence and use of other material, of a literary or archival kind, which supplements the older narrative presentation. In a variety of ways, the attempt may be made at penetrating through the Chronicles form of the narrative to see how far new insights into the eighth century situation may be discovered. But, alongside this and not automatically dependent on one particular presupposition about the probability or improbability of the later form containing valid original evidence, there is a second level which looks to see not what the narrative tells about the eighth century, but what it may reveal about other and later situations, in particular that of the present narrator. The relationship between narrative and history is then a complex one, since more than one historical level is presupposed.

In some degree such a discussion can only be undertaken within a much wider frame of reference. The understanding of the author's whole intention and the understanding of an individual narrative or section run together; detailed discussion of the smaller units builds an impression which may or may not be confirmed by a consideration of the whole. And in this area, as in others, we need to be cautious in assuming that there is a precise singleness of purpose about such a work. Consistency of a general kind may be clear enough; there may be a degree of unity which holds the work together. But to claim such a degree of consistency is not necessarily to suppose that at every point precisely the same emphasis is found. In some respects our nearest analogy for the nature of the Chronicler's turn of mind appears to be that of expositor: he is concerned that the readers or hearers should acquire a particular insight into the material being presented, and learn to understand in a somewhat new way what is already familiar. A primary aim of the work is clearly to make the older traditions meaningful to a later generation.

A general impression created by the Ahaz material is clear enough: it is to be read in close association with what follows. The Chronicler has built upon the already relatively modest hints of Kings, where the condemnation of Ahaz is followed by the partly idealized presentation of Hezekiah. The evolution of the portraits of these two kings may be seen first in Kings, with indications that underlying this we may assume a less idealized story; it may be seen further in the presentation to be found in the book of Isaiah, which reveals a fuller development of the contrast, though sometimes implicitly rather than explicitly; and alongside this, not entirely unrelated to Isaiah, is the much more elaborate presentation of Chronicles. The full stylization of Hezekiah here has as its foil the stylization of Ahaz; and this is exemplified in the detail.

(1) 28.1-4 offer the conventional condemnation of an evil king, expanded with a series of typical phrases, bringing together numerous aspects of apostasy which are mentioned in other contexts but are here built into a total statement. The opening is balanced by the end, both in the description of idolatrous and irreligious acts (cf. chs. 23–25), and in the final summary which refuses proper royal burial (cf. chs. 26–27).

(2) Verses 5-7 divide the Syro-Ephraimite threat, presented so clearly in Kings as an alliance, into two component parts: it becomes a double disaster. First, the Syrians bring defeat and captivity, involving an exile to Damascus. Secondly, the northern kingdom brings a defeat and major slaughter; the reason is specified as Judah's apostasy. A list of notabilities who lost their lives is added. The older form of the story is doubled by the separation; the basis for the disaster is given a specific explanation; and the narrator has added precise details of a kind which give a deceptive impression of exact information. We are familiar with the process by which the later form of a story acquires more detail; the names mentioned here are all common enough, and there is little likelihood of historical basis for such additions. They are part of a good storyteller's technique, and we may give credit to the Chronicler for his skill. This section is balanced by the more complex vv. 16-21.

(3) Verses 8-15 form the centre of the narrative as a story of exile and return. Captives taken to Samaria are in due course returned to Jericho, the point of entry and appropriately the point of re-entry to the land. Their return is brought about by the words of a prophet Oded, who preaches a sermon on northern apostasy and on the apostasy of Judah which has given the north the victory (a theme perhaps linked to Jeremiah material). The name Oded is another familiar one (cf. 2 Chron. 15.1), connected with prophetic activity; the use of a known name is not to be regarded as evidence of lack of imagination but to stress the consistency of divine judgment. A similar technique may be observed in Kings. The mention of named leaders who oppose the holding of the captives in response to the prophetic sermon again illustrates the narrator's technique with familiar names, only one (Hadlai) being at all unusual; we may perhaps see some deliberation in the choice of names, not least because one is the same as that of

Hezekiah (though differently transliterated in English versions). We may legitimately suspect that the theme of exile and restoration (cf. Williamson too) has helped in the shaping of this narrative, and that it may be read with the overtones of the Babylonian experience clearly in mind.

(4) In vv. 16-22 the pattern of vv. 5-7 is repeated in a new form: two further attacks—by Edom and Philistia—balance the Syria and Israel pair. The first is bald and without details; the second seems to rely heavily on older Philistine traditions, notably in the Samson and Samuel narratives. The brief explanatory comment of v. 6 is here repeated in a more elaborate form in v. 19. But this second pair of attacks is framed in the appeal by Ahaz to Assyria (v. 16) and its consequences, the reversal of help into affliction (vv. 20-21). The futility of that appeal is therefore here expounded in detail.

(5) In vv. 22-25, 26-27 themes found in 2 Kings 16 are used but without detail. A similar technique may be observed in 2 Chronicles 32 in its relation to 2 Kings 18–20. Apostasy in worshipping the gods of Syria also links back to v. 5; and the actions of Ahaz in the temple in effect anticipate the disasters to the temple at the hands of the Babylonians and prepare the way for the reforms of Hezekiah which echo and reverse Ahaz's actions.

This brief account does not attempt a detailed examination of this narrative. But it does suggest something of the literary and expository skill of the Chronicler. Here, as elsewhere, we may recognize the degree to which his narratives are to be understood as expositions, invitations to read and to hear the older and familiar stories in a new light. They show a good feel for structure. They exemplify particular modes of exegesis, and strongly suggest that one of the most important aspects of our study of the books of Chronicles is to see the ways in which, in the period of his activity, the earlier literature of Israel is acquiring new meanings and new applications. (Clearly in this instance the full impact of the Ahaz account is only felt if the sequel in Hezekiah is read with it.)

3. *Achaemenid Policy*

The chronological lacunae and misunderstandings of the biblical text have already been mentioned; the lacunae are in fact such that we have little or no information, other than some speculative reconstruction on the basis of uncertainly datable texts, for substantial parts of the period.

In some respects more serious are the problems of offering entirely satisfactory interpretations of Achaemenid policy, in large measure because of the often persisting rose-tinted view of the period which has been derived from ancient material, both biblical and non-biblical, but which has been understood in a one-sided manner. The common drawing of sharp contrasts between Assyrian and Babylonian policies on the one hand and those of the Persians on the other—to the great advantage of the latter—has built substantially on the biblical and other documentation; but that evidence has not always been examined sufficiently strictly to assess its proper value for picturing what life under the Persians was really like. The matter cannot be examined here in detail, but recent discussions (see especially R.J. van der Spek 1983) show the falsity of the oversimple contrast, as also the much greater delicacy of interpretation needed of the texts. It is possible to cite examples of Persian protection of religious cults; it is also possible to see the ruthlessness of Persian reaction to any indication of rebellious activity. In the light of these general statements, it is desirable to examine some of the aspects of the evidence for Achaemenid policy and to attempt some assessment of the value of the biblical evidence within that context.

The claim, clear in the Cyrus cylinder, for protection of the Persian ruler by the deity Marduk and hence for his status in Babylon, finds an intelligible counterpart when we assume that kingship in Judah can be regarded as revived with Persian involvement in the restoration of the temple, with its royal connotations, and the inference that the Persian ruler claimed a royal succession there to the previously deposed line. The fact that Cyrus appears to trace his claims back to the great Assyrian rulers of Babylon of the seventh century— thereby in effect treating not only Nabonidus but all the Neo-Babylonian rulers as an unsatisfactory interim—suggests a comparable situation for Judah. We do not, of course, know anything of royal claims for Judah in the period after 587, except in the possible, even probable, recognition of Gedaliah as king, and the existence of Ishmael, the claimant to legitimacy, as an example either of a genuine attempt at Davidic restoration or of an upstart (like Babylonian claimants at the beginning of Darius's reign), supporting legitimation with a spurious Davidic ancestry. The claims of Darius in Jerusalem (see Ezra 5–6) may be properly related to his uncertainties in succession. The elaboration of his claims, particularly in the Behistun texts, argues for their being less than generally acceptable; as R.N. Frye comments sardonically, 'Darius won' (Frye 1984: 102); there is nothing that succeeds like success— especially in claims to legitimate succession. Such evidence as we have further for Jerusalem, as also for Elephantine, argues for Persian royal claims to control both political and religious organization.

In assessing the biblical texts, we need to take into account the pressures on the Judaean community to accept these claims; we need also to consider the probable degree to which the texts have been modified to make them more acceptable to the community itself. We need also to be cautious in assuming that what looks like satisfied political subservience is really quite so straightforward. Interpretation of the status of Zerubbabel remains a matter for debate; but this much is certain, namely that claims to his royal status could be regarded as denying Persian claims. However precisely Zerubbabel himself regarded the matter, the holding together of a status as Persian nominee and of pressures to reclaim Davidic rule— whether or not Zerubbabel was actually of the royal line— must have been a matter of some delicacy. We may observe that there is some parallel in the case of Nehemiah, where again, whatever precisely lies behind the texts, Nehemiah could have found himself—perhaps did find himself—in the position of defending his actions in Jerusalem against a charge of claiming kingship in Judah. In Nehemiah's case, assuming such a delicate position, the evidence suggests that he was able to refute any charges brought against him by his opponents; in the case of Zerubbabel, we have only conjecture to offer as to whether he too, if charged, defended himself successfully, as is

perhaps implied by the completion of the temple; or failed to do
so and was removed from office and replaced by another governor believed to be more reliable. In both instances interest
centres in part on the question of what happened; but more
significantly on the light that such a situation may shed on the
attitude of the rulers and on the ways in which we may detect
a subject people reacting to them.

Implicit in this is a questioning of the common impression
that Persian authority was accepted with complacency; that,
for example, the Chronicler was quiescent in political matters—which may or may not be true; that the period was one
of peace and contentment, a picture that underlies the discussion of concepts of Persian kingship undertaken by Klaus
Koch (Frei and Koch 1984: 49-54). The realities of the political
situation appear to be both harsher and more varied than a
simple verdict would imply.

If we are to get nearer to an understanding, then there are
at any rate two other areas which warrant attention. One is
the broader question of how the figures of Cyrus and Darius
have come to be idealized, not simply in the biblical texts but
much more widely. The other is the recognition that stylization has taken place in the biblical presentation of Achaemenid
rulers. While this is evident in the actual narratives in the
books of Ezra and Nehemiah, it appears still more clearly in
the legendary material of Esther and Daniel: to some extent
there, stylization has been taken to a logical conclusion.

In Ezra, Cyrus and Darius are pictured as offering protection to the Jewish community. This is at its most vivid in Ezra
1 and 3, and it is also underlined in the opening of ch. 4 by the
insistence that only those authorized by Cyrus may join in the
temple restoration; the ideal figure of Cyrus is here used in
relation to some conflict of interest where we should be cautious in making an identification—except for being sure that
the 'Samaritan' explanation is either anachronistic or is a
later superimposition. We should rather recognize the probability that a conflict of views among groups within the community is being conducted with the kind of vituperation which
is all too common in religio-political quarrels. Darius in Ezra
5–6 is also pictured in ideal terms, protecting the Jewish
community against its immediate neighbours and overlords in

the lower ranks of Persian administration, and as re-enacting the Cyrus edict and protecting the community under Persian law; though in this narrative, the motif is now made subservient to the operation of the divine will mediated by the prophets. Much the same may be said of the figure of Artaxerxes in the Ezra narrative: the royal authority, which is shown as providing imperial sanction for the community's law (cf. Frei and Koch 1984, especially p. 17), is protective of the community, understood from a particular angle. But alongside these there is a different picture in the Aramaic narrative of Ezra 4 where a complaint against the community by its immediate neighbours and by the lower officials is accepted by royal authority when it is presented as a threat to the imperial economy. Another picture of local conflicts impinging on imperial policy appears in the Nehemiah narratives. And more qualified or negative views appear in the prayers in Ezra 9 and Nehemiah 9.

In the prophetic collections of Haggai and Zechariah 1–8, similar problems are present. If Hag. 2.20-23 really presents Zerubbabel as a 'messianic' figure—Davidic or not—we have here an implicit protest against Persian religious claims to the succession to the Davidic monarchy. A contrasting rejection of royal claims to political power may be detectable in Zechariah 3. A full reading of these two prophetic texts, now assimilated by the comparability of their presentation, may enable us to detect a much greater diversity of views within the Jewish community—though this is only what we might expect.

With Esther, we move to a different level in which the Persian ruler, who is in many respects a legendary figure, offers both threat and protection: the ambivalence makes for a tension between the absolutism of Persian control and the acknowledgment of the Jewish community, figured in the persons of Esther and Mordecai. In Daniel, the process goes further: on the one hand, the stories of threat to individual Jewish heroes are subsumed under the broader concept of the acceptance by alien rulers of the truth of Jewish faith (cf. also Judith); on the other, the great empires whose pictures lead up to the contemporary threat to the Jewish community in the second century BCE are without exception bad. There is no room for a more favourable attitude; and the fact that Greek rule brings the worse and final king does not in reality present a refined historical judgment but rather climactic development to usher in the last moment. With this, any idealization of Persian (or any other) rule has gone.

In a period which is at so many points lacking in precise historical evidence, the recovery of history does not depend merely on the sifting of the narratives to discover what might be the events upon which they could ultimately rest. It is more to be developed from a sensitivity to the shades of emphasis which appear in stories and other material, which do not necessarily of themselves provide clues to actual events, but do suggest pointers to attitudes and conflicts and the painful development of religious life and thought.

Chapter 4

SOME RELIGIOUS PROBLEMS OF THE PERSIAN PERIOD[1]

In the discussion of both the history and the religion of ancient
Israel, the Babylonian conquest of Judah, at the beginning of
the sixth century BCE and of the period during which some
part of the Judaean community was exiled in Babylonia, has
normally and rightly been seen as a dividing point. The importance of this disastrous experience of defeat and disruption is
evident, and the awareness that it brought about a considerable measure of rethinking as well as changes in political and
religious life, must affect our understanding both of the period
of Babylonian rule and of the restoration period that follows
under the Persians. We should not overestimate the break.
The life of a community continues even through such major
disasters, and the ability of a people to absorb such experience
represents part of the process by which change and development take place. In my *Exile and Restoration* (1968), I devoted
a good deal of attention to these broader questions, and also to
the way in which the theme of 'exile' could come to be not
merely a recollection of past disaster but a symbol for later
experiences of distress. This I believe to be an important part of
the process of assimilation, but also an indication of one of the
ways in which subsequent experiences can be given a coherence and meaning which makes it possible to live through
them too.

A somewhat similar comment needs to be made about the
period of the restoration. The second part of that same study

1. This essay represents the text of a guest lecture delivered at International Christian University, Tokyo, Japan for the Society for Old Testament Study in October 1983, and published in International Christian University Publication IV-B; Humanities. Christianity and Culture (Tokyo: International Christian University, 1984).

Exile and Restoration is devoted to discussing some of the problems, both historical and religious, in the understanding of the first years of Persian rule over Judah. Since that publication, I have devoted a good deal of time to trying to elucidate further the problems both of that first period and of the subsequent two hundred years of Persian rule. One of the results of this further study has been to bring home to me even more clearly the great uncertainties which still affect any attempt at providing a coherent account of the early years, the period of the rebuilding of the temple, roughly from 538 to 515 BCE. Another, and I believe more significant one, has been the recognition that the variety of accounts of that period itself witnesses to the importance it had in subsequent years. The fact that we may detect so great a variety of accounts, both in the form of descriptions of the period itself—as in the opening chapters of the book of Ezra where more than one such presentation is to be found—and in attempts at offering a broader interpretation of what the restoration really meant—so in the narratives of Ezra and Nehemiah, as well as in the material now to be found in the book of Daniel, and in indications that later writings too continued such attempts—points to ways in which the experience of restoration, with its inevitable disappointments and setbacks, came to be used as part of a continuing way of looking at the past in order to look at the problems of the contemporary scene.

To understand what we may see as the lasting significance of the experience and interpretation of this period of restoration, we need to look at the period itself. To do that adequately also involves some measure of backward look to see how we may be able to understand the kind of impact that the exilic age may have had on the nature of the community and on its understanding of itself. Many indeed of the issues involved can be drawn together in the question of how the small Jewish community in Judah under the Persians, together with the wider groups of Jews in other areas—Babylonia, Egypt, and elsewhere—understood themselves. How did they define themselves in relation to what they believed about their own past? What kind of picture did they have of their connections, both of continuity and discontinuity, with that past?

I propose to examine three areas of thought: the nature of
the community; the question of continuity; and the problems of
divergent and dissenting views.

1. *The Nature of the Community: Nation into Church*

A comment which has often been repeated is that 'Israel went
into exile a nation and returned a church'. I cannot now recall
who first said that, nor in what context the words were used.
The context could be important for its proper understanding,
since this may well have provided some degree of qualification
of the statement to make it more adequate as a summary.
Taken as a statement, it is doubtful if it can be considered as
any more than a half-truth, and the effect of a half-truth is
often more dangerous than that of a recognizable falsehood,
since the degree of truth which it may contain can easily
make for more credibility being given to it than it really
deserves.

It is an attempt at defining the difference between the
nature of Israel in the pre-exilic and the post-exilic periods.
Clearly it starts from the recognition that the well-defined
system of monarchical government of the pre-exilic period
has given way to one in which, eventually, the rule was to be
that of high priests, though this does not become explicit for
two centuries, perhaps more. We may note that, unlike many
comments which are made about the differences between
these two periods, this one offers a positive appraisal. To be a
'church', however precisely we define the term, is to be a religious community of some kind; it carries the notion of a community more close-knit and perhaps more uniform than
could be possible for a 'nation', a political organization, however much of religious grounding such a nation may have. All
too often, oversimple statements are made about the pre-exilic
period as being that of the prophets, and hence often thought to
have close affinities with the New Testament, with a picture of
Jesus and the early church as bypassing the intermediate
period and reaching back to the prophets, so that a new
prophetic age is thought to have begun. The post-exilic period,
by contrast, has often been thought to be dominated by law and
priestly things, and hence to be at a lower level religiously.

That this is a travesty is, I hope, clear; I do not propose to argue it here. While the balance in Old Testament study still often swings towards the earlier period, a greater interest in the later period has been encouraging to observe. In numerous ways, in the last decades, this change may be observed, though such implicit lower evaluation of the later period survives in many standard works; a recent study by Joseph Blenkinsopp has demonstrated how far such assumptions have been implicit in the devaluation of the post-exilic period in Christian works, especially in some theologies of the Old Testament. An example of a clear shift may be seen in the new edition of Schürer's *History of the Jewish People in the Age of Jesus Christ*, where in volume 2 the original essay on 'life under the law' had to be completely rewritten to eradicate the misunderstandings of Judaism which it revealed. The increasing concern for a right understanding of the Jewish context of the New Testament is to be seen in much recent work.

But while the statement 'nation into church' has this possible advantage over some of the comparisons and contrasts between pre-exilic and post-exilic life, we may doubt whether it is an adequate description. It may easily imply a too simple shift, as if the change were from a political to a non-political community. That in its turn supposes that a 'church' can be defined in such a way as to avoid any political categories, with the supposition that a 'church' is non-political, an entity which can be regarded as totally separate from the political world.

It is clear that the Israel of the pre-exilic period, at least through the four centuries covered by the monarchy, was a political entity in which it would be inappropriate to think in terms of separation between church and state. This is not to suggest that there were not differences of religious level and belief, though this is an area in which the evidence is very piecemeal and problematic, and not to be simplified into the notion of a pure centre preserving ancient practice and of various improper religious ideas and beliefs held by some fringe groups; nor, indeed, to the alternative of thinking that purity was maintained in outlying areas—an idea fostered by the supposition that such men as Elijah and Amos came from such uncontaminated environments in contrast to the laxity of the cities and in particular the capitals; Isaiah after all belonged to Jerusalem. There is evidence of the place of religion as a part of statecraft; temples and administration belong together (cf. Ahlström 1982). But the position is a complex one, and it is the more difficult to describe because we have to make considerable allowance for the degree to which our sources describe an idealized or schematic view, in which a period of ancient loyalty and purity is followed by one of the intrusion of alien religious belief and practice. Such an idealization is entirely intelligible, but it has its significance theologically rather than historically.

Israel as a politico-religious unit shows a situation in which religion is very much concentrated on the community; it is expressed particularly clearly in the association which exists between temple and kingdom. But in so far as Israel was a nation, the centrality of a temple, which expressed the well-being of the kingdom and catered for its needs, is apparent. When Amos dared at Bethel to attack religious and political and social life, he was a threat to the kingdom: the shrine was a shrine of the kingdom, and he could, with some justice, be accused of 'conspiracy' against it. The use of such a weighted political term indicates the seriousness of the threat. And it was when Jeremiah threatened a destruction of the Jerusalem temple like that of Shiloh (Jer. 7 and 26) that we find a narrative indicating the severest threat to his life, together with the note that another such prophet, Uriah, had in fact been executed.

There was also, as we may observe in the comparable claims for Moab in the Mesha inscription, a relationship which could be expressed in such terms as 'Chemosh was angry with his people': deity and people belong together, and such belonging implied not only special relationship and privilege, but also special responsibility. If the Mesha inscription implies this, it is small wonder that we find in Israel's thought so strong a tradition of the critique of political and religious life, which could on occasion go so far as to repudiate the idea of a specially protected position, and could bind together privilege and responsibility: 'You only have I cared for of all the families on earth: therefore I hold you responsible for all your sins' (Amos 3.2). Thus there are indications of both reality and ideal in the concept of Israel as nation and as people of God. We may consider how far such a reform as that of Josiah, which quite clearly had its strongly national and prestige aspects, was an attempt at reformulating the idea of a national entity which is also a religious entity. We may also raise the question, relevant to wider aspects of our subject, whether it failed simply because of the political pressures which brought disaster upon Judah—though it could still be pointed to as what ought to have been, and was probably in some considerable degree written up so as to set out the ideal—or whether there are inbuilt and irresolvable problems about attempting to make such an equation between a political entity and a religious community.

The fact that in the last years of the kingdom of Judah such an attempt at bringing about a satisfactory reformulation of politico-religious structures could be made, and could be seen to have failed, might then in some measure point up the need for rethinking the nature of the community and might justify the belief that what emerged after the exile was to be something other than the 'nation' as a political and religious unity, that some redefinition of its nature would be necessary. It is clear that some of the forms would prove to have gone for ever—the monarchy in particular, though this was not necessarily perceived at the time. But how far can we see differences which justify the choice of some other term to define its nature? And is the term 'church' the right one?

What emerges after the exile, when we get within sight of some clearer picture of the community of early Persian years, is in fact also a political entity, though its precise status is a matter of much debate. It is, clearly enough, a provincial unit of the Persian empire. It is a century or so later that we have independent evidence to see it as an administrative unit with its own title, Yehud, though there are strong reasons for thinking that, whatever changes may have taken place during that century, the same essential unit was there at the outset. Its status may have been different; its relationship with neighbouring Samaria remains uncertain; the position of its officials—such as we know by name—is unclear; the use of names of governors known to us from non-biblical materials is made difficult by the lack of clear chronological criteria. So we are in uncertainty regarding the precise nature of the administration; the lack of sure information about governors—or indeed at what point that title becomes appropriate—and about the nature of the political organization, have sometimes seemed to suggest a sort of political vacuum in which religious elements could claim a central place. Recent attempts at filling the gaps by the using of governors' names to provide a sequence after the tenure of Zerubbabel (so Talmon 1976) would still provide no detail. If accepted—and I consider the proposal very uncertain—it would however underline the position of a civil officer as governor, thus emphasizing the political nature of the organization.

Such indications of a strongly political aspect to the post-exilic community's life is made clear by two further factors. One is the degree of criticism which we find of a community which did not sufficiently re-establish the religious organization, typified by the temple, and was condemned for its slowness and reluctance to do so. This evidence in both Haggai and Zechariah indicates strong criticisms of the religious life of the community, and much emphasis also on both rebuke and encouragement. The second is the recognition that the accounts which we have, both implicitly in these prophetic books and in narrative form in Ezra 1–6, show a markedly theological bias in the presentation of the restoration, with prominence given to the priestly leadership alongside the secular. The degree to which these materials have modified their sources is a matter of debate, yet it is clear that there is at numerous points what appears to be a depreciation of the Davidic figure of Zerubbabel alongside Jeshua the priest; part of the material lays stress on the prophetic impetus to restoration and the more political elements are in the background; there is emphasis on religious continuity rather than political. When we recognize that, whatever the precise relationship of the books of Ezra–Nehemiah to the books of Chronicles, there is in the latter a similarly strong theological emphasis, this would suggest that the presentation of the restoration and of subsequent life under the Persians—in the Nehemiah and Ezra narratives—is offering a consistently theological account as part of an attempt at seeing the history of the people in a new guise. The explicit movement to such an emphasis is part of a whole range of thought which may be seen to have its counterpart in the Deuteronomic and the Priestly presentations of the earlier elements in the story.

It is in the light of these considerations that we may ask whether it is appropriate to speak of the restoration community in terms of 'church'. No doubt part of the difficulty of definition would lie in differences of understanding of the term itself; our judgment of the matter may be influenced by the particular model we have in mind. There were those who could describe the post-exilic community in terms of a 'remnant'; strong arguments can be adduced for suggesting that such a concept, though often thought to be of earlier origin, really belongs to that period (cf. e.g. Werner 1982: 89-147). The remnant as that which survives disaster would be an appropriate term for such a community (cf. Haggai and possibly also Zech. 3 and Isa. 37.31-32 = 2 Kgs 19.30-31). There were those who would describe it as 'the sons of the exile' (Ezra 4.1), implying some degree of descent through the actualities of the exile experience, and claiming a particular kind of continuity with the past. The indications are of a considerable variety of views and of different types of claim made.

Now this does point in the direction of the understanding of the community as a church in the sense that it was an *ekklesia*, a community called out, set apart, a separated entity. This is an idea which fits with some aspects of Israel's tradition, expressed for example in the comment 'Out of Egypt I called my son' (Hos. 11.1.), and the theme of the bringing of Abraham out of Ur of the Chaldees. In both cases they are ideas which were to be developed—within and beyond the Old Testament—into themes of 'being brought out of a land of alien religious practice' (so already the forefathers in Josh. 24.2, where they are described as having left their ancestors who served other gods beyond the river), and more fully developed in targumic interpretations of the environment of Abraham as threatening and idolatrous, and in the association of all manner of religious evil with Egypt as in the latter half of the Wisdom of Solomon. There is here a symbolic presentation of Israel's religion as set apart, and of Israel as a people separated from its environment. It was to be undergirded by various attempts at defining more closely the limits of the community by descent, and at preserving it from external and hence dangerous influence by separation, particularly in such matters as marriage (cf. Deuteronomy and the Ezra and Nehemiah narratives).

This would suggest that what we have in the restoration is not the immediate establishment of a different system, but rather that, in a way that is characteristic of much simplification of history, the dividing point of the exile is made into a marker to set up a contrast between a period when identity of religion and community was assumed, with attendant disadvantages of overmuch political control of religion or interference in it, and one when there was to be a different kind of definition, eventually to be valid when the political conditions changed and Judaism was deprived even of a separate subservient existence, though still regarding itself as a community and therefore needing to redefine itself; and when Christianity, as one of the successors of Old Testament religion, was also defining itself and had as yet no political definition to offer.

2. *The Question of Continuity*

In any attempt at self-understanding, the Jewish community after the exile needed to come to terms with the past. In part we may expect this to be expressed in the drawing of contrasts: the consideration of how and why the past led to disaster—a marked theme of the Deuteronomistic writings—and hence to direct or implicit indications of how the future is to be organized. But even more we may see how the later community needed to be assured that the contemporary experience could be seen to cohere with the past, representing a revision of its values but a continuity with them.

The most obvious area concerns the temple, destroyed and rebuilt. There has been much discussion about what happened to the temple area after the destruction by the Babylonians so fully stated in 2 Kings 25 and reiterated in 2 Chronicles 36. There are hints, notably in Jeremiah 41, of some continuance of practice on the holy site, presumably sufficiently cleared and reinstated by some appropriate ritual of purification. It is not possible to judge the matter from the indications in Ezra 1–6, since the emphasis there on restoration is clearly offered in a context of complete rebuilding, the setting up again of the altar, the carrying through of building work comparable with that of Solomon (so Ezra 3). But in fact by the very degree to which comparability with the Solomonic building is stressed here, continuity is underlined. Both in Ezra 3, where the comparison between the old and new temples is linked to a great religious celebration, and in Haggai 2, where a dismayed view of the new temple as inferior is the occasion for an oracle of promise of a coming new age of glorification, the relation between the two is equally stressed. Further we may note that, just as the Deuteronomistic writings preserved in the first part of 1 Kings the account of the building of the temple, with its climax in the Solomonic prayer of 1 Kings 8 which assumes the moment of disaster and thus in reality looks back on that temple, so too the Chroniclers' account preserves a very closely repeated text of that account of the Solomonic building, and this in a work which belongs to a later period still, and surely therefore with the aim of reaffirming that the current temple is genuinely *the* temple. Rebuilding does not invalidate continuity.

Along with this we may observe the use of related motifs. That of the temple vessels appears in Ezra 1 and 5–6, as also in Isaiah 52, and further in the Ezra narratives and in a different form in Jeremiah 28 (I have elsewhere discussed this as a continuity theme [Ackroyd 1972]). The degree to which the theme of the return of the vessels belonging to the first temple is stressed makes it clear that belief in the possession of these, as well as the continuing provision of such vessels, emphasizes the sense of identity of the later temple with the earlier.

Similarly, the stress on the priesthood and its ordering reveals both a contemporary concern for correct and valid worship, and also a belief in the continuity of the present priesthood with that of the earlier temple. Much of the material in this area is concerned with the even more ancient authentication of the priesthood by tracing it back to Aaron. The priestly genealogies and the lists, for example in 1 Chronicles 24, bring this out. But the purpose served by such genealogies and lists is related to the contemporary scene. And we may note two specific aspects of the concern: in Ezra 2 and in Nehemiah 7 the same list is used for different purposes, but both forms contain a section which in listing priestly families points to the problem of true descent which raises doubts about certain priests who are precluded from priestly function until the matter is resolved; in Ezra 8, the account of Ezra's return stresses the vital importance of his having with him men of the family of Levi. The proper observance of worship without these cult officials would be impossible; they are themselves guarantors of the genuineness of the establishment.

A further and related area concerns the continuance of the Davidic line. It was evidently significant that Zerubbabel, of that line, was chosen by the Persians for a position of authority in the period of Darius, and, according to some elements in Ezra 1–6, he was closely involved in temple rebuilding. While we may observe in Hag. 2.20-23 what appears to be a much more explicitly political statement of his function as divine executive, it is evident from the relative lack of such material in the Persian period—Zechariah 9 may represent another such element—that a greater stress rests elsewhere than in the hope of a restored Davidic dynasty. The secondary position of the Davidic figure, and that a very insignificant one, in Ezra 8.2, shows the degree to which Davidic hope has receded. It is in relation to this that we may see the importance of the emphasis in 1 and 2 Chronicles on the function of the Davidic monarchy in relation to the cult and the temple. The story of that monarchy, as related in this late presentation, shows how much the function of the Davidic ruler is that of the maintainer of the cult; it is also to be observed that, in a notable instance, disaster falls on a good ruler, Uzziah, for infringing the restrictions on entry into and functioning in the temple (2 Chron. 26). A parallel development may be seen in the last chapters of Ezekiel where the prince, the secular ruler, has responsibility for providing for sacrificial worship and has his own privileged position in the temple precincts, but has no right of entry beyond that (Ezek. 44.1-3; 45.17; 46.2). Thus the concept of the Davidic line—though this is not explicit in the Ezekiel material (cf. Levenson 1976)—preserves the emphasis on cultic continuity rather than political; it retains its religious rather than its political function. The ruling authorities in the community are governors whose relationship to the Davidic house is made explicit only in the case of Zerubbabel.

3. *Differences and Dissensions*

A close examination of the biblical documentation for the restoration period offers some clues to divisions of opinion within the community. To some extent these differences are concealed by the bringing together of disparate elements: thus in Ezra 1–6 alternative presentations of the restoration, which lay different emphases and show different individuals and groups involved, are now presented as if they formed a continuous and coherent narrative. The two prophets Haggai and Zechariah, who appear in Ezra 5 as a pair, have been eventually presented within an editorial structure which is designed to make them speak with one voice (Beuken 1967); yet a closer look reveals that their emphasis is different, and while it would be overstating the position to regard their views as sharply conflicting, the differences are important for our understanding of the lines of thought in the period. Attempts have been made at defining more closely different parties in this period (e.g. Hanson 1975; Smith 1971); but these are not entirely convincing, either because they use material whose precise date and purpose is uncertain (thus Isa. 56–66 and Zech. 9–14), or build too large constructions on evidence which is either minimal or problematic of interpretation (for example, the vexed problem of the meaning of Zech. 3.1-7 where Joshua the high priest is both accused and honoured). Our difficulty, so far as the early period of Persian rule is concerned, is that we have so little of precise evidence even though we may strongly suspect the existence of sharply differing views. Analogy from later periods, when restoration after disaster may be seen—in the period of Antiochus IV Epiphanes in the second century BCE, or after the destruction of the temple in CE 70—makes it probable that there was no unanimity concerning the nature of the community or on problems of life and practice. We have, however, little basis for more than generalization.

As we have seen, there are some indications of a Davidic hope, but the very limitation of this suggests that it was restricted to a small part of the community or that, again as we have seen it, was largely subjected to a theological re-interpretation. In the following period, with the advent of Nehemiah, we obtain a clearer picture, in spite of the obvious one-sidedness of the account. The opposition to Nehemiah and the support for Tobiah, the accusations against Nehemiah for having royal pretensions, but his continuing position of favour and support from the Persian authorities, suggest a complex period of conflicting views. Clearly the Nehemiah account presents the story from one angle only, but even so it preserves enough to suggest that there were those who were deeply suspicious of his position and aims. To some extent, though here the hints are minimal, the same may be said of Ezra, for we have mention of those who opposed him (Ezra 10.13-15).

The fact that even within such edited and unified accounts we also have such indications of divergence of view suggests that the reality was more complex. And indeed, both in the narratives now gathered in Ezra 1–6 and from the later emergence of the Samaritan community we may infer the sharpness of division. Whatever the true origin and nature of the various opposition narratives in Ezra 4, they point to a sharp hostility both from outside the community but also from within, from those who at least claimed to belong to it. The acceptance of some from outside on limited terms (Ezra 6.21) implies the rejection of the rest. The possible reinterpretation of the passages of conflict in the light of the later Samaritan divergence means that the original intention is obscured. That division, whose real development belongs to the end of the Persian period or more probably to the Hellenistic, is an indicator that, within such a small community as that of Judah and the related Jewish groups elsewhere, there were to be sharp divisions, eventually to be expressed in separatism. Again we may see how the analogy of the second century BCE, where the sharply defined groupings which we know from Qumran and the New Testament as well as from Josephus and some classical sources can be pictured with relative clarity, suggests that such differences were not new, but express the variety of reactions to the problems of restoration.

Conclusion

These comments on some aspects of the religious situation in the early Persian period, and on the problems with which we may see the community then confronted, are inevitably tentative. I would like, however, in concluding to suggest that they may not be entirely irrelevant to the consideration of a problem which is recurrent in the life of any religious community. This is the question how far what the religion itself asks of that community, and the patterns which the religion demands that the community impose upon itself, can or should be realized in a political context.

We have come in recent years to know quite a lot about one particular religious community which emerges from within the Jewish life of the last centuries BCE, that of Qumran. In some degree at least, this represents one of the ways in which the attempt may be made at meeting the problem: this is by secession, withdrawal into a separated community, concentrated, as we may judge, on discovering the meaning of ancient tradition for itself, and looking to a moment, near or far, when a new age would bring about the possibility or the reality of the ideal religious life envisaged. We do not know—perhaps never will know—what became of the members of that community who survived the disasters of the Jewish War period around 70 CE. Were they absorbed into one or more of the religious groups, both Jewish and Christian, which we can see at that stage, and how far may their ideals have influenced subsequent developments? Or is there no more than a blank? We can also point to numerous examples, in different religious traditions, certainly frequent in the Christian line, of those who similarly have seen in secession the only way in which a satisfactory expression could be given to their religious beliefs and practices.

We may recognize that, in the degree of the protest in such groups against contemporary political and ecclesiastical life, there is an important contribution to the kind of self-criticism which must belong to any religious organization. Alongside such endeavours, we may see other attempts, equally varied, at establishing a politico-religious entity, a state or nation conformed to the requirements of a shared religious faith. In earlier centuries, there were many who moved from Europe to the new lands of North America, with that kind of religious ideal, clearly expressed in some degree also as a kind of secession. Once established in their new home, they engaged in establishing a society which would seek to enshrine their beliefs in the concrete realities of political order. The story of such attempts is a sad one, especially when it is seen how often they felt themselves required to deprive their members of the very freedom which they claimed to have sought. Such endeavours were matched in Europe too by attempts at establishing the organization of a Christian society within existing political systems, equally, all too often, with a loss of freedom which eventually led to protest and collapse.

Does this perhaps suggest that one aspect of the relevance of Old Testament material to questions of political and religious organization is to point to the problems inherent in such attempts? We may be aware of the tensions which existed, within Israel as a nation and within the post-exilic Jewish community as a provincial unit, though it was more than that, between the religious beliefs and their consequent demands upon life and the political organization by which a society is ordered. In recent years, we have seen the establishment of a Jewish state which hovers somewhat uneasily between secular and religious thinking; we have seen the attempts of Islamic fundamentalists to establish a totally ordered Islamic state; we have become acutely aware of how delicate are the relationships between religious ideals and demands and the realities of political life. And the pressures are, I suspect, the greater for us because, while we have not yet learned what freedom really means, we are at least much more cautious than our forefathers were about being sure that we know how the tensions are to be resolved. Or are we? Have we yet discovered what it means to combine order and tolerance? How often do we aspire to a certainty and hence to a dogmatism in religious matters, which, if we examine it, is an impropriety of thought in that it presumes knowledge where faith is what we have?

And what effect does this have for a Christian community in a country like this (i.e. Japan) which is predominantly non-Christian? And that is a question which may equally be asked of the countries of the so-called West, including my own, where Christianity is seen to be a minority movement in spite of the impact of Christian culture on the shaping of our institutions and attitudes.

Chapter 5

HISTORICAL PROBLEMS
OF THE EARLY ACHAEMENIAN PERIOD[1]

In 1968, I included in my *Exile and Restoration* a discussion of
the restoration period in Judah under the early Persian rulers,
the kings of the early Achaemenian period. More recently, in
a review of post-exilic history in *Tradition and Interpretation*
(1979), in a lecture entitled 'Archaeology, Politics and Religion
in the Persian Period' (1982a; Chapter 2 above) and again in a
chapter in the first volume of the *Cambridge History of Judaism* ('The Jewish Community in Palestine in the Persian
Period'), I have returned to the topic; indeed, in a number of
other ways I have attempted to deal with particular aspects
and problems of that period as part of a continuing concern
with a more adequate interpretation of the evidence available
to us for historical reconstruction. In spite of new evidence,
and particularly archaeological evidence, now usefully sum-
marized in Ephraim Stern's *The Material Culture of the
Land of the Bible in the Persian Period* (1982), we are still
dependent to a very large extent on the same documentation.
Refinements in our assessment of the problems must rest
mainly on new questioning of our sources, and it is useful to
observe that this is being done both in relation to the biblical
texts so vital to the understanding of the development of that
narrower part of the Near East which we know conveniently
as Palestine, but also for the more substantial Greek texts
which, for the most part, provide our fullest information about
the Persians by handling their relationships with the Greek
world. What is of importance here is the way in which new
questions are being asked about these texts, particularly the

1. Reprinted from the author's article in *Orient* 20 (1984): 1-15.

writings of Herodotus, in the recognition that we cannot hope to make use of such ancient writings for historical reconstruction unless we have adequately assessed the nature of the texts themselves and therefore have recognized what kind of questions we must ask and what kind of information we legitimately hope to gain. I was able in May of 1983 to share in a 'workshop' in the Classical Department of the University of Groningen, in which attention was devoted to just such problems; and since most of the discussion concerned the wider areas rather than merely Palestine, it was immensely valuable to observe how the same paucity of information affects scholars in other fields in this still so little-known period.

My intention in this present discussion is to look again at the biblical sources for this early Achaemenian period, and to limit my discussion to those biblical texts which may with certainty be regarded as reflecting the period, though we may need to go a little beyond this in order to fill out the picture properly. The primary text is Ezra 1–6; to this we must add elements in the prophetic collections of Haggai and Zechariah; and I intend to make brief reference to the Ezra and Nehemiah traditions without discussing the texts in detail. I am aware that there are those (e.g. Hanson) who are confident that other texts (in his case Isa. 56–66) are to be used as sources for this period. But I have too great doubt about the correctness of his interpretations of the texts to follow him; and I see here the great danger of using a text whose dating remains a matter of debate for the filling in of gaps in our knowledge of an obscure period. The use of such material must, I believe, be secondary to the endeavour to establish as clear a picture as we may of the period; into such a picture we may be able to fit further material, though always with a considerable degree of caution.

Ezra 1–6 offers a difficult group of texts to the interpreter. In a recent issue of the *Journal of Theological Studies*, Williamson has offered a study of its composition. He considers the detail of each of the sections into which he subdivides these chapters, but his main concern is to point to the overall function of the whole, seeing it as related to a later period, and aimed at providing the link between the story of Judah up to the exile which is found in the books of Chronicles and the narratives of Ezra and Nehemiah in Ezra 7 to Nehemiah 13 which he believes to have been available to the compiler of Ezra 1–6. I am not here concerned with this eventual building together of the material; I would differ from him at a number of points, though I think he is right in seeing a degree of unity of purpose here. I do not share his view of the relationship between Chronicles on the one hand and Ezra–Nehemiah on the other. But these differences are less significant than the attempt at discovering what the materials are. My own purpose differs from his in looking rather more at the earlier stages of meaning of the texts and only then at their use as a whole. Whatever may be said about eventual unity or unification, it appears to me to be clear that we have in these chapters a rich variety of material; and whatever its sources, it is now used to provide an overall picture of the restoration period. But within that the chapters show, I believe, considerable differences of emphasis and suggest, as does other evidence, that we are confronted with an embarrassingly rich diversity of material. Nor is it by any means clear that it is now possible for different elements to be welded together without doing violence to them.

We may look briefly at each element within Ezra 1–6. To do this demands decision on how the material is to be divided into its component parts, and this inevitably means that there are different possibilities. In general, however, we may take the sections as being: ch. 1; ch. 2, essentially as an interlude, though none the less important for that; ch. 3, with which 4.1-5 is often associated, though it is not clear that these verses really belong, and, in my view, the conclusion of ch. 3 is to be found in the final verses of ch. 6, 6.19-22; and ch. 5.1–6.18 (in Aramaic), with which perhaps 4.24 belongs. The intervening section 4.6-23 (24) must clearly be treated as a separate element since chronologically it is out of place (compare also its different position in the parallel 1 Esdras text), though it would be wrong to ignore this intrusive element in the final assessment of the section.

(1) *Ezra 1* is, as it stands, designed as a continuation of 2 Chronicles 36. Whatever the true explanation of the literary relationship, it is clear that we are intended to regard this as the sequel, and indeed it is not easy to see the ending of 2 Chronicles 36 as a satisfactory conclusion to the books of

Chronicles, whether or not the overlapping verses are considered to belong there or at the beginning of Ezra 1. In the latter position they appear to be essential; but equally without them 2 Chronicles 36 has an unexpectedly negative ending in view of the picture of exile and restoration which appears in 1 Chronicles 9 as an introduction to the narrative of the kingdom.

Ezra 1 contains three elements: the authorization for the rebuilding of the temple by Cyrus; the theme of the temple vessels; the designation of Sheshbazzar as the agent of restoration. All these elements in fact reappear in the Aramaic account of 5.1–6.18; there is clearly a relationship between the two, but in other respects the handling of the themes is different, and in any case the perspective of the Aramaic material is different. The nature of the relationship between the two texts is a matter for consideration. It is clear, however, that Ezra 1 concentrates on the authenticity of the restored shrine. It makes use of the Cyrus motif, properly seen as related to the Cyrus cylinder in that both are here concerned with the validation of Cyrus as king—the cylinder in relation to his position in Babylon and to Marduk and his shrine (cf. Kuhrt 1983), Ezra 1 in relation to his position in Jerusalem/Judah as successor to the royal line and as restorer of the temple and hence of the deity of the temple. It is, of course, clear that the biblical text has a different slant in its use of this motif, and this difference is brought out by the appointment of Sheshbazzar, the *nāśîʾ*, high officer, prince, of Judah; and more specifically by the enumeration of the temple vessels, for this underlines, both by the numbers and by the stress on restoration of the original vessels, that the restored temple will be in legitimate continuity with its predecessor. What for the Judaean community may be seen as a concern with religious continuity and validation, may be understood as concerned, so far as Cyrus is involved, with the continuity of dynasty and hence legitimacy for him and his line in relation to the preceding dynasty.

(2) *Ezra 2* does not advance the narrative, but provides a punctuation of it by making use of a list, also found in Nehemiah 7 where it serves a different though somewhat similar function, by way of identifying the nature of the restored community, drawing together various elements, different

styles of list, into a single whole. Its function within the narrative sequence may be seen as providing some echo of the listing of 1 Chronicles 9, though that has its closer relation to Nehemiah 11, and by now anticipating the re-establishment of Jerusalem as this is subsequently to be associated with Nehemiah. It is evident that, whatever the precise relationship between the two forms of the list, and Williamson has argued very cogently for the Nehemiah form being prior to the Ezra 2 form, neither belongs strictly to its context. Both passages make use of a list which has a broader function than that with which it is now associated. It is nevertheless clear that by the use here of a composite list, purportedly bringing together various groups that had returned, as may be seen by the names in v. 2, a concept of the wholeness of the restored community is being emphasized. In addition, the inclusion at the end of the list, as an appendix to the priestly names, of a group which is shown to be unable to prove its proper descent and is therefore adjudged to be unfit for priestly office until the question of status has been resolved (so vv. 61-63), shows that the list as at present constituted, and used, is concerned with a definition of the restored community, and is making a particular point about the purity and separateness of that community. This is important in relation to the appearance subsequently of sections of material in chs. 4–6 which provide further comment on this particular aspect of the community's nature.

The ending of the passage is to be found in 3.1 which, as may be seen from Nehemiah 7–8, forms part of the narrative sequence there. It now provides a sort of chronological link between ch. 1 and 3.2ff., and evidently telescopes the period of the restoration so as to suggest that what is described in 3.2-7 took place in the seventh month of the same year in which Sheshbazzar arrived in Jerusalem, the first year of Cyrus.

(3) *Ezra 3.2-13,* as we have just seen, is clearly intended to be associated with the first year of Cyrus, but it is in fact quite separate. It consists of two elements: in vv. 2-7, there is a description of the re-establishment of the altar, and, according to v. 6, this was in position by the first day of the seventh month; this makes it clear that the altar had already been put back in order before the month actually began. Indeed, closer

examination of the text suggests that there are really two elements within this opening section: an account of the setting up of the altar in vv. 2-5, in which notably Jeshua the priest and his associates, and Zerubbabel the Davidic descendant and his kinsmen are involved. The placing of Jeshua first (only here) may indicate a desire to stress the priestly prerogative; Zerubbabel appears here to that extent subordinated, the Davidic element set lower than the priestly, which is characteristic of the books of Ezra and Nehemiah (cf. Ezra 8), and also in effect can be seen as an appropriate continuation of the way the Davidic theme is handled in Chronicles, where the royal functions are shown to be primarily those of instituting and maintaining temple and cult. Conformity to the Mosaic law is stressed (vv. 2 and 4-5) and emphasis on the correct celebration of the autumnal feast. Also appearing here, and providing a link to the material of ch. 4, is the theme of 'terror at the peoples of the lands', a motif which invites a contrast with the latter part of the chapter where a different impact is produced. In the ending of this passage (vv. 6-7), there appears to be a résumé, indicating that the use of the new altar began on the first day of the seventh month, that is the autumnal new year, and explaining that the temple was not yet re-established—understanding the root *ysd* here in the sense of 'firmly accomplished' rather than supposing that it refers to an initial stage of the building. Emphasis follows, with clear analogy to the Solomonic temple building, on the employment of the appropriate Phoenician craftsmen and materials (cf. 1 Kgs 5 and more precisely 2 Chron. 2; cf. also 1 Chron. 22). These verses emphasize the continuity of the post-exilic temple with the pre-exilic in a different manner from that of ch. 1, where the temple vessels provide the theme, a theme which is absent from ch. 3. Verses 6-7 also provide a link to the second part of the chapter, where in vv. 8-13 we again meet with Zerubbabel and Jeshua, but in the reverse and normal order. Stress here is upon the activity of the whole community returned from exile, upon the appointment of Levites, and upon the liturgical celebration of the completing of the temple (again recognizing *ysd* as having this sense). The passage culminates in vv. 12-13 with the recognition of the re-established temple, with stress on both weeping and laughter, clearly to be understood as liturgical forms. It is often affirmed that this contrast between weeping and laughter is based on Hag. 2.3 where an unfavourable comparison between the new temple and the old is an occasion for a contrasting oracle proclaiming the glorification of the new shrine. But this suggestion of a link in fact reads the Haggai text too literally, and fails to recognize that the Ezra text is describing an occasion where the two elements of weeping and laughter are component elements in the worship. (The text in 3.12 may be overloaded as a result of a later inclusion of elements from Haggai.) The final phrase indicating that the sound of this celebration was heard afar off may be seen as the answer to the theme of fear in 3.3; now the peoples of the lands will hear the celebration of the new-built temple and know that the situation is reversed.

The true sequel to this passage would appear to be in 6.19-22. The celebration of the passover follows at the beginning of the next year (the spring new year), and we note that there is stress on the purification of priests and Levites (v. 20), and also all the returned exiles who are now joined by those from the peoples of the land who have separated themselves from pollution; there appears to be a further development here of the theme in ch. 3, as well as an emphasis which we found indicated in ch. 2 on purity. The peoples which appear in 3.3 as threatening, and in 3.13 as hearing the triumphant celebration, are here subordinated to the extent that some from among them are separated to become part of the renewed religious community.

Williamson's analysis and discussion of these passages differs at a number of points from my own; but I would agree with him that there is in this part of the material a highly theologized presentation of the restoration with the rebuilding and celebration of the temple at its centre.

(4) *Ezra 4.1-5.* It is common to treat the opening of ch. 4 as part of the preceding narrative, and it is true that the appearance here of Zerubbabel, at first alone and then with Jeshua in v. 3, provides a clear link with what precedes; there is a link too in the use of the expression 'heads of fathers' houses', i.e. family leaders or representatives, which appears also in 3.12; but the use of this expression is different in the two contexts and real links are not at all clear. That there may be seen to be

an echo in vv. 4-5 of the theme of fear in 3.3 suggests that at
whatever stage this material was included here, that theme,
already handled and in effect answered by the end of ch. 3, has
here been re-used at a different level. In view of the odd reference to Esarhaddon, as the king of Assyria who had brought
what would appear to be aliens into the land—and this
appears to be a kind of exegesis of the story of Samaria in 2
Kings 17—it would seem likely that this passage too, whatever
its origin, is now used at a double level. On the one level, it is
concerned to provide an explanation of material now found in
5.1–6.18; on the other level, it is concerned with polemic at a
later date against the Samaritan religious community, and to
this extent it provides also a link with the following passage,
4.8-23, which emphasizes the settlement of aliens in Samaria
and elsewhere 'Beyond the River', and, again whatever its
original function in the book, would appear now to be concerned too with the Samaritan polemic.

Whether there is any historical basis in this material
remains uncertain. Much has been made of the naming of
Esarhaddon; links have been suggested with the obscure date
in Isa. 7.8 which refers to a sixty-five-year period; Esarhaddon's campaigns in the west suggest that he might have followed the same policy as his predecessors. But in view of the
confusions about rulers in these books, including the remarkable reference to the king of Assyria in 6.22, we may more
naturally suppose that the compiler had only vague notions of
Assyrian history, and that he was probably utilizing another
piece of anti-Samaritan material associating their origins
with another Assyrian ruler.

(5) *Ezra (4.24) 5.1–6.18* provides an Aramaic account of the
rebuilding of the temple. It utilizes the figure of Sheshbazzar
(5.14, 16) and also the temple vessel theme (5.15), and this
provides an overlap with ch. 1. But the overlap is in reality
minimal, and the function of Sheshbazzar is differently
described, both in that he is precisely described as governor
(*peḥâ*) and that he is described as involved in actual temple
rebuilding over a continuing period of time. More distinctive is
the emphasis on divine protection (5.5), and that on prophetic
guidance and support, with the naming of the two prophets
Haggai and Zechariah. It is puzzling to find Zerubbabel and

Jeshua in 5.2, though we may make a comparison here with
the text of Hag. 2.11-14 where a short narrative gives them a
similar position. There are no obvious linguistic overlaps, so
that direct relationship is not determinable. But the non-mention of these two leaders in the remainder of the Aramaic
account—often explained as due to the removal of Zerubbabel
and presumably Jeshua for rebellious pretensions, though
such a supposition is without any clear foundation—is best
explained as indicating a narrative of the rebuilding without
the naming of these two, and hence the recognition that their
names are intrusive in the text in 5.2. The present text is due to
a conflation of narrative motifs, and is also to be seen as a
middle term between the narratives of Ezra 1 and 3 and that
of Haggai; it serves too to provide evidence of the process by
which the two prophetic figures have eventually been joined
together in a pairing which makes their separate and distinct
emphases less easy to discern.

This Aramaic narrative also makes use of the Cyrus theme
found in ch. 1, with a much more detailed use of the edict
motif, and with a more elaborate theological interpretation set
out in the report sent to Darius. In that and in the reply, with
its substantial detail and its emphasis on royal protection for
the shrine, we may see an alternative and fuller elaboration of
the position of the Persian kings in relation to Jerusalem and
its royal temple (cf. 6.10), interpreted theologically in relation
to the validation of the shrine rebuilt under divinely given
prophetic authority and under royal protection. There is close
resemblance between this use of the divine and royal motifs
and what we may find in both the Ezra and Nehemiah traditions.

(6) To this brief review of Ezra 1–6 we may add simply a
note on the other passages in ch. 4. In 4.6-23 (24) we have a
collection of documentary material. It begins in v. 6 with a
brief and totally unattached note on the period of Xerxes. This
is followed by an equally unattached note on the period of
Artaxerxes. Both of these are in Hebrew, and they appear to be
placed here to indicate the sequel to the opposition to Jewish
restoration from the days of Cyrus to Darius in 4.5, under succeeding rulers. These verses may be seen then to provide a
chronological link with ch. 7 where the name of Artaxerxes is

picked up to introduce the reversal which was eventually to come about under Ezra, a reversal which in effect now overshadows these early stages of restoration, and which may be held to begin to pave the way for the eventual pre-eminence of Ezra in the Persian period so far as the Jewish community was concerned. In ch. 4, these two Hebrew elements are followed by the fuller Aramaic narrative, with its documents cited, also set in the reign of Artaxerxes but clearly unrelated to 4.7—the names are totally different, and only the ruler's name provides a link. The join is made by the explanatory note on the use of Aramaic in the second half of v. 7. This longer narrative again in effect falls outside the period with which we are concerned, but its significance may be seen in that it provides obliquely a glorification of Jerusalem, extolling the greatness of the former kings in Jerusalem and their rule over the whole province 'Beyond the River' (4.20), clearly a reference to the Davidic–Solomonic empire, and thereby suggesting not only the past but the future. In a number of respects a near parallel may be seen in Judith 5 where Achior the leader of the Ammonites advises the Assyrian general Holofernes that the Jewish people is unconquerable so long as it remains obedient to its God. The real meaning of the Ezra 4 passage is that there will be a full restoration of the Jewish community, with a supremacy equal to that of the Davidic period. It represents a different type of comment on post-exilic distresses. It is not in any way concerned with the building of the temple, but with the rebuilding of city and wall. To that extent it is comparable to the Nehemiah narrative, though there is no real ground for associating it with what appears in Nehemiah 1.

The fact that 1 Esdras places this section differently, making it follow immediately on the material of Ezra 1 and conflating the material of 4.7-8 (cf. 1 Esd. 2.16) and thus utilizing it to bridge the gap between the period of Cyrus and that of Darius, again with a total disregard of the realities of Persian history, shows that we are dealing with a quite separate element which has been employed in alternative ways in two versions of the material.

The effect of this survey of Ezra 1–6 is, I believe, to indicate that we have here at least three quite separate accounts of the restoration period: ch. 1, ch. 3 together with 6.19-22, and 5.1–

6.18. In each case we may recognize distinctive elements; they have some measure of overlap, and this may suggest some evidence of a harmonizing process. They are all now highly theological in their interpretation of the period, but the ways in which they express their interpretation are not all at one level. The reconstruction of a historical sequence from this material must inevitably remain very uncertain. It is not simply a question of attempting to distinguish between one set of events under Cyrus and another set placed in the reign of Darius; it would seem rather that for the account of Ezra 1, restoration was effected by Sheshbazzar in the period of Cyrus; thus this account emphasizes, with links to Isaiah 44–45, that there was immediate response to the divine impetus through Cyrus and the restoration of the temple followed at once. The account in ch. 3 and 6.19-22 knows nothing of any preceding action, and clearly envisages the move from the setting up of the altar to the completion of the temple as one process under Zerubbabel and Jeshua. 5.1–6.18 can be seen to offer the largest view, and it may itself represent one attempt at synthesis: the activity of Sheshbazzar under Cyrus moves without break into the next stage of activity under Darius; the text in 5.1-2 clearly suggests a beginning of work: 'Then (i.e. in response to the prophecies of Haggai and Zechariah) they set themselves (literally 'they rose up') to rebuild the temple', but the Sheshbazzar reference in 5.14-16 stresses that there has been no interruption in the rebuilding process. To that extent, this Aramaic account differs radically from the alternative in which the gap between the periods of Cyrus and Darius is bridged by explaining how and why there was interruption in the rebuilding. These two explanations, both intelligible but, we may suspect, both reconstructions, cannot really be reconciled. We are left with evidence of two periods of activity; we have no real basis for explaining the relationship between them.

For completeness, we need to go a little further. As if three alternative accounts were not enough, we may see the existence of a fourth, and perhaps of more still.

(a) *The book of Haggai* provides our first. While most of the book consists of prophetic oracles introduced by precise dates, there is a short narrative section in 1.11-14. In fact the use of dates, which reveal a concern with the precise occasion of the divine word, suggests a certain archival interest on the part of the compiler of the book, and there are clear indications of a relationship between the dating formulae and the Priestly Work in the Pentateuch. There are also links with the Chronicler's style. This would seem to suggest that the shape of the book is in part at least directed towards providing not a narrative but an interpretative statement about the meaning of the restoration period to which Haggai addressed his message. At one level, we may naturally be concerned with the nature of the prophetic message and its relationship to the contemporary aspirations of the Jewish community; this is particularly the case with the final Zerubbabel oracle which speaks in royal terms. But at another level, we may see the compiler making his own contribution to the nature of the restoration period. It is yet another account of that period. It associates the rebuilding with another style of theological interpretation. A different basis is provided for the summons to build. It is linked to the economic problems of the period and to a plainly stated view of priorities: unless the temple is rebuilt there can be no prosperity for the community. By way of underlining this, the oracles in ch. 2 demonstrate the consequence of rebuilding: a glorification of the temple by the presence of the deity and the gifts of the nations (2.1-9); a coming age of material prosperity dating from the completion of the temple (2.15-19), and a new age with a new Davidic ruler (2.20-23). The centre to this presentation is the brief but clear account of the response of leaders and people (here described as the 'remnant') to the summons to rebuild, with the implication, confirmed by the comparison between rebuilt and former temple in 2.2-3, that the rebuilding was carried straight through to its completion.

I have for some years been inclined to believe that we may see in these verses in ch. 1 a fragment of another restoration narrative. If that is a correct view, then we may postulate the existence of another narrative source in which the figure of Haggai is pre-eminent, and this may be set over against the Aramaic presentation in Ezra 5.1–6.18 where the two prophets Haggai and Zechariah appear as a pair. This is the more interesting in view of the fact that a consideration of the Zechariah material suggests that there we have a rather different position and one which does not completely accord with the Haggai picture.

(b) In *Zechariah 1–8* the amount of material actually concerned with the rebuilding of the temple is very limited, though it is present indirectly in passages concerned with the restoration of Jerusalem. This is clear from 2.11-17 where the presence of the deity in the people's midst clearly envisages the restored temple. Direct reference appears at the end of ch. 6 in a summarizing statement which is concerned with the relation between obedience and blessing. In chs. 7–8, as has often been observed, we appear to be handling material which moves beyond the theme of the rebuilding of the temple, and indeed in 8.9-10 looks back from some distance at it.

The only passage in which more specific statement is made is in 4.6b-10a, which intrudes into the vision and interpretation of the gold lampstand and the olive trees; it is echoed in the difficult passage in 6.12-14 where the link with the figure of the Branch points also to the ending of ch. 3. Neither in ch. 3 nor in ch. 6 is Zerubbabel mentioned by name, and it may be right to suppose that his name has been eliminated in a process of reinterpretation pointing to a later understanding of the nature of the temple with stress on priesthood rather than on any royal figure.

The passage in ch. 4 remains an enigma. No satisfying explanation has been given for its intrusive presence in the middle of the vision, and commentators have been very ready to move it elsewhere. The problem with shifting this odd piece of text is that it then becomes virtually impossible to explain why it ever came to stand where it does. We can, of course, postulate an accidental dislocation of the text, but this is a poor substitute for a real explanation. It is more satisfactory to suppose that the compiler who put it there knew what he was doing; and the oddity, to our way of thinking, of such a positioning, is in fact on a par with a series of other apparently inappropriate placings of biblical material. I have had occasion in recent studies to refer particularly to Isa. 6.1–9.6 and chs. 36–39; there is also Amos 7.(9)10-17. In each case an otherwise coherent text is broken by an insertion; and we do better to look for possible explanations rather than suppose accident.

In the case of Zechariah 4, there are two points to note. One is that the theme of the rebuilding of the temple by Zerubbabel, by being inserted into the vision, gains the authority of that vision. The divine word to Zerubbabel is undergirded by the revelation of the lamp in the shrine as the symbol of the divine presence which watches over the whole earth. The rebuilding of the temple is thus placed in a cosmic context. The other is that, while there are links here with other passages in Zechariah, particularly in the theme of v. 9b, 'You will know that Yahweh of hosts has sent me to you' (cf. 2.12, 13, 15; 6.15), in other respects there are links with Haggai, particularly in the theme of the completion of the temple (4.9). The glorification of Zerubbabel himself parallels that of Hag. 2.20-23. Since in Zech. 8.9-10 we have another passage which appears to be more closely linked to Haggai than to the other Zechariah material, we may perhaps see the incorporation of both these passages as part of the process by which the two prophetic collections of Haggai and Zechariah 1–8 were given a more unified structure, part also of that process by which they were paired as they appear in Ezra 5.1–6.18.

This does not amount to another account of the restoration, but it does reveal yet another element in that process of interpretation of the restoration period which gives us so much material with different viewpoints and so little precision in drawing the material together.

The present survey is incomplete; it leaves open the further question of how the restoration period was looked at yet elsewhere in our sources. Without discussing the later sequels in any detail, I would simply draw attention to the fact that both Ezra and Nehemiah are also pictured as the agents of restoration. Whatever our judgment of their chronological placing and interrelationship, it is clear that eventually they both come to be regarded as responsible for the restoration itself. In the case of Ezra, this is apparent in the later portrayal of 2 Esdras, but it is also present in Ezra 7 where the genealogy of Ezra, which describes him as the son of the priest who went into exile in 587, shows him to be thought of as direct successor; this is not to eliminate the intervening generations, for the genealogy is clearly concerned to lay stress on legitimacy; but it does pave the way for viewing him as the true and only restorer. In a similar way, Nehemiah appears in 2 Maccabees 1–2 as such a true restorer, and it is my own belief that the opening of Nehemiah 1 which refers to the ruined condition of Jerusalem, whatever its original connotation may have been, does not now look to some immediate cause of distress but back to the disaster of 587, and sees Nehemiah as the first and real rebuilder of city and people, thus effectively depreciating the significance of any intermediate stage.

Thus if we add up, we may see the presence of three possible accounts of restoration in Ezra 1–6; a fourth in Haggai and hints of a fifth in Zechariah 1–8; and, with the interest in this period by no means dead, a sixth and seventh in the Ezra and Nehemiah traditions. Of this wealth of material it may fairly be said that it does not resolve our attempts at discovering historical reality; it indicates the significance with which the period of restoration was invested, for the greater the wealth of tradition and interpretation, the greater the significance of a particular moment must be held to be so far as the successors to that moment are concerned. Furthermore, we may not be far wrong in estimating that the significance of devoting so much attention to that period in the past when restoration took place is not simply that of recording and interpreting a great moment in history: it is more importantly a reflection on whatever contemporary circumstances we may suggest. I suspect that we may have clues here to endeavours at looking at subsequent events, and particularly at the long-delayed but still-awaited hope of full restoration, with a Judah independent of external restrictions. Perhaps it is not accidental that in the ordering of the Hebrew canon, Ezra–Nehemiah, so much concerned with one period of restoration, should have been placed next to the book of Daniel which, under the guise of being involved in the same broad period of disaster and recovery, the sixth century BCE, is in reality concerned with the period of disaster and hoped-for recovery of the second century, in the pressures of the reign of Antiochus IV Epiphanes.

Chapter 6

FAITH AND ITS REFORMULATION IN THE
POST-EXILIC PERIOD: I. SOURCES[1]

The British Broadcasting Corporation produced some few years ago one of its most notable television serials. It was entitled 'The Long Search', and was a serious attempt at inquiring into the nature of religious practice, belief and experience. The general impact was often moving and illuminating—both in the sympathetic and critical opening up of the breadth of Christian practice, and in the wide variety of what was shown of the spectrum of religions from east to west. Its success was in no small measure due to the sensitivity of its central inquirer, Ronald Eyre.

When his book on the making of 'The Long Search' was published, an interview with him was reported in which, as I recollect, he was asked what he felt had been achieved for himself in the series. His reply was, 'I have rearranged my uncertainties'.[2] Of course, there is a place in religion for confidence, and for confident action based upon conviction. But that is not the same thing as certainty, and there must always, as I think, be in true religion a measure of uncertainty, not least because, however we may express the centralities of our beliefs, they imply the reality of something beyond ourselves, something 'other'. We may or may not give to this the title 'God', though in many instances this is a convenient if in fact often rather misleading term behind which a very wide vari-

1. Reprinted from the author's article in *Theology Digest* 27 (1979): 323-34.
2. In his book, *Ronald Eyre on the Long Search* (Eyre 1979: 280), he gives this as '*The Long Search* has radically rearranged my ignorance'. I cite this for the record; but I find my recollected version more illuminating.

ety of ideas can co-exist. The unknowability of God can, somewhat inconsistently, be said to be the only certainty in an otherwise uncertain area of thought and experience. We may not greatly care for Pascal's expression of this in terms of a wager, perhaps because for some of us betting on anything is rather repugnant. We may prefer what at first sight sounds like certainty: Martin Luther's 'Here I stand; I can do no other'; but this is in reality an affirmation of confidence in a context of awareness of the uncertain.

This introduction, which appears to have nothing to do with the particular theme of these two studies (Chapters 6 and 7), is in my thinking related to that theme in two specific ways. First, it is related in my own work, now over some thirty years, to attempt to elucidate what the exilic and post-exilic period is about. In a number of larger and smaller studies over these years—and the present discussion is part of a further attempt at defining the area in which I am currently though spasmodically engaged—I have tried to penetrate the complexities of a period about which we know at one and the same time a great deal, in the sense that we have material which is relevant, and very little, in the sense that there are such gaps in our knowledge that we do not know how to fit together what we do know. If I could make any general comment on the progress of my work over these thirty years, it could very well be in Ronald Eyre's words: 'I have rearranged my uncertainties.'

This is an aspect of my writing which some have criticized as timid, but which I see as cautious—it is familiar that one scholar's demonstration of the truth is to another scholar wild hypothesis, and that one scholar's caution is to another an unwillingness to see what stares everyone in the face. But the more I work in the area, the less sure I become that I can really pinpoint as precisely as is desirable the essential moments of thought and experience.

Second, uncertainty is a not inappropriate term to use in relation to the problematic position of the Old Testament community in the years following on the collapse of the kingdom of Judah under Babylonian pressure, the divergent experience of different groups in different places—Palestine, Babylonia, Egypt and perhaps others too—the differences of emphasis which must attend any attempt at reformulation of belief as also at reorganization of social and political life in a new context.

As soon as that is said, it calls for qualification. It is typical of human thinking about both past and future that over-simple time divisions are made. During a period of crisis—such as the second world war of 1939–45—there is an understandable supposition that when the crisis ends, when peace is signed, then will be the moment for rethinking, for reorganizing, for putting into effect what is needed in a new political and social situation. If some planning ahead is done, it is still with such a term in view. But in reality, the moment of peace is no more than a continuation of the past; there is no break, though there is a welcome alleviation of particular pressures. A country may decide, as Great Britain did in 1945, to reject the war-time leadership and majority party in favour of an alternative; it cannot cut itself off from the shaping of its life and thought which have been going on all the time.

We speak, understandably and indeed rightly, of the crisis in the Old Testament period which is marked by the final stages of Babylonian onslaught, the collapse of the kingdom of Judah, the loss of its royal house, of its temple and religious leadership, of its national status, all reaching a climax in 587 BCE. We may then speak—as indeed the title of these studies implies—of the need for reorganization, for reformulation of faith, as if this could take place without the past hanging over it, and also as if somehow there were a moment of leisure in which that reorganization, that reformulation, could be undertaken. In reality, the kingdom of Judah, with one relatively brief period under Josiah as at least a partial exception, had not existed as an independent entity for over a century. Its last two kings who ruled for more than a brief space, though both of the Davidic house—Jehoiakim and Zedekiah—were on the throne by foreign permission and with foreign support, the first from Egypt, the second from Babylon. The attempt of 'the people of the land'—whoever precisely is meant by that designation—to put another Davidic ruler, Jehoahaz, on the throne in 609 at the death of Josiah, was doomed to failure; the natural successor to Jehoiakim in 598–597, Jehoiachin, was to be taken captive to Babylon, where some focus of hope for the future centred on him, but he was never to return to the throne (2 Kgs 25.27-30). The monarchy was already so much changed and its status so much in question that the rethinking had in a sense already begun. Even with the collapse, it is by no means clear how far there were those who saw this as totally the end of that particular political institution. Gedaliah, appointed by the Babylonians—and what status did he actually have?—provided one focus, for a brief moment, until he was assassinated, most probably by one who, as a Davidide, looked for the 'rightful' succession. The later descendant of the family, Zerubbabel, was to be a centre of some urgent hopes for Davidic restoration (so especially in Haggai), but it came to nothing, and the rethinking which could be said to belong to the first moment of disaster could in a sense only be taken a full stage further when that frustrated hope may have suggested a somewhat cooler look at Davidic ideas, already adumbrated in Isaiah 55 and to be taken to a much fuller and more consequential rethinking in the books of Chronicles; but this alongside an evident continuation of Davidic ideals, attested in a variety of Old Testament materials—though their dating and provenance are often very uncertain—and found more explicitly and precisely in materials from beyond the Old Testament period.

There is—as this one example shows—not one moment of reformulation, but an ongoing if spasmodic process. A cross-section of life and thought at any one moment, if we were able to make it, would show a wide spectrum. The limitations of our sources tend to force us into concentrating on particular moments for attempting such a cross-section—and here particularly the years from the rise of Cyrus to the completion of the restored temple dated to 515 BCE. But such particular moments, however much we may see the reason for their being picked on by subsequent writers and compilers, are not the only moments in which rethinking, reformulation, is going on. We have here, as in other instances, to ask ourselves also just why a later generation gives us so much material attached to one moment and so little for others which may have been equally or more important. There is a degree of stylizing in the presentation which distorts, and at every point we have to be asking not just 'What does this text tell us?' but also 'Why does it tell us this and not something else?'

And that brings me to the first division of my subject: *the sources of our information*. What is the material, biblical and non-biblical, on the basis of which we can discuss the whole topic of 'the reformulation of the faith'?

1. *Problem of Sources*

The problem of sources is a complex one. It is immediately clear that we are almost entirely lacking in narrative material dealing with the period of the exile: the last part of 2 Kings relates with some degree of detail certain aspects of the two stages of the collapse of Judah. It is a selective and significantly interpretative account. It includes also two brief notes on subsequent events: the appointment and assassination of Gedaliah with its consequence in flight to Egypt (2 Kgs 15.22-26), and the release of Jehoiachin in 562 BCE (25.27-30). The placing of these two at the end of the work produces an ambivalent climax: hope centred on Gedaliah and the people with him is negated totally; hope centred on Jehoiachin is an open-ended prospect for the future. Both in fact underline a single point, already brought out in the previous sections: except for those who had met their death (cf. 25.18-21) effectively all of the Judaean community that mattered was in exile. While nothing is said of the outcome of the flight to Egypt, it is difficult to see any prospect of the future here. It has been held that the final comment on Jehoiachin is also negative, with the implication that the release from prison and the giving of status at the Babylonian royal table higher than that of the other captive kings—surely a folkloristic motif—does not have its natural sense of genuine and lasting favour, but is merely a comment on the already presumed dead Jehoiachin; the favour was temporary only. (This negative view seems to be implied by the curious NEB translation, 'he lived as a pensioner of the king', a rendering which suggests a different view than that implied by the rendering of the corresponding but almost identical expression in 2 Sam. 9.13 of Mephibosheth at David's court.) What leads up to these final comments contains both the indication that 'Judah went into exile' (25.21), with its implication of total exile, and the only people that were left after the two captures of Jerusalem were 'the poor of the land'—this is stated twice, at 24.14 in reference to the year 597, and at 25.12 in reference to the year 587. It is in effect picked up in 25.22 and 26 where it is indicated that even the few left did not remain long in the land.

The recognition of these points in the text suggests that reconstruction of the history of Palestine during the exile on the basis of the last part of 2 Kings is very hazardous indeed. It may be held that the *dallat hā'āreṣ* , the 'poor of the land' (NEB 'the weakest class of people' is rather fanciful) were the dispossessed, though this would be more clearly expressed if they were described as *'anāšîm rēqîm*, 'empty men' (cf. Judg. 11.3, where NEB again misses the point with its 'idle men'), the opposite of *benê ḥail*, 'men of substance'. It has then been argued that with the departure of the property owners, these unlanded persons took over properties, and hence that when there were returnees from Babylonia—or indeed from elsewhere—problems of property provided a major cause of social unrest. Now it is quite reasonable to suppose that such problems of ownership would arise after a gap of somewhere over fifty years between the deportations and the return. But it may be doubted if this can be grounded in the Kings text. That text is concerned with a particular theological point: hope for the future lies with those in Babylonia and not with any other group. Such population as remained in the land, according to this presentation, did not remain there long, and so far as the future is concerned there is not the slightest indication of a continuing community. The historical (as distinct from the theological) judgment here given of the situation is very difficult to credit. But we cannot use what can be seen to be essentially theological interpretation as the basis for historical reconstruction without very clear confirmatory evidence from elsewhere.

2. *The Future is Judah?*

Support for this negative view of Judah is to be found in our two other direct sources, Jeremiah and Chronicles. The last chapter of Jeremiah (52) contains a closely parallel, indeed almost identical, text to that of the end of 2 Kings. It goes further in that it mentions a third deportation beyond the two given in 2 Kings: deportees in 582 (Jer. 52.30). It thus adds to the emphasis on removal of populations. It also omits all mention of Gedaliah. This omission could be because Jeremiah 40–44 provides a much fuller account of the Gedaliah interlude and its sequel in Egypt; more probably it represents the view of the final compiler of the book that the Judaean episode was of no lasting significance. Indeed that view is to be seen in the retention of the Jehoiachin element at the end of Jeremiah 52, and also in the way in which the Gedaliah episode is now presented. Recent study (see Pohlmann 1978) has provided fuller support independently for a view which I myself put forward some years ago (Ackroyd 1968a: 55ff.; Ackroyd 1971a), namely that the underlying narrative material in Jeremiah envisages that hope for the future lies with the Judaean community with which Jeremiah himself is described as electing to stay; and when, after the assassination of Gedaliah, Jeremiah's advice is still to stay, the disregarding of this leads to the almost total obliteration of the refugees in Egypt. Indeed the original text of Jeremiah 44 has probably been overlaid with glosses at vv. 14 and 28 to reduce the negative effect of the originally total pronouncement of doom—perhaps with reference to the existence of Jewish communities in Egypt at a later date. The same point, that the future lies in Judah, is effectively made in the symbolic action in Jeremiah 32. Here the redemption of Jeremiah's family land is made explicit in the elaborate sermon by which the significance of this action is drawn out (Jer. 32.26-44, in response to the prayer put into the mouth of Jeremiah in 32.17-25).

In 2 Chronicles 36 a much briefer account of the last days of Judah is even more explicit. Here vv. 11-21 set out the total disaster and the total removal of the population in so far as it survived the warfare. The land remained empty—all the days of its being desolated—until the time of the Persians; it was observing a total sabbath rest, so there was no question of any cultivation of the land.

Of course this is not historical statement; it is theological interpretation. And in offering this, the Chronicler both generally (so in the comments of 36.15f. on prophetic activity of a continuing kind) and specifically (so in the attribution to Jeremiah of the seventy-year prophecy in 36.21), extends the brevity of the 2 Kings comment on the fulfilment of the prophetic word 'as Yahweh had decreed' (24.13). The interpreter to whom we owe the books of Kings and indeed the narratives which precede them as they now cohere in a continuous theological work had already at numerous points illustrated the principle of the prophetic word and its fulfilment, gearing the one to the other with precision. At certain points— in the David narrative, for example, or in the link made between Jeroboam I of the north in 1 Kings 13 and Josiah in 2 Kings 23—specific cross-reference assists the reader. This final expression of the fulfilment of the prophetic word is not so linked, but it is hardly likely to be merely general; and in fact it is most naturally linked to the Isaiah-Hezekiah narrative in which the king, by what is effectively a symbolic action, hands over to the Babylonians as the eventual conquerors everything in the land of Judah (2 Kgs 20.12-19 = Isa. 39). The exile is there precisely anticipated and indeed may be said to be initiated by Hezekiah's actions: there can be no drawing back from it now.

(The Chronicler does not use this motif. His allusion to this moment in the Hezekiah material makes a different point. But he reserves the theme of the exile for a following moment, when he portrays Manasseh as exile and captive in Babylon, thus anticipating the events of the following century; he has provided a significant pointer also to the theme of restoration by showing the wicked Manasseh as a repentant and restored ruler who carries through reforms.)

Thus both here and at the end of his account of the fall of Jerusalem, with a seventy-year term put to the exile, the Chronicler updates and clarifies the theme of restoration. We must further understand the Chronicler's presentation with reference to the preface to his whole narrative. Genealogies in 1 Chronicles 1–8 provide from traditional material the basis for the concept of the community as one which can demonstrate its ancestry back to the very beginning of human history. In 1 Chronicles 9 the theme of the restoration is set out, also in genealogical form, utilizing material which is also partly used in Nehemiah 11, to demonstrate the link to the record of the past—'So all Israel was registered, recorded in the book of Israel's kings, and Judah was carried into exile to Babylon because of their rebellion' (1 Chron. 9.2). Whatever may ultimately be said about the literary relationship between the books of Chronicles and the books of Ezra–Nehemiah, the material of 1 and 2 Chronicles encloses its narrative within the clearly defined belief in the relationship between exile and restoration. (An analogy to this may be seen in the Priestly Work, which, it may be argued, ends without any description of the actual occupation of Canaan—staying at the point at which the tribes stand on the threshold, rightly ordered religiously, with the allocation of territory planned and the possession of the land anticipated. But this depends on assumptions which are inevitably somewhat uncertain—assumptions about the end of the work and the degree to which combination of that work with the Deuteronomic material may have produced some measure of dislocation.)

This brief survey of the material relevant to the exilic period already overlaps the nature of restoration. This again is a period which is not in fact very satisfactorily definable, since it is more natural to assume that the moment attempts at recovery after disaster begin to be made is really the point at which we may speak of restoration. Hence, ideally—and here again our evidence is problematic—we should begin discussing the nature of restoration in a consideration of how, in the years after the disaster to Jerusalem, members of the community, whether there or elsewhere, began to adjust themselves to the revival of life and to make the adjustment of faith necessary to meet a new situation. If we define restoration, as is normally done, in terms of the changed political situation brought about by the establishment of Persian rule— and this is what the Old Testament material enjoins on us— then we find ourselves again confronted with complex evidence and with selectively and theologically treated material. For the moment, a look at the opening chapters of Ezra reveals this: there is no single, coherent account here, however much a superficial reading may seem to suggest a sequence of stages. There are loosely connected elements of material, and if we read in parallel the account as it is presented in 1 Esdras, we can detect another dimension added to it. The narrative of

Sheshbazzar in Ezra 1 is one account; it can be read as a self-contained whole, since there is no immediate link to it in the elements which follow. Only in Ezra 5–6 is there a reference back. The presentation of Cyrus as divinely led to initiate the rebuilding of the temple in Jerusalem and the support of the rebuilding by the associates of the Jews in Babylonia (with its links to Exodus themes) and the enumerating of the temple vessels taken from Jerusalem and now committed to Sheshbazzar, provide a clear picture of what can be read as the essential of restoration. This theme is now undergirded by the placing in Ezra 2 of the list of returned exiles which is also utilized in Nehemiah 7. This serves to identify the ancestral connections of the restored community, underlining the point by distinguishing a group which could not establish satisfactory ancestry, including priests who were temporarily disqualified from officiating because their status was in doubt. We may note the functioning of the governor (*tiršātāh*, Ezra 2.63) in forbidding their participation; the problem of localizing the passage chronologically prevents us from utilizing this information as clearly as we might wish, but the term used distinguishes this unnamed figure in any case from Sheshbazzar the officer (*nāsî'*, Ezra 1.8).

A new narrative in Ezra 3 describes the re-establishing of the altar and the rebuilding of the temple, associating it with the Davidide Zerubbabel and the priest Jeshua. Ostensibly the sequel to this narrative appears in the opposition material of Ezra 4.1ff., but there are differences between this material and the preceding which raise doubts; the Hebrew text does not mention Jeshua in 4.2, and while the name may be added on the basis of the 1 Esdras text and its occurrence in v. 3, the possibility of harmonization of an original narrative containing Zerubbabel alone must be considered. More clearly we may see that the community is described as engaged in the rebuilding in ch. 3, where the emphasis is on priests and Levites and returned exiles, contrasting with ch. 4, where it is Zerubbabel (and possibly Jeshua) and the heads of families— all of whom appear in the previous narrative only rather subordinately to priests and Levites (cf. 3.12). The presence in the remainder of Ezra 4 of other opposition narratives, of which the whole Aramaic section is differently placed in 1 Esdras, raises a doubt about assuming that we have here a true chronological sequence. The more natural continuation of Ezra 3 is in the final Hebrew fragment in 6.19-22, recording the celebration of the completion of the building, or at least a further stage of it since the final verse speaks only of 'work on the temple' and not specifically of 'completion'.

While Ezra 4 provides something of a hotch-potch of elements, some clearly quite out of context, dealing with opposition—hence providing some important interpretations of the problems of restoration—the narrative in Aramaic of 5.1–6.18 provides another and apparently independent account of the progress of the restoration. The mention of Zerubbabel and Jeshua only in 5.2 suggests a harmonizing element, for otherwise the narrative is concerned with the prophets Haggai and Zechariah and the elders of the community. Reference back in 5.14 to Sheshbazzar's appointment as governor (*peḥāh*) provides an apparent, though not precise, link with ch. 1. Subsequent reference to the governor without any name (6.7) leaves doubt whether this is still Sheshbazzar or some other. The narrative is virtually complete in itself and can be read as an alternative account of the rebuilding, culminating in a dated completion of the temple in 515 BCE (6.15–sixth year of Darius).

3. *Historical Context*

Reconstruction of the course of events on the basis of this placing together of evidently disparate elements of material is very uncertain. And the uncertainty in regard to this period is matched by the equally problematic account which follows of the activity of the two leaders Ezra and Nehemiah. Within the limits of time here, I do not propose to do more than make brief reference to these later stages of restoration; but they illustrate similar problems of reconstruction, not least by the way in which partly parallel accounts—and perhaps mutually interacting accounts—of the two leaders prevent us from now establishing with certainty in what order they came, what relationship really existed between them, and precisely what functions they performed.

The consideration of the narrative material points to the problems of reconstructing a clear historical context within which to set the picturing of rethinking; without such a context, we are liable to misunderstand more obviously interpretative material, particularly in prophetic collections, because of the danger that we may be tempted to construct from them, with all their uncertainties, a picture of how society must have looked in order for such prophetic oracles and comments to have been produced, and then to use such reconstructions to fill in the all too many gaps in the narrative sources. What in fact I would wish to underline here is the importance of discovering, as precisely as we may, just what are the intentions of narratives which at first sight look like historical accounts.

We must indeed recognize—and this has already been indicated—that the very selection and arrangement and presentation of narratives itself involves an aspect of the very process of reformulation with which we are concerned. To recognize that the materials in all our sources for the period of the exile now present a picture which concentrates virtually our entire attention upon the exiles in Babylonia is clearly to raise problems for the understanding of the history; but such materials do set out one particular (and very evidently influential) view of the way in which the events were to be understood. In doing this, they lay a particular emphasis. In effect they are saying: The future lies with those who are in exile, not with those in Palestine; and that means that the interpretation of experience and the reformulation of belief must be in the full consciousness that it is those for whom the exile is a physical reality who count. This may carry with it the implication—when we recognize that historically the idea of an empty land is impossible—that any endeavour at re-establishing the community's life in Palestine is of no lasting consequence. (Here we may again remind ourselves of an underlying different view in the Jeremiah material.) Any attempt, such as may be reasonably surmised, at restoring worship in the shrine at Jerusalem and reordering social and political and religious institutions in Palestine, is to be regarded as a non-starter. (That this will create problems at a later point when those who return from Babylon encounter the realities of a Palestinian community which claims its continuity in the land, must be clear. It is perhaps hardly surprising that accusations of impurity of religious practice—contamination with the uncleanness of the other and hence alien inhabitants of the land—are to be detected.) The inverse of this is the statement that 'everyone with them who separated himself from the impurity of the peoples of the land so as to approach Yahweh the God of Israel' (Ezra 6.21) joined in the passover celebration along with the purified who had returned from the exile. Already in this there is recognition of the unreality of the picture drawn of the exilic period, but there is set out an alternative possibility: either the members of the community must have gone through the experience of exile in Babylonia; or they must have separated themselves from impurity, from contamination associated with the peoples of the land. This represents an understanding of the exile as an experience of purification; in effect it means that one approach to the whole experience is to see it not simply in historical terms but also in terms of detachment from the past, a past described so largely in the narrative works in terms of failure and loss of true religious adherence.

At the same time we may observe a shift in understanding of the earlier traditions of Israel. The great theme of the deliverance from Egypt, and so an interpretation of the distresses of the exile as providing the occasion for a new great act of deliverance, is one which pervades much of the latter part of the book of Isaiah. But it has often been observed that there is a sharp contrast between the experience of Israel in Egypt and that of Israel in Babylon; the latter, by and large, is seen in terms of judgment for Israel's failure, though this does not exclude the frequent use of themes of lament, expressions of distress, such as are to be found in the poems of the book of Lamentations. Such themes are indeed also to be found in the latter part of the book of Isaiah. The shift comes as the earlier experience is reinterpreted in terms of the alien quality of life in Egypt. In some of the presentations of the tradition, to return to Egypt is to show lack of faith in the ways of God. For example, the picture of those who went to Egypt in Jeremiah 42–44 as finally lost in idolatrous practice is expressive of the conviction that Egypt is a place of alien life, of alien gods—a theme eventually to be elaborated in such a writing as the much later Wisdom of Solomon. This theme is already present in the Exodus narratives when the people express a preference for being slaves in Egypt to dying in the wilderness (Exod. 14.12), or when they yearn for the fleshpots of Egypt (Exod. 16.3), or when return to Egypt appears more attractive than entry into Canaan (Num. 14.3-4). In the royal law of Deuteronomy, the king is not to 'cause the people to return to Egypt', for Yahweh said 'You shall never go back that way' (Deut. 17.16).

The particular approach to the experience as now presented means that there is pressure to interpret it in one way. This in its turn may be seen to correspond in some degree to the Deuteronomic presentation; for no sensitive reader of Deuteronomy in the sixth century BCE—or indeed later—could fail to be moved by the reiterated 'When you enter the land which Yahweh your God gives you', in the reflection that his immediate experience was of a land lost. This must be evident for those in Babylonia, for whom actual return to the land may be a strongly motivating factor—though we may observe that there is no indication that all the descendants of those who were taken to Babylonia did actually return. The existence of an important community in Babylonia (and in time to come in other places), a community for which return to the land was not necessarily a primary factor, opens up the prospect of an alternative style of interpretation, an understanding which in due course may be set in sharp contrast to the views of those for whom the actuality of return is central. That such an urge to return has been a very important factor in much later Jewish thinking, and that it eventually underlies the political developments of the past century and more particularly of very recent years, is clear. It nevertheless remains a fact that not all religiously loyal Jews take this view; and also not all religiously loyal Jews see in the current political situation an adequate expression of the concept of return to the land. The possibility of alternative modes of interpretation can be seen already in those biblical materials in which we may detect differing understandings of the way the experience is to be appropriated.

We may observe also that the experience of alienation from the land can come to be expressed in terms which are not

directly connected with exile; a poet of the post-exilic period
period, whose words are very difficult to date, could speak of
the divine promise of the land, tracing it from the traditions of
Abraham through to the current situation. But that current
situation is contrasted with the true possession of the land:

> See how we today are slaves; the land which you gave to our
> forefathers so that we might enjoy its fruits and its produce,
> see we are slaves in it. What it produces goes entirely to the
> kings whom you have set over us in our sins; they control
> our bodies, take what they please of our cattle, and we are in
> great distress (Neh. 9.36-37).

4. *Political / Religious Web*

The theme of exile, of loss of the land, is thus capable of different interpretations. Equally this is true of the themes of
restoration. The variety of presentations in Ezra 1–6, with the
attribution of the central role to one or another of the leaders of
the early Persian period, indicates a shared conviction in the
reality of divine power to restore. The themes of restoration
are now skilfully interwoven with others of opposition to the
community, and this makes restoration stand out sharply
against a dark background. In some degree we may detect
further aspects of this in the prophetic literature of the period,
and particular features of the prophetic material will form
part of the second stage of this discussion. But at once we may
detect differences of political and religious emphasis, and the
unravelling of these is by no means easy. Thus in Haggai we
see a conviction that a direct relationship holds between current economic distresses and the failure to rebuild the temple
(so especially Hag. 1); we see a degree of despondency at the
rebuilding as it does take place; we see accusations of impurity
which strike at the very root of a new religious community (so
Hag. 2). We also see, interwoven with these elements, the
conviction that divine intervention must come. We read of
great cosmic revelation of God, a shaking of heaven and earth
and of the nations, the outcome of which will be a glorifying of
the temple at Jerusalem to a central place in the world's life;
and we also find a comparable intervention, expressed in virtually identical terminology, pointing to the establishment of a

Davidic ruler as executive of the divine will (so Hag. 2). The interrelationship of the political and the religious here is clear, but the balance between them is not easy to assess. In the opening chapters of Zechariah we may detect a concern at the delay in restoration, and the possibility that the same political events which are associated with Haggai's conviction of divine intervention are here differently viewed. The cessation of political turmoil—a turmoil which may be the instigation of Haggai's particular expressions—is here interpreted not as being an indicator of divine inactivity but as the moment of divine intervention. There is here a different understanding of the relationship between the historical situation and the deity's action. If the various sections of both these prophetic collections are provided with dates which set them into the political world of the first years of Darius the Persian (around 520 BCE), there is, however, none of the reiterated emphasis on the divine leading of Persian rulers from Cyrus onwards—Cyrus, Darius, Artaxerxes—towards the restoration of the Jewish community. There is a confidence in divine action, but a more sombre view of the political world.

Yet—and here we come back to an earlier point—the uncertainties of political history leave us with doubts in the reconstruction of religious thought. The variety is apparent; the precise attachment of that variety remains uncertain.

Chapter 7

FAITH AND ITS REFORMULATION IN THE
POST-EXILIC PERIOD: II. PROPHETIC MATERIAL[1]

In the first part of this study (Chapter 6), we looked at some
aspects of the evidence for the period, the traditions preserved
and presented, with a view to detecting indications of the way
in which both the disaster and the restoration were viewed.
The understanding of the disaster, the placing of it in context,
and the interpretation of restoration (and the determining of
its relationship to the past), are all central elements in appreciating how the community—and various groups within it—
adjusted themselves, their way of life and their beliefs, to the
realities of new situations.

The process of understanding the disaster involves a reap-
praisal of institutions and beliefs. Insofar as the physical aspect
of disaster includes the destruction of particular institutions,
the community has to come to terms with their cessation; are
they to be regarded as belonging now only to the past or do
they still carry significance for present and future? If they are
to be restored, in what ways must their nature be rethought in
the light of the changed circumstances?

1. *When Prophecy Fails*

One of the areas in which this process of adjustment may be
detected is that of prophetic literature. The formation of the
prophetic books, with all the complexities of analysis that the
study of this involves and with the inevitable uncertainties of
interpretation and differences of assessment, bears witness to

1. Reprinted from the author's article in *Theology Digest* 27 (1979):
335-46.

the ongoing process by which the understanding of the divine word, mediated through the prophet, is interpreted. There is a sense in which the prophetic word is bound to win: if it is fulfilled, then there is confirmation of its truth and of the status of the prophet in the life of the community. That status is, of course, not dependent on fulfilment, since, however limited our knowledge of precisely how the prophets operated and how they related to the particular social and religious structures of ancient Israel, it is clear that they occupied a place of authority, by virtue of their status, by virtue of an acknowledged special relationship to the deity, and by the recognizable power of their words. Through the stories of the prophets we may see this clearly, though we may recognize that there is something of a love–hate relationship between community and prophet, and more sharply still between leaders and prophets—a conflict that should not be over-simply generalized, since there are many factors involved.

Part, however, of the eventual acceptance of prophetic words as lastingly authoritative is the acknowledgment that pronouncements of whatever kind are seen to be fulfilled. The relationship between actual pronouncement and historical event seen as fulfilment may be much more complex than the kind of exact correspondence which sometimes serves to underline a point in prophetic narratives. Thus the precise relationship between the prophetic word of Ezekiel and the death of Pelatiah in Ezekiel 11, or that between the word of Jeremiah and the death of Hananiah in Jeremiah 28, may be considerably more complex than the present form of the material indicates; yet the very telling of those stories undergirds prophetic authority. This is then a contributory factor to the second aspect. If the prophet's word is not fulfilled, it does not automatically follow that he is discredited. This is an area of investigation recently pursued with much illumination by Robert Carroll in his stimulating study *When Prophecy Failed* (Carroll 1979). The postponement of fulfilment to a future date, the modification of a pronouncement to fit a new situation, the reinterpretation of the prophetic words to bring out a new meaning—these are all possible mechanisms for preserving what is accepted as a divinely given message with its particular status and impact.

We may see the disaster to Judah as providing a particularly arresting confirmation of words of judgment spoken by earlier prophets. The words of Amos and Hosea had a primary reference to the situation in the northern kingdom in the mid-eighth century BCE and a fulfilment in the collapse of that kingdom under the power of Assyria; yet it is clear that further understanding of that message was to be seen in the ongoing situation in Judah. In both Isaiah and Micah, the theme of the doom of the north provides a basis for warning to Judah; and the same kind of emphasis is to be found elaborated much more extensively in Jeremiah and Ezekiel, nearer the time of the final disaster to Judah. Such reapplication of prophetic words is evident, though there are many problems in detail in detecting the degree to which modification has taken place within the material itself. As with narratives, the reading of a prophecy in a new context itself invites the appropriation of what is said to that new situation, and this may take place even without verbal modification. The same is clear in the Psalms, though it is often more difficult to detect there with precision because of the almost total lack of direct historical allusion even where precise events may be suspected.

A typical example in a prophetic text may be seen in Hosea 3. The problems of interpreting the experience of Hosea as indicated in chs. 1 and 3 are only one aspect of the study of the text. Whatever may be the context for interpreting the strangely allusive account in ch. 3 of the acquiring of a woman (not named and therefore not immediately identifiable, and whose relationship to Hosea remains indeterminate, except that a full sexual or marital relationship is evidently not immediately in view), the theme is now interpreted in terms the community being deprived of a range of normal religious and political institutions. 'Indeed for a long period Israel will remain without king or prince, without sacrifice or sacred pillar, without ephod or teraphim' (3.4). The statement envisages a period of cessation of institutions, but one which is limited, even though the phrase 'many days' is indeterminate and suggests a long period. A further comment follows, perhaps or perhaps not an integral continuation of the first one: 'Afterwards Israel will turn back and seek Yahweh their God, and David their king;

and they will show reverence towards Yahweh and his benevolence in time to come' (3.5).

2. *Davidic Monarchy*

We may here pick up again a theme already handled briefly (see Chapter 6, Part 2), that of the problem of the Davidic monarchy. In the Hosea material this theme is set in the wider context of monarchy more generally, since it is evident that there is a range of sayings in the book of Hosea concerned with problems of the status of the king in the northern kingdom, of the political contrivances, with the accusation of lack of divine authority, and the tracing of royal failure back into a remote and uncertain past. It remains debatable how far this material is totally negative as regards kingship, and perhaps our inability to give a definite answer derives from the overlaying of one level of interpretation with another: critique of a specific political and religious situation overlaid with critique of an institution bound up with political disaster, and this in turn overlaid with the final collapse of all kingship in Israel and Judah, i.e., the cessation of the Davidic line so far as political reality was concerned. Here the text of Hosea 3 invites reflection upon this as deprivation, and as a period to be regarded as abnormal. In effect it appears to suggest that loss of kingship, like loss of various religious emblems and practices, is to be seen as unnatural. For this interpreter, reformulation of the Davidic idea lies at the end of an indeterminate interval.

With this we may contrast the positive and negative aspects to be found in the book of Ezekiel. Davidic reference there is not frequent. Negative and hostile comments on the royal house, repeated in symbolic action (Ezek. 12.1-15) and allegorical prophecy (Ezek. 17.19), provide a prelude to passages which contrast sharply in speaking of a Davidic ruler, a true shepherd, a ruler of a united Israel (Ezek. 34.37; only here is *melek* [king] used). The contrast is so sharp that these Davidic promises must be seen as part of the reinterpretation. They contrast yet again with the modest place accorded to the prince (*nāsî'*) in the final chapters of the book. While a position of honour and responsibility is here given to the prince—never

referred to as a king (the term *melek* is used only in a derogatory reference in 43.7, 9)—the stress here is still negative. His
conduct is to be a contrast with the oppression with which
former rulers treated the people. While the prince has his
position in relation to the worship of the people, it is that of
provider rather than that of active participant. It is not difficult to detect in the final presentation of the book of Ezekiel at
least three different levels of understanding: the negative one
which represents virtually a repudiation of kingship, the positive one which expresses the hope of a restored and ideal
Davidic monarchy, and the strongly priestly one in which the
ruler occupies a place, but a subordinate one.

Here, set alongside what we have already noted, is an indication that the process of reformulation is no simple restatement of earlier belief and practice. It is of a piece with the
negative and positive elements in the Deuteronomic writings:
kingship is both a disaster and a divine institution, and the
holding together of negative and positive elements remains a
witness to the ambiguity of a whole period of experience. The
entire lack of royal material in the laws in the first four books
of the Old Testament and the very small place given to royal
law in Deuteronomy may together be seen as indicative of
hesitation, or indeed of eventual loss of kingship as a factor in
post-exilic thought. Yet not in fact entirely so, since flutters of
Davidic hope echo in the continued use of the Psalms; and
later thought anticipated more than one anointed figure. But
the emphasis which earlier belonged to Davidic status shifts to
the high priest, as the descendant of Aaron, but also in some
degree as inheritor of the function of Moses—a figure conceived in part in royal and in part in priestly and prophetic
terms.

3. *Role of Hezekiah*

There is yet one more line of thought related to this which we
may tentatively trace. I suggested earlier that the eventual
comment in 2 Kings that the disaster came to Judah 'as Yahweh had decreed' (24.13) is to be linked with the initiation of
this doom in the words and actions of Hezekiah (2 Kgs 20).
That might seem to imply a negative view of Hezekiah, but

this is not borne out by an examination of the whole of the material. There is here a structural problem in the books of the Deuteronomic history. The establishment of David in 2 Samuel 7 is linked verbally back to the opening of Deuteronomy 12; David's intention to build a temple is fulfilled in Solomon; the vicissitudes of that temple reach their positive climax in the reform of Josiah, in the moment before the final disaster. That reform, while depicted as too late to avert the fall of Jerusalem and the destruction of the temple, nevertheless serves to undergird the belief in a life lived in accordance with the Deuteronomic law in the land which Yahweh gives to his people, with a central shrine as appointed by God himself. This life, though not yet realized, is anticipated as a hope, a hope rooted in the conviction of the reality of the first entry to the land and its sequels. In this structure, the narratives of Hezekiah, so extensive and marked uniquely in the books of Kings by the appearance in them of one of the great prophetic figures, that of Isaiah, the prophet who was in the course of time to achieve primary status in the prophetic tradition, stand out too boldly and break the pattern. When we look further to the books of Chronicles, we see that, with a different emphasis, the figure of Hezekiah has become pre-eminent, overshadowing with his reforming activity that of Josiah. It seems evident that we have here indications of a further development, beyond that of the original shaping of the Deuteronomic history, a fuller statement of the significance of the traditions of the past and a fuller pointer to the future.

Indeed (and this is a theme that I have pursued in a number of studies—Ackroyd 1987b [1972]) Hezekiah has already in the narratives in 2 Kings 18–20 moved beyond his original role, difficult as that is to detect, but in some measure discernible within the book of Isaiah in the somewhat equivocal handling of the period of disaster which attended the Assyrian invasions in this reign. If, as appears probable, the isolation of Jerusalem in a devastated Judah in Isaiah 1 portrays that period, then this negative view matches the doom emphasis so prevalent in the opening chapters of the book, not least in the black pictures of Isaiah 6. Something of the same gloom pervades chs. 28ff., though both there and in the opening chapters we may detect the revaluation of the

message of doom in confident recall of the great deeds of
Yahweh in the past: the prospects of a renewed Exodus
experience and of a renewed Davidic monarchy are both to be
found alongside the negative material. I am not here
attempting to give precision to the stages of this development
in the Isaianic tradition, only to point to that tradition as the
repository of a rich and ongoing reformulation of the faith.
And it is a reformulation which points again and again to
moments of reflection after the major disaster of the exile.

Now within this lies the Hezekiah tradition, placed as it is
not only in 2 Kings but also within the book of Isaiah at
chs. 36–39. There is a particular significance in its position in
the latter book, since it provides a historical context for the
message of deliverance from exile which precedes it in
chs. 34–35 (itself preceded by Davidic promise and themes of
judgment and hope in chs. 32–33) and which follows it in
chs. 40ff. But within itself it provides a counter to the doom-
laden prophecies of the opening chapters and more precisely a
balance to the material of Isa. 6.1–9.6 with its pronouncements of judgment upon the Davidic king in the figure of Ahaz
and its anticipations of a new Davidic ruler in the oracle of 9.1-
6. This latter figure, often in later tradition identified as
Hezekiah, points forward to the interpretation of Hezekiah
offered in chs. 36–39, where the faithful figure of the king
withstands the Assyrian onslaught and meets with reward in
the total overthrow of the Assyrian enemy (36–37); meets
with a word of personal judgment withdrawn in a new
promise of life, here commented in the poem which uses
images of death and restoration to life (38); and prefigures the
disaster of exile in the symbolic action by which, acting within
the context of divine purpose, he hands over Judah to the
Babylonians (39).

The negative interpretation of this last element misses the
real point of the narrative. We may observe that the Chronicler, alluding to it, points it out as a moment when, even with
the withdrawal of divine help ('God abandoned him, to test
him, to know his true nature,' 2 Chron. 32.31), Hezekiah
proved himself faithful. In the Kings/Isaiah text, just as his illness and recovery is a type of exile and restoration, so too the
relations with the Babylonian envoys are a prefiguring and

enacting of the exile as a necessary moment beyond which lies hope for the future.

Earlier forms of the Hezekiah traditions undoubtedly underlie the present two forms of the material, in 2 Kings 18–20 and Isaiah 36–39; any reconstruction of these earlier forms would be purely hypothetical, though we may observe that there are indications of a less favourable view of Hezekiah if we consider the historical situation and some other clues, as for example Isaiah 20. But as the material now stands, there is on the one hand in 2 Kings a use of the developed material to point forward both to disaster and to hope, and on the other hand in the book of Isaiah a precise relating of the narratives to the immediately contextual message of hope.

The complexity of reformulation in this one area of the Davidic theme stands out in its rich variety in the material we have considered. It is not a single line of thought, but a many-coloured texture, with negative and positive elements woven together. Beyond it lie other ideas of monarchy: the precise estimate of Zerubbabel, presented with differing shades in Haggai, Zechariah 1–8 and Ezra 1–6; the undercurrent of monarchical intentions which we may detect in the Nehemiah narrative (was it for nothing that he was accused by his enemies of planning rebellion and seeking kingship for himself? [Nehemiah 6]); the eventual establishment of independent monarchy in the 2nd century BCE in the Maccabaean/Hasmonaean family, not acceptable to some but clearly idealised by others as we may see in the varied material of 1 and 2 Maccabees; and beyond this yet again both the actualities of kingship in the family of Herod, with the attempt at attachment to the Hasmonaean line and with the varying endeavours, some quite considerably successful, at keeping the favour of Rome in the extremely delicate political situation of the time. (And that the Herod family was not without its supporters is indicated at the very least by the references to Herodians in the gospels.) Side by side with this is the ongoing undercurrent of Davidic and idealized hope, which expresses itself in the hailing of Jesus as son of David and in the genealogies by which the gospels of both Matthew and Luke seek in irreconcilable fashion to establish Davidic lineage for him.

4. *Cultic Continuity*

A look again at the passage in Hosea 3 points to a further
theme, that of cultic continuity. There are two conflicting tendencies in thought in this area. On the one hand we may
detect important indications of the process by which older holy
places and practices are totally repudiated at a moment of
religious crisis: a notable example is to be seen in the report of
Hezekiah's destruction of the bronze snake which was associated by tradition with Moses (2 Kgs 18.4; cf Num. 21.4-9); on
a wider scale, the Deuteronomic emphasis on the total
destruction of everything connected with the earlier inhabitants and their religion is an idealized presentation of the
theme of break with the alien past. On the other hand, we may
see the concern for continuity, represented by sanctuary
legends which attach an experience of Yahweh to a holy place
earlier associated with another deity (so Bethel, cf. Gen. 28).
The two tendencies work in some degree in opposite directions,
each representing an important element in religious development. A break with the past or with the alien is one aspect of
adjustment to a new situation; an affirmation of continuity
with the past is another aspect. The two together provide a
clue to the understanding of the problems not only of the exilic
age but of other critical moments of reform and change.

In the presentation of the history, the theme of temple and
priesthood is a prominent one; the exodus/wilderness traditions provide a partly alternative, partly complementary presentation of the more ultimate ancestry of what came to be
seen as the one true shrine of Jerusalem and the one true
priestly Aaronite/Zadokite line. The claims made for the permanent quality of both temple and priestly line stress the continuity of practice, the authenticity and authority, with which
religious life can hold to the past while adjusting to the present.
The disaster of the Babylonian conquest was not the only crisis
in Israel's history: other moments of military attack and of
despoliation of the temple appear in the narratives. But it is
presented as having a finality and completeness which makes
it raise fundamental questions about the validity of the institutions themselves. If the temple is destroyed and the priesthood
shattered and exiled in an unclean land—very much the

stress of the message of Ezekiel with its strong concern for cultic continuity—what future can there be? That this could be said to mark absolute finality was clearly the view of some members of the community. We may observe—even though lack of evidence must enjoin caution—that other ancient communities appear to have disappeared virtually without trace, with loss of their religious centre. We can in fact only speculate on what became of the exiled members of the northern kingdom, though continuity can be traced in the surviving members of that community in Palestine; or what became of Moabites and Ammonites and others, with again the possibility, indeed probability, of survival in their successors in the later biblical period.

That the religion of Judah did not so disappear is to be seen in relation to the acceptance by some members of the community of the propriety of disaster. That it created problems of insecurity is evident from the distressful utterances of the book of Lamentations and of a number of Psalms, as well as the agonised laments of prophecy. But that it could be given a context is indicated both in prophetic material which pronounced the inevitability of disaster and in the interpretation of legal material, both in Deuteronomy and in the Priestly Work, as indicating the dire consequences of failure. The disaster could thereby be assimilated into the religious thinking of the community.

This would again point to various possible ways in which restoration and hence reformulation could take place. We may see the probability of what we might term 'simple restoration' of the older system as presenting the way forward for some members of the community: simply to rebuild, to re-establish a replica of the older buildings and procedures. There is a more positive side to this in the clarification of the relationship between the restored temple and the pre-exilic temple: thus the Chronicler repeats, with relatively little modification, the description of the Solomonic building. This is in effect to say: the temple now is the same as the temple then, its validity and status are unchanged. At a different level, the last chapters of Ezekiel present a divinely ordained blueprint of the restored temple in which modifications are clearly present, not least in the localization by which temple and city are separated. But detailed examination of the texts shows some measure of straight reproduction of the earlier pattern without the specific functions of certain features being made clear. Where, as most often, no specific detail is provided—as in Haggai and Zechariah and the opening chapters of Ezra—the assumption is simply made that new and old are on a level; and where, as in Haggai, contrast is drawn between new and old to the disadvantage of the new, the evidently recognizable deficiencies of the new are answered by the assurance of an imminent glorification of the new temple with the coming both of the treasures of the nations and of the glory, the very presence, of the deity.

Identity , or at the very least close relationship, between new and old is established by the affirmation of cultic continuity. This is expressed by the reinterpretation of older cultic legislation, particularly observable in such a compilation as Leviticus; by priestly genealogies in which, in the post-exilic period (cf. 1 Chron. 24ff.), the modifications which have inevitably taken place are given validity and authority in links to the past; and by stress on the precise and tangible links between the objects of the new temple and those of the old. It is notable that the theme of restoration of the temple vessels occupies a substantial place in the writings of the Chronicler, as also in the narratives of Jeremiah in Jeremiah 27–28, and in Isaiah 52 and at an even later date in Daniel 5. Especially in the book of Ezra, not only in the first stages at the decree of Cyrus in ch. 1, but again underlined in the Ezra narrative itself in chs. 7–8, the emphasis on temple vessels, supposedly recovered from Babylonian captivity, or offered as a further complement to the Jerusalem shrine, provides a linkage between different stages of the restoration as here depicted (Clements 1965; Brueggemann 1977; Davies 1974).

5. *Contrast of Old and New*

In this area of presentation, we may observe an element of the same kind of hesitation that is present in the royal theme. The underlining of a sense of contrast between the new temple and the old, answered by the promise of a coming moment of glory (so Hag. 2, see above; and cf. the celebration with ritual weeping and joy in Ezra 3), is in itself a qualifying statement: the moment of true restoration is not yet. The reiteration of restoration themes by the combining of different strands of material in the opening chapters of the book of Ezra, and the combining of these with opposition material, which provides qualifiers to the confident hopes in the narratives; the continuation of these sections with the now twofold accounts of the re-establishment of the community in the Ezra and Nehemiah sections—all these point to the incompleteness underlined in the last parts of the material by indications of the unsatisfactory state of affairs (cf. the final verses of Neh. 9 already cited; and Neh. 13 for another aspect). Neither Ezra nor Nehemiah is in fact described as involved in actual temple restoration—though the latter acquires this status later in 2 Maccabees and the former has acquired in 2 Esdras the status of total restorer of life after the exile expressed particularly in the scriptures. But the reiteration of the theme of the temple vessels in the Ezra material, and the stress on reformation of religious matters in the second part of the Nehemiah narratives, show the continuing of essentially the same themes here too. It has become increasingly clear in recent work on the Chronicler (Ackroyd 1974, 1981, 1982b [repr. Ackroyd 1987b, chs. 9, 7, 10]) that the body of writings in 1 and 2 Chronicles, Ezra, Nehemiah (which certainly belongs together, however precisely its dating and authorship may be delineated) does not present a complacent picture of a theocratic community seeing in its present life the realization of eschatological hope; there is a degree of hesitation, of anxious looking forward, of realisation that all is not yet right with the community, which suggests that here we have an ongoing concern with what restoration means, with a particular awareness of the unsatisfactory nature of the attempts which are made at establishing a fully acceptable way of community life.

Underlying this we may recognize the ongoing concept of exile, of loss of land. The theme of the relationship between land and community has been much examined in recent years (cf. Ackroyd 1976, 1977a [repr. here as Chapters 12, 13]; Mosis 1973; also cf. Walten 1973), with the recognition also that the temple has a special relation to the concept of land. It is not my purpose here to attempt a further discussion of this area of thought, except to point to the presence within temple ideology of the idea of a divine realm, a divine area of territory for which the prototype is presented in the J story of creation in Genesis 2. The garden that Yahweh plants for himself and commits to the first man to tend for his (Yahweh's) use, has sufficient analogies with other indications of the dwelling place of the deity for it to be clear that, while its present use has shifted its function, it belongs in this area of thought. We may see here a link with the view that the notion that the whole land—or in other contexts the whole earth—belongs to Yahweh, is expressed in the recognition of his absolute control of that part of it on which the temple is built. The centrality of the temple land in the idealized geography of Ezekiel 40–48 is one clear expression of it. Other aspects of this thought are found in the relation between the existence of the temple and the well-being of the community: Haggai 1, as an example of such thought, continues a much older tradition of religio-political understanding.

This has several aspects relevant to the theme of our study. If one aspect of the exilic disaster is loss of land, one element in restoration is its recovery. This may be seen in the implicit hope of a new entry into the land which is present in both the Priestly Work and in Deuteronomy. As already indicated, the reality of the experience is not to be seen as restricted to those who have actually undergone the physical experience of deportation. Alienation is part of the experience of those who live under the rule of foreign powers. Restoration in the sense of physical return to the land is a real part of one type of understanding of what the recovery of the land may be. It is also expressed in the long succession of nationalistic movements, particularly well documented for us in the period of Greek and Roman rule, but by no means absent in the earlier periods too. Through the whole period when Israel and Judah were under foreign rule, the desire for independence, expressed in various rebellious activities, is in part a desire for control of the land which, in the more theological writings, is regarded as the possession of the deity, lent to Israel and therefore inalienable. In this context too we must understand the hopes centred, at least for some members of the community, in the figure of Zerubbabel; as we may also believe it likely that, whatever precisely Nehemiah's own position—and we have only a substantially propaganda document from which we may speculate—there were those who hoped and no doubt worked for the establishment of independence under him. The extent of response to rebellion in the 2nd century BCE, and the continuing pattern in the last century BCE and the 1st century CE, underline this.

6. *Local / Universal Tension*

Along with this goes the fact that not all those who were exiled from Palestine returned. The modern parallel lies close to hand. There are those who see in the establishment of the modern state of Israel a fulfilment of the always present desire for return, a significant factor in much Jewish thinking down the centuries, and a potent motive, especially when strengthened by the unacceptable conditions of diaspora life as these have so often been experienced with greater or lesser degrees of hostility from non-Jewish neighbours—Christian and otherwise. Yet it must be recognized that a considerable proportion of the Jewish community still lives elsewhere in the world; and within the modern state of Israel itself there are very varied estimates of its religious status. There are those who would argue that a true conception of Judaism demands the desire to return to and recover the land; but this view is not universally held. In the biblical material there is one work—the book of Esther—which has an explicitly diaspora setting, and it clearly does not at any point raise the question of whether Jews should continue to live away from their land; its assumptions are entirely set within an alien environment. The same is at least in part true of some elements in Daniel and in the Joseph story. No doubt one of the reasons for the popularity of Esther with Jews is that it provides a certain analogy to later experience, pointing to the long-standing distress of Jewish life in an alien environment, as also to the loyalty to the faith of those it portrays as heroic. It is also clear that many Jews, over the centuries, have understood the concept of land in a less than material sense, in this offering an interpretation of biblical promise in a way comparable to that of Christian thought. The Christian reinterpretation of the temple concept in terms of Jesus himself—a line of thought represented in various ways within the New Testament—allows for the reality of the presence of God within the world which is his, while not insisting on a particular kind of localization. We may observe that there is often here a tension between a stress on the localizing of manifestations of God—stress on holy place, on building—and the recognition of the temporary quality of such localization; a similar tension may be observed between concepts of a church as associated with a nation and those of universality. While the tensions exist, it is not to be argued that there is a simple balance to be found, since there are so many factors which enter into the particular emphasis.

These reflections on later developments of thought are intended to be no more than pointers, and need much closer discussion and investigation. They are intended to suggest that the theme with which we are occupied is an extremely complex one. There is a process by which a long-held religious faith, confronted by disruption of belief and institutions—and this is an experience which confronts every religious community at some stage of its existence, and one which many would feel to be particularly acute in our contemporary society—can react to the disruption and can assimilate it into its system, and this process leads to the working out of a variety of ways in which reformulation can take place. Perhaps the most obvious aspect of such an experience, but in some ways still one of the most difficult to accept, is this recognition that any such critical moment evokes not one but many responses. The variety that may be detected in the exilic and post-exilic period—detected rather than fully described because of the limitations of our information—is not to be seen as a break-up of orthodoxy, if indeed such a term is really an appropriate one. It is rather an attestation of the richness with which the religious interpretation of life can express itself; and that in part derives—and we are again in the realm of 'our uncertainties'—from the intangible nature of the ideas with which we are operating. If variety of belief within a single system looks to some people like the way to chaos and hence to even greater dilemmas, we may at least console ourselves with the thought that complete singleness of belief, a single unified system acknowledged as alone valid, is a too narrow a concept, too limiting an understanding; it is an approach which stultifies and becomes barren, rather than a potentially developing and enriching experience. In our contemporary uncertainties this may not be an immediately consoling thought; but set against the background of the period with which we have been concerned, we may recognize that it was the achievement of men and women of that ancient community to survive the disaster, not in the narrow sense of living through it, but in the deeper sense of making of it part of their way of understanding themselves, the world in which they lived, and the nature of the God whom they worshipped.

Chapter 8

A SUBJECT PEOPLE: JUDAH UNDER PERSIAN RULE[1]

1. *Persians and Jews*

These studies in the Haskell series concern three interrelated topics: Persians and Jews; the Jews and other peoples; the Jews and themselves. But, as often happens, the neatness of division by title may easily conceal the overlapping nature of the actual discussion. Jewish relationship with and attitude towards the Persians are clearly in part a topic which overlaps with questions of Jewish attitudes and relationships to other peoples in general; but it is convenient to distinguish between the relationship with the superior power, the ruling imperial authority, and that with other subject peoples with whom there is at least a common level of experience in being subject to that imperial power—though the topic of relationship with these other peoples is only in part concerned with the question of standing under Persian authority. Similarly, one aspect of the problem of Jewish self-understanding and self-definition in this period involves the way in which the community saw itself in relation to imperial power; and another is the way in which it saw itself over against other surrounding peoples, though this topic extends more broadly into issues concerning the tradition from the past within which the new political situation was to be understood. If, therefore, the studies move in some measure in overlaping circles, we may nevertheless hope that these circles do not merely revolve, as it were, upon their own axes, but that they also produce some measure of progression towards a fuller and more adequate understanding of the community within which there was being formu-

1. This essay represents the text of the author's Haskell Lectures delivered at Oberlin College, Oberlin, Ohio in 1984.

lated so much of the literature which we know as the Old Testament, or as the Hebrew Bible. It is that literature which remains, and is likely to remain, our main source of understanding of that community at whatever period of its life in biblical times, and indeed, in considerable measure in later times, too; it also provides the base on which is built the substantial structures of the later religious life of both the Jewish and the Christian communities with their differing stances towards the base upon which they rest.

a. *A Subject People*
It was not, in fact, new for the Jewish community of the Persian period to find itself a subject people. Quite apart from that element in the religious tradition which placed the origins of the people in the ferment of oppression in Egypt, and the recognition of the degree to which the Palestinian area was in earlier times a region whose control was a concern to Egyptian and Hittite rulers, we may recognize a degree of intervention at least from the very early years of the first millennium BCE. Shishak of Egypt, protector of the fugitive Jeroboam (1 Kgs 11), and invader of the territory of the two kingdoms in the period of Rehoboam and Jeroboam (1 Kgs 14), is known to us (if not completely lucidly) from his own inscriptional material. He is the first named ruler of Egypt in the Old Testament. The nature of his intervention in Palestine remains less than clear. Within a century, the threat was to be felt from Assyria, and by the end of the ninth century, however much political independence was retained by the two kingdoms of Israel and Judah, that political independence was to a considerable degree overshadowed by Assyria. Jehu's submission to Assyria is indicative of the power that threatened, and which remained as a threat only in so far as the political and economic aims of Assyria did not press that empire to thrust out to take complete control of the western lands. The logical sequel was the political instability of the second half of the eighth century BCE, the fall successively to Assyrian conquest and control of the various kingdoms, including the northern kingdom of Israel. Judah, partly by political contrivance, partly by judicious submission and payment of tribute, did not suffer the magnitude of the disaster

that overtook the north; but it lost its real independence and we may suspect that only a combination of luck and the vagaries of Assyrian politics and domestic troubles prevented a similar disaster at the time when Hezekiah, a foolish political operator if ever there was one, was playing at power politics in the last years of the eighth century. His successor, Manasseh, more wisely preserved peace by submission.

There was a moment of relief under Josiah, when Assyrian power was weak and Babylon did not yet threaten, but it was of brief duration. The last years of Judah are marked by subservience, with the only uncertainty being that of whether, in the outcome, it would be Egypt or Babylon which would control its destinies. It is clearer to us now that it was to Judaean politicians and people then which way the political scene would change; submission to Babylon, advocated by Jeremiah and one significant group of political leaders, was to prove inevitable, if accepted only reluctantly by heroic patriots, like Ishmael of the royal house. You will observe that I use contemporary terminology in speaking of Ishmael as a 'heroic patriot', where perhaps more appropriately, he might be called a bloody assassin and terrorist; his technique is familiar, with the use of both murder and blackmail. We have no measure of his success; only a report of aspects of his failure. He is unlikely to have been the sole representative of his kind.

So when Judah came, with the turn of events, to be part of a new political system, as Persia under Cyrus took over from Babylon as supreme, and as the western lands, including Palestine, found themselves inevitably accepting the new domination, it was not so much a new situation as a continuation of the old. To speak of a change from liberty to servitude would be inappropriate. If there was recollection of political liberty for a short space under Josiah, our sources do not really give much scope for it. The account of that period is dominated by the picture of religious reform, and ends in what we may well see to be political failure. The days of Josiah were remembered by those who wrote the story not as a time when the days of the old kingdom were restored, but as one when religious reformation could indicate that, had the law been obeyed, circumstances (if not necessarily political circumstances) could have been different. They told this story in order to make it clear, as Deuteronomy makes it clear, that a renewed entry into the land, whether actual or symbolic, demanded an obedience to the law of the God who gave them the land, without which a new life in the land would be no more successful than the first period of occupation had been (cf. also Jer. 7). Political hope was not lost; but the recognition of Persian authority was a matter of political realism.

It was to remain a matter of political realism. This does not mean that acceptance was universal, though discovering the evidence in this is difficult and largely hypothetical. That there were those who resented Persian authority and would wish to attempt rebellion against it is likely enough. Our sources, however, provide no direct indication of this, and reading between the lines is less than satisfactory in building up a picture. It would, however, be surprising if there were no such attempt in the two centuries of Persian rule; just as we may see evidence of such political activity in the succeeding periods of Greek and Roman rule.

What, then, did being a subject people under Persians mean? Precise evidence for Judah remains difficult to discover. We may recognize that the normal features of foreign rule are likely to have been clear enough. Foreign control involves some aspects of occupation and direct control; it may involve the deportation of individuals or groups, and that is attested for Persians as for other imperial powers. It certainly involved taxation in one form or another; since imperial power is concerned with economic needs, control of trade and the payment of tolls and duties on trade are a commonplace. It involves also the presence of foreign government officials and of troops; the archaeological evidence is meagre, and so it is for the whole area of the Persian empire, but some indications of Persian military or government installations remain.

The question of religious influence or control remains elusive. A debate still continues about the nature and degree of such religious pressures in the earlier policy of the Assyrians; the religious aberrations associated with Manasseh, the subservient, appear to show more evidence of the presence, on a continuing basis, of religious practices familiar already in earlier years, and forming in large measure part of the reality of Judaean religion rather than being foreign and imperially imposed departures from it. Our picture of Judaean religion often tends to be more ideal than real. The degree of influence of Persian religion on the development of Judaism and of Christianity remains another area of debate, and the main issues fall, so far as our information goes, rather outside the period with which we are concerned. The question whether either the earlier imperial powers or the Persians demanded the recognition and worship of the imperial gods, remains debated; distinguishing between the formal acknowledgment of the god or gods of a controlling power or of an equal in a treaty form, on the one hand, and the enforced acceptance of another form of religious belief or at least respect to a deity who could make claims to superior power, on the other hand, remains a difficult and debated issue. The Jews of Elephantine could sign documents, involving negotiations with their Egyptian counterparts, which included reference to Egyptian deities; but the courtesy of a legal negotiation does not imply the acceptance formally of worship of a deity so invoked. We may wonder how far the external political control actually involved more than this, though it is an area in which we might expect to find differences of view as to what constituted religious control and as to what was involved in a formal acknowledgment of the existence of other religious systems.

b. *The Nature of Persian Rule*
It will not be surprising if there has been some expectation that these general and rather negative comments would soon be balanced by some contrasting statements about the difference between the policies of earlier empires and those of the Persians. Everyone knows that 'the Assyrian came down like a wolf on the fold'; equally it has generally been assumed that the rule of Persia was tolerant, that the religions of subject peoples were respected. For is it not the case that Cyrus authorized the rebuilding of the temple in Jerusalem, and that this authorization was subsequently reaffirmed by Darius? And subsequent Persian rulers, even if we are not sure which Artaxerxes is the relevant one in each instance, gave authority to Ezra and to Nehemiah to restore Jewish life and to rebuild the walls of the city and re-establish its political and economic life. The indications of such a concern with Jewish life, both

religious and political, must be taken seriously; but the evidence needs to be examined and assessed. The picture of Persian rule as tolerant by contrast with its predecessors must itself be examined, and what emerges is by no means so simple. At the same time, it must be recognized that the bad name of the Assyrians, however much no doubt deserved by the indications of ruthlessness and cruelty, needs to be assessed with greater justice to the context of such ruthlessness, as well as to other aspects of Assyrian policy which suggest that this is not the whole truth.

None of the great empires of the past—nor indeed the great empires of more modern times—can be described simply in terms of benevolence towards those over whom they ruled. An exaggerated picture of any such power in simplified terms, whether good or bad, is unlikely to do justice to the very complex motivations of imperial expansion. The economic motives underlying the pressure to extend and to control trade lead on very easily into fuller political control whenever it appears that without such control trade is at the mercy of changing political fortunes or lack of political stability in the relevant area. The extension of civilizing influence as a cover for the extension of political and military control did not begin with Alexander the Great. Political control will demand whatever action is deemed necessary for the sake of security. Persian policy, like that of its predecessors, led to extended control; it was in the fifth century to lead on into the great and eventually unsuccessful conflicts with Greece, and through much of that century also to a fluctuating situation in relation to Egypt, quite apart from similar exercises in other areas remote from that which is our immediate concern. The Persians had taken over the control of the empire from the Babylonians; the latter in their turn had taken it over from the Assyrians. Each in turn sought to justify its position and to validate its claim. It used religious appeal as one element in this; it claimed a right to succession to the previous power; it would, when appropriate, denigrate the previous rulers and claim the benefits of the restored order brought by the new power.

In making such claims, and in exercising its rule, it would engage in whatever were the normal procedures for enforcing conformity. Persian handling of opposition, whether in

subject peoples or in rebellious officials, was in accordance with
the standards of the time, neither better nor worse. While not
all Herodotus's stories of cruelty and atrocity are to be believed,
sufficient is indicated to show that the Persians could be as
cruel as they believed necessary to the pressures of an urgent
situation. When they suppressed rebellion, it was with a com-
prehensible firmness and with brutality. The years of Persian
rule were years of much warfare, and with that went consequent hardships for those they ruled, whether directly
involved or not—then as now, wars have to be paid for in hard
cash as well as in economic and other miseries.

We can gather instances, in addition to those of the Old
Testament, to show Persian interest in the religious organization of subject peoples. We find a later Persian concern with
the Jewish shrine at Elephantine, destroyed by Egyptian
nationalists—more patriotic heroes, no doubt. We find respect
paid by Persian rulers to Egyptian and Greek religious institutions. But alongside this, we find evidence of determined and
hostile action against religious groups or institutions which did
not toe the line. Even in the now confused narratives of Ezra
1–6, alongside the indications of interest and support, we find
the attribution to the Persians of a willingness to stop the Jews
in what they are doing. Ezra 4 contains a group of passages,
admittedly chronologically out of place, used to indicate the
withdrawal of Persian royal favour with the result that the
temple building, begun under Cyrus, was halted until the
reign of Darius. That the material so used is, in fact, not concerned with the temple, does not affect the point that the picture given of Persian rule is not even there quite as simple and
one-sided as it is sometimes made out to be. Nor, as it has often
been observed, is there the slightest indication that Persian
rulers acknowledge the superior status of the God of Israel,
any more than the claim of the Cyrus cylinder that Marduk
had specially chosen him to restore the god to his rightful place
in Babylon can be used to make Cyrus into a worshipper of
that deity. Politics and religion here go closely hand in hand,
and the Persians, like other rulers, could perceive that a subject people may well be more content to accept alien rule if
some concessions are made to its susceptibilities, some regard
paid to its particular religious and other institutions. This is not

tolerance, as we may understand the term: that would be an anachronism. Perhaps it is better described in terms of political realism.

What is the truth of the matter? A Hebrew prophet could speak of Nebuchadnezzar of Babylon as 'my servant' (Jer. 25.9); another could speak of Cyrus of Persia as 'my anointed' (Isa. 45.1). The fact that the eventual picture of the former is of the destroyer of Jerusalem and its temple, and of his reduction to folly and madness in later stories told about him (Dan. 3–4), and that the picture of the latter is favourable because of his authorization of the rebuilding of the temple (Ezra 1), does not make the one religiously more acceptable, or politically less so. It is a perfectly natural development which makes these pictures cohere. There is no special political validity in a portrayal of the great empires—Babylonia, Media, Persia, Greece—in a descending order of merit (so Dan. 2), or in that which represents them all by one or another fearsome beast (so Dan. 7, and cf. Dan. 8). They were imperial powers, ruling over subject peoples, and we would hardly expect accurate historical assessment from such a viewpoint. A change of rule may bring nostalgia for an earlier imperial power by contrast with the immediacies of political distress; this does not of itself mean that the earlier ruler was in reality the more tolerable.

Examination of the 'Cyrus cylinder' as a foundation document for the Marduk temple restored by Cyrus shows the degree to which this is concerned with claiming the legitimacy of Cyrus's position in Babylon, as successor to previous royal dynasties, and with particular reference to the Assyrian Ashurbanipal, a previous restorer of the shrine. The parallels with Ashurbanipal texts are particularly close. This may suggest that Cyrus was claiming to bring back to Babylon the legitimacy of a previous age, regarding the intervening rulers as a kind of interregnum, and himself as the restorer of true rule, with Marduk as the god of Babylon in his proper place. Relationship between the Cyrus cylinder and earlier Assyrian inscriptions both reveals the pattern being followed and also draws attention to the comparable claims to pious actions made by those earlier Assyrian rulers. Nabonidus, too, may be seen as making similar claims, suggesting that, as a rebel on the Babylonian throne, he was needing to legitimate himself as 'true' successor.

In the light of this, the authorization of the rebuilding of the temple at Jerusalem in Ezra 1 may be seen as claiming a comparable position for Cyrus there in relation to the royal dynasty of David, now as it were restored in himself (cf. also Isa. 44.28; 45.1). The reiteration of this theme in Ezra 5–6 makes essentially the same point, and illustrates it further with the injunction by Darius for prayer to be made in the temple for the king and his sons (6.10); the royal dynasty of Persia, to which Darius himself was now claiming to be the legitimate successor, is to be the object of special attention in the rebuilt temple. From the point of view of Persia, we may thus see the possibility that the restoration of the temple in Judah was one point at which the legitimacy of the Persian royal house could be seen exemplified. How far such legitimation can be traced elsewhere is not clear, but there is some indication of a similar position in other places, at least at Ur and Uruk. The authorization for the rebuilding of the temple, therefore, would from the Persian side be one aspect of the process by which Persian rule over the whole existing empire could be seen to be imposed and accepted. Indications of Persian concern with the rituals of Egyptian worship perhaps provides yet another such pointer.

We may see that this suggests two points about the position of the Jews in relation to Persian authority. On the one hand, the Jews in accepting the commission to rebuild the temple could be regarded as recognizing Persian royal status in Jerusalem/Judah. If the Persian ruler was the Davidic successor, so far as legitimacy was concerned, then the acceptance of Persian rule implied the relinquishing of any claim to restore the Davidic line. Some further comment on this will be in order subsequently. On the other hand, we may recognize that the interest of the compiler of the opening chapters of the book of Ezra was in a restoration centred on the temple. For that compiler, as indeed for other writers in the post-exilic period, a more serious question than the more narrowly political one was that of religious continuity with the past. To that question of continuity, Persian claims could contribute something important. The first temple, built by Solomon, is presented in 1

Kings as constructed as a result of divine command: the command is linked to the passage in 2 Samuel 7 which shows
David as initiating the proposal to build a temple, a plan denied
to him by divine injunction mediated by Nathan the prophet—
with the neatly turned comment, 'You will not build a house
(i.e. temple) for me: I will build a house (i.e. dynasty) for you'—
but qualified further by the note that David's son (i.e. Solomon)
would build the temple. (In the later presentation by the
Chronicler, this position is further extended by making David
responsible for all the planning of the temple, as the recipient
of the divine outline for the building; Solomon still builds the
temple, but the authorization goes back to David.)

If we may understand the Persian rulers as claiming the
Davidic succession, then we may see a parallel between the
divinely ordained David and Solomon responsible for the first
temple, and the divinely 'stirred up' Cyrus as responsible for
its renewal. It is a 'Davidic' ruler in each case who can be
regarded as mediating the authority, and therefore under-
girding the legitimacy of the temple. Royal house and royal
shrine go together. The temple is not simply a place of worship,
though it is that; it is also a symbol of divine rule through the
king, and a centre of royal administration for the proper control of the land. The restoration of the temple is effectively the
restoration of the community. Another presentation of this
theme is offered in Haggai 1; but it can be seen as the obverse
of this, in that it stresses that without a rebuilt temple there
can be no proper natural order. The temple stands central to
the life of the land, and therefore to well-being, expressed in
terms of the giving of rain and dew and hence of good crops
(cf. also in Hag. 2.16-19).

It is not therefore surprising that the presentation of the first
Persian rulers strikes us as so favourable. For the Jewish
community this was not simply a takeover by a new imperial
power: it was an imperial power which, in the course of its
taking control of the empire and claiming royal succession,
could be seen to be performing the proper acts of royalty. The
restoration of the temple, and therefore the possibility of well-
being, could be seen as part of the new order, and to that
extent, whatever else might need to be said about Persian rule
and the problem of being subject to it, there was something

positive which could be grasped. It was not that the Persians
were tolerant of another religion, still less that they actively
accepted it; in so far as such language appears to be used, or
such a conclusion seems to be inferable in the biblical text, it is
because of the style in which the story is presented. But this is
not unlike that of the Cyrus cylinder, where not altogether
different statements are made about the relationship between
Cyrus and Marduk.

The favourable impression created by Ezra 1 is continued in
some parts of what follows. The new-built temple is presented
as analogous to that of Solomon in Ezra 3. In Ezra 5–6, a reiteration of the theme of Persian authorization is given in a
divergent account, in which inquiry into the rebuilding activity in Jerusalem in the time of Darius leads to a reaffirmation
of the legal authority upon which this building is going forward—indeed, according to Ezra 5.16, has been going forward
without interruption since the time when Sheshbazzar was
first commissioned. To underline the point, the narrator here
goes another stage further by noting at 6.14 that the restoration of the community, here particularly in relation to its
temple, went forward under three Persian rulers: Cyrus,
Darius and Artaxerxes. The anticipation of the further narratives by the introduction of that third name takes us already
into the subsequent events associated with Ezra and Nehemiah; the narrator is concerned to show the unity of the various events, and does so by a simple archival note which cuts
across the chronology.

The presentation of this theme can clearly be substantially
extended by an account of the way in which other aspects of
restoration are associated with direct Persian action in the
instance of both Ezra and Nehemiah. The story of Ezra shows
the same underlining of the divine control of events: Ezra
receives from the Persian king all that he asks, because of
God's hand upon him (Ezra 7.6). The authority given to Ezra
to impose the law upon all the members of the Jewish community in the province 'Beyond the River' incorporates also
an appropriate development and enrichment of the equip-
ment and worship of the temple at Jerusalem: Artaxerxes is
thus presented as comparable with those good Davidic rulers
who have been portrayed in 2 Chronicles as restoring the wor-

ship of the temple, particularly after periods of regression. Financial support from the royal Persian treasury reveals the same concern of the royal house for the shrine which is under its protection as was to be expected from a native Judaean ruler. The journey of Ezra, emphasized as under divine protection, leads to that glorification of the temple, and so naturally into the giving and exposition of the law and to the celebration of a renewed and reformed festival of Tabernacles (Neh. 8). Associated with it is the purification of the community; but that is a matter for subsequent discussion.

The Nehemiah story offers a rather different picture, concentrated on the rebuilding and reordering of Jerusalem and the Judaean community. It equally shows the divinely controlled favour with which the Persian ruler acts, but it is directed towards another aspect of royal activity, namely that of the protection of the community, in the building of the walls, a type of activity associated with a number of Judaean rulers of the earlier period, in that their building, or rather rebuilding, of cities and fortifications is regarded as a proper manifestation of royal power. Nehemiah too, and in this like Ezra, is presented as one who in proper royal fashion upholds the observance of law, himself as governor setting the example to his subordinates in the maintenance of justice. Nehemiah too is presented, particularly in the final section which deals with his second period of office, as a religious reformer, an upholder of the royal protection of proper religious observance.

The impression created by these various narratives is of a protecting royal power. Behind the narratives, we may detect some indications of Persian policy, and we may very tentatively go further to expect that, in the appointment of both Ezra and Nehemiah (even if in either case, and perhaps in both, royal favouritism may have been a factor) some element in the contemporary political situation may have provided the occasion for sending royal appointees at these particular junctures to Jerusalem with its possible significiance in relation to Persian aims or anxieties in Egypt. The possible dates for the appointments, and these are uncertain, could coincide with moments of particular insecurity in the area; but any precise correlation of appointment and events is impossible.

What we may properly suppose is that the Persian rulers must have recognized the importance of security in the area.

Taken by themselves, the narratives might seem to suggest a degree of favour and benevolence on the Persian side which gives a good impression of Persian behaviour. The wider study of evidence about Persian policy indicates that this would be a one-sided impression, to be balanced by our knowledge of other aspects of Persian rule.

c. *The Unacceptability of Persian Rule*
A fuller consideration of the biblical evidence provides other indications of Jewish attitudes and makes it clear that all was not so smooth and comfortable as appears at first sight. There have indeed been attempts at demonstrating that the Persian policy bore harshly upon the Jews at more than one point during the two centuries of Persian rule. Julius Morgenstern produced over the years a series of studies in which he believed he was able to demonstrate that the year 485 BCE, at the beginning of the reign of Xerxes, was a disastrous moment for the Jews in Palestine. His interpretation of a wide range of biblical texts has not found acceptance. Its initial premise, that the accession of a new imperial ruler will very probably be a moment of upheaval, is readily paralleled from other contexts in the ancient near east; it does not therefore lack verisimilitude. But the arguments from the texts are speculative, and the build-up of the reconstructed event unconvincing, not least because of the way in which Morgenstern has added more and more material, thus producing an accumulation which makes the lack of any clear reference to the event the more problematic.

Rather more credence might be given to the supposition that another disastrous period occurred in the mid-fourth century BCE. There are some indications of a moment of stress, and attempts have been made to find archaeological data to match the proposal. But both the historical and the archaeological evidence are too uncertain for there to be any real coherence, and the proposal remains no more than a hypothesis for which substantive support is lacking.

We may be able to get somewhat nearer by examining a small group of texts which may provide pointers to particular attitudes. The first of these is in the curiously misplaced Aramaic complaint in Ezra 4.8-23, associated with the reign of one of the rulers named Artaxerxes. It is not possible to ascertain which ruler is involved, since no chronology is available. It has most often been assumed that it must be Artaxerxes I (465–424); this is on the further assumption, first that the stopping of the building of the walls and of the city (not the temple) here related must lie just before the activities of Nehemiah; and second, that Nehemiah is himself to be placed in the reign of Artaxerxes I. Neither of these assumptions can be verified, though both are most often made by commentators. Our interest lies rather in the attitudes suggested by this little piece of narrative. It records a complaint against the Jews who are rebuilding their city; we need not at present concern ourselves with the identity of the complainants. In the course of their complaint, they advise the Persian ruler that the city of Jerusalem has a reputation for rebelliousness, that if the rebuilding goes ahead there is a risk of taxation loss to the king, and the reason they give for this is that in the past, great kings ruled in Jerusalem and that their domain extended to the whole province of 'Beyond the River'. Artexerxes is described as taking the hint, and ordering the forcible cessation of the work.

The story is now used, rather inappropriately, to explain the delay on the restoration of the temple, a matter to which it does not refer. But its significance, as a story, lies rather in the way in which it puts into the mouth of opponents of the Jews statements about Jewish history. These sentiments are clearly to be regarded as those of Jews themselves, for the tradition that the kings in Jerusalem ruled 'from the Sea to the River' is one which is to be found in Ps. 89.25 and also implicitly in 2 Sam. 8.3 (where the MT lacks the name 'Euphrates', added in later scribal tradition). The original meaning of the expression in the psalm appears to be connected with the concept of the universal rule of the divinely appointed Davidic king; it is a piece of royal and theological glorification, akin to other presentations of the king as the conqueror of all nations ranged against Jerusalem (e.g. Ps. 2). By using this motif, and putting it into the mouth of opponents, the narrator has obliquely expressed a hope: it is the hope of a restored rule from Jeru-

salem over the whole area, and it may be intended to suggest
the re-establishment of the Davidic monarchy. The great
kings of the past in Ezra 4 can be seen to be anticipations of
great kings of the future. No such future is possible under the
present condition of servitude. The Persian ruler's reaction,
taking this threat seriously, is itself another way of underlining the hope.

If the hope here is oblique—and it has its parallels in other
indirectly stated glorifications of Jewish life, e.g. in Judith 5 in
the words of Achior the Ammonite—the position is more
direct in Hag. 2.20-23. Here the figure of Zerubbabel, the
Davidic descendant who for a time was governor of Judah
under Persian authority, is invested with a royal authority by
divine decree which depicts him as the servant, the royal
figure, and as the signet ring, the royal executive officer. This
expression of hope in a Davidic renewal, if politically
expressed, would inevitably have come into some conflict with
Persian claims; for if the Persian rulers saw themselves as
successors to the Davidic line, they could not admit another
claimant's rights. The passage is one of the bases on which it
has been argued that the Persians removed Zerubbabel from
office; but the evidence for such a removal is very thin, and we
should certainly have expected to see some indications of more
precise intervention in Jewish affairs than can be detected in
the narratives of Ezra 1-6. The interpretation of the passage
is complicated by the fact that both it and the preceding section
in Hag. 2.6-9, which deals with the future glorification of the
temple, are introduced by pictures of a theophany and of the
universal overthrow of kingdoms, pictures which may correspond to political reality—and have been thought to allude to
the upheavals at the beginning of Darius the Great's reign,
when he fought off his rivals and established himself on the
throne in the years 522 to 520. But the language is also capable
of interpretation at another level, that of a purely divine intervention: in that case, both the future glory of the temple and
the future Davidic ruler may be seen as projections into the
future. In any event, there is here an indication that the hope
of such a Davidic restoration was alive; and with this we may
perhaps associate other prophetic passages in which this hope
is expressed, though we are in great uncertainty over the

dating of such oracles. Zechariah 9 contains one such; but to what period does this belong? Royal oracles in the prophetic books are among the most debated elements, for it remains unclear how far they represent pronouncements in relation to a new Davidic ruler or the birth of a Davidic heir (so e.g. Isa. 9.2-7), or how far they are later expressions of hope, as in the fairly clearly additional materials of Jer. 23.5-6; 33.14-18, 19-22, 23-26; and Ezek. 37.24-25. But these later additions themselves, which may belong to the Babylonian period or to the Persian (or even later) certainly indicate the continuing vitality of the Davidic hope.

Inevitably with such material, the picture is less than precise since dating is so uncertain. Yet it is clear that we cannot entirely satisfactorily account for the presence of a strong Davidic hope in later centuries, down into the Qumran texts and the New Testament, without postulating some continuing strand of thought. The fact that the books of Chronicles contain a different kind of Davidic hope, concentrated on the function of the Davidic monarchy in the establishment of worship, may suggest some measure of polemic against the more political aspects of anticipation.

Another type of reflection, of a fairly general kind, is to be found in the two prayer-psalm passages incorporated in the narratives at Ezra 9 and Nehemiah 9. The former in Ezra 9.9 appears to accept that the favour of Persian rulers has been divinely ordained; yet the context of this reflection in vv. 8-9 is that of consciousness of bondage, and this condition of servitude is seen as only partly relieved by the Persian protection which has permitted the restoration of the temple and has allowed the Jewish community to exist. Neh. 9.6-37, in a long reflective passage concerning the land and the promises of its being given to Israel, reaches its climax, after the review of past failure, in a comment on the servile position of the present community, and the loss of the produce and wealth of the land to the kings 'whom you have set over us because of our sins' (v. 37). The community remains in a condition of distress. The passage is hardly dateable, except to recognize that it reflects post-exilic conditions. It does not necessarily belong to the narrative in which it now stands, but may be a quite independent poem inserted into the context. But, placed alongside the pas-

sage in Ezra 9, it suggests another aspect of Jewish response to
the current political and social situation. Living as a subject
people is by no means to be regarded as an ideal state. Distress
is real, and the problems of economic life are urgent. If there is
no hint here of any attempt at gaining release from the Persian overlordship, at least there is no easy acceptance of it.

It is sometimes urged that there was a degree of complacency about life in the Persian period. In particular, it is
thought that the presentation in the books of Chronicles
argues for a belief that the final age has in effect come, and is
embodied in the theocratic or hierocratic system now in being;
and that this involves an acceptance of Persian rule as benevolent and tolerant. That this picture of the Persian period is
erroneous has, I hope, been sufficiently shown. It has not been
my intention to denigrate the Persians, but rather to present a
more sober appraisal of what life must have been like under
such alien rule.

In fact, both with the Chronicles–Ezra–Nehemiah complex, and elsewhere in the writings which can be directly
attributed to this period, we may detect considerable pressures
towards looking critically at the current situation, and hope-
fully to a more distant future. It we take into account also the
final shaping of much of the earlier Old Testament material,
and ask ourselves why it survived as it did, we may find it
proper to see there too the imprint of a longing for renewed
life. Some part of this can be seen in the later prophetic texts,
with their critical comments on contemporary life; something
may be seen in the building up of the collection of psalms
which now form the Psalter, with so dominant an emphasis
on distress and lament. Perhaps we may need to consider too
how large a place is occupied, in the presenting of the story of
the people in the past, by threats to that people's life. The
recording of the stresses on the forefathers; the place given to
the deliverance from servitude in Egypt, and to the wilderness
wanderings; the theological explication of the history of the
period of the monarchy through to disaster—all these leave
open the question: what lies in the future for the Jewish community? What is its nature and place?

2. *The Jews and Other People*

At the beginning of the last section I indicated that the sub-division of the subject inevitably involves some measure of overlap. The relationship between the Jewish community in the Persian period with its rulers is, of course, part of the larger topic of the relationship between the Jews and other peoples in general. But inevitably there is a difference, in view of the overruling position occupied by the Persians. Also, we may observe that the contacts between Jews and Persians are to a considerable extent unknown to us; and where we do get indications of contacts, as in the various narratives of the restoration period, or in those of Ezra and Nehemiah, we observe a degree of stylization, even fictionalization, in the pre-sentations.

Zerubbabel, pictured in the story told in 1 Esdras as the third of three guardsmen engaged in a contest of wits in the pres-ence of Darius the Great, has a small overlap with the figure whom we may discern in the narratives in Ezra 1–6 and in Haggai and Zechariah 1–8. It may indeed by proper to believe that he was appointed by Darius, as that story relates, but we have no precise evidence for such an appointment. But the story is clearly fiction, and it makes use of folk-tale motifs, notably those which depict a trial by which the favoured can-didate, usually the last, or the youngest, wins the hand of the princess and half the kingdom for his resolution of a problem which confronts the fairy-tale king. Nehemiah, the royal cup-bearer and favourite, may to some degree be in a different position; but the motif of the foreigner who rises to a position of honour at an alien court is like that of Moses, Mordecai and Daniel, and many other such figures. If, as may be the case, royal favour plays a part in the designation of Nehemiah as governor, the scenery for the encounter between king and Jew, with the queen also present, bears some resemblance to the more elaborate account of Esther and Mordecai and their dealings with the Persian court, there evidently fictionalized. And in some degree the same is true also of Ezra, designated to reform the Jewish community, under favourable protection of the deity, and pictured as both bold and hesitant as he under-takes that duty: not liking to ask for military protection on the journey, because of his assuring the king that divine protection was all-sufficient—a nice motif of trust and hestitation which places Ezra alongside other heroic characters of the biblical story who both believe and hestitate to believe.

When it comes to contacts in Palestine, the archaeological evidence for the Persian presence remains very meagre: some buildings appear to be residences or outposts of Persian military and administrative control, but Persian artefacts are few, surprisingly so considering two hundred years of Persian rule. Persian presence was felt in taxation and administration, rather than in culture and material influence. The Persian officials who appear are shadowy figures, notably in Ezra 4 and again in Ezra 5; in neither case is it entirely clear who is involved. They stand in the background in the Nehemiah narrative, agents of the promised Persian support for Nehemiah's restoration activity. The Bagohi of the Elephantine letters, governor of Judah to whom appeal is made in the reign of Darius II, is not known to us from elsewhere; we do not know whether he was Persian or Jewish—though our knowledge of other named governors who were Jewish and his name itself, which, in the form Bigvai, appears in lists in Ezra and Nehemiah (Ezra 2.2 = Neh. 7.7; Ezra 8.14; Neh. 10.17 [EVV 16]), suggest that he was more probably Jewish. He invites comparison also with the Bagoses of the Josephus narrative (*Ant.* 11.7.1 §297) which tells of the murder by the high priest Johanan of his brother Joshua; but this Bagoses is another shadowy figure, and we do not really know to what period he belonged. He could, as is often supposed, be the Persian general of Artaxerxes (II or III: cf. Diodorus xvi, 47)—so Josephus may have thought—or the governor of Judah already mentioned, still in office under Artaxerxes II.

If contacts of Jews and Persians are difficult to assess and in any case few in number, those with other peoples have at least a sense of greater immediacy. For these were the near neighbors of the post-exilic Judaeans. There are impressions of real contact, largely (though not entirely) hostile; there are other indications of contact in which a closer relationship is envisaged, though such contact is introduced by way of pointing to the impropriety of such links. An examination of the material in detail does not give any very clear picture; and we may again suspect some measure at least of stylized presentation, a presentation which may make the evidence of greater importance for our last topic, 'The Jews and Themselves', because it is in self-definition over against others and over against those within the community who differ about the way in which relationships with non-Jews are to be established, that such evidence may be expounded. There is often a strong suspicion that the other peoples being presented are less portrayals of real people than stylized lay figures whose presence is really more concerned with indicating how and how not to react.

In what follows no attempt had been made at handling all the biblical texts which might be considered in some way relevant to the discussion. One reason for this is that the decision whether and how far the present forms of the texts reflect the Persian period remains one which must be regarded as less than verifiable: for example, confident statements that this or that passage in the three major prophetic collections, in the books of Isaiah, Jeremiah and Ezekiel, belong to the fifth or the fourth century often seem to demonstrate the ingenuity of the commentator rather than the discovery of precise evidence; even in what is here handled there must be a degree of hesitation about its use, and a recognition that other interpretations are also possible.

a. *Hostility and Separation*

It is, of course, no matter for surprise that expressions of hostility are to be found towards the imperial rulers, the Babylonians, whose oppression is now a thing of the past. We may observe, in the presence of large scale treatments of Babylon in the foreign nation oracles, in Isaiah 13–14 (perhaps in part originally concerned with Assyria), in the diatribes of Isaiah 46 and 47, and in Jeremiah 50–51 (as also in Jeremiah 25 and elsewhere), an anticipation of and a reflection upon the downfall of that imperial power. More particularly, we may note that in such passages, and even more clearly in such a passage as Psalm 137 and in other sections where no clear identity of the enemy is given (e.g. in some sections of Isa. 24–27), the figure of Babylon is becoming more a symbol of the outside and hostile world than an actuality. We are already on the way towards that symbolic portrayal of Babylon in the figures of its rulers in Daniel 2–5, and to the Babylon of later writers such as the author of the Revelation of John in the New Testament.

Such conventions may also in some degree underlie the presentation of the overthrow of the hostile powers in Zech. 2.1-4 (EVV 1.18-21). The figure four is used both for the horns which symbolize hostile royal power, and for the smiths, craftsmen, agents, who 'terrify' them—the term seems odd, but we should recognize that it is not inappropriate to the overthrow of hostile powers, and that it may incorporate the theme of panic at the presence of God which is to be found in the discomfiture of the nations of Canaan at the conquest. The passage, standing within the oracles of Zechariah and therefore associated by the chronological framework with the beginning of the reign of Darius I, cannot be given a precise context. The supposition that Zechariah was active as a prophet before that date, and perhaps in Babylonia, could presumably take it back to a date twenty or so years earlier when Babylon was about to be overthrown by the Persians; or, perhaps more probably, it could reflect a more immediately contemporary awareness of the upheavals in Babylon, and the claimants to the restoration of the royal line of Nebuchadnezzar who appeared at that moment, in due course to be put down by Darius. (Cf. also the summons to escape in Zech. 2.10 [EVV 6]).We may, however, see here too a wider and more symbolic use of the theme of the overthrow of the nations; for this is not in fact simply Babylon, the major oppressor: it is the four nations, that is, all the nations, with the figure understood from its relation to the 'four winds of heaven' (Zech. 6.5), who are here overthrown. It is the picture of the onslaught of all the nations against Jerusalem: all the alien powers are subdued and destroyed. There is here a development of and a comment on the preceding passage which speaks of the divine wrath against the oppressors, the 'nations which are complacent', which, when divine wrath was but a little against Judah, exceeded the limits by the disaster which they brought (Zech. 1.15).

Such a broad expression of hostility is, by its very nature, not precisely applicable to a particular situation. It may, it is true, utilize the wider terminology in order to provide an interpretative context for the contemporary moment: the uncertainties of the early years of Persian rule, the political pressures of the years of Cambyses' advance into Egypt, his death and the battle for the succession, may have suggested that a moment for the overthrow of all the hostile peoples had come. Perhaps we may more probably see such material as offering a subsequent understanding of the period in terms of hope of a new age, freed from the pressures of the outside world. The opening verses of Obadiah provide another indication of Edom's involvement (cf. also Ps. 137), as do some indications of Edomite pressure into the southern territory of Judah during the Babylonian period; but they point even more clearly to the use of Edom, like Babylon, as a symbol of that outside and hostile world against which the community sought divine protection. The broader understanding of such hopes of overthrow relates to the question of the delimitation and protection of the community, and hence to its self-definition (the topic of section 3). But we should not in fact attempt to draw too sharp a line of division between the contemporary experiences of the community, which would involve some degree of hostility to the surrounding areas, and the symbolic representation of this in pictures of total overthrow, pictures which could provide the context for thinking of relief from immediate pressures.

It is perhaps here that we may assess the relationship between political reality and theological reflection in the opening part of the so-called book of Malachi—'so called' since it has no real name and its prophetic figure is clearly fictional. If we really knew with any precision where this collection of material belongs, we might the more easily assess how far the actualities of political pressures on Judah from the Edomites underlie the hostile comparison between Edom and Judah, the unfavoured and the favoured sons, represented in the figures of Esau and Jacob. The possibility of such actuality must be there; but here again, as in other prophetic oracles against Edom (for example, in Isa. 34 and Ezek. 35), we may be dealing as much or more with symbolic use of terms. The stress on the choice of Jacob carries with it an implicit hostility to Esau; the point of the presentation may lie more with offering an understanding of what the Jewish community is and therefore what it ought to be, than with engaging in expressions of

Schadenfreude against an old rival seen embodied in a contemporary political foe.

To these may be added those foreign nation oracles which handle the other neighbours of Judah and which may possibly belong to this later period. The problem here is that there are few instances in which any kind of precision can be given to the situation to which they were addressed. The nations included, apart from Babylon and Egypt (notably in Jer. 46 and Ezek. 29–32), are for the most part the near neighbours—Tyre, Ammon, Philistia, Moab, Damascus, in addition to Edom already mentioned. It is arguable that all or most of these belong to a period earlier than that with which we are concerned, though all the major collections of foreign nation oracles—those in Isaiah, Jeremiah and Ezekiel—could, in view of what we may suspect of the process of formation of these three major collections, include elements which represent either new oracles from the later period or updating of earlier oracles to meet new situations. What seems, however, to be proper here is to recognize that, whatever their specific origin, these groups of oracles have come to occupy a prominent place in the prophetic tradition; and if we are right in assuming that the preservation of that tradition involves the recognition of its continuing relevance to the needs of the community in the later period, then we may at least ask what kind of function they might then perform, and what kind of attitude is reflected in a community which found such oracles against the nations needful.

To this kind of question, we may, I believe, make two kinds of response: the one is that the nations included in the list may have a certain artificial status, viewed not so much as the historical entities with which we are familiar from earlier conflicts, but rather as presenting in a unified manner the concept of a hostile outside world. That the Jewish community found such material meaningful, suggests some measure of protection against the outside world. The theme of the onslaught of the nations (and we shall see this again in Zech. 14) has become a symbolic one. The other point is a related one and may be illustrated in all three prophetic collections though in somewhat different ways. It is that the foreign nation theme is linked to the idea of a final overthrow of that outside hostile world. This is particularly clear in Jeremiah 25, where the reversal of the concept of Babylon as the instrument of divine judgment into a judgment upon Babylon is associated with a broader picture of the overthrow of the nations, and to that the Greek text adds by its placing of the foreign nation oracles at this point. In Ezekiel, though less precisely, the foreign nation collection is later followed, as a preliminary to the understanding of restoration in 40–48, by the evidently non-historical presentation of the overthrow of the enemy in 38–39. Possibly, the function of Isaiah 24–27 in relation to the preceding foreign nation oracles of 13–23 is designed to be similar. It is to be noted that here the theme of restoration is bound into the overthrow of the enemy.

Thus we may observe that, if we look at the broader range of expression of hostility to the nations in the later writings, the function appears to have a positive as well as a negative aspect. It comes to represent not simply judgment upon individual nations, but rather universal judgment; and the hope of restoration lies beyond this, the new age appearing out of that universal judgment. The last element provides a link with the second aspect of this present discussion.

But before we move to that, we must look more closely at specific material which bears on the theme of separation, material in which we may also see in anticipation one element in the discussion of the Jews and themselves which is the topic of the third section. This is material which is concerned with the relationships which should exist between Jews and non-Jews, and therefore centres on practical questions concerning intermarriage and exclusiveness.

The question of intermarriage is, of course, rooted in legal material, and it is not our concern here to explore the earlier stages of this and the degree to which an endogamous system existed in Israel. The desirability of marriage within certain clan and tribe areas is clear both in story and law; it is not in itself expressive of hostility to the outside world, but concerns itself rather with the life and well-being of the community, as well as with questions of property and inheritance. But it is clear that this material is widely interpreted in the Old Testament in terms of defence against alien religion, and we may observe that the story of Jacob and Esau incorporates this element, projecting it back we may assume, and understanding Jacob's (and indeed before him Isaac's) need to find a wife among his own kinsfolk in the area to which ancestry traditions pointed; in contrast, Esau marries outside the community, thus demonstrating his unfitness as the carrier of the religious tradition. The association of this theme with the conquest and hence with the repudiation, even total destruction, of the peoples of Canaan, characteristically in the Deuteronomic material, represents an extension of the concept to take in comment on the alien religion of Canaan and the demand for the community to be uncontaminated by it. It is part of that process of idealization by which a picture of a pure community from the pre-settlement period is contrasted with that which followed, in which alien religious practice comes in from the outside, especially associated with foreign contacts, among which are those of royal marriages and diplomatic arrangements. The picture of the foreign queen—most clearly Jezebel, but she is not alone—who brings in alien religion, becomes a paradigm for seeing religious failure as due to outside influence rather than understanding it from within the community's life.

It is therefore a logical extension to find insistence in two of the main leaders of the Persian period, Ezra and Nehemiah, on the need to break off foreign marriage contacts in order to ensure religious purity. The general similarity between the presentations of these two leaders, not only in this particular element, suggests the probability of some degree of parallel development of the traditions, but there are also differences. We may observe that the Nehemiah tradition, found in Nehemiah 13, places the theme in the context of the problem created by opponents, and implies that the relationships between the governing family of Sanballat in Samaria and some members of the Jerusalem community are as much concerned with such contamination as the marriages with women from surrounding areas, who, bringing with them their own language, produce a situation in which children are growing up who cannot speak the language of Judah. The whole context is that of religious reform, and this produces the effect of suggesting that the reaction against foreign wives is also of religious origin. The analogy of Solomon (Neh. 13) whose marriages with foreign women caused him to sin—and again the implication is religious impropriety—also suggests this. But the actual statements about foreign marriages appear to be linked narrowly to the language question. The intermarriage between the priestly family and that of Sanballat is condemned for defiling the priesthood and breaking the priestly covenant; we may suspect that political motives underlay the marriage and also underlay the opposition to it. We may perhaps therefore find a clue here to a different view of the social problem than that to be found essentially in either the Deuteronomic or the Ezra material.

The Ezra narrative presents a much clearer and more decisive picture. The theme is to be found in Ezra 9–10—and there are some indications that more than one source may be present here—and again in the opening of Nehemiah 9, where the brief allusion to it suggests the existence of yet another form of the material, possibly, since Ezra's name does not appear, belonging to yet another source. The Ezra 9–10 material is the clearer, for not only does it condemn foreign marriages, but it also makes explicit the reason for the condemnation, namely association with the abominations of the peoples of the lands (Ezra 9.1), and the mixing of the 'holy seed' with that of the peoples of the lands (9.2). The prayer psalm in which the distress at this situation is commented upon (9.6-15) gives fuller and explicit expression to the religious corruption involved, again with precise reference to religious abominations. The formal carrying through of divorce procedures is related at length, and in this respect too we may see a difference from the Nehemiah material in which only a requirement to avoid such intermarriage in future is laid down.

The degree to which this presentation is formalized may be seen from the way in which it is set out in the opening of Ezra 9 with the list of peoples from whom the community has failed to separate themselves: Canaanites, Hittites, Perizzites, Jebusites, Ammonites, Moabites, Egyptians, Amorites. It is clear first that this list closely resembles lists of the nations to be found in the narratives and the legal material; second, that there is a formalism in the presentation which shows that we are not dealing here with a precise statement about contemporary conditions, but with a concept of the community as separate from the peoples as in the settlement period. The Ezra story represents a projection into events of a concept of separation.

It is possible that the element in the list found in both Ezra 2 and Nehemiah 7 where certain people, including priests, were unable to provide satisfactory evidence of their descent and hence to show whether or not they were really members of Israel, represents a similar concern with foreignness; so far as the priests among these are concerned, they were excluded from officiating until a proper priestly decision could be made; this was done by order of the governor (Ezra 2.59-63 = Neh. 7.61-65), but there is no specific mention of the possibility of foreign marriage or foreign descent.

One last small group of passages raises another question. In Ezra 4.1-3, what are described as 'adversaries of Judah and Benjamin' attempt to join the building of the temple on the grounds that they are loyal Yahweh worshippers since they were brought into the land by Esarhaddon, king of Assyria—a story which looks like an alternative to the account in 2 Kings 17. The rejection of their claim is on the grounds that the community commissioned by Cyrus has the right to rebuild. This polemic has ultimately come to be regarded as reflecting the Samaritan schism, but if so it would be anachronistic here. It clearly represents an exclusivist attitude, and a view of the community as consisting only of the true Israel, that is Judah and Benjamin. Alongside this, we may set the statement of Ezra 6.21 in which the community celebrating the passover is described as consisting of the Israel which had returned from exile, and joined by all who had separated themselves from the pollutions of the peoples of the land to worship Yahweh. However limiting this may be, it envisages a community which can be joined by others than those returned from exile; it lays the stress, as in the foreign marriage material in Ezra 9, on separation from religious improprieties belonging to the local inhabitants—and the plural expression here would seem, like the list of nations in Ezra 9, to point to an idealized use of settlement motifs. Again there is no allusion to foreign marriages, though again it could be that the distinction between the returned exiles and those in Palestine which is explicit here is

based on the assumption of a strict adherence to the code in the
former and laxity in the latter.

b. *Outreach Incorporation*

This last element represents not a more liberal view but a
stress on the importance of the separatist concept; only with
such separation can membership of the community exist. And
there is no obvious reason for equating the content of these last
verses of Ezra 6 with the material at the opening of Ezra 4,
though it has often been assumed that they are directly connected. We may see that there are two possible levels: in Ezra 4
there appears a claim to be members of the community from
those whose loyalty to Yahweh is not sufficient to counterbal-
ance their alien origins; in Ezra 6 a willingness to accept those
who, while not of the group returned from exile, are nevertheless prepared to repudiate any links with the religious practices associated with the nations of Canaan and thereby to
indicate their full loyalty to Yahweh. The two are not really
the same, though they now form part of an attempt at a
unified presentation.

It is important to recognize that there was not and never
had been a purely separatist attitude. We may recognize that
many of the heroes of Israel's remoter past are associated with
wives from outside the community, and only here and there,
as in the case of the challenge to Moses in Numbers 12, do we
find an explicit question raised on the matter. In that instance,
we see that the challenge is rejected, though we may recognize
that the ground shifts somewhat to suggest that the real point
at issue is the exclusivity of Moses' position, and that the marriage motif provides only a starting point for a more serious
discussion of authority. We may recognize that the policies of
rulers in marriage questions, as in other communities, derive
rather from political advantage than from points of principle.
It would appear probable that one of the areas at issue between
Nehemiah and the highly supported Tobiah is that of political
advantage achieved through interrelationship, including
marriage bonds, with the neighbouring communities. It is evident that there was an influential group in Jerusalem which
took a different view of the proper means for establishing and
developing the life of the community from that represented by

Nehemiah. We may note that the little Jewish outpost at Elephantine, (known to us mainly for the fifth century BCE to
which the documents themselves belong) shows a measure of
intermarriage and certainly of other close relationships with
the Egyptians among whom it existed. It has already been
noted that the formal acknowledgment of Egyptian deities in
legal documents does not of itself imply worship of those
deities; we might expect there to be some, taking a stricter line,
who might view with apprehension such a degree of openess
to broader contacts. Yet that Jewish group maintained relationships with both Jerusalem and Samaria, the two centres
from which they might expect support in their conflicts with
local Egyptian patriots, and the documents reveal no antagonism, so far as we may judge, to either their religious or their
social conduct. Whatever interpretation we may offer of the
various deity titles, not now the Egyptian ones but the Palestinian, which appear in their documents, it is clear that the
Elephantine Jews were regarded as an appropriate part of the
Jewish community.

The very fact that some measure of opposition is noted to the
activity of Ezra in regard to foreign marriages—so in Ezra
10.15—makes it explicit that there were those who saw the
matter differently; and one of those there named was a Levite.
In fact, the ideal of separatism, with a concern for the stricter
definition of the Jewish community—again a topic which
overlaps into the third section—is one which has never been
strictly adopted, even if in many cases in later years the
enforced exclusion of Jewish communities from their neighbours brought about both a greater degree of the practice of
separateness and also a stronger justification of it for the protection of the community. The degree of assimilation is clearly
attested by the substantial conformity of Jews to the contexts
in which they lived, so that Jews from different parts of the
world, however strictly adhering to their ancestral faith, show
in large measure the physical characteristics of those among
whom they have lived. The issues at debate must concern us
again subsequently.

For the moment we may observe another aspect of the same
concern. This is witnessed by the presence of material which
develops another aspect of older tradition, the counterpart to

the theme of the onslaught of the nations against Jerusalem; indeed that theme itself often incorporates the more positive element alongside the prospect of the overthrow of the nations, for, as we may see at the end of Psalm 2, which is so clear an example of the presentation of the onslaught theme, the acceptance of the rule of the Davidic king by the nations, and by implication their acceptance of the superior power of the God in whose name that Davidic king occupies his anointed position and wields his authority, involves a relationship between the outside world and Yahweh, God of Israel, expressive of the absolute authority of that deity.

Incorporated in this is the further and related theme of the centrality of Jerusalem and its shrine. The geographical idealism which places Jerusalem at the centre of the tribes (so Ezek. 47–48), as a similar idealism placed the ark on the march at the centre of the tribal organization (Num. 2), may leave open where the nations stand in relation to that centre. But the issue is not in doubt where the concept of the exaltation of Jerusalem and its temple is made clear, as in the twice occurring oracle, in Isa. 2.1-4 and Mic. 4.1-5, which portrays the nations coming in pilgrimage in their acknowledgment of the divine word which issues from Zion and which brings peace and order to the world. The date and origin of that particular oracle are a matter of debate; it appears evident that the Micah form, with its comment on the worship by each nation of its own deity, has a more primitive theology than does the Isaiah form which lacks that particular phrase. The position is clearer in other passages. In Hag. 2.6-9, the centrality of the shrine, its glorification by God, and the coming to it of the desirable things of the nations, does not clarify the attitude of the nations, though it implies their acknowledgment of Yahweh. Zech. 8.20-23 offers a further stage, in which the presence of the nations depends upon their acceptance that God is with the Jewish community and that adherence, or acknowledgment, relates to the protection which can be found in the members of that community. In Zechariah 9, again a passage for which a precise date is not available (though it would appear clear that we are dealing with at least the Persian period, though possibly even later), another aspect appears, both more limiting, since it concerns only immedi-

ately surrounding areas, and more radical, since it involves
the incorporation into the Jewish community of alien areas
and alien population, in this instance the Philistine territory
and people, who become a clan of Judah (Zech. 9.7). As it
stands, the passage is in the context of a renewed Davidic
monarchy, and this suggests the expression of a hope of the
restoring of the idealized territory of that monarchy, including
the Philistine area which does not in actual fact appear to
have been incorporated by David but only kept at bay. With
such a more political prospect, we might properly refer—even
though the situation lies beyond our period—to the defeat of
the Idumaeans in the second century BCE by John Hyrcanus,
of the Maccabaean/Hasmonaean family, and the forcible
incorporation of that people into the Jewish community—an
attempt at resolving the political problems of the period,
though one which could hardly commend itself nor could it be
expected to produce a stable situation. Such a belligerent
incorporation does, however, offer yet another picture of how
the outside world could be regarded, though in this particular
instance, we may recognize that there are difficult problems in
understanding the traditions of relationship between Judah
and Edom, and it is by no means clear what kind of relationship existed between the religious systems of the two communities.

At a more positive level, we may observe the broader outlook
of Zechariah 14, where the theme of the onslaught and overthrow of the nations in the opening part of that chapter is followed by another presentation of the centrality of Jerusalem
and Judah, here with the interpretation of the whole land of
Judah as constituting a holy precinct, a temple area fully
equipped for the nations to accept the full acknowledgement of
the people's deity, with a threat of exclusion to those who do
not so acknowledge. The pilgrimage of the nations to
Jerusalem has come to be expressed in a fuller and more precise form. Perhaps we can also place beside this the picture of
Egypt and Assyria in Isaiah 19 as forming two partners with
Judah in the people of God—though this passage seems more
probably to allude to the presence in those two areas of a Jewish diaspora which shares with Judah in being that people.
Similarly, the controversial Mal. 1.11, which speaks of the

honouring of the name of God wherever worship is offered, could imply that all worship is in reality the worship of the one God, though the more probable interpretation would seem to be that such worship is acceptable wherever there are members of the Jewish community to offer it.

The equivocal nature of the evidence leaves open the conclusions which can be drawn. A decision, where that is possible, on the likely meaning of individual passages, would provide only evidence for the way in which the issue was viewed at a particular moment. The sequel was to show a degree of openess to the outside world, the incorporation full or partial, into the community of God-fearers and proselytes; and such incorporation remained a feature, though most often a very subordinate one, in later centuries. It provided the fullest statement of the acknowledgment of Yahweh that forms another element in the understanding of the relationship between the Jews and other peoples.

c. *The Recognition of Judaism*

We have already seen two examples of the acknowledgment of Judaism by the outside world: Ezra 4, with its stress on the greatness of Israel's past, put in the mouth of outsiders, underlines the status of the Jewish community even in its subject state; and (in association with that) we may note the speech of Achior the Ammonite in Judith 5, in which it is an alien who most clearly articulates the nature of Jewish faith and its power when its adherents are loyal to it. Such a theme is in fact to be found in numerous stories in older narratives. Rahab the harlot at Jericho is found to be one who gains protection in the overthrow of that city not so much for her rescue of the spies but rather for her acknowledgment of the supremacy of Israel's God. Naaman the Aramaean finds healing at the hands of the same God. If these, and other such stories, are relatively isolated instances, they constitute the context in which a wider development may take place. The theme of the alien who recognizes the supremacy of Judaism is one which is developed later both in Jewish and in Christian contexts. There is here a story motif which has strength in that it puts into the mouth of an outsider what the community itself wishes to affirm. It in fact at one and the same time stresses the propriety of the claim and the possibility that such a recognition can be made by one who stands outside. We observe that the overthrow of the hostile nations in Ezekiel 38–39 reaches its climax, as now presented, in the picture of the nations as witnesses of what God has done for Israel; and the motif of witnesses, who thereby affirm the reality of God's saving power, is one which is used in a variety of ways—at one level it is used as a basis of appeal to the deity to act, lest his inactivity should be misconstrued; it underlies the conviction, expressed especially in Ezekiel but also elsewhere, that God acts for the sake of his name, that is, both in expression of his true nature and that his name should not be dishonoured. The picture of the nations observing and commenting on the activity of God and on the fortunes of the community is to be found negatively in Lamentations, positively in Isaiah 52–53 and 60–62. We may also observe it in the way in which an older narrative is given a new guise, as when the Chronicler, telling the story of Hezekiah and devoting most of his attention to the carrying out of religious reform (2 Chron. 29–31), comes, when he alludes to the Assyrian invasion and its withdrawal, to show the nations giving honour to Hezekiah as a consequence of that act of deliverance (32.23). The relation of this to passages which speak of the acceptance of the supremacy of God is clear. We may also consider how far the Chronicler's portrayal of David and Solomon, which occupies so large a part of the work, is directed towards expressing less a picture of the past than an ideal for present and future; and how far the idea of a Davidic-Solomonic 'Enlightenment', which has led to the placing of numerous Old Testament works, actual or hypothesized, in that period, is in reality the outcome of such a portrayal rather than a result of more sober historical assessment. But that is only to recognize that what a community says about its past will be at least as much a statement about its present position and its understanding of itself; and with that we are moving into the theme of the next section.

3. *The Jews and Themselves*

The general title of these studies uses the term 'Judah', but in the titles of the separate studies, it is appropriate that we have shifted slightly to speak of the 'Jews', by which is meant that community which derives its name from association with Judah. Sometimes a distinction needs to be made between Judahites, that is inhabitants of Judah, and Jews, that is members of the religious community which now has a history subsequent to this period of more than two millennia. The terminology is always somewhat confusing, not least because it is difficult to decide when we should begin to speak of Jews and Judaism—just as it is difficult to know in what different senses we should use the term Israel, both in reference to the biblical period and to later times. In the present context the term Jews rather than Judah is particularly appropriate, in order to allow for the broader perspective in which the community must be seen: namely, that there were those in Judah who are to be seen as at the centre, but there are also others (in the dispersion, that is) for this period, mainly the Egyptian and Babylonian Jews, and also, as we may surmise, Jews who lived outside Judah but still within the broader area of Palestine; their links with the centre at Jerusalem need to be considered.

It must again be recalled that clarity of a historical kind is not available for this period, and that detailed knowledge of life and thought equally remains so patchy that any reconstruction is bound to be very tentative. Also, that, as we might reasonably expect, there is no single strand of thought; nor, as has been suggested in numerous recent studies, should we assume an opposition simply between two parties or groups. Such evidence as we have points rather to a greater variety and complexity; opposition, while sometimes clearly sharpened to direct confrontation, includes differing shades of view, overlapping and interrelated alternatives which exist side by side. And if we may judge by later theological controversies, down to our own time, we should not expect to find logically worked out positions, wholly consistent with themselves, but rather the holding together of sometimes virtually mutually exclusive ideas, indicating the problem of theological formulation and the degree to which any statement involves qualifiers which may include some measure of negation. When we add to this the reflection that there is a political element in the positions held—as there must be—we hardly need reminding of the ability of politicians—and their supporters—to hold more than one view at the same time. And such a comment is not cynical but realistic.

At this point we should make a distinction between what could be described as three directions of thinking: backwards—the consideration of the relationship of the community to its own past; sideways—that is how the community or its component members and groups looked at itself and at the demarcation between itself and what lay outside; and forwards—the ways in which hope for the future, the expression of ideals, can be seen in this period. Each of these is a broad topic, and covers a wide range both of material and of possible interpretation. No attempt will therefore be made at comprehensiveness, but only at some indications of ways in which, as it appears to me, we may see the process of thinking going on.

a. *Looking Back*

The problem of how the people of Judah reacted to the disaster which brought to an end kingdom and temple is one which has been many times discussed, and I have myself in various ways contributed to that discussion. There is no need now to emphasize the degree to which a break with the past, an interruption of the normalities of life, demands rethinking, which must include both the assimilation of disaster and the working out of a method by which continuity with the past may be achieved. For the community in the Persian period, now some years after the disaster itself, the problem remained; but we need to be clear that the intervening half century cannot be regarded as a vacuum, however much material in our literary sources appears designed to suggest that it was only after that interval that any real progress towards rethinking emerged. We cannot suppose that either those left in Judah and around or those in Babylonia and elsewhere merely waited until Babylon was replaced by Persia and a new political situation invited rethinking. We need not doubt that there was a new impetus with that change of rule, however much we may be aware that change of ruler did not necessarily involve real change of status. But what then happened cannot be detached from what we must suppose to have happened in the intervening years.

Questions of religious and political continuity inevitably invite alternative answers. The end of the Davidic monarchy came in 587; but not the end of the Davidic concept. We do not know the precise status of Gedaliah, the Babylonian appointee at that moment, though there are clues to suggest that he was vested with a royal status; we do know that Ishmael who claimed Davidic descent—which Gedaliah could not claim—attempted a coup, and failed. But we may reasonably suppose that he was not alone and that there were those who, whether or not they would have accepted his claim to succession, would have welcomed a revival of the Davidic monarchy. As we have seen, the Persian rulers claimed that succession for themselves; but that did not mean the death of a Davidic hope of a native kind. Speculation about the emphasis on the king being of native birth in the so-called kingship law of Deut. 17.14-20 has normally looked to problems of the monarchical period for its explanation; but the various elements in that kingship passage do not fit any one situation, so far as we may detect, and we may question whether perhaps its final form, with the welding together of various injunctions about kings and their conduct, might not also reflect on the future, after 587, and perhaps even on the problems of a period in which the king, as the Persian ruler, was an alien.

The degree to which the Deuteronomic History harbours a hope of Davidic succession remains uncertain, though the end of 2 Kings points in that direction. We have seen already that Ezra 4, associated with a somewhat later date, expresses obliquely a hope of Davidic restoration. We have also noted the oracle of Zerubbabel in Hag. 2.21-23, and the wide range of Davidic royal oracles to be found in the prophetic books, with the probability that a number of these belong to the post-exilic period. The degree to which the royal psalms, still used in the worship of the post-exilic period, were re-interpreted as it were 'democratically', with reference to the community or to the needs of individuals, remains a matter of debate; as also how far they were reinterpreted in anticipation of a final David ruler, a messiah. We cannot exclude the possibility that, at least for some members of the community, they could constitute a kind of secret code by which the current Davidic descendant—and we have family lines which trace that descent, genealogies eventually to appear in more than one form in the New Testament—could be seen to be the real Davidic ruler rather than the Persian king. (With the fall of the English Stewart house, loyalists to the line, we may recall, drank to 'the king', but, so it is related, by holding their glasses over a container of water, in reality drank to 'the king over the water', the Stewart claimant to the throne.) It would be stretching the evidence to speak of a Davidic party; for some it might be sufficiently articulated to suggest looking for the right moment, the political shift, the change in Persian control, which could bring that Davidic figure to an independent throne. More broadly, we may suppose, there would be those who, if and when a change did come, would look with favour at such a recovery of the past.

Support for some measure of such hope of recovery may be seen in what appear to be the negative views, the critique of such hopes, the denial that political development should go in that direction. If it is too strong a term to call this a polemic against political Davidic hope, it may nevertheless be proper to see a rejection of that or a hesitant attitude to it in the offering of an alternative view of the significance of the figure of David. Zerubbabel provides a focus here, since he is the one Davidide with whom a specific oracle is associated. His lineage, though not entirely clear, is sufficiently stated in Haggai and in Ezra 3–4 (also 5.2); in Zechariah he is named only in 4.6b-10a, and without lineage, but the passage is intrusive, and too much should not be built upon it. Yet while Davidic lineage is clear, there is no emphasis upon it. When Ishmael is mentioned, his Davidic descent is explicit (Jer. 41.1); but such a statement is never made for Zerubbabel. Whatever Davidic hopes may have centred on him, such hopes were at best secondary for the compilers of both Ezra and the two prophetic books. The failure to draw out the Davidic background suggests at best a neutral attitude, perhaps an even more cautious view. As a Davidide, he was an acceptable governor to the Persians; no doubt also to the Jewish community; but no more than this, at least for those who were to tell the story as we have it. The proposal that among the names of governors known to us from excavated seal impressions (but not stratified) we are to see successors and relatives of Zerubbabel remains too hazardous to be more than conjecture. A shift away from a more explicit political hope may be suggested by the failure to identify Zerubbabel by name in Zechariah 3 and 6, where we rather expect to find him, and where indeed it has often been argued, and perhaps rightly, that his name has been deliberately suppressed. But the argument is from silence, and cannot be regarded as proved, however attractive it appears. It would seem that the Davidic theme was at a lower level in those circles in which these prophetic books were shaped, circles perhaps connected with those in which the Priestly work was formed; as also in the circles in which the material of Ezra was shaped, where Ezra 8 again suggests by its placing of the Davidic members of Ezra's party in a second position, that Davidic hopes were not given any high priority.

Or perhaps, if we take account of the way in which the theme is handled in the books of Chronicles, we should see in the high estimate there of the figure of David, and of Solomon his son and successor, the presentation of an alternative view: David is the founder and organizer of temple worship, including the priestly and other personnel; Solomon carries through the building of the temple which David has prepared and committed to him. In the sequel, the theme of the temple and its relation to the Davidic monarchy is stressed in narratives of reformers and anti-reformers. And if, as the biblical text invites us—and without here any discussion of the problems of literary relationship—we read on into Ezra and Nehemiah, we may see how the authenticating of the post-exilic temple is given the authority not of the Davidic house but of the Persian rulers who saw themselves, and appear to this extent to be accepted, as the successors to that house. True continuity, as associated with the Davidic line, is thus declared to be in the temple, the worship and the priesthood. If this does not directly repudiate the more political aspects, it may at least be seen to give them a less than central place.

A further possibility emerges along this line, the pointer to an alternative to Davidic monarchy of a non-Davidic kind. Here we may consider the position of Nehemiah, and later tradition invites us to do this with a look forward to the second century BCE and the establishment of the Hasmonaean monarchy which was non-Davidic. Attempts to trace a Davidic ancestry for Nehemiah do not appear to be valid; nothing in the text really points in that direction. But the presentation of Nehemiah does offer royal features. The heading for the memoirs (and these in a number of ways invite comparison with royal inscriptions of the ancient Near East in which kings glorify themselves—though actually it is their scribes who do this), 'words' or 'acts' of Nehemiah, may have a prophetic connotation, but also suggests the 'annals', more fully 'the acts of the days', comparable to those which, according to Est. 6.1, were read to the Persian king one night when he could not sleep. Such a record is appropriate to royalty. And we observe also that as religious reformer, and as promulgator and upholder of law, he engages in activities proper to the office of king.

Now to some extent we may explain this as due to the transfer of royal prerogatives to the post-exilic governors, under the aegis of the Persian authorities. But we find also that one of the accusations against Nehemiah is couched in the form: 'You are becoming to them a king', and that there are prophets proclaiming: 'A king in Judah' (Neh. 6.6-7). Now, of course, these are the accusations of opponents, threatening to make trouble for Nehemiah with the Persian ruler. We are not told whether they carried out their threat; if they did, Nehemiah evidently succeeded in exonerating himself, though such an accusation might have been a reason for his return to Persia (Neh. 13.6). Nevertheless, whatever Nehemiah's own views may have been—and professions of innocence do not always reveal the whole truth—we could properly surmise that there might be some who saw in him a viable alternative to a now fading or lost hope of Davidic restoration. Better, they might think, a man high in Persian favour and one who with vigour and courage brings about a new hope for Judah, than some less than effective personage whose sole claim to position lies in remote descent from the Davidic line. The possibility of this is in a small measure enhanced by the presence in 2 Maccabees 1–2 of a portrayal of Nehemiah which, again without using royal terminology, shows him as a restorer of temple and city, the only true restorer in fact, and sets him alongside Judas the Maccabee, first great representative of the family that was to provide the only genuine native royal house for Judah, itself an alternative to the Davidic line. If a supporter of the Hasmonaeans saw the link with Nehemiah as a useful one, then he may be saying both something about the claims to status of the Hasmonaeans and also something about the way in which Nehemiah was still regarded in some circles (cf. also Ecclus 49.13).

There is another aspect of restoration which is relevant here: that of the land itself. It is clear in the Deuteronomic writings, with the particular stress in Deuteronomy itself, that the giving of the land to Israel provides the basis upon which they are in due course to be obedient to the law. The implication of that whole presentation, with its indications that the loss of the land has already been experienced by the people (so especially Deut. 30 and 1 Kgs 8), is that when a new possession of the land is granted, the example of past failure will underline the requirement of obedience if the same fate is not to overtake the people yet again. In the Chronicler's presentation of the narrative, the theme of loss of the land by the removal of all its inhabitants is differently handled; the land itself, so the implication seems to be, is not lost, but it is vacated in order that it may enjoy its sabbaths, that is, make up for the failure of its people (cf. also Lev. 26). The land is there; but it must wait for a new population.

Now in this presentation we may look back to the theme of the land and its settlement as presented by the Chronicler, and see that in 1 Chron. 13.5, it is made clear that the whole land, without exception, is in the possession of the people at the time of the reign of David. The territory extends from the Nile (Shihor) to the extreme north. And in repeating the text of 2 Sam. 8.3, 1 Chron. 18.3 actually includes the name of the Euphrates which is missing in the Samuel text. The possession of the land is therefore a concomitant of the position occupied by the Davidic house, and, in view of what has been seen of that house and its concern with the worship of the temple, it can be seen that the relationship between temple and land, the dwelling place of the deity and the land which is his, points to the re-establishment of the temple by divine authority, mediated through the Persian rulers, as constituting a restatement of the ownership of the land. The land, which is God's, is given again—or better its position as given to Israel is reaffirmed—so that the original position is seen to be recovered.

We may observe that the sources available to us for the post-exilic period do not deal with one aspect of this situation which must presumably have raised considerable difficulties. According to the ending of 2 Kings, some of the 'poorest of the land' were brought in to care for the land after the taking into exile of some of the population. The question has often been raised as to what consequences must have followed from this in the Persian period when some of those returning from Babylonia would find their land occupied by others. It is often supposed that considerable social and economic, as well as legal, problems would result. But we do not appear to have any direct reflection of it. (It has been seen as background to Zech. 5.1-4, but this is hypothesis.) We might perhaps properly suppose that these questions would be resolved by legal decision, perhaps in some instances by compromise. It is possible that lists which deal with the occupants of the land in the post-exilic period, in 1 Chronicles 9, partly overlapping Nehemiah 11, and in Ezra 2 (= Nehemiah 7), contain elements which reflect questions of land occupation. But these problems seem to be overshadowed by the more general emphasis on the land being again occupied by the people who constitute the true Israel.

But with this go two other clues. In Ezra 4, which we have already considered in relation to the concept of the Davidic monarchy, it is clear that the whole area of 'Beyond the River' is regarded as having been under the control of that monarchy. Thus the full ownership of the land is here too implied though not directly stated. In Nehemiah 9, in a prayer-psalm, the question of ownership of the land is treated at length, in a survey which deals with that ownership not from the settlement period—as the Deuteronomic writings indicate—but from the patriarchal period. This psalm thus has similarities to what is quoted in 1 Chronicles 16, which jumps from the patriarchs to the settlement; it assumes, as the genealogies do, that the real ownership of the land was continuous from the patriarchs onwards, and that the sojourn in Egypt, not handled by the Chronicler, can be regarded as somewhat analogous to the period of exile, a temporary absence from the land not a loss of it. The psalm in Nehemiah 9 goes on in its latter part to indicate that the actual situation is not as the portrayal of the past would suggest: Israel, the post-exilic community, is indeed in the land, and to that extent the promises hold; but its possession of the land is limited by the fact that alien rulers dominate it, and that its produce is taken by these aliens whom they are still compelled to serve. Within that complex of writings which we know as Chronicles–Ezra–Nehemiah, the theme of the land is presented with both a positive and a negative aspect. Continuity with the past is there, but the present situation belies the reality which should exist.

With this we may also consider relating those elements in the book of Jeremiah which concentrate our attention on the future in Judah. The background to this, particularly in Jeremiah 40–42, is the portrayal of Jeremiah as staying in Judah with Gedaliah, rather than going to Babylonia; and the further affirmation of a future in Judah when the leaders, after the death of Gedaliah, resolve to go to Egypt. A similar stress is to be found in the symbol of the redemption of the piece of family land in Jeremiah 32, with the sermonic exposition that follows: the land will again be occupied, Judah will again recover its status. As the book of Jeremiah is now ordered, this stress has been overlaid with the emphasis on a future through the Babylonian community, but we may see that the preservation of this pro-Judah material now serves to point up the recovery of the land in the post-exilic Judaean community. The later stages of the shaping of the Jeremiah tradition provide this further level of meaning; the texts can be read as confirming restoration in and to the land.

b. *Looking at Themselves*

How did the community think of itself in its present situation? This is a difficult question to answer, though to some extent what has just been said indicates one aspect of it in relation to the land. We must allow for alternative possibilities co-existing.

In some respects the answer provided by Ezra 1–6 seems clear: various expressions are used to describe those who are members of the community, but they suggest that the restored people consists in those who have been in exile (*golah*). The same is true for the remaining material in the books of Ezra and Nehemiah which cover the narrative of Ezra himself (the language is not used in the Nehemiah narratives). The same passages also, but less commonly, speak of those who have come from the captivity (*shebi*), the term which is also used in the Nehemiah material, though only in fact in the opening verses of Nehemiah 1. More specifically, the term exile (*golah*) is used of the whole community. At the celebration of the dedication of the temple (6.21), it consists of 'those who have returned from the exile' together with those who have separated themselves from the abominations of the nations of the land, and very similar terminology is used in Neh. 10.29 (28). In the time of Ezra, reference is made to the sin (*ma^{c}al*) of the exiles (*golah*) (9.4), which clearly refers to the whole group with which the narrative is concerned; and this is made even clearer when it is stated that those who fail to appear when mixed marriages are dealt with, are to be separated from the 'assembly (*qahal*) of the exile' (*golah*) (10.6). Thus, if we place these expressions together we may see a concept of a community which is a community of the exile, but it is one from which there is a separation out of those who have failed to conform to its requirements, and there is also a separation in of those who have withdrawn from outside contamination.

Such a concept of the community, if taken literally, would appear to claim that only those who had actually been in exile and who had returned, whether at one period or another, could be considered its members—with the provisos just indicated. But these provisos in fact make it clear that there are conditions imposed on those who claim such a position, and failure to abide by those conditions can result in exclusion; and at the same time, it is clear that it is also possible for those who cannot claim such a position, nevertheless to be included under certain conditions. The concept is not therefore understood in a purely literal sense; it would appear to be partly a matter of reality, partly a matter of ideal. The use of such terminology suggests an attempt at providing a satisfactory definition, and at indicating the relationship between the post-exilic community, as understood in this particular context, and the experiences of the sixth century BCE. It may be seen as one expression of that kind of thought which, as for example in 2 Chronicles 36, depicts the land as emptied of inhabitants; or which, as for example, in Jeremiah 24 and Ezekiel 11, depicts the inhabitants of Jerusalem as bad in contrast to those in Babylonia. Before such statements are treated as generalizations, they need to be considered in relation to the context in which they belong, namely as part of a polemic against the Judaean community under its king Zedekiah upon which both Jeremiah and Ezekiel pronounce virtually inevitable judgment (only Jeremiah indeed appears to allow for the possibility that submission to the Babylonians might provide some measure of relief).

At another point, in the heading to the list which appears both in Ezra 2 and Nehemiah 7, those who belong to the community are described as 'the members of the province (*medinah*, the administrative district) who came up from the captivity of the exile'; and their names are listed after a note of numerous leaders. Since that note includes widely separated figures such as Zerubbabel and Nehemiah—and perhaps also Bigvai who might be the Bagoas of the late fifth century—it is clear that we have an attempt at indicating membership on a broader scale. It is also clear from the mixed character of the list that it is made up of originally separate elements, and that in its two occurrences it performs similar but not identical functions. In Ezra 2, it is designed to define the earliest returned community; in Nehemiah 7 that which existed in the time of Nehemiah, a document to which he made appeal for the authenticating of the contemporary position. It is also of note that it includes the indication that there were some of priestly line who failed to demonstrate their proper descent, and that their position remained at least subject to susequent judgment before they, as priests, could officiate. It does not appear that they were excluded from the community, but only from the exercise of their office. But there is in this an indication of the basis on which membership could be claimed— namely, to be able to trace oneself back to those who came from the captivity of the exile with a notable leader, even if the failure to demonstrate this fully would seem to be of moment only for the cult officers. From what we know of genealogies in the biblical world and elsewhere, we may recognize a degree of both truth and fiction here: genealogies, while they reflect memory of interconnections of families and generations, are also susceptible to adjustment to express in that form the accepted legitimacies of particular periods. There is perhaps a hint here of the process by which those whose ancestors had not in fact been in Babylon could claim a descent which made them part of the community.

Other lines of demarcation or description may be seen. The framework to the Haggai oracles—though not the oracles themselves—call for an address to the leaders and to the 'remnant of the people', possibly influenced by the opening words of the oracle that follows: 'Whoever among you who is a survivor (one who remains)...' (Hag. 2.3), but suggesting an understanding of the community as remnant, a concept which appears to have developed more clearly in this period than at an earlier date in the more technical and theological sense which it acquires. The oracle itself goes on to specify leaders and ordinary people, literally 'people of the land' that is, local inhabitants (Hag. 2.2, 3, 4). Possibly a similar thought may be seen in Zechariah 3 if the high priest Joshua, there restored to honour, vested in clear robes as fit for the official priestly duties, represents not simply himself as high priest thus validated, but also the people, the Jerusalem which God has chosen again, the 'brand plucked from the fire' as a symbol of a preserved and rescued remnant; but the terminology is different and the interpretation debated.

Other claimants to membership of the community, and therefore claimants to share in the rebuilding of the temple, are described as meeting with rebuttal. Ezra 4.1-5, another controversial passage, speaks of adversaries of the true people, who professed longstanding loyalty to the same God and to be true worshippers; but they are refused on the ground that there is a separation between those commissioned to build by the royal authority of Cyrus and all others. The basis of that aspect of the community's membership is to have been commissioned by the king whose authority derived, as these narratives present it, directly from God. We know nothing of who these opponents were; they are set now in conjunction with other opposition themes in Ezra 4, most of which belong to another period. Are they real or symbolic figures? In any case, are they perhaps used to provide a delimiting view to the community as it is regarded by some of its members?

Another aspect of definition is provided by the Ezra story. Two levels of thought may be seen here:

(1) Central to the Ezra tradition is the reading and exposition of the law described in Nehemiah 8; it provides one of the bases for the development of the view that the post-exilic community was law-oriented, which is a partial truth, and for the consequential belief that it was legalistic in its attitude. The latter represents a serious distortion of the proper understanding of the community, and indeed of the development of Jewish thought: obedience to the law, right practice, is always subordinated to the sense of the relationship with God, to the religious motivation in response which places first the recognition of God's self-revelation: Torah is not law, though that is how it may properly come to be understood; it is divine directive which involves divine self-revelation. That a religious system may become legalistic in its attitudes is evident: in the Old Testament it may be seen in prophetic criticism of cult practice as representing an externalizing of religion, a criticism which does not reject cult but raises questions about its observance and understanding. Christian religious tradition is shot through with legalistic misunderstanding. Jewish discussion of obedience to the law may easily become too interested in detail to see the underlying principles, but essentially it is a discussion of how obedience is to be properly achieved, given the problems of any situation in which obedience is required.

The law-orientation of the post-exilic Jewish community is to be seen in a love for the awareness of God's self-revelation; a contemplation of that self-revelation; a consciousness of the need for a proper response. Life under the law is a life of joyous response, as a psalm such as Psalm 19 amply illustrates. The rich piety of prayer and right living which is so clearly shown in Jewish writings and stories (e.g. Tobit) reveals the inner nature of the religious community which is no more undermined by examples of impropriety and legalistic casuistry than Christian religious life is negated by hypocrisy and cant. It is a community, as the story of Nehemiah 8 presents it, which responds in distress and rejoices to the reading and exposition of the law, revealing a deepened religious consciousness.

Such reading of the law is ostensibly linked to the royal commission to Ezra described in Ezra 7, though we may note that, as the material is now arranged, there is not only an interruption between the two created by the foreign marriage section of Ezra 9–10 (and of course, in the present text, the whole Nehemiah narrative of Nehemiah 1–7), but also no indication of any specific relationship between the commission and the reading of the law. We might at the very least have expected some comment such as 'Ezra read the law, in accordance with the royal commission'. This invites consideration of the possibility that a story of religious reform has now been given the wider context of this commission with what we may think to be its political aspects. Quite apart from questions of why a Persian ruler should have commissioned Ezra—what the Persians stood to gain from such an appointment—there is the question of the concept of obedience to or adherence to the law as a mark of membership of the Jewish community.

The royal commission gives authority for the imposition of the law on the Jews within the whole province of 'Beyond the River', the area, that is, of Syria-Palestine, which, as we saw earlier in Ezra 4, can be taken to represent something like the area of the idealized Davidic kingdom. The exact geographical delimitation is not here our concern. Not only the Jews in Jerusalem and Judah are involved in acceptance of the law—such is the picture given by the reading of the law in Nehemiah 8—but also the wider Jewish community scattered over the whole area of the province. Since there are evident religious links between the northern part of the country, the old kingdom of Israel area, and Judah, we may suppose that many of the Jews involved would be living in that area; but there could have been considerable other Jewish groups or communities scattered throughout the area, and these too are seen to belong. There is here a political concept: membership of the Jewish community is here not just localized in Judah, it extends over a much wider area. Should we perhaps detect here an attempt at the solution of a delicate politico-religious matter? If political boundaries and religious affiliation coincide, there is no difficulty. But such coincidence is rare, and drawing political boundaries to take account of religious affiliations invariably produces discrepancies: as attest the problems of dividing Ireland, or the Indian subcontinent, or Palestine or Cyprus. Later Roman attempts at political organization in Palestine may be seen to express various ways of trying to resolve the dilemma, though other factors clearly operate as well. Should we see the Ezra commission as one such attempt? If so, it is one which may be seen to take account of religious susceptibility by allowing all who so regard themselves to be treated as Jews, accepting the law as their basis of life, but continuing to live whether in Judah and Jerusalem or in any of the areas within 'Beyond the River' where they now are. No movement of population is implied; royal authority for the policy can be assumed to include some measure of royal protection for those so treated. Nothing in the accounts or in the commission gives us any clue as to how the day to day practicalities of the policy would be handled.

It is, I think, not easy to see how far such a policy is to be regarded as practicable: problems inevitably arise between members of different religious groups living side by side in the one place, as the Jewish community in Elephantine in the fifth century witnesses: harmonious interrelationship and bitter hostility can both be seen operating. No amount of royal recognition and protection will obviate that; and we have no information as to how far comparable policies of recognition and protection are extended to other minority groups. Nor can we be entirely sure how far we are dealing with a sober historical presentation and how far with an idealized picture, in which the claim to Jewish rights within the whole province in reality represents a claim to a territorial possession, pointing to a hope of a return to idealized Davidic independence. Either way we discover something about the community considering its position and defining itself.

(2) The second aspect of the Ezra material points to another kind of sensitivity to the community's nature: it is the indication in Ezra of those 'who are in awe at the words of the God of Israel concerning the faithlessness of the community (*golah*)' (9.4); action is urged 'according to the counsel of God (the Lord—or is it "the counsel of my lord", i.e. Ezra?) and of those who are in awe at the commandment of our God' (10.3). By

itself this could mean no more than that there were those whose reverence for God was such that they responded to the appeal of Ezra, and to that extent formed a supporting group. But since the theme of 'those who fear God' is to be found elsewhere—in two phrases in Isa. 66.2 and 5, where the same Hebrew word is used as in the Ezra passages; and in Mal. 3.16 and 4.2 (MT 3.2), with a different word—the possibility can be considered whether there is here a pointer to a group, associated with Ezra in the one group of narratives, and in the prophetic material set apart with some degree of opposition to others, suggesting at least the beginnings of the growth of a partially separatist movement. This kind of group in a more unfavourable situation, could find itself unable to endure the pressures and would move out, as the Qumran community appears to have done, and as indeed we may think it possible that the so-called Samaritans—the 'keepers', *Shomerim*, the loyal ones—were to do. It must be doubtful whether there is evidence of a religious party; but there is certainly the basis upon which a group which saw itself as somewhat isolated by stricter rules and stricter obedience might begin to become a party. There is a question here whether some members of the community may begin to think of themselves as a group within the community, and so in some degree at least as themselves constituting the true community over against other claimants. There would be no reason to suppose the existence of only one such group of those who made particular insistence on loyalty: puritanical groups may easily proliferate if they become intolerant of those against whom they protest. Further indications of such pressures may be found in some of the obscure oracles of Deutero-Zechariah, where a contrast is expressed between faithful and disloyal, as perhaps in Zechariah 11, and 13.7-9.

The evidence adduced does not, as can be seen, point to precise pictures of the community; it suggests rather a variety of lines of thought, several ways, not always entirely distinct, of defining the community in this period. If we think more broadly, we may see such a group of Jews as those at Elephantine, conscious of coherence and aware of a relationship to Jerusalem but in which we may detect religious views and practices which are to say the least somewhat equivocal. We may see in stories told in this period and later—though the presence of the stories in books which reached their final form at a later date does not exclude the possibility that the stories themselves have a previous history—in which loyalty is variously expressed, whether in Judah (so in Judith), or in the more distant diaspora of Babylonia and beyond (in Tobit and Esther), as also in Daniel, where the stories are set in Babylonia even though we may see their real context as Judah. The problems of loyalty which are a repeated concern in the Hellenistic period may have been greater than under previous rule; they are unlikely to have been entirely unfamiliar.

c. *Looking Forwards*
It is to be expected that a community will also express what it believes about itself by the ideals which it projects. This is a point at which two of the major Old Testament works are relevant: the Priestly Work, of which the date of final composition remains debatable but still fits more probably, in my view, into the Persian period than earlier, a work in which the ideals of present and future are presented in the guise of a description of the past; the Chronicler, and again leaving aside the question of how much belongs to one work, in which there is an account of the past, the Davidic–Solomonic period, which expresses both the authority for the current religious order and the hope for its real and full re-establishment, and in which there is also a degree of dissatisfaction with the present which suggests a forward look. I think we may wonder also whether the idealized concept of the new temple and land which we find in Ezekiel 40–48—normally regarded as belonging to the period of the exile, before the rebuilding of the temple—may not in reality, like other utopian presentations, represent both a critique of the actualities of the post-exilic temple and the religious and social order of the restored community, and a pointer to the ways in which, in an ideal situation, these would be rectified, and a presentation of that ideal in terms which, if not precisely realizable, nevertheless provide a measure against which practicalities can be judged.

Wider expressions of hope for the future are to be found in many of the prophetic texts. The projection of hope into a future may be seen to present a comment on the present situation. Such texts, which are to be found throughout the prophetic writings, though their precise dating is invariably a matter of debate, are likely in some measure to reflect the Persian period. The fact of their existence shows a confidence in the reality of God in the contemporary situation as well as in the coming of a future which will serve to clarify that situation. Such a projection into the future is not to be depicted solely in terms of disappointment in the present; it may rather be seen as a way of speaking of total hope and restoration, of a resolution of the theological problems of the present, by a confident statement of who God is and how he acts.

The foregoing picture of the subject people under Persian rule is clearly at many points impressionist. Sometimes it may look something like one of those Claude Monet pictures of the London scene in what once could have been called a typical London fog'—no longer typical since the clean air acts came into force, though river mist remains and one may hope will always remain a feature of that scene. We see the bridges and the Houses of Parliament through the haze; in some respects they may be considered more artistically viable than if reproduced photographically. Perhaps such a picture is what most suits the Persian period, though there are many points at which some greater precision in the evidence and in its interpretation is much to be desired. But the impression of a community needs to hold together different aspects: it is not all of one piece, and the divergencies are not themselves simple. There are differences of view, but that is not in itself an unhealthy symptom. There is evidence of a rich interpretative activity, which draws on the writings and traditions of the past to understand the present and to contemplate the future. If firm conclusions are difficult to draw, there is no lack of possible ways of looking at the period; and while there is difference of opinion there is hope.

Chapter 9

THE INTERPRETATION OF THE EXILE AND RESTORATION[1]

The events of the sixth century BCE produced a manifold reaction among the members of the Jewish community, and from its prophets and thinkers there emerged various writings expressing these reactions: in the prophecies of Jeremiah, Ezekiel, and Deutero-Isaiah, and in the historico-theological works of the Deuteronomic and Priestly schools.[2] We may also recognize the way in which, from these various reactions, centring on the idea of the acceptance of the reality of divine judgment and looking towards the hope that a new people of God might be truly responsive to his renewed and continuing grace, lines of interpretation stretch out into the following period. The handling of the sixth century BCE is not solely a problem of historical reconstruction; it is also a matter of seeing how a historic experience could become a symbol of a certain understanding of the life of a people.

1. *Exile*

In an important passage which occurs twice in the book of Jeremiah, the substitution of a new *confessio fidei* is indicated:

1. Reprinted from the author's article in *Canadian Journal of Theology* 14 (1968): 3-12 (= the last chapter of *Exile and Restoration* [Ackroyd 1968a], cf. the following note from the original article).
2. This article represents part of the conclusion of a forthcoming study of the whole period of the exile and restoration; it has been presented in this form at several universities and theological schools in Canada and the United States. I am grateful for the comments and questions which it has aroused.

So, the days are coming—oracle of Yahweh,
when it shall no longer be said:
> As Yahweh lives who brought up the people of
> Israel from the land of Egypt,

but
> As Yahweh lives who brought up the people of
> Israel from the north-land and from all the
> lands into which he had driven them; and I will bring
> them back upon the land which I gave to their
> forefathers (Jer. 16.14-15 and, with some variants, 23.7-9).

A 'new Exodus' is to be the central element in the faith, in the place of the 'old Exodus'; such is indeed very much the emphasis of Deutero-Isaiah. But when we look at later passages in which the *confessio fidei* is again expressed (in Neh. 9 or Jdt. 5) we find that, though some reference is certainly made to the later events, there is no substitution of a new act of deliverance for the original one. A very modest reference is made to the exile and to the change of fortunes which followed it:

> So you gave them into the power of the foreign peoples, but in your great mercy you did not make an end of them nor forsake them, for you are a God merciful and gracious (Neh. 9.30-31).

> But when they had departed from the way which he appointed for them, they were utterly defeated in many battles and were led away captive to a foreign country...But now they have returned to their God, and have come back from the places (lit. 'dispersion') to which they were scattered, and have occupied Jerusalem, where their sanctuary is, and have settled in the hill country, because it was uninhabited (Jdt. 5.18-19).

In other words, the assessment is not made in terms of the Exodus, of a new act of deliverance, but rather in terms of the continuing mercy and grace of God which operates in spite of the fact that justice demanded the destruction of people and land. Such an emphasis is particularly characteristic of the Chronicler, who, while alluding to the Exodus theme in sermons and prayers, passes over the event itself altogether. He thus offers what is essentially a non-historical interpretation of his people's past and present experience.

There is a recognition here that the exile is not in fact comparable with the period of the Exodus. At no point in the Exodus narratives is it suggested that the people in Egypt were brought into subjection by reason of their own sinfulness. The *vaticinium ex eventu* of Gen. 15.13-14 offers simply a 'factual' statement of the experience of slavery, and whereas a link could have been made between the envy and sin of Joseph's brothers and the subsequent events seen as punishment, instead the link is made between men's evil intentions and God's overruling goodness (Gen. 50.50). But the exile could not be so treated. It is true that estimates of it varied, but in general the stress lies on the punishment, acknowledged to be just, of the people's failure. So restoration, as viewed by those who experienced it and by those who later considered it, is not simply a great act of deliverance viewed against the background of the evil of the nations (though themes connected with this play their part in the pictorial representation of the restoration); it is an act of mercy, a restoration brought about solely by the willingness of God to have his people again in their own land. It is 'for his name's sake'.

Alongside this kind of development of thought, we may see that of the Chronicler, who is deeply conscious of the providential care of God, but who also attempts a more precise description of the exile so as to bring out its inner meaning. The narrative of the final disaster to Jerusalem is punctuated by statements of the reasons for it:

> Yahweh the God of their fathers sent to them by the agency of his messengers, and kept on sending, because he had pity on his people and his dwelling-place. But they simply kept on mocking the messengers of God and despising his words and scoffing at his prophets until the anger of Yahweh came up against his people till there could be no healing (2 Chron. 36.15-16).

When the disaster takes place, this comment is made:

> He exiled to Babylon the remnant which survived violent death, and they became slaves to him and his descendants until the rule of the kingdom of Persia. This was to fulfil the word of Yahweh by the mouth of Jeremiah: Until the land has *paid off* its sabbaths. All the days of desolation it kept sabbath, to complete seventy years (36.20-21).

The allusion to Jeremiah, which in fact covers only the one phrase 'seventy years' (Jer. 25.11; 29.10), is accompanied by an allusion to the final peroration of the 'Holiness Code' in Leviticus 26:

> If then their uncircumcised heart is humbled and they then *pay off* their iniquity, then I will remember my covenant with Jacob and my covenant with Isaac; even my covenant with Abraham I will remember, and the land I will remember. The land will be abandoned by them and it will *pay off* its sabbaths in its desolation without them and they will *pay off* their iniquity (Lev. 26.41-43, cf. 34).

The interpretation of the exile by the Chronicler thus depends upon a passage in which the exile is regarded as related to the disobedience of the people, but is also given a more precise meaning in relation to the sabbath.

Here we must recognize two possible interpretations of the root *rāṣā*, here in relation to the people's sin; so too the third occurrence. It could also have this meaning in its second occurrence in relation to the sabbaths. In some way, not clearly specified, the period of the exile means a paying off or counting off of sabbaths (or sabbatical years) which have not been properly observed and are therefore now to be substituted for in an enforced observance. The emphasis is on punishment and atonement; through the exile the sins of the past are dealt with—as also in Isa. 40.2, where the same root is used. But an alternative interpretation may be obtained by treating the root here as meaning 'to enjoy' and more particularly 'to be acceptable (to God)'. In this case we might say—using modern terminology—that the Leviticus passage plays upon two distinct roots. The people are *paying off* their sin, and while they do so the land in its desolated state is *enjoying* its sabbaths and hence is being made acceptable to God. There is a period of enforced fallowness, comparable with the sabbath years of the law (cf. Lev. 25). The fact that the Chronicler quotes only the one phrase from the Leviticus context suggests that this was the interpretation in his mind. The exile is not viewed by him simply in terms of punishment—though this is evident enough in the context—but also in terms of the recuperation needed for the new life of the post-exilic period.

Such a link with the seven-year law (and also with the Jubilee laws of Lev. 25.8ff.) is also presupposed by the later use of the same idea in Daniel 9. Here the interpretation of the seventy-year period, taken literally in some measure by both Zechariah (1.12) and the Chronicler, is linked with the weeks of years which mark the sabbath periods of years, and the whole period from the fall of Jerusalem to the restoration under Judas Maccabaeus becomes a period of sabbaths. It is in effect an exile lasting 490 years. With this interpretation we reach an understanding of the exile and restoration which takes us well beyond the consideration of the sixth century. For here the exile is no longer a historic event to be dated in one period; it is much nearer to being a condition from which only the final age will bring release. Bound to the historical reality of an exile which actually took place in the sixth century, the experience of exile as such has become the symbol of a period, viewed in terms of punishment but also in terms of promise (cf. Dan. 9.24). The understanding of the exile is clearly enlarged beyond the temporal framework of seventy years and the precise period covered by Babylonian captivity in the stricter sense. The desecration of the Temple by Antiochus Epiphanes is here regarded as a continuation of that desecration which belonged to the exilic age. A true limit to the exile is now being set.

It is in this way of thinking that we may see the truth of that type of interpretation of the post-exilic age, found particularly in the writings of C.C. Torrey. Such an interpretation stresses the fact that the exile gradually came to be seen as of paramount importance, as a great divide between the earlier and later stages, but one which it was necessary to traverse if the new age was to be reached. Only those who had gone through the exile, whether actually or spiritually, could be thought of as belonging to the people of God. The rebuilt Temple was dedicated by returned exiles and those who, forsaking the abominations of the land, joined themselves to them (Ezra 6.21). The Chronicler shows too that in the times of apostasy in the past—at the division of the kingdom, or in the reigns of Hezekiah and Josiah—there could be held out the possibility that the faithful who thus separated themselves could rejoin the community (cf. 2 Chron. 11.13ff.; 30; 34.6-7, 33). This is an

appeal for a gathered community, based on the recognition
that the experience of the exile, the experience of judgment,
can be appropriated in either of two ways: (1) by virtue of
having gone through it (proof of this may be furnished by
means of genealogies, real or fictitious), and so the impetus
again and again is shown as coming from returned exiles—
the 'remnant' of 2 Chron. 36.20—or (2) by accepting its significance by the abandonment of what belongs to it, namely
uncleanness, pollution of the land. (Cf. the interpretation of
Josh. 24 as representing an appropriation of the Exodus events
as religious history by those who had not actually experienced
them.) In this the Chronicler is properly elaborating that
aspect of prophetic teaching which stressed the absolute
necessity of exile (cf. Jeremiah and Ezekiel), the principle that
God's dealings with his people in the future must depend upon
a repudiation and destruction, of which the exile provides the
classic instance.

Later echoes of this kind of teaching are to be found in the
reinterpretation of the exilic period and the restoration, in
Daniel and other apocalyptic works. We may also wonder to
what extent it is an element in New Testament thinking as
well, for while it is clear that Exodus terminology is often
dominant (e.g. in the concept of redemption), the theme of
captivity to sin suggests other overtones too. Certainly Babylon
becomes the symbol for the hostile world which is eventually to
be overthrown by God in the final age (cf. Rev. 16.12ff., 19;
18.2ff.), and Babylonian captivity becomes the symbol for the
bondage from which release is to be found (cf. Rev. 18.4ff., and
also the use of the term 'Babylonish Captivity' in the mediaeval period). These are indications of the way in which the
terminology of exile and restoration has entered into later
thinking.

2. Restoration

The thought of the exilic age concerning restoration and its
nature also had its repercussions in the period that followed,
and these may be conveniently considered under the three
themes of the Temple, the New Age, and the People's
Response.

(i) *The Temple*. It is sometimes suggested or implied that, at the fall of Jerusalem, the point had been reached when, under the influence of the personal and spiritualized religious conceptions of Jeremiah, it would be possible to see the end of the institutional religion of the pre-exilic period (cf. recently Gottwald 1964: 267). Not infrequently such statements are followed by a tracing of the evolution of new institutions during the exilic period: sabbath, synagogue, circumcision, as substitutes for the older practices. More important, the point is then made that, after this high degree of spiritualization (typified further in Deutero-Isaiah), there is a sad decline into the bricks-and-mortar Temple mentality of post-exilic Judaism. Quite apart from the inadequacy of such an evaluation of Jeremiah, which misses the deeper significance of his strictures upon contemporary religious practice, it is clear that in fact the post-exilic period represents a natural development from the thought of the exilic age in the direction of a right understanding of the nature of the presence of God, of which the Temple is the most potent symbol (cf. Clements 1965, esp. 135-40). It is not that the Temple as such is a guarantee, any more than Jeremiah would permit it to be one, but that it is the outward sign of that manifestation of divine presence and power which is essential for any kind of reorganization or establishment of the common life. Stress upon the centrality of God in exilic and early post-exilic prophecy and other writings makes it clear that there is here no necessarily narrow or pedestrian thinking, but a legitimate attempt, in the terms most readily available, to solve that most persistent dilemma of religious experience, the gulf between God and the human person. The Temple is the symbol of that presence which God chooses to give. It is as improper to concentrate our whole attention upon the recurrent human tendency—to see the symbol as the reality—as it is to judge the contemporaries of the pre-exilic prophets solely in terms of the condemnations uttered by the latter, or the Pharisees in the time of Jesus solely in terms of his most virulent criticisms. The essential basis of thought about the Temple is that of the mediation of divine life and power at the will of the deity himself. From this various lines develop.

We may see, in the post-exilic period, the development of that deepened love of the Temple, that adherence to Zion, which is expressed so richly in the Psalter (itself coming to be the vehicle not only of public worship but also of intense private devotion). The temple remains a major focus of religious life even for those (either outside Palestine or in its remoter areas) who could hope to visit the Temple itself only very rarely, if at all. The picture which the Chronicler provides of joyous worship, the evident ardour and love for the Temple, even if often tinged with superstition, which are reflected in the opposition to both Jesus and Stephen—these are indications of how deeply rooted this affection became. If it came to be wrongly superstitious, we must nevertheless attest to the fact that the final destruction of the Temple in 70 CE did not result in that disastrous end to Judaism which must have occurred had there been nothing but superstitious veneration. On the contrary, Judaism survived that disaster without losing the essential value of the Temple as focus.

Further, we may see how the thought of the exilic age, and after, concerning the extension of the principle of the divine dwelling of the Temple to the idea of a holy city, a holy land, was an indication both of the limitations of a too narrowly based conception, and also of the richness of the idea. The centrality of Zion, not only for the life of Judaism but also for the life of the world, made it logical to think in terms of a holy land. See for example the last chapter of the book of Zechariah, where the multitude of worshippers necessitates the sanctifying of all the vessels in Jerusalem and Judah to serve the needs of those who come to the holy city (Zech. 14.20-21). This provision is made for the survivors of the nations, who, having gone against Jerusalem, now come to worship annually at the feast of booths. The place which is occupied in the conceptions of the final age by pictures of a new and heavenly Jerusalem is another aspect of this development.

In the New Testament, these lines of thought are elaborated in the understanding of Jesus himself as the Temple, as that place in which God chooses to manifest himself and in which, therefore, his power and presence are made known and operative. Thus the Christian community did not abandon Temple ideology, but rather concentrated it in the understanding of a person in whom the glory of God was revealed, and in whom God could be said to 'tabernacle among men', as he had chosen to reveal himself in the shrine. The destruction of the Temple is linked with the death of Jesus; its restoration is effected in his resurrection. Neither Gerizim nor Jerusalem offers finality, but worship will be in him (Jn 4.21; cf. also Rev. 21.22). From this view of Jesus there develops the understanding of the Christian community as itself the Temple of which Christ is the chief corner-stone (1 Cor. 3.16-17). By further extension, this idea applies to each member of that community, whose body is itself a Temple of God (1 Cor. 6.19).

(ii) *The New Age.* The expectation that a new age was about to dawn, so amply expressed in the prophetic writings of the exilic and restoration periods, and linked both with political happenings and still more with the revealed willingness of God to come again to his people, is an aspect of thought which finds large-scale development in the subsequent centuries. Thought on this subject is so rich that any summary does less than justice to the hopes which were expressed not only in new works, particularly in the later years of the post-exilic period, in apocalyptic writings both canonical and extra-canonical, but also in the reinterpretation of older works (notably of particular passages of psalmody and prophecy). Much of this material is very familiar because of its recognized importance for the understanding of the New Testament, and also because of the expression of this kind of thinking in the Qumran documents. I propose to comment only very briefly on three points.

The first is the recognition that the new age is of cosmic significance, and involves not simply the final establishment of God's promises to Israel, but also a complete renewal of the life of the world. This prospect is expressed in terms of a reversal of the present untoward condition of nature (cf. Isa. 55.12-13; 65.25; 11.6-9; and also e.g. Rom. 8.19-22). This statement of reversal is to be seen against the background of thought disclosed in the older material in the opening chapters of Genesis (Gen. 2–3), which is now, in the final form of the Priestly Work, given a new context and a new significance in relation to the later creation material of Genesis 1, with its reiterated emphasis on the goodness of God's creation. The same view of the world is further expressed in the account of the repeated failures and promises which follow on the initial failure of humanity, with its consequences in the life of the natural world (cf. e.g. Gen. 6.1-4, 5-7; 11.1-9). In the ultimate reordering, the centrality of Israel is a centrality of promise, and expresses to the nations the purpose of God towards all people. The narrowness of particularism and the breadth of universalism are held together in the understanding that what God does for his people of his own choosing is significant for, and is to be recognized as significant by, all the nations.

The second point concerns the place of the Davidic line in relation to this new age. This is expressed in various prophetic writings of the period (Ezekiel, Deutero-Isaiah, Haggai, Zechariah) as well as in elaborations of earlier prophetic material, where older royal oracles have probably been given a wider connotation. The emphasis in this material varies. The Davidic hope is hardly present as a real hope for the future in the Deuteronomic history, though the adumbration of a future Davidic line is there. In the Priestly Work it has found no place, except in so far as the royal house is replaced by the priesthood. But subsequently, in the Chronicler, a compromise line of development is found, in which the concentration of attention on what David achieved means that, while the Davidic monarchy no longer exists, and virtually no hope remains for its restoration, what Davidic monarchy essentially stood for is achieved in the life of the purified post-exilic community, in its Temple and worship. The Davidic hope has there been refined, and again we may see how the Chronicler directs attention to theological, rather than to historical, realities.

Alongside this there are other lines of thought, culminating in the more purely political Davidic-type hopes of later nationalistic groups (Mowinckel 1965: 155ff.). On the one hand, some modifications in this way of thinking would appear to be linked to the actual political conditions; thus the modification of Ezekiel's projected organization can be traced in the dual leadership envisaged in Haggai and Zechariah, and subsequently further modification resulted from the the increasingly prominent position of the high priest (Bevan 1912: 5-6), representing a link back to the Priestly Work; on the other hand, the idealistic conceptions of the exilic age, themselves linked with still older ideals, are at work to give rise to other, less obviously politically connected, thought. The linkage between the new age and a central figure who both embodies divine rule and is himself the guarantee of its reality is an idea of considerable importance for later Messianic thought.

The third point concerns the deferment and actuality of a new age. It is evident from what we know of the history of the post-exilic period that the new age, anticipated by both the exilic and restoration thinkers, did not materialize. To that extent, therefore, there is always an element of deferment in the vision of the new age. (The same point may be noted in the thinking of New Testament times concerning the parousia.) But to picture the development of eschatological thought solely in terms of deferment would be erroneous. The projection into the future of the hopes of a new age is not simply a matter of dissatisfaction with the present, of disillusionment resulting from the deferment of hope. It is a recognition rather of the future fullness of what is already tasted as reality. The prophets of the restoration period were both idealists and realists; as such they were able to see in the realities of a not very encouraging situation the earnest of what they believed to be present, namely, a new age with the glory of God at the very centre of the community's life. To us the age of the Chronicler, in the aftermath of Ezra's reform and with the Samaritan schism an ugly reality and a serious challenge, may well seem somewhat of a disappointment, in view of the high hopes which were evident in the work of Ezra. But to the Chronicler, whose sense of the realities is equally acute, this was the age of the fulfilment of promise. The reality of the embodiment of the rule of God in history which the New Testament proclaims is not a denial of that earlier sense of its reality, but a deepening and enlarging of its meaning. Nor does the fact that the new age has still not fully come alter the reality of Christian confidence that it is possible to live here and now in the context of that new age.

(iii) *The People's Response.* The problem for the exilic thinkers, in the face of failure, was to find a means by which the

future people should really embody the divine will. Having laid
their stress upon the priority of divine action, and the reality of
the new age in which the new life would be lived, they were
much concerned with this question of mechanism. The development of thought connected with this problem is again very
broad; it may be briefly analysed along three main lines. In the
first place, there is the response of piety, which we have
already linked with the idea of the Temple. The maintenance
of worship, the development of the synagogue, the marked
emphasis on prayer which becomes increasingly clear in the
later post-exilic years, all indicated a deep concern with the
inner life of both individual and community to ensure the
condition in which the blessings of God can be appropriately
received. In the second place, the evolution of law, already a
dominant element in earlier thinking, but coming to occupy
an increasingly important place in the later period, and especially in post-biblical Jewish writings, is marked both by a concern with the purity of the people's life—shown especially in
the mass of ritual law—and also by the concern to cover every
aspect of life—shown in the inevitable development of casuistry. While such casuistry has been criticized, it was at heart
a right casuistry, for though, like all legal developments in
religion, it readily came to be thought of in terms which denied
the divine prerogative and suggested the possibility of coming
to terms with God, it nevertheless expressed the recognition
that no part of life is outside the concern of God, and that the
completely fit community is one in which all life is brought
under his control. The New Testament criticisms of the wrong
understanding of law must never conceal the fact that the
Christian movement found itself deeply indebted to that sense
of divine control which belonged to the Jewish community in
which the early church came into being, and from which it
only gradually separated itself, nor the fact that the church
found it immediately essential, with a renewed understanding
of the place which law occupies in the religious life, to evolve its
own ethical teaching on the basis of the older law and of the
fundamental principles which its founder had stressed. In the
third place, the increasing importance of wisdom material in
the post-exilic period is itself a witness to this same concern
with the fitness of the community. If we are right in under-

standing wisdom as part of that mechanism by which life is to be rightly ordered, so that the counsel of the wise can stand alongside the *tōrā* of the priest and the word of the prophet (Jer. 18.18; cf. Ezek. 7.26), then it is clear that the sometimes apparently pedestrian concerns of the wisdom teachers are in fact directed towards that right ordering of life which is part of the necessary response of the community and all its members. The recognition of this role of wisdom may perhaps be reflected in the greatly increased influence of wisdom thought in both Old Testament and apocryphal works. (On this last point, cf. the recent study of H.H. Guthrie, *Wisdom and Canon* [1966], esp. 10-28.)

From all that has been said, it follows that both the idea of the exile, as symbol of divine judgment accepted and experienced, and the idea of restoration, expressed in concern for the right response to what God has done, may be seen to be influential in determining some of the patterns in that rich texture of thought which we may trace in the post-exilic period—that often obscure, but immeasurably important, part of Old Testament history, without which neither the developments of the intertestamental period nor the appearance and impact of Christianity can be understood.

Chapter 10

HISTORY AND THEOLOGY IN THE WRITINGS
OF THE CHRONICLER[1]

It would seem as if the Greek title of the two books of Chronicles, *Ta Paraleipomena* ('The things omitted') has left a certain legacy of doubt about the value of the work of the Chronicler. In liturgical use[2] as well as in reconstructions of the history, particularly those of a more conservative kind, the tendency has often been for passages from 1 and 2 Chronicles to be inserted or utilized at what appear to be appropriate places when Samuel and Kings are being read or the history of that period is being surveyed, by way of supplementing the material covered in those books. As a result, the Chronicler is relatively rarely read for himself, and his particular kind of presentation is not seen for what it is. Only when we go on into the post-exilic period and consider the content of the books of Ezra and Nehemiah, which form the final parts of the work as we now have it, is there a clearer recognition of the contribution which the Chronicler made, though inevitably to read only the last chapters of a work gives a somewhat curious impression of its meaning. And added to this is the problem that reconstruction of the post-exilic history on the basis of the books of Ezra–Nehemiah is fraught with so many difficulties, and the differences in presentation between 1 and 2 Chronicles and the books of Samuel and Kings suggest such doubts, that even here, bogged down in historical and literary uncertainties, we may feel something of impatience.

---

1. Reprinted from the author's article in *Concordia Theological Monthly* 38 (1967): 501-15.
2. See, for example, the current lectionary of the Church of England.

Now perhaps we must acknowledge that it is partly the Chronicler's own fault. (For the moment I am treating the whole work as one, whether or not some parts of it were added at a later stage or at later stages to an originally smaller compilation.) The work begins in a manner which is not immediately calculated to inspire excitement at either his historical contribution or his theological penetration. 'Adam, Seth, Enosh,' he begins in his opening verse, and with little interruption the series proceeds through nine whole chapters, at least a tenth of the whole work. It was chapters like these which so puzzled the Scottish child whose father religiously read the Bible aloud day by day, chapter by chapter from cover to cover; for the child could not but wonder at so large a family as that of the 'Begats'. And unless we are to emulate the woman who, so it is said, learned the names by heart, because, as she explained, she hoped one day to meet all these people in heaven, we are unlikely to be much moved by the monotonous and repetitious style. Yet this part of the work, dull though it may be and certainly not directly edifying, has its place in our proper appreciation of the whole.

The negative attitude persists.[1] In an otherwise most illuminating recent treatment of the development in the understanding of Old Testament material in the post-exilic period entitled *Wisdom and Canon*, H.H. Guthrie describes as 'unrealistically ecclesiastical' the Chronicler's 'attempt at claiming for Nehemiah's and Ezra's accomplishments the status of a present once again coterminous with God's activity' (Guthrie 1966: 9). To this study I shall make further reference, as I believe it provides an important insight into post-exilic thought, an insight which in fact helps us to see the Chronicler's place more clearly when once his work is brought into focus. We have moved beyond the negative approach of C.C. Torrey, though not always appreciating the understanding and insight that accompanied his erroneous estimate of the exilic age. But much of the discussion is still in

---

1. G. von Rad (von Rad 1962: I.348) takes a negative view, still in this closely dependent on Wellhausen. At the end of the section (p. 354) he makes a curiously thin concession to the merits of the Chronicler's concern with the praise of God.

danger of turning on the wrong issues, though there have been notable moves towards a more adequate appraisal of the Chronicler as a theologian. This can be seen already in Martin Noth (Noth 1957: 110-80) and Wilhelm Rudolph (Rudolph 1955b; as also in Rudolph 1954: 401-409), as well as more recently in the studies in the *Journal of Biblical Literature* by W.F. Stinespring (Stinespring 1961) and Robert North (North 1963). The purpose of the present study is to attempt to carry further the investigation of the Chronicler's contribution as a theologian of high significance for our understanding of the development of the thought of the post-exilic age.

1.

It may be convenient if, before we go on to look at the theological issues, we attempt to resolve, though without fully solving, the literary problems which confront us in this now very substantial work. It is useless to deny that there is still great uncertainty and disagreement about the processes by which the work came into being; and to refer to 'The Chronicler' as if he were a single, almost identifiable, author, begs many questions that have to be answered.

In many ways the use of the term 'school of the Chronicler' would be more appropriate, and although it is probably right to believe that within any such school there is likely to have been one great influential personality—perhaps more than one— yet the complexities in the formation of such a work as this may well suggest that we are dealing with the gradual shaping, over a relatively long period, of the traditions out of which the work is formed. To say this specifically at every point is to become unnecessarily pedantic; references to the Chronicler in what follows, therefore, presuppose an awareness that we are more likely to be dealing with a particular type of theological tradition to which various people have contributed over a period of time, but with a community of thought linking them together. If there are inconsistencies within the work—and such may well be observed in all Old Testament traditions— this may be explained by such a process of composition, though I believe in fact that such inconsistencies are less evident in this work than in other Old Testament works comparable with it, except in so far as the use of sources not totally re-written for their present context sometimes leaves unresolved roughnesses.

It is now clear (cf. Cross 1961: 188-91; Cross 1964: 292-97; Lemke 1965) that the text of Samuel/Kings underlying the Chronicler's work is close in many respects to that of the LXX/Qumran—an old Palestinian text—than to that of the Masoretic tradition.[1] We may legitimately claim that the first stage towards the work of the Chronicler as we have it rests in the existence of this particular type of text of Samuel/Kings (and of other material utilized by the compilers alongside the text eventually destined to become the Masoretic text) and that the existence of such alternatives, natural enough when each copy of a work may be regarded, in at least a limited sense, as a new edition, reveals already a measure of differen-tiation in the appraisal of the past. At whatever point we place the textual deviation, it may still shed light on the richness and diversity of the theological handling of the traditions.

The present text of the Chronicler's work represents a development from this. Recently D.N. Freedman (Freedman 1961) has revived the view, earlier to be found in a similar form, for example, in A.C. Welch (Welch 1939), that the first 'edition' belongs to about 515 BCE and was designed to cover only that aspect of the survey which represents an explana-tion of the true nature of Davidic monarchy. That the Chron-icler has something to say about the Davidic monarchy is evi-dent, but I shall comment on this point later. I am not per-suaded that it is demonstrable that such an earlier form of the material as Freedman proposes may properly be termed the 'work of the Chronicler'; but it is conceivable that a first stage toward the evolution of the material as we now have it was a selection from the previously existing Deuteronomic History, a selection which omitted all the earlier stages and concentrated simply on the period from David to Jehoiachin, or perhaps, by way of indicating the revival of Davidic hope, from David to

1. Cf. also Gerleman 1948: 9-12, for similar evidence concerning 1 Chron. 1–9, shown to be closer to the Samaritan than to the Maso-retic tradition. F.M. Cross (Cross 1964: 297) regards this too as evi-dence of a Palestinian text, and indeed as providing the oldest witness to such a text's existence.

Zerubbabel. We might compare with this the suggestion that 1 Esdras is a selection from the Chronicler's work, picking out from that work simply the three great moments of religious reform and revival—Josiah, Jeshua, and Ezra.[1] What we understand by the Chronicler's particular emphasis in regard to the history may have been due to his work being built upon what was only a partial survey—a survey in which already some at least of the notable omissions had been made which so characterize the whole over against its predecessors.[2] But such a stage is hypothetical only—a perhaps quite useful working hypothesis, but no more. The acceptance of such a selection from the material and its use in the larger work which we now have implies at least some measure of continuity with this kind of thinking.

It is, I think, reasonable to view the central moment of the Chronicler's activity as coming after that of Ezra, so that the whole of the previous history is summed up in the most recent and, to the Chronicler's theology, in many ways most significant moment. Freedman believes that this represents a substantial shift in emphasis, but this too, as I shall hope to show, seems not as clear as he supposes. It would seem proper to associate with this period too the main genealogical introduction, and the whole survey to Ezra, while we may allow the probability that there has been some subsequent expansion at certain points in the genealogies and some in the David section of 1 Chronicles. But these additions are so much in the spirit of the work that there seems to be no need to make sharp distinctions, as, for example, is done by Galling (Galling 1954), between a first and second Chronicler, but rather to regard these as linked stages in the development of the present more elaborate text.[3]

---

1. Cf. Rudolph 1955b: xiv-xv. S. Mowinckel (1964a: 12-18) argues against this view. But its separate preservation still needs to be explained.

2. Cf. the suggestion of J. Lewy, cited by R. North: 'a history not of the *people* Israel but of the *city* Jerusalem' (North 1969: 368n.).

3. There are reasons for thinking that some of the genealogical material may have been modified in the second century BCE (cf. Ackroyd 1953: 126-27).

Galling would appear to be right in regarding the Nehemiah material as a later insertion (Galling 1954: 9-10; cf. also Mowinckel 1964b), worked into its present position as a result of a natural misunderstanding of the chronology that allowed Nehemiah and Ezra to overlap because both were erroneously associated with the same Persian ruler. (Such a chronological error can be paralleled in the rather confused accounts of the Persian period in Josephus's *Antiquities*,[1] and we may compare also the identifying of Micah the prophet and Micaiah [1 Kgs 22.28] and the possible use in 1 Kgs 13 of an Amos legend from the period of Jeroboam II in the form of an anonymous prophetic legend set in the reign of Jeroboam I.[2]) On the assumption that the Nehemiah material was later inserted, the problems of the lack of real relationship between Ezra and Nehemiah are resolved. Nehemiah, as is now virtually proved, worked in the reign of Artaxerxes I, and Ezra most probably in the reign of Artaxerxes II, a position recently carefully reargued by J.A. Emerton (Emerton 1966). No textual emendation has then to be undertaken in Ezra 7, for the date of Ezra can stand. The apparent misunderstanding of history by the Chronicler no longer exists, and the literary problems are reduced largely to the recognition that the conflation of the Nehemiah and Ezra material has resulted from the placing of the Nehemiah sections as seemed most appropriate—partly before and partly after the narrative of Ezra's reform, the reading of the Law and its sequels—and a measure of harmonization has then subsequently followed in much the same way as harmonization can be observed in the

1. *Ant.* 11.297-312. The confusion is, as we now know, in part at least the result of there having been three governors named Sanballat. Cf. the evidence of the Samaria papyri, F.M. Cross, *BA* 26 (1963), pp. 109-21. Cf. also on the whole question, H.H. Rowley, *BJRL* 38 (1955–56), 166-98 = *Men of God* (London, 1963), pp. 246-76, and 'The Samaritan Schism in Legend and History' in *Israel's Prophetic Heritage* (ed. B.W. Anderson and W. Harrelson; London, 1962), pp. 208-22.
2. This is, of course, only a hypothesis. Cf. Eissfeldt 1965: 46, 290. The contacts between the opening part of 1 Kgs 13 and the book of Amos are quite striking—attack on the altar (cf. Amos 9.1ff.), earthquake (cf. Amos 1.1; 9.1), confrontation with the prophet (by Jeroboam in 1 Kgs, by Amaziah on Jeroboam's behalf in Amos 7.10ff.). The 1 Kgs legend is of course now intricately bound up with other elements.

smoothing of rough edges in the combined Pentateuchal traditions, both in the Masoretic text and in some measure even
more clearly in the Samaritan. This view is also in some measure confirmed by 1 Esdras, in which the Nehemiah material
is absent, and also by the clear independence of the figure of
Nehemiah in the traditions both used by Jesus ben Sira and in
2 Maccabees.[1]

It is not the intention of this study to enter in detail into the
literary problems, but only to suggest this as a possible series of
stages in the evolution of the material as a background to the
study of the theological viewpoint of the Chronicler. It is a
work with a complex history, and yet it presents a largely
coherent and significant theological interpretation of the
whole period with which it deals.

2.

In his recent commentary on the two books of Chronicles and
on Ezra/Nehemiah,[2] J.M. Myers has presented a full-scale
coverage of the work with a very definitely positive appraisal.
Yet in spite of all its merits in points of detail, Myer's treatment begins with a statement that provides a good example of
the way in which the discussion can easily turn on the wrong
issues. Commenting on earlier tendencies to disregard the
Chronicler he writes: 'When it had to be dealt with, it was done
grudgingly, often with misunderstanding, misgiving, or
downright hostility...Archaeological and historical studies
have now rendered it more respectable and have shown it to
be at times more accurate than some of its parallel sources'
(p. xv). (Reference could be made here to studies that stress
the good historical information available in the Chronicler's
version of the history. Many of these, particularly by Israeli
scholars and by W.F. Albright and others sharing his general
approach,[3] have developed this by tracing the relationships

---

1. Ecclus 49.13; 2 Macc. 2.13.
2. Anchor Bible 12–14 (New York, 1965).
3. References are given to many such studies by Myers both in his
bibliographies and frequently in the notes. Cf. also Albright 1942: 27,
and references in Richardson 1958: 9-12.

between material found only in Chronicles and in ancient monuments and documents.)

Exaggerated claims have probably been made for this historical value of the Chronicler's material, yet we may certainly recognize the probability that the source text of Chronicles in a deviant version of Samuel/Kings was subsequently modified by the inclusion in it of additional information, traditional or annalistic, from various sources, and that some of this is of independent historical value. It must, however, be admitted that there are other narratives which have little or no historical probability, for example the curiously presented story in 2 Chronicles 28 concerning the strife between Israel and Judah during the reign of Ahaz; whatever of historicity may underlie this, namely, the reality of such strife, is now totally overlaid with improbabilities. For the sections covering the post-exilic period, we have no precise means of checking the reliability of the account, and it seems clear that there are many points at which it is difficult to reconcile what we do know with what is here related; but here too there is little doubt that older material was being used and that at least some of the source material has good historical value.

But immediately we are back at the point of using the historical or supposedly historical data in the Chronicler's work to fill gaps, and immediately too we are in danger of making the assumption that the importance of the work lies in its historical information and that by implication the respectability of the Chronicler as a contributor to the Old Testament canon is relative to his historical reliability. The recent trend towards rehabilitation in these terms is in danger of creating a false image of his contribution by allowing considerations of historical accuracy to outweigh considerations of theological acumen. However good his sources, it is the way he uses them which ultimately counts. It is not a fair judgment of his work to single out what is historically verifiable without also considering very carefully how he shapes this material into a coherent work. Thus his treatment of the restoration period in Ezra 1–6 shows a fair disregard of chronology—as the work now stands—and a considerable element of confusion in his virtual conflation of Sheshbazzar and Zerubbabel material. In handling Ezra, it seems most probably—judging both by the dates provided and by the nature of Ezra's work as we may discover it—that he has ordered it for theological reasons, so that the ending of foreign marriages should precede rather than follow the reading and acceptance of the Law (cf. Eissfeldt 1965: 547ff.). His significance as a theologian is not dependent on the historical reliability of his sources; even if it were demonstrated that at every point his account was historically speaking inferior—as used often to be affirmed—we should still have to ask what kind of theological judgment he makes and how far we may assess this judgment as valid.

The danger, here as elsewhere in handling Old Testament material, is of confusing historical verification with theological validation; and then, particularly among scholars with a more conservative inclination who tend to welcome points of confirmation of the Old Testament record from archaeological evidence or Near Eastern comparative material, of failing to realize that this is not so very far from the older but still not altogether defunct view that to assail the accuracy of the biblical record at any single point is to bring down the whole edifice of faith like a house of cards. Biblical faith is rooted in historic experience. Certainly. But its relationship to verifiable historical events is more subtle than to be supported by mere historicity or undermined by recognition of historical inaccuracy.[1]

3.

It is clear that when we approach the question of the Chronicler's theology, we cannot satisfactorily do so by means of the detail of his work. This may be seen from the recent studies of the textual problems, which reveal that we cannot now state with confidence that at any given point the Chronicler has rewritten his source from a particular theological viewpoint, for it is conceivable, and may indeed be very probable, that many of the small points of difference between Samuel/Kings etc. on the one hand and Chronicles on the other are due to a stage in textual history that antedates the Chronicler. Many of these differences may in fact merely reflect stylistic changes

1. Cf. Childs (1967) for a recent contribution to this problem.

or modifications in linguistic usage and have no further significance at all. The argument should not, however, be overstated;[1] and in particular it must be said that if we can get an adequate overall picture of the Chronicler's theology, it may well be that some of the small points may be reasonably explicable on this basis, in default of evidence to the contrary. We have also here, however, to beware of overtidiness in the estimating of theological viewpoint. It is well known that total self-consistency is rarely achieved by any writer. (One of the fascinations of reading detective stories is watching to see whether you can catch the author out!) In so far as the Chronicler's work represents a school rather than an individual, differences may be due to stages in its development. The preservation within the work of older source material, even if rewritten, may result in inconsistency, an inconsistency which is resolved in part by the new context providing a new motivation and thus contributing to the neutralizing of the older matter. The use of liturgical and other such material may give at times the impression of a difference of outlook that is not in fact present. (The significance of this last point will become clear in a moment.[2])

1. When Lemke rightly criticizes those who sought theological motivation in every change (e.g. Brunet 1953, 1954), it must at the same time be said that his final comment to the effect that we must concentrate on 'nonsynoptic parts of his history in which he seems to be composing independently of any canonical sources' (1954: 363 n. 4) seems somewhat naive. For one thing it is by no means clear when the Chronicler is independent of his sources; he certainly is not entirely so in Ezra/Nehemiah, and many recent studies suggest that apparently original sections may be based on earlier material. For another, while argument from small detail will not do, argument from larger differences is less subject to uncertainty. And as has already been indicated, even if the change had already been made in an earlier form of the material, it is still part of what we now have to interpret. Thus the Chronicler may not be responsible for identifying the threshing floor with the temple site, and this in turn with Mount Moriah (1 Chron. 22.1; 2 Chron. 3.1); in fact, it is improbable that he invented these two identifications, the first possible but totally unproven, the second highly improbable. But his utilization of them is not without significance in his handling of the David traditions.

2. Cf. below the comments on D.N. Freedman.

4.

The Chronicler was not the first to survey the history of his people, nor was he to be the last. Something may be learned about him by the extent and nature of his survey in comparison with others. At a much earlier period, such theological expositions of the past are to be found in the work of the Yahwist, itself quite possibly a reworking of earlier forms still; and the same is true of the Elohistic presentation, which is in large measure a reworking of the same and similar themes. Their coverage is different. J begins at Creation and extends possibly to David; E from Abraham and continuing perhaps to the divided monarchy. The finishing point is so difficult to establish with certainty that inevitably the assessment of these works remains in some measure in doubt; and it is also at many points not altogether clear how far they can be separated from each other and from the larger works in which they are now embedded.

More complete and therefore more satisfactory for our understanding of their theological viewpoint are the two great surveys of the Deuteronomic History and the Priestly Work, both incorporating much earlier material (including parts of J and E), but now to be understood as final presentations, offering a total interpretation of the past, covering different areas, and concerned in some measure with different problems. The Deuteronomic History belongs in its final form to the mid-sixth century, surveying from the Exodus to the contemporary situation; it is not improbable that the Priestly Work comes from very much the same period, still anticipating and therefore uncertain about the outcome of the problematic exilic period. The latter's presentation runs from Creation to the threshold of the conquest, so far as can be judged from its present form, though some dislocation of its conclusion may be postulated. This much less historical treatment points forward to an important feature of the Chronicler's work.

The Chronicler offers a different and in some respects a more comprehensive survey. Like the Priestly writers, he goes back to the very beginnings, to the first man; like the Deuteronomists, he covers the whole period of the monarchy but extends the narrative further to include other material down nearly to his own time. His survey is, however, in other respects more limited in the abbreviated coverage of the whole period before Saul, in the selection of material for the period of the monarchy and after, in which many substantial gaps are left, in the virtual ignoring of the north, and in the very limited selection of post-exilic events.

After the Chronicler, a further such survey may be found, for example, in Josephus's *Antiquities*, evidently composed with a strongly apologetic motive.

What has already been said about not treating the Chronicler's work merely as a historical source is again important here. If we say, quite correctly, that the Chronicler covers the period from Creation to Ezra, we immediately suggest a comparison with the area of coverage of the earlier surveys *in historical terms*. It is quite evident that the Chronicler is dependent on material found in a different form in our versions of these earlier works. He uses in particular the Deuteronomic presentation of the history as an essential basis for his own work. But at the same time, he is really closer to the Priestly Work, not so much (as used to be said) because of his interest in priestly things, but rather because he is less concerned with the presentation and interpretation of history and more concerned with the theologizing of past and present experience.

We may properly ask by what process it comes about that the Priestly Work offers a theological study solely in terms of the early period; and part of the answer to this must be that this period is seen as normative. It is not just past history; it is meaningful history, relevant to contemporary experience. H.H. Guthrie in his *Wisdom and Canon* (1966) stresses the important point that increasingly in the post-exilic period the older narratives come to be used as vehicles for exhibiting wisdom, as edifying stories. So he says of the first part of the material that 'the narrative from Adam to Moses came to be seen as a wisdom tale certifying the validity of the Mosaic instruction set down in Exodus, Leviticus, Numbers, and Deuteronomy' (1966: 27), and similarly (and this provides a further comment on the separation of Deuteronomy into the Torah and the Former Prophets, the remainder of the Deuteronomic History, as placed side by side with the Latter):

'the narrative from Joshua to Jehoiachin became the tale preceding the instruction to be found in the corpus of the latter prophets from Isaiah to Malachi' (1966: 27).[1] What is here insufficiently seen is that this dehistoricizing of the narratives is already in substantial measure present in the Priestly Work and perhaps less obviously in the Deuteronomic History. Neither work (nor even their earlier predecessors) is to be regarded simply in terms of historical narrative, but both are rather to be thought of in terms of theological interpretation of a contemporary situation in the light of the recounting of already familiar material. The Chronicler is not, as Guthrie thinks, making an unrealistic attempt at providing a new historical presentation, a new updating of the *Heilsgeschichte;* he offers a further and more far-reaching dehistoricizing of what he sees as the essential elements in the community's previous history.

5.

This can be made clear from two main features of the Chronicler's presentation and theology: the absence of the Exodus and the interpretation of the Davidic theme.

The first—an apparently negative feature—is of considerable importance when we set the Chronicler's work over against the earlier surveys. The significance given to the Exodus in the historical books, and in psalmody and prophecy—the latter in both pre-exilic material and in such exilic prophecy as that of Deutero-Isaiah—has been highlighted by the whole trend of the *Heilsgeschichte* approach to Old Testament theology in recent years. This motif is clearly of very great significance especially where it is central to a particular body of material. But increasingly it has been observed that the

1. It must be pointed out that Guthrie rejects the hypothesis of a Deuteronomistic History (cf. 34 n. 7), though the point is not argued in his short study. The comment made here is my own deduction from what seems to me to be his illuminating suggestions. I am less inclined to see his next point as sound, namely, that the whole of the first two parts of the canon provide an introduction to the instruction of the third. Strangely, he does not mention the book of Job as offering an excellent example of the kind of wisdom-tale he is using as basis.

emphasis given to this as *the* central motif inevitably distorts the total picture. It is not only that Wisdom falls outside this pattern, but in fact much more than Wisdom; and not least among works which either play down or virtually ignore the Exodus theme is the contribution of the Chronicler.[1] Yet it is clear that he is not alone in this. For such bypassing of Sinai or subordinating of the Exodus motifs is also to be found in large measure in the Jerusalem traditions. We may note that the Isaiah prophecies contain less of Exodus allusion than do those of Amos, Hosea and Micah. Subsequent prophetic developments, particularly in Deutero-Isaiah (and rather less and differently in Ezekiel), represent a fusion of the different elements and show the variegated pattern that could be produced. It has also been observed that the Priestly Work, concentrated though it is on the normative period and laying much stress on the ordering of people and cult in the wilderness, does not really concern itself with the Sinai covenant in the way that the earlier works had done and as the Deuteronomic History does. The real foundation of God's relationship with His people is rooted much further back, in the Abrahamic covenant, and this itself is the context of the primeval history. God's purpose for His people begins in Creation, not at the Exodus. The Chronicler is the inheritor of this richness and variety, but he makes his own particular stress. He adopts a device already much used by the Priestly writer to bridge gaps between material, that of the genealogy. The list of names, so easily read as a mere catalogue, is in fact an assurance of the ultimate origin of the relationship. 'Adam, Seth, Enosh'—that is where Israel, the true Israel, begins.[2] There is a certain solemnity about it, a sonorousness, an evocation of what goes back to the remotest antiquity, that which has always been. Divine grace does not begin in history; it is always at work. So the Chronicler—and in this respect he in a measure resembles the Deuteronomic Historian who also assumes knowledge of traditions he does not relate—passes over the period of the

1. North (1969: 378) comments on the omission of the Exodus references in 1 Chron. 17 (cf. 2 Sam. 7) and in 2 Chron. 6.11 (cf. 1 Kgs 8.21), though inconsistently the reference remains in v. 5.

2. G. von Rad (1962: 352-53) points to the frequent use of the root *bḥr*, but he offers a very forced view of the theology underlying this.

Exodus, not because he is unaware of it, and he knows that his readers are also familiar with its narratives (how could they not be?), but because the real moment of his theological interpretation lies elsewhere.[1]

D.N. Freedman in his recent study[2] has assumed that because the central moment lies in the Davidic tradition, the Ezra material must be a later addition to the original work: it not only represents a recall to the Exodus legal tradition but also includes a prayer in Nehemiah 9 (attributed in the LXX to Ezra) which devotes not a little attention to the Exodus theme as central theologically. But if we are to make the Chronicler consistent in this, we shall also have to say that some if not all of the Levitical sermons of Chronicles are insertions and that the use of Exodus motifs, for example in Ezra 1, which Freedman must allow to be either part of or related to his 515 BCE Chronicler's work, must also be due to a later attempt to make the Chronicler conform. It is much more natural to suppose[3] that in such passages the Chronicler is making use of liturgical and homiletical material familiar to him; in this, Exodus themes and allusions were frequently to be found. He is not thereby contradicting his main emphasis, but he reveals familiarity with other theological motifs. Indeed there is much

---

1. North (1969: 377-78) lists possible lines of approach to this silence on the Exodus. He refers to Freedman's view, which is discussed in the next paragraph here. He cites Noth as indicating that the Pentateuch had just been published and that silence meant assent; this is not impossible, though for the understanding of the Chronicler we must stress what he actually says. Rudolph views it as part of the polemic against the Samaritans; the Exodus, which they too could claim, was less sure as a foundation for his argument than the Davidic monarchy. Certainly legitimacy of Jerusalem is an important theme. Brunet thinks he regards Sinai as a provisional step towards David, but this is nowhere made explicit. North himself stresses that for the Chronicler the basic vehicle of Israel's chosenness is not Moses on Sinai but David on Zion and that he is also endeavoring to correct P and explain the cultus more realistically. These views are not mutually exclusive, and it may be wondered whether in fact there are various contributory factors to the Chronicler's attitude. My own views are developed subsequently.

2. *CBQ* 23 (1961), 436-42.

3. Freedman (437) does in fact allow for what he terms 'stereotyped references'.

to be said for modifying the old view that the Chronicler was a Levitical singer[1] (because of his predilection for music and worship generally and because he seems at times to be arguing for the status of Levitical singers) and for ranking him rather with the Levitical preachers, from whose store of homiletical material he draws so frequently and so appropriately (cf. von Rad 1966, Mason 1977). With his concern for law and particularly ritual law and the purity of the community—themes which recur repeatedly—the Chronicler is developing further the tradition of both the Priestly and Deuteronomic schools in seeing that the whole life of the community and its suitability and acceptability as the people of God depend upon a law ultimately associated with Sinai, though ratified and applied in a series of decisive moments of which the Davidic is the first and that of Ezra the most recent.

6.

On the more positive side we have the Chronicler's stress on David and Jerusalem. The emphasis on the unity of all Israel under David probably has an element of anti-Samaritan polemic (cf. Rudolph 1954: 404; Rudolph 1955a: ix; von Rad 1962: I.348). But although we may rightly believe the contemporary situation to have influenced the Chronicler, the polemical element is perhaps less than the need for reinterpretation of the Davidic–Jerusalem tradition which faced the post-exilic community. If there were those who saw in Zerubbabel the revival of a Davidic hope in extreme nationalist terms, by the time at which the Chronicler was active Davidic hope had clearly receded. While, as Stinespring has stressed, much interest centres on Davidic descent, for 1 Chronicles 3 gives a substantial list of Zerubbabel descendants (1961: 210),[2] the prospect of a restored Davidic monarchy was minimal by the fourth century. No doubt some circles still cherished it, and later centuries were to see recrudescence of

1. So recently again Stinespring (1961: 210).
2. Some of the Davidic material may belong to the later strata of the work.

the hope in political Messianic terms. But at this point it was hardly viable.

Why then the stress? By contrast with the Deuteronomic Historian, who, preserving both promonarchical and anti-monarchical material, depicts the monarchy as a divine blessing but also as a historically and theologically questionable institution, the Chronicler has given us an idealized picture. As both Stinespring and North have emphasized, there is here an eschatological element in the Chronicler's work—but it is not in terms of the future of the Davidic monarchy and hence a hope for the future,[1] nor is it, as North maintains, 'a deliberately archaizing treatment of a genuine eschatological messianic hope (1969: 378ff.). It is rather the embodiment of the David/Jerusalem theme no longer in political but in theological terms, in relation to the life and worship of the little Judaean community of his own time. In stressing this, I find myself closely in sympathy with Rudolph's emphasis on a 'realized eschatology,' but I think it needs to be differently expressed in terms of a re-embodiment of the Davidic ideal in terms of what temple and cultus now mean.

The Chronicler sees David as the ideal. To the Davidic period is traced the unity of the people; the loyalty of all the tribes is expressed again and again, and David's appointment as king at Hebron is described as by representatives of all, 'all of one mind' (1 Chron. 12.38). To David is traced both the intention to build the temple and the preparation of all that is needed for its construction according to the divine plan (1 Chron. 28.19; cf. v. 11). Its whole organization and worship were prepared; its officials designated and their duties made precise. The temple site was divinely chosen as an act of grace in a moment of David's own failure and repentance (1 Chron. 21–22.1). The choice of Solomon as builder and successor is confirmed, the man of peace in contrast to David's involvement in war (1 Chron. 22.8ff.). The Chronicler has thus paid respect to the tradition of Solomon's building, but he has given it a new and

---

1. North (1969: 378) cites A. Noordtzij (1940: 161-68) and J. Swart, (1911: pp. 3, 97) for the view that the failure of David's house points to the future, and hence to the Messianism of intertestamental and New Testament times. It is noted that the genealogy of Zerubbabel is virtually that of Jesus in Mt. 1.

richer context. David, Jerusalem, the temple, the priesthood—motifs which appear already linked together in the intricate version of the material in Samuel, but still not fully co-ordinated—are all here shown to be part of one unified theological structure. In this the themes North separates out and analyses (1969: 369-70; cf. also Freedman 1961: 436) as those of legitimacy and cultus are seen really to be only aspects of the one theme of David. His fourth theme—retribution—is in part a development of the already existing stress in the Deuteronomic History, and indeed also in other Old Testament writings; but in the Chronicler it is in fact overshadowed by the emphasis laid upon divine grace.[1] For while at certain points the Chronicler elaborates the theme of retribution and makes history where necessary fit a scheme, he also makes it clear that the eventual outcome is due not to retributive action but to repeated and continuing acts of grace tied to the central theme.

For David is but the type of the divine grace revealed to the true Israel.[2] The theme is repeated in faithful kings who show themselves to be on the side of faith over against apostasy—the wars in which the true Israel is engaged (that is, Judah etc.) are wars of faith against apostasy, holy wars taken out of the merely historical context into the theological.[3] Without faith no army avails; with faith the enemy goes to disaster at the recognition of the presence of God (cf. Abijah's speech in 2 Chron. 13, and the examples of Asa in 2 Chron. 14–15 and of Jehoshaphat in 2 Chron. 19–20). A new David arises in Hezekiah (cf. Moriarty 1965: 401), when with the fall of the Northern Kingdom there is once again only one kingdom, and opportunity is found for the faithful to join (2 Chron. 30); the vision appears of a united Israel, celebrating its first united feast since the kingdom's disruption.[4] Even Manasseh pro-

---

1. Cf. Rudolph 1955a: xx. This aspect is missed by von Rad (1962: 348-49).
2. Cf. the unqualified promise to David—e.g. in 1 Chron. 17.12-14 (contrast 2 Sam. 7). Freedman 1961: 438; North 1969: 378.
3. On this theme cf. also de Vaux 1961: 258-59 and esp. 266-67, on Qumran. Stinespring 1961: 217. Cf. also J.A. Soggin, *VT* 10 (1960), p. 81.
4. Cf. 2 Chron. 30.26 and the summary in vv. 20-21.

vides an example of repentance and grace; disaster is delayed by Josiah's obedience, but in the end the failure to heed the warnings brings about the inevitable judgment.

7.

This sounds like historical survey, and it is, of course, linked with the order of events, the succession of kings. But it is already in the process of being dehistoricized; the events are only partly real, the battles are no longer actually fought. And with the exile this becomes clear in that to the Chronicler the exile is both an event which took place but also, and this is more important, a symbol of the reality of divine judgment and grace. In spite of repeated prophetic warnings (2 Chron. 36.15-16), the people would not hear; the last king, Zedekiah, refused to heed Jeremiah (2 Chron. 36.12). The exile overtook them. But it was not just deserved disaster, not just another example of retributive justice; it was also a respite for the land which could now become acceptable after seventy years of sabbath rest (2 Chron. 36.21), and the promised act of grace was to be seen in Cyrus.[1]

From now on, hope lies with the exiles; not because they are exiles but because they have undergone judgment. The Chronicler builds upon prophetic words which showed that the hope for the future lay only with them; the exile as symbol of judgment is to be experienced or to be accepted. Rebuilding, when it comes, is by those who have been through the judgment —whether in person or in their forefathers (and hence the importance of genealogy)—or by those who have separated themselves, acknowledging judgment.[2]

And what has been lost can be recovered, but not in the same form. The Davidic line is cut off—Jehoiachin's release from prison finds no place in the Chronicler's narrative to suggest a

---

1. I have discussed this point more fully in an article on 'The Interpretation of Exile and Restoration' in *The Canadian Journal of Theology* 14 (1968), 3-12. It is important to see here the value of the stress laid down by Torrey, though this does not require our acceptance of his views of the sixth century. (See Chapter 9, below.)

2. Cf. Ezra 6.21.

line of hope.[1] If Sheshbazzar was a Davidide,[2] which is uncertain, no stress is laid on this; nor even on the certain Davidide status of Zerubbabel. It is the rebuilding of the temple, closely parallel with the building by Solomon (cf. Freedman 1961: 439), which marks the real revival of the Davidic hope, and this fits precisely with the Chronicler's emphasis in his narrative of David himself. Jerusalem with its shrine is again the focal point, the centre of a purified people. The Davidic hope, taken out of history, is embodied in temple and cultus, ordained by David and now renewed, which represent its true value, an enduring witness to divine grace and power to purify.[3] The old institutions are recovered—continuity is preserved by temple vessels and a legitimate priestly line (cf. Ezra 2.61-62). All Israel, the true Israel, rejoiced to celebrate the dedication feast. And with Ezra's reform and the purifying of the community from foreign contaminating elements, there is once again a true people of God, the recipient of divine promise, obedient to the Law, the sign of the continuing grace and blessing of God.

H.H. Guthrie (1966: 3ff.) points to the process by which the ancient faith is repeatedly shown to be still meaningful. He goes on to demonstrate how in later years the historical material became the vehicle of teaching, the setting in story for an example of life (1966: 21ff.). And thereby it is dehistoricized, and so we meet with it again in the New Testament, where Paul, for example, uses Old Testament narratives as a basis for edification (cf. 1 Cor. 10).

But this process of dehistoricization is older. It is the great contribution of the Chronicler that he takes up on the one hand the themes of the Deuteronomic Historian and traces their further development in the later period; and at the same

1. It is of course possible that the text of Kings available to the Chronicler did not include this item, but it is even so not improbable that he was aware of the incident. Cf. Baltzer 1961: 30-31.

2. Freedman (1961: 439) follows the line that it is an alternative for Shenazzar, both being corruptions of Sin-ab-usur. But if so, why is he described as 'prince (*nāsî*) of Judah', whereas Zerubbabel is given his father's name?

3. A different application of the David theme may be seen in Deutero-Isaiah (cf. Eissfeldt 1962).

time he takes up the Priestly concern with purity and legitimacy and right organization.[1] He links these, not in a simple re-presentation of history but in a demonstration of the way in which historical experience has become theological experience. The community is shown that the real values of the past are enshrined in the present, that Davidic monarchy and all that it betokens of divine grace is exemplified in temple and cultus, that a community joined in the joyous worship of God, a community purified and renewed, is the recipient of divine promise. This may be seen to be related to later, both Jewish and Christian, ways of understanding Old Testament events as of more than historical significance.

---

1. Cf. North (1969: 369, 374ff.), on the reconciling of different elements. Freedman (1961: 441) in effect sees this only in the Ezra/Nehemiah material which he regards as later addition.

Chapter 11

THE THEOLOGY OF THE CHRONICLER[1]

The obscurity of the earliest periods of Old Testament history—those of the patriarchs and of the Exodus, Wilderness and Conquest—is matched only by the obscurity of the post-exilic period. Whereas in some measure at least the problem of the earlier periods derives from the richness and complexity of the evidence from which attempts are made at reconstructing a historical sequence, the problem of the period from the rebuilding of the temple (c. 515 BCE) to the coming of Alexander the Great (336–323)—and even beyond this into the third century BCE—stems not so much from complexity in the evidence as from the (almost total) lack of it.

It is true that we know from the biblical records of two notable personalities of this period, Ezra and Nehemiah. But the very existence of the former has been doubted, Ezra being supposed by some to be nothing but a figment of the Chronicler's imagination—an unnecessarily extravagant notion—and the uncertainties which exist about the order of their appearance and the dating to which Ezra is to be assigned make for substantial difficulties in historical reconstruction

---

1. Reprinted from the author's article in *Lexington Theological Quarterly* 8 (1973): 101-16. This study represents, in part, a further development of ideas set out in the writer's earlier essay 'History and Theology in the Writings of the Chronicler', *Concordia Theological Monthly* 38 (1967): 501-15 (reprinted here as Chapter 10); in part, a deposit from the writing of the commentary *I and II Chronicles, Ezra, Nehemiah* (Torch Commentary Series; London: SCM, 1973); and in part—section III in particular—the substance of a paper contributed to a discussion on Old Testament theology at the congress held in Los Angeles in September, 1972, under the general theme 'The Humanizing of Man'. The essay in its present form served as the basis for a lecture delivered at Lexington Theological Seminary and elsewhere.

for the period of about 50 years—the latter half of the fifth century BCE—to which they appear to belong. There is the evidence of Josephus whose account of this period raises yet other problems. There are some important archaeological discoveries, notably the Elephantine and Samaria papyri. Excavations are beginning to shed more light on this period. External history and particularly the relationships between Persia and Greece and Persia and Egypt provide an important background, but one which it is not always possible to relate with certainty to the biblical material. Internal history, however, remains very difficult to reconstruct except at a few points.

It is the more tantalizing in that it can be quite reasonably suggested that a number of Old Testament writings belong to this period. Among the prophets, the words of Haggai and Zechariah (1–8) were compiled in their present form; the second part of the book of Zechariah (9–14) and the book of Malachi probably belong to this period, though the evidence for a precise historical attachment is lacking in them—even in Malachi, which has for long been placed with some assurance in about 470 BCE. Joel and Jonah and Ruth may belong here; so may Job, though there is a strong trendency to push the date of Job back at least into the previous century. Other elements in the prophetic books and some parts of Proverbs may belong here. Perhaps most significant, the shaping of the Tetrateuch, Genesis–Numbers, the 'Priestly Work', that great theological exposition of the origins of Israel, almost certainly belongs here. But the difficulty is that in all this material we are provided with no precise historical evidence and no precise historical definition. Unless we are to adopt the method of those who date virtually undateable works in periods about which little is known and then proceed to write the history of the unknown periods on the basis of the works assigned to them—a way of proceeding adopted particularly readily by some commentators on the Psalms—we are only able to make the most tentative statements about the relationship between events and writings in the period with which we are dealing, however sure we may be that the form and content of much of the Old Testament material owe a great deal to the needs and aspirations and experiences of the post-exilic community.

The work of the Chronicler—1 and 2 Chronicles, Ezra, and Nehemiah—is not a complete unity. It seems probable that there have been additions to what may be regarded as its more original form, and, in particular, the Nehemiah material is perhaps best understood as such an addition. But in spite of this, there is a sufficient unity of thought and presentation for the work to be treated as a whole; and the fact that the climax of the work is quite evidently in the activity of Ezra makes it most natural to see it as essentially a product of the fourth century BCE, sufficiently after the period of Ezra (here assumed to be around 398 BCE) for there to be both perspective and a measure of idealization. The point cannot be fully demonstrated, but a date of around 350 BCE, before the advent of Greek power, would appear to fit the evidence most nearly. The fixing of the date is tentative and we must not therefore fall into the trap already mentioned of reconstructing the history of an unknown period on the basis of such a dating of a work. We may, however, cautiously draw out from this work some understanding of the way of thought, the style of interpretation of its author or compiler and in some measure the needs of the community to which it was directed. If we term this author or compiler 'the Chronicler', this is partly for convenience. It may well be that we should think rather of the Chronicler as the representative of a particular school of thought, a member of a particular group within the community; yet it is proper also to give credit to the creative thinking of a leading individual within such a group, and to give to that leading individual a title which sufficiently identifies him.

1. *The Avoidance of Misconceptions*

If this work is to be properly understood, we must be clear about what it is and what it is not. It must be firmly insisted that it is neither a history book—and here is the obvious disadvantage of the term 'the Chronicler' for its author, itself the result of the Hebrew title 'the annals' (literally 'the words [things, matters] of the days), rendered as 'Chronicles'—nor is it a supplement to the earlier narratives to be found primarily in the books of Samuel and Kings—and here the title in the

Greek translation, the Septuagint, is misleading: 'the things left out'. These two titles have led to much misunderstanding. In their different ways they have contributed to the supposition that this work is to be judged as a historical narrative. As a result it has been largely discredited and ignored, for it is quite evident that much of the narrative is very unsatisfactory if it is viewed as history. Taken as history, it may be compared unfavourably in many respects with its earlier counterparts. The opposite view of the work has also been taken, based partly in the supposition that it may be used to fill the obvious gaps in the earlier narratives and partly on the assumption, which is not necessarily an entirely erroneous one, that the Chronicler had access to source material which was either not available to the earlier writers or simply not used by them. The probability is that some of the material which is to be found in the Chronicler's work and is unparalleled elsewhere is based on older sources; but its significance lies not in that but in the way in which it is used.

For the real point is to see the Chronicler not as a poor historian or as a good historian, but as an interpreter. He handles the older traditions; he incorporates newer material in them; he rearranges, comments, elaborates, sermonizes—all with the purposes of bringing home to his readers (or perhaps his hearers, for the style is very strongly homiletic), the meaning for themselves of what is being related and expounded. Often we may observe that he assumes that his readers know the story being told, or that they know the form in which the story existed in the older presentations; by an allusion, by a brief summary, by a comment, he invites a particular kind of understanding, pointing in the direction of a particular moral or theological insight.

It is, of course, proper to add that interpretation is equally the concern of the earlier compilers of the Deuteronomic History, that work which runs from Joshua to 2 Kings (including Deuteronomy in reality as its foundation statement), and which presents in the guise of history, and often with much important historical information, a narrative which equally offers interpretation, judgment, homily, encouragement and warning to the community of the exilic age. Neither the Chronicler nor the Deuteronomist is to be understood in narrow terms as a historian; they are both theologians and it is in this that their real significance lies.

In order to understand the work of the Chronicler we need to see the whole as well as examining the component parts; we need to consider the overall purpose and method, and observe how, in various ways, these are expressed in individual narratives and homilies. The detail of such a study is the function of a commentary; what is attempted here is a consideration of the wider purpose.

2. *The Method of Presentation*

An examination of the central part of the work, the portrayal of the monarchical period from the death of Solomon to the exile (2 Chron. 10–36), shows a skilful patterning. It is possible to see some use of this method in the older presentation in 2 Kings; contrasting rulers follow one another—Ahaz, Hezekiah, Manasseh (Amon), Josiah, Jehoiakim—in a way which suggests that history is at least in some measure subordinated to interpretation. The Chronicler uses the same device in the case of Ahaz and Hezekiah. For him, the former (2 Chron. 28) is the most evil of the kings of Judah, and the latter (2 Chron. 29–32) is the ideal, proving his faith even in moments of military threat and testing (so esp. in ch. 32).

But most often, the Chronicler uses a more subtle pattern of apostasy and repentance, obedience and faith, disobedience and unbelief. Thus Rehoboam, the first king of the true kingdom from which the apostate North has separated itself, is shown to find strength and well-being when the faithful, priests and Levites and laity, from the north join him. Success leads to pride and faithlessness; this in its turn leads to judgment in the form of Egyptian attack. Prophetic comment brings submission and the averting of divine wrath, and the reign ends in prosperity (2 Chron. 11–12).

It is a neat ordering of themes. The relation to history is less important than the portrayal of the nature of faith and pride. The good king Jehoshaphat, the reformer of justice—a theme not found in the older material and perhaps in reality suggested by the exposition of his name ('Yahweh judges')—is also the encourager of faith in his people in times of danger.

But he is led into alliance with the apostate north and must inevitably be condemned (2 Chron. 17–20). Most striking of all, Manasseh, the most evil ruler according to the earlier account—and there portrayed as the prime cause of Judah's downfall (cf. 2 Kgs 21; 23.26-27)—begins his reign in this evil and apostate fashion, with the result that judgment falls and he is taken captive to Babylon, a captivity which serves as a type for the judgment on Judah which is to come. In captivity he repents; restored to his throne, he becomes a model, reforming king (2 Chron. 33). In this improbable narrative, historically speaking, the Chronicler makes an important point about the possibility and the nature of restoration for the community.

Thus, in the reigns of individual rulers, and by the arrangement of one ruler alongside another, the Chronicler presents a pattern which is variegated yet constant. It reaches its climax in the moment of judgment in the exile, the moment at which it is possible for the reader to look back and to see how the detail of the narrative is coordinated into the overall pattern to which judgment is the proper resolution.

This particular example of the patterning of material in the work of the Chronicler is the clearest and most extensive. The construction of smaller units within the work reveals also a highly skilled arrangement and balance, pointing to a literary artist. The ordering of the Solomon narratives, in part dependent on the earlier forms, provides a good example of a literary unit built up in a pattern out of its component parts.

It is possible also to look even more broadly at the work and detect an overall theological scheme. Without imposing too rigid or precise a definition of this, it may be tentatively described in terms of 'exile' and 'restoration'. The opening part of the work, the long genealogical tables of 1 Chronicles 1–9, reaches its climax in the setting out of exile and restoration in ch. 9. At this point the writer offers what is in effect a summary of the whole intention of his work, his desire to show how and on what basis the restored community has come into being and to what it owes its existence. 1 Chronicles 10–2 Chronicles 9, the section which concerns the reigns of David and Solomon—united in the theme of the temple, its ordering and its building—is related as beginning in the failure of Saul (only the final disaster to Saul is related in 1 Chron. 10), and taken further in the judgment upon David which issues in the choice of the temple site (1 Chron. 21–22.1). It is from a moment of judgment and disaster that the high point of Israel's history arises. 2 Chronicles 10–36 together with Ezra 1–6, viewed now as a larger unit, shows judgment and exile and restoration culminating in the dedicating of the rebuilt temple in a restored and purified community (Ezra 6.13-18, 19-22). The work of Ezra, described in a theological rather than a chronological order (Ezra 9–10; Neh. 8–10 in which the themes of Ezra 9–10 belong in reality after the description of the reading of the law in Neh. 8), shows a new restoration in the acceptance of the law and the making of a new covenant, a restoration which is set against the background of ignorance of the law and disobedience to it and the contamination of the community with the alien influence. The Nehemiah material, though separate in origin from the remainder, nevertheless reveals a comparable pattern in this respect, in that it portrays disaster to Jerusalem as the preface to the restoration of the city and the people.

In relation to this broad presentation we may see certain incorporated emphases. Restoration is possible only out of judgment; it can only be through exile that the community comes to hope. The implicit concentration on the exiles in Babylon in the Deuteronomic History—the poor of the land left behind (2 Kgs 25.12), the governorship of Gedaliah ending in disaster (2 Kgs 25.22-26)—is here made into an explicit statement that nothing whatever remained in the land at the time of exile. The whole community is handed over to Nebuchadrezzar; the land is left desolate, to enjoy its lost sabbaths (2 Chron. 36.15-21). Only the returned exiles and those who have expressed their sharing of that experience in the repudiation of alien contamination join in the rededication of the temple (Ezra 6.21).

A unity is established in the work by the Davidic theme. The first climax is reached in the ordering of worship under David, the planning of the temple on its divinely appointed site, the designation of Solomon as the one chosen to build. Care for the temple marks the obedient descendants of David; neglect and apostasy are the most heinous sins. The reality of the Davidic

idea is to be found in the re-established temple, both at its
rebuilding and at its reordering under Ezra. The theme is not
that of monarchy, but a reinterpretation of the relationship
between king and cult in terms of the absolute centrality of the
worship of God. Such worship is possible only for the true people, whose nature is set out in genealogies, and whose continuity is made plain by the same device; it is a people which incorporates the whole faithful body of those who accept the worship of the temple and obedience to the law.

We may, in such points as these, detect the concern of the
Chronicler with his own age, with the problem which confronted the little Jewish community, subject to Persian rule, if
it was to think of itself as the true heir to the past traditions
and to express its position rightly in worship and obedience.

3. *The Chronicler as an 'Old Testament Theologian'*

But we may, I believe, go a stage further and see the Chronicler's presentation and endeavour to unify, to draw together
the diverse strands of Israel's thought into a more coherent
whole. We may be even more precise in our delineation of him
as a theologian, and see him as one who aimed at presenting a
unifying concept of the nature of the Jewish religious community and hence of its theology and the meaning of its rich
and varied traditions.

His was not the first such attempt at unification, nor was it to
be the last. But it is of particular significance that it is, within
the Old Testament, the most comprehensive such attempt,
going considerably further in its unifying endeavours than its
pedecessors. It points forward to other attempts at unification
to be found in later Jewish and Christian writings, and while it
would be straining the evidence to describe it as the first
'theology of the Old Testament', it nevertheless, in its endeavour to be comprehensive and yet true to the tradition, anticipates some more modern essays which have sought the
essential centre of Old Testament theological thought and
have attempted to trace the relationships between the various
strands which make up the whole. Like modern essays of this
nature, the work of the Chronicler has also come in for sharp
criticism. We may observe that von Rad, whose comments on

the Chronicler are rather lukewarm, sees in the imposition of what he regards as an individualizing standard of judgment an inevitable dissolution of the appreciation of the whole sweep of Israel's history. There is some truth in this criticism, but not, I think, a complete understanding of what is being done. Similarly, we may observe that just as those who have concentrated their attention in the elucidation of Old Testament theology on the great acts of God have found whole areas of Old Testament material either not entirely to their taste or difficult to fit into a neat pattern, so too the Chronicler may with propriety be seen to be less percipient in regard to some aspects of the tradition than to others. In offering a critique of his theology, however, there is more value to be found in assessing his positive achievement, since we may see here some relationship between a pluriform theological tradition and attempts at clarifying what unity this tradition may be held to contain.

It is one of the curious features of von Rad's *Theology of the Old Testament* that he appears—in spite of much perceptive writing on the work of the Chronicler in earlier studies—to have so limited an appreciation of the Chronicler's theology. Essentially, he stands, like so many more, in that negative line which devalues the Chronicler as belonging to a late and therefore less significant moment of Israel's thought, the *Epigonentum* of the post-exilic period. One feels that, essentially, von Rad sees the Chronicler's failure in the devaluing of history (or *Heilsgeschichte*) in the sometimes evidently atomistic treatment of the reigns of individual kings of Judah; though in this quite proper recognition that each king, is, as it were, the subject of a single sermon, he fails to see that the presentation of the Judaean monarchy, which forms only one part of the whole work, does in fact provide a series of illustrations, similar though not identical, of the nature of the response or lack of response, the faith and the unbelief, which, as we have seen, the Chronicler portrays as belonging to the whole character of his people's life and experience. Essentially, it is the historical element or its lack which leads either to an undervaluing of the Chronicler or to extravagant claims for his defence. An apology is made for his theology: he is said to be percipient in the matter of divine grace, even if his outlook is limited to a belief that the true community has embodied itself

in the life of his own time and he therefore lacks a proper outlook towards the future (so, though too briefly to be entirely
just, we might describe Rudolph's assessment). Or, by careful
correlation of the special material to be found in the Chronicler with archaeological and topographical information, or by
endeavours to show how his different presentation is truer to
the actual situation, an attempt is made to salvage historical
accuracy and so get the Chronicler into the proper and
accepted sequence of those who find theology in history and in
historical action and interpretation.

Such approaches do not do justice to the work of the Chronicler; nor would it be proper to make extravagant claims, in
the spirit of those who would rather argue a new case than
make a merely modest reassessment. It may well be that *sub
specie aeternitatis* the theology of the Chronicler will not rank
so very high. Its assessment must be seen against the background of what must still be admitted to be a very little-known
period. The only fair method of handling his work is to ask
what kind of theological and other problems appear to have
confronted him, and to ask how he handled them. On the basis
of such an inquiry an assessment may be made which is
neither narrowly negative nor unrealistically approving. But
it may be nearer to being a proper one.

Four aspects of the Chronicler's thought may be seen to be
relevant to the question of his handling of a pluriform tradition
in relation to the needs of a particular situation.

(1) The older emphasis on the priestly or cultic preoccupa-
tion of the Chronicler—aligning him with P—gave way to a
newer insistence that his real ancestry in thought was to be
found in the Deuteronomists. A fairer assessment, confirmed
both at the literary level and at the theological, is that he com-
bines the two types of interpretation. It is, of course, possible to
excise from the Chronicler everything that belongs to the
Priestly strand (e.g. by regarding 1 Chron. 1–9 as a later addition), but this, in a sense, only postpones the problem. (If those
chapters were a later addition, then we should only be forced
into saying that whoever added them represents this literary
uniting of the two strands.) It is easier to take the work essentially as it stands and see that its dependence at the literary
level is on both the Tetrateuch, the 'Priestly work', and the

Deuteronomic History, the D-work. At the theological level, there is both the awareness that the judgment and mercy of God may be seen to be exemplified in history, even if that history is frequently retold in homiletic language to make the point in relation to particular narratives; and there is also the recognition that the relationship between people and deity is one of dependence expressed in obedience to the law and commitment to the practices of worship. There is a combination of that theological strand which lays emphasis on humanity's obligation to obedience and faith, with its complement—which sees the inability of humankind to respond exemplified in judgment and met by divine grace.

Whatever our precise judgment upon the relationship between the P and D strands of thought—whether we accept a view which sees some form of P-work alongside a D-work, or the alternatives in which P and D represent different stages in the evolution of the material—there still remains clear to us a fairly marked contrast between these two lines of thinking. The reconciliation in one body of literature of the two represents a significant attempt at establishing a theological uniformity where in fact there is a pluriformity of tradition and interpretation. The final acceptance of the Pentateuch as *Torah*—whether it is the result of a truncating of a Hexateuch, itself the result of a complex and long time of development, or the result of an incorporating of a Deuteronomy separated from the historical work for which it provides the theological basis into a somewhat incomplete union with the 'Priestly work' of the Tetrateuch—this acceptance represents the combining of two ways of thinking. Much of the subsequent harmonizing process—discernible in Deuteronomic passages in the Tetrateuch and in a reshaping of the end of the work in both Numbers and Deuteronomy (and this harmonizing process, we may note, is carried further and differently by the Samaritan community)—and much also of subsequent exegesis designed to show that the different approaches are in fact to be seen as one—is indicative of the somewhat artificial nature of the combining of the two strands. Alongside what we may detect of editing and harmonizing and exegetical procedures here, we may place the work of the Chronicler. Using substantial elements of both corpuses of material, subordinat-

ing them to his own particular viewpoint, he offers another
line of unification.

Now it would be going beyond the evidence to suggest that
there existed in post-exilic Judaism two parties within the
community, the 'Priestly' and the 'Deuteronomic'. It has
sometimes been thought possible to detect in some of the
Chronicler's lists, particularly where these concern different
groups of Levitical officials, if not precisely struggles for power,
yet at least some manoeuvring for position in the post-exilic
community. The community of that period would be quite
unique—so far as our experience of human behaviour goes—
if there were not such manoeuvres. It is quite conceivable—
though so far as we are concerned the tracks have been pretty
well covered—that the Chronicler was himself arguing a case
for some particular group. But the significant point is that in
doing whatever precisely he is doing, he is claiming validity for
these two great traditions, not coming down so heavily on one
side or the other as to suggest that they are mutually exclusive.

To this we may add, having regard for the prophetic quota-
tions and the psalm-passages and the allusions to the Exodus
and the like which appear most clearly in the homiletic passages but also elsewhere, that his range extends more broadly
than this. If there are more direct allusions to Deuteronomy
than to other material, this is nevertheless balanced by the
wide range of prophetic quotation and by the recognition of the
validity of prophetic teaching. 'Believe in Yahweh your God
and you will be established; believe his prophets and you will
succeed' (2 Chron. 20.20, with the clearest of verbal allusions
to Isa. 7.9). This particular passage, set side by side with references to the Mosaic law and the Chronicler's use of the
Deuteronomic History, comes very near to being a statement
of canonical authority for the whole range of writings now to
be found in the first two sections of the Hebrew canon,
regarded as 'wholes', to be understood in the context of a conviction of the unity of their testimony. Is the Chronicler thus
perhaps the first theologian of the canon?

(2) The centrality of the David material to a very large part
of the Chronicler's work appears from 1 Chronicles 10 to
2 Chronicles 9 explicitly, and implicity also to the end of

2 Chronicles. The re-establishment of the temple and worship in the two stages of rebuilding and the work of Ezra represents a recovery of the situation under David and Solomon and complements the David material (cf. Ezra 3.10, and more generally the restoration of the vessels and sacrifices). This centrality may be viewed in a variety of ways. On the one hand, the place given to this theme is so great that it is hardly surprising that von Rad describes the Chronicler as a guardian of the messianic tradition ('Wächter der messianischen Tradition').[1] The elaboration of the Davidic genealogical material, probably a secondary development, would seem to point to an even greater concern with the Davidic ideal, as does the prominence given to a Davidic descendant in the list of those who returned with Ezra. The existence in the post-exilic period—traceable in often undateable messianic oracles and in the later speculations concerning the son of David—of a strongly messianic tradition, probably in some circles more politically oriented, in others directed more towards ideals of obedience, would suggest that the Chronicler is taking up a position in relation to these. The consideration of one element in that development, the Zerubbabel oracles of Haggai and Zechariah, suggests, with all the difficulties of interpretation, a strong political slant to some of these speculations, and it may be significant that the Chronicler's use of the Haggai–Zechariah tradition in Ezra 5–6 lacks this political aspect.

The Chronicler—with his concept of a Davidic ideal, and his evident belief that the true expression of what David meant and means to the community lies in the ordering of temple and worship, and particularly music and praise—would appear to come down rather firmly on the non-political, quietistic side in this area of thought. But we may ask whether, with his degree of emphasis on David, there may not be an endeavour here at drawing together two lines of thought, a recognition of the validity of the Davidic tradition in its various expressions and a belief that this kind of thought has a significant part to play in holding together a community which—if we may judge from two centuries later and beyond—could be so sharply divided on political and religious

---

1. Von Rad 1957–60: I.347 (= [ET] 1962: I.351).

issues that party splits among the religiously convinced became a commonplace. The Chronicler's concern with these issues is no narrowly academic one. Whether or not he composed the prayers in Ezra 9 and Nehemiah 9, the fact that they find a place in the work makes them a legitimate pointer to a particular insight into the problems of the period. Here we see a combining of a strong sense of the divine hand at work in the benevolent activities of Persian rulers with an equally realistic recognition of the slave-condition of a community whose land is the holy land as promised to Abraham, but which cannot now enjoy that land because of its slave position. Here all the tension between political distress and religious awareness is brought to a head. If the Chronicler was a theological quietist, we must nevertheless add to that definition a qualifier to the effect that he was also sensitive to the realities of a subject people's condition.

(3) The emphasis on David, and the drawing of parallels between Moses and David (e.g. in 1 Chron. 28, which concerns the plan of the temple and the plan of the tabernacle, and the ordering of the rebuilt temple, with its fulness of worship [associated with David] and its properly established priesthood [associated with Mosaic law]), point to a further aspect of the Chronicler's theological policy. It has been observed, and rightly, that when a division between Jews and Samaritans took place—and the precise decision on this is a matter of great delicacy—the latter could claim, and did, the same historic origin, the same Mosiac law, and a priestly line which they regarded as absolutely authentic. For them, as their later statements set it out, the break came in the period of settlement, and the establishment of the Davidic monarchy could be seen as a departure from the true line. It has often been supposed that the Chronicler was setting out a statement, in some measure a polemic, against Samaritan claims. The final form of the work may allow this—though it seems less likely that it is true of the earlier stages—but what is epitomized in the Samaritan viewpoint and divergence from Jerusalem Judaism may be regarded rather as an example, the clearest we have, of critical attitudes towards that Judaism's claims. In the face of such critical attitudes, the Chronicler, building upon earlier thought, lays claim to the centrality of the

Davidic tradition and its unity with other aspects of the tradition.

We might cautiously compare the position of the Chronicler with the position taken in later apocalyptic writings, so highly venerated in certain areas of Judaism and in certain Christian circles. In apocalyptic literature a claim is made (cf. e.g. 2 Esd. 14.45ff.) that the higher wisdom is to be found in writings other than those of the accepted canon of scripture. The rejection of this view by Judaism, as we may see in Josephus's *Contra Apionem*, may be undertaken on the basis that there is a canonical period, from Moses to Artaxerxes; what purports to go back further or what belongs later may be edifying, but it is not scripture. Similarly, those who claimed the greater antiquity of their tradition, whether it was alleged to go back to Moses or beyond, were to see in the Chronicler a countercheck in his claim that it is that earlier tradition as it is expressed in the Davidic context which is valid. The earlier, or supposedly earlier, traditions are seen through a particular lens. The lack of description of the Exodus events, which evokes such a feeling of antipathy to many who read the Chronicler's writings, is not in any way due to a lack of knowledge of them on the Chronicler's part—or so it must appear, unless we go carefully through and excise every allusion to them. The homilies in particular reach back to this moment. But the community is being invited to read its earlier traditions in a particular manner, to see them expounded in relation to what are here seen as the central moments—David, Jerusalem, and the temple.

(4) We may see in this last point an indication of the degree to which the Chronicler, in presenting a unification of theology, inevitably also makes claims to absoluteness. The community, as he defines it, is centred on Jerusalem; this necessarily involves a certain element of rigidity in the reading of the earlier traditions. As von Rad observes (1957–60: I.350 = 1962: I.353 [ET]), the address by Abijah in 2 Chronicles 13 provides a very clear exposition of the Chronicler's theology. Let those who have withdrawn from the true line of faith return; let them not fight against the true religion, for this would be to fight against God himself. Yet in this definition there is both a degree of confidence regarding the true centre

and a marked element of conciliation towards those who are outside. If it is the true community which celebrates the dedication of the rebuilt temple, it is possible for those who separate themselves from the pollutions of the peoples of the lands to join with them (Ezra 6.21). If it is the true people of Judah which celebrates the passover with Hezekiah, it is with the adherence of those who are willing to respond. And their acceptability, even though they are not purified according to the proper procedures, is recognized as made possible by the response of God himself to the king's prayer (2 Chron. 30.18-20). If the centre of the community, the priesthood responsible for the maintenance of worship, is to be properly maintained, there must be strictness of marriage relationship (Ezra 10); but the genealogies bear witness to the incorporation into the community of many groups which can only be regarded as loosely connected with Israel's ancestry. If obedience to the law is to be the mark of membership in the community, it is nevertheless thereby made clear that a willingness to undertake that obedience ranks above a mere claim to ancestry and even to practice (cf. Ezra 7 and 4.1ff.). There is in this a strong element of adherence to a centrally held conviction—the ancient traditions in all their variety are to be read through these particular spectacles—and a measure of ecumenicity which makes an appeal to those who will associate themselves with that conviction. There is no room for the loosely held supposition that everything is moderately true; there is provision only for the impact of a firm faith and a firm understanding of the community as the inheritor of its faith.

The sketching of these points is an attempt to show how this one theologian within the Old Testament period has handled the problem of a rich and diversely interpreted tradition. He stands in this tradition as one example—a clear one because seen within a self-contained work—of the drive towards unity, towards orthodoxy, which we may detect within theological development. Such a move has both its strengths and its weaknesses. It cannot mark a final resting point, for it will be subject to revision. But it represents a major contribution at a certain moment; to examine it enables us to lift the curtain at one corner to show the working of people's minds at one particular level. It provides a valuable focal point in an endeavour to understand the life and thought of the post-exilic community.

Chapter 12

GOD AND PEOPLE IN THE CHRONICLER'S PRESENTATION OF EZRA[1]

The original title proposed for this discussion was 'God and People in the Writings of the Chronicler', but I have thought it sensible, in view of the limitations of space, to look only at one representative section of the Chronicler's writings, that part in which he handles the figure of Ezra. I hope this may be regarded as justifiable.

It may be that there are still some to whom either subject needs some measure of justification, for the writings of the Chronicler are not always viewed with particular favour.[2] Because they occupy a secondary place in the canon of scripture—the last two books of the Writings, or a sequel to the historical books, and sandwiched between them and the

---

1. Reprinted from the author's essay in *La notion biblique de Dieu* (ed. J. Coppens; BETL, 41; Gembloux: J. Duculot, 1976 [1985]), 145-62.

2. It is probable—and Professor Walther Zimmerli has himself stressed this to me privately—that the abiding influence of Wellhausen's negative assessment is to be seen in this (cf. Wellhausen, 1883: ch. 6; = ET: Wellhausen 1957: 171-228). This continuing influence may be seen at various points: In the general understanding of the significance of the Chronicler (so e.g. von Rad, cf. below); in the view taken of his sources and of the nature of the work (so e.g. Rudolph, Willi, cf. below); in the criticism of the attemtps to find authentic early sources which, it is supposed by some, may serve to validate the work at a historical level (cf. Ackroyd 1967, repr. as Chapter 10 in the present volume, and the recent work of Welten, cf. below). The importance and in many features the soundness of Wellhausen's study tend to be overlooked. But what is really lacking there and in so much that has been written subsequently, is any real appreciation of the Chronicler as theologian, the Chronicler as deeply concerned with the problems and needs of those for whom he wrote. A considerable rectifying of this may be seen in the work of Mosis (cf. below).

rather dubious book of Esther—they have tended to be viewed as having a lesser importance, though various types of endeavour have been made to show their particular historical usefulness. For the post-exilic period they are—and to some appear rather regrettably so—a main source of information; but the use of them as a 'historical source' remains very problematic. The endeavour to find in the Chronicler remains of ancient historical information in the material which is not paralleled in the older books represents one way of addressing this problem, though we may doubt if it is really a satisfactory procedure.[1] Their lower value has to many scholars seemed evident, either because they take on from their Septuagint title the quality of merely 'the things left out', or because it is believed that their author's interests are at a lower religious and theological level than that of their greater predecessors.

Even Gerhard von Rad, who made important contributions to a better understanding of the Chronicler, remains at the end somewhat patronizing in his attitude, commenting on the replacement of 'adherence to Yahweh' by the 'recognition of and adherence to his cult place', and ending his comments with the rather curious note: 'Nevertheless we may properly ask whether a theology which saw the existence of Israel before Yahweh as so strongly determined by the offering of praise, can really be so very far from the right track' (von Rad 1962: 353-54). One has the strong suspicion that the main trend of Protestant scholarship has been to write off the Chronicler (very often along with the Priestly writer) as priestly, concerned with the cult, and therefore at a lower level than the prophetic, the religion of the word. It is hardly a matter for surprise, though it may be a matter for criticism, that von Rad's first volume, based on his own particular presuppositions, devotes 240 pages to the Hexateuch and the books that follow to 2 Kings, and eight pages to the Chronicler. If Martin Noth has made a much fairer assessment both proportionally and theologically (1957: 110-80), the influence of this negative treatment has remained marked and Noth's

---

1. Welten (1973) in a study of certain elements of the Chronicler's special material, shows how inadequate are the attempts to trace this back to genuine pre-exilic sources.

presentation has been less influential than other aspects of his work (cf. Knight 1973: 164-66). I have ventured to be critical of the recent handbooks of Old Testament theology by Professor Zimmerli and by Professor Fohrer for their dismissal of the Chronicler in a perfunctory manner.[1]

The tide has begun to turn, and it is perhaps significant that the most coherent and illuminating treatment of the Chronicler in the last few years has come from a Roman Catholic scholar, R. Mosis; I largely share its approach and outlook, and I shall refer to it again. My own first stimulus to look more attentively in this direction came from the work of Wilhelm Rudolph, and specifically from the pleasant task of translating for him his paper 'Problems of the Books of Chronicles' (Rudolph 1954), which he presented at the Society for Old Testament Study in the summer of 1954. As a result, I gave a short course of lectures at a summer school and undertook to write a commentary. The commentary was in my mind for rather a longer period than was proper, but eventually appeared in 1973.[2] Progress towards it was in fact represented by the consideration of the problems of interpreting the period of restoration after the exile (Ackroyd 1968a) and by a number of studies either directed to aspects of the Chronicler's

1. Cf. reviews in SOTS *Book List 1973*, p. 51 and *Expository Times* 85 (1973–1974), pp. 40ff., commenting on W. Zimmerli, *Grundriss der alttestamentlichen Theologie* (Theologische Wissenschaft, 3; Stuttgart, 1972), and G. Fohrer, *Theologische Grundstrukturen des Alten Testaments* (Theologische Bibliothek, 24; Berlin, 1972). Zimmerli has a mention of David and temple music as an application of Mosaic law (99), of the thesis of Willi and the element of renewal of hope (159, 206), and some few references to individual passages relevant to particular questions. Fohrer has a single sentence on p. 141, and no treatment of the Chronicler in a number of passages (e.g. 121ff., where the handling of the tradition in the narrative works is discussed); the lack of an index makes it impossible to be certain whether there are other odd allusions, but the parallel *Geschichte der israelitischen Religion* (Berlin, 1968; ET, Nashville, 1972, London, 1973), devotes one page (370-71) to the Chronicler, and similarly only two pages (365-66) to the Priestly writer. But cf. now the second edition of Zimmerli (1976), 159-61.

2. *I and II Chronicles, Ezra, Nehemiah* (London, 1973).

work as such,[1] or concerned with wider questions of exegesis in which the Chronicler's handling of particular sections serves to illuminate the problems of handling the material of the books of Kings and of prophetic writings.[2] The result has been the confirming of the impression that these writings must be given due weight both in the assessment of Old Testament theology and in the appreciation of the politico-religious development of the post-exilic community, which has also been given less attention in scholarly study than it deserves.

Interest in this later period is growing, not least in modern Israeli circles and among archaeologists for whom the Persian period has often appeared to offer only marginal concern. The change has also shown itself both in an increasing number of articles devoted to the material in these books, and also in a number of important monographs and other studies.[3] The fuller investigation of this whole area reveals how many unsolved problems there are; and we may note one of the particular problems of study in the field of the Chronicler. What is written tends often to be specific either to a small area or to a particular problem and may thus only with difficulty approach the major questions of interpretation. Or it may tend to generalization and a resulting over-simplification, which I know to be the risk of writing a relatively short and limited commentary on so large a work, and which is certainly a risk in this present short study. Awareness of the limitations of the present study is an important qualification to what is to be said. It may nevertheless serve to offer some comments in this context which may open up elements in the whole theme with which this Colloquium is concerned. At the same time, I hope it may provide some comment on a question which has been thought by many scholars to have been given a definitive answer by W. Rudolph, namely the supposition that the

1. See Ackroyd 1967, 1970a, 1973b, 1977a, repr. as Chapters 10, 1, 11 and 13 (respectively) in the present volume.

2. Ackroyd 1968b, 1974, repr. as chs. 8, 9 in Ackroyd 1987b.

3. A new bibliography of Chronicles, Ezra, Nehemiah, to be published by the Pontifical Biblical Institute, Rome, is being compiled by Kent H. Richards of Denver. Among recent important works, to which reference will be made, are Willi 1972; Mosis 1973; Welten 1973; In der Smitten 1973.

Chronicler has no outlook to the future. It is very substantially questioned by Mosis, but there are many who continue to stress this so-called 'non-eschatological' character of the Chronicler's writings.[1]

Any discussion of the Chronicler's writings must inevitably be prefaced by some consideration of the literary problems. These may be limited here to two points in relation to the Ezra material. First, it must be recognized that whatever the precise nature of the historical sequence, the Nehemiah and Ezra narratives are originally quite separate and their dovetailing is the result of a later operation. Whether this was done by the Chronicler (so most recently In der Smitten) or subsequently (as I am inclined to believe), we must consider the two figures initially in their separate functioning. One difficulty here is in the precise defining of the Ezra material; clearly this appears in Ezra 7–10, clearly too in Nehemiah 8. Nehemiah 9 is most probably part of the same presentation; Nehemiah 10 remains uncertain, though it appears to me to be more probably an originally Ezra section than to belong to Nehemiah as it has now in part been ordered. Second, it must be clear that the presentation of Ezra is complex. Whatever the precise nature of Ezra's mission, we now read this through the Chronicler's eyes. If it is adjudged that there is more than one stage in the Chronicler's presentation, the position becomes even more complex.

I propose to develop the discussion in three themes: 1. the 'Exodus'; 2. the lawgiver; 3. the land.

1. *The 'Exodus' theme in Ezra*

Klaus Koch (1974) sees in the basic Ezra material ways in which he believes Ezra himself envisaged his function in relation to the Exodus. He describes the march to Jerusalem as a cultic procession, a second Exodus as fulfilment of prophetic expectation. He sees allusions in points of detail: in the dating of

---

1. This applies, for example, to a new work: *The Dawn of Apocalyptic* by Paul D. Hanson, to be published shortly by Fortress Press, Philadelphia, of which I have been able to see a typescript and to which I make this brief reference by kind permission of the author. (Now published: cf. Hanson 1975.)

the return on New Year's day (7.9, cf. Exod. 12 which dates the Exodus in the first month);[1] in the insistence on the presence of Levites (8.15ff., cf. Num. 10.13ff., cf. also 1 Chron. 13.15); in the theme of the temple vessels (8.24ff., cf. Isa. 52), and that of protection on the journey. We may then compare the activities of Ezra on his arrival with the first occupation of the land.

It is clear to me, as it is to Koch, that underlying the present form of the Ezra material there are sources[2] and that these have been woven into a now complex structure by the Chronicler. In particular, I am of the opinion that there is, in Ezra 10 and Nehemiah 9, material not originally concerned with Ezra, but similar in purport, suggesting that Ezra's was not the only attempt at reform in this general period (and indeed Neh. 13 provides another parallel).[3] I am therefore more inclined to see the presentation of Ezra's work in Exodus terms as due to the Chronicler himself, and thus as shedding light on the latter's outlook. For him, the moment of Ezra was yet one more stage towards the re-establishment of his people, and as such stands in parallel with earlier moments, particularly that described in Ezra 1, where, equally in dependence on the idea of fulfilment of prophecy (and closely linked to 2 Chron. 36 which lays the foundation for the sequel)[4] we may see clear analogies drawn (especially the 'spoiling of the Egyptians'). We may, indeed, go further than this, for one of the evident patterns of the Chronicler's work is that of a moment of revival, of restoration, out of a moment of judgment, of distress. I have ventured to call this an 'exile and restoration' pattern;[5] it is set out initially at 1 Chronicles 9; subsequently in

1. Koch notes some of the dating problems here. The chronology of Exod. 12 is by no means clear, but 12.2 insists that whatever the precise dating of the Exodus itself, closely linked to Passover dating, the moment marks not only the beginning of a new year, but the beginning of a new era. U. Cassuto (1967: 137) paraphrases: 'You are now beginning to count a new year; now the new year will bring you a change of destiny.'
2. See now the analysis of W.T. In der Smitten (1973).
3. Cf. my commentary (Ackroyd 1973a: 257, 299-300, 313-14); also Chapter 1 above, 46-47, 57-58.
4. Cf. Mosis 1973: 211; cf. also Vogt 1966, esp. 46, 157ff.
5. Cf. Chapter 11, section 2, above.

the Saul opening to the David narratives (1 Chron. 10),[1] and, as Mosis has shown, the pattern recurs in the subsequent narratives. In this, the material of 2 Chronicles 36–Ezra 1 and that of Ezra 7 may be seen to follow as further and more elaborate examples. In the light of the Exodus themes here used, it may be proper to see the Chronicler working also from the prophecies of Deutero-Isaiah, where the second Exodus theme is employed, as interpreting the disaster of exile as comparable with the distress of Israel in Egypt, following a line suggested by the revision of the covenant formula in Jeremiah 16 and 23, so that deliverance from Egypt is now replaced by deliverance and gathering from the north country, or from all the lands.[2] In this way, the Chronicler, who appears to make no use of the Exodus theme as such, bypassing that moment in his presentation, in fact uses the theme as part of an overall pattern.

It is significant for our present discussion that this is so. It underlines the continuity of theological presentation in the Chronicler with what precedes. We must recognize that, even without direct use of the narratives, the Chronicler is basically concerned to reiterate the older theological theme. For him, God is the God who delivers out of distress. His view of the distress is more fully coloured by the experiences of the exilic age and after, and there is therefore a deeper apprehension of the deliverance as being from a disaster brought upon the community by its own failure. In this he is taking further the Deuteronomic theology with its recognition of the rightness of the judgment of exile, and the prospect of a future which is tied in with the acceptance of that judgment, and indeed he provides a link with that type of thought (found in later rabbinic writings but adumbrated in the OT) in which Egypt is not simply a place of sojourn and oppression, but of evil and idolatry.

By way of underlining this point, the sequel to the coming of Ezra in Ezra 9–10 concentrates on the theme of the people and its condition. This has been anticipated in one of the themes of the opening section of the Ezra narrative (the need

---

1. Cf. Chapter 13 below; Mosis 1973: 17-43.
2. Cf. Ackroyd 1968a: 238-39 (see also Chapter 9 above).

for Levites), and suggest that the Exodus theme is here being developed along with the theme of divine protection in the wilderness. In Ezra 8.21ff. we have what has always appeared as a slightly odd incident, Ezra's embarrassment over the question of military protection for the journey. I suggest that this represents a deliberate recalling of the themes of the wilderness narrative. On the one hand, the theme is of divine protection, typified there by the pillar of cloud by day and of fire by night; it is a repeated emphasis of the wilderness narratives as now presented that there was such continuous protection. On the other hand, there is the theme of lack of faith, which results in the people's desire to return to Egypt, their fear at the pursuing Egyptians, the disobedience of even their leaders at various moments.[1] Here Ezra is depicted, almost with humour, as the leader who has proclaimed his absolute faith, but who secretly doubts the power and protection of God.[2] The significance of the incident is underlined by the poetic quotation of 8.23 (not recognized as poetry in the majority of translations and editions):

> The hand of our God is for blessing upon all who seek him,
> but his might and his anger are against those who forsake
> him.

Obedience and faith bring divine blessing; the forsaking of the divine will brings disaster.

It is this theme that is then further developed in the consideration of the community's condition in Ezra 9–10. We may observe here that the foreign marriage issue is one which is handled with very full dependence upon Deuteronomic teaching, in the list of the nations in 9.1 and in the often markedly Deuteronomic language of the 'prayer of Ezra' (cf. Steck 1967: 64ff.), while at the same time the stress on purity and on pollution of the land strongly suggests links also with the Priestly teaching (cf. Myers 1965: 73; Rudolph 1949; 93;

---

1. Cf. Coats 1968: 70, 78, though this point is not specifically handled. Cf. also Tunyogi 1969: esp. 115-16 and n. 14.
2. Koch (1974) speaks of Ezra's 'determined refusal of any official military guard' and contrasts this with the attitude of Nehemiah. But the two appear to be entirely unrelated, and Ezra's embarrassment—*bô'štî*—seems to mark anything but a determined refusal.

Koch 1974). The prayer is, as In der Smitten emphasizes (1973: 26), an instruction in the guise of a prayer, concerned to point out the threats to the *p‡lēṭāh*, the surviving community, as a result of the mixed marriages which threaten to put the community in the same situation as the nations which defiled the land into which God brought his people (a theme closely linked to Lev. 18.24f. and cf. Ezek. 36.17 where it is also applied to Israel).

Thus the theme of Exodus and wilderness is taken a stage further with a pointer to the occupation of the land. Before there can be a full establishment of the new community, there must be an abandonment of the mixed marriages which corrupt religious life, lest the land be again defiled. It is one of the first clear pointers to the hazards of the situation in which the people of God finds itself, and a corrective to the too easy supposition (repeated in this context by In der Smitten) that the Chronicler sees 'eschatological expectations of the pre-exilic prophets...realized and fulfilled in the post-exilic Jerusalem religious community'. In der Smitten in fact, underlining this, nevertheless goes on to recognize the threat to this 'state of salvation, this time of fulfilment'. But he supposes the Chronicler to see here an insoluble problem, regarding the question: 'Now...what are we to say after this?' (9.10) as having a somewhat hopeless tone. 'The situation of a salvation already present but not yet visibile, remains for the Chronicler an unresolved problem' (In der Smitten 1973: 27-28). But there is something more to be said than this (cf. below).

2. *The Lawgiver*

It follows naturally from the preceding discussion that we should find Ezra as the giver, the new giver, of the law, in Nehemiah 8, which is the true sequel to the narratives of Ezra 7–10 (as it stands in fact in 1 Esdras). It is clear that for the Chronicler there is a parallel between the lawgiving and renewal of covenant of Nehemiah 8–10 and that to be found in the Josiah narratives in 2 Chronicles 34–35. And we may note the significance of the fact that now that the monarchy has ceased to exist, the law-giving is directly associated with a priestly figure. Klaus Koch (1974) has emphasized the

significance of the priestly genealogy of Ezra in Ezra 7.1ff. and
in particular the directness of the link which is made there
with Seraiah the last chief-priest before the exile. Ezra is thus
declared to be the true successor to the pre-exilic line. He takes
over the function of the pre-exilic king in the giving of law. He
is for the Chronicler the successor to both the ancient figures
of Moses and of Aaron.

This point is made clearer if we observe the way in which
the Chronicler establishes his cross-references to the past.
There are various types of linkage made. The correspondence
between David and Moses is stressed at the bringing up of the
Ark (1 Chron. 15.15; David decrees [15.2] what Moses had
decreed); in the ordering of the temple and its staff (cf. 1
Chron. 9.17ff.; 21.29–22.1); and a correspondence between
David and Aaron is noted in the ordering of the priesthood
(24.19). A chiastic arrangement of correspondence has been
noted by Pohlmann (1970: 148; cf. Mosis 1973: 218-19), so that
Hezekiah is compared to Solomon (2 Chron. 30.26); Josiah to
Samuel (35.18); and Ezra to Joshua (Neh. 8.17). Thus the
moment of Ezra's giving of the law is linked to the successor to
Moses, the Tabernacles celebration of Nehemiah 8 corresponding to the Passover observed by Joshua (Josh. 5.10-12)
and it may this be said to represent a carrying through of the
injunctions of Moses to Joshua that the law should be put into
effect (Deut. 32.45-47; Josh. 1.7-9). It is significant for the next
part of our discussion that this correspondence with Joshua is
made.

Such a portrayal of Ezra certainly does not correspond precisely with what appears in the authorization given to him by
Artaxerxes (Ezra 7.12-26). That edict has its political context[1]
and it is proper to recognize that the Chronicler's portrayal of
Ezra has shifted the emphasis from the more purely political
to the religious, to the reenactment of Exodus, lawgiving and
beyond. Both K. Koch and recently W.T. In der Smitten have
stressed the degree of development in the picture of Ezra in
the writings of the Chronicler, a feature which in fact is also of
significance in the consideration of the relationship between

---

1. Cf. e.g. In der Smitten 1973: 110ff.; cf. also Ackroyd 1970a: 11ff.,
33ff. (= Chapter 1, 13ff., 46ff., present volume).

his presentation of the post-exilic period and his presentation of the pre-exilic. In both we may observe the same very radical reshaping of his sources to serve the particular purposes of his work. It is in such a development that we may observe what the Chronicler is concerned to say. For him the moment of Ezra is that of the reacceptance of the law, newly given and newly interpreted; and, in the context of the Artaxerxes decree which enjoins the uniting of the whole community in terms of the law, it is evident that this involves a reconstituting of the people of God.

In making use of the Artaxerxes material, the Chronicler only partly related it to the reading of the law by Ezra. The separation between the narratives is brought about partly by the journey description, but more by the placing of the foreign marriage action before the law-giving, in spite of some indications within the material which may suggest that it ought to come later.[1] One effect of this is to loosen the link.

The king of Persia is depicted as acting under divine authority (so especially in Ezra 7.27-29). But we may observe that the Chronicler has so described the coming of Ezra as to subordinate the Persian ruler's action to the Ezra story as he now presents it. The coming of Ezra is introduced as a sequel loosely linked chronologically[2] to the rebuilding of the temple (7.1); the whole of 7.1-10 is concentrated on Ezra's position and his ordering, under God, of the journey to Jerusalem. The king has granted his requests—the point makes clear that in the Chronicler's view the initiative rested with Ezra,—and this was because God was operating in Ezra's favour (7.6). The decree itself authorizes and supports religious reorganization in Jerusalem, and unification of members of the whole people within the province 'Beyond the River'. The subsequent actions of Ezra make no reference to that broader action—

---

1. So e.g. Eissfeldt 1964: 743-44 (= ET, 1965: 547ff.); Rudolph 1955b: 85. For criticism of this view, cf. Pohlmann 1970: 129ff.

2. Note that 'the seventh year' (Ezra 7.7) of Artaxerxes follows on 'the sixth year' (6.15) of Darius. This may be due sinply to the chronological information available to the Chronicler; but one may suspect that he saw a theological link in the sequence of figures, and was less than interested in the order of Persian rulers (cf. the chronological oddities of Ezra 4).

perhaps it was in the event not possible thus to resolve the difficult problem of the politico-legal unity of a community which had its members scattered over the whole area in addition to the central concentration around Jerusalem.[1] But the Chronicler takes no account of this lack of coherence; for him the essential lies in the re-establishment of the rule of the law of Moses, now brought afresh to the community by Ezra. Klaus Koch rightly underlines the emphasis on all Israel in this aspect of the description of Ezra, and notes the preference for the number 12 in various contexts (cf. also Vogt 1966: 47ff.). It is clear that the Chronicler regarded Ezra's work as bringing about the re-establishment of the whole people of God, and in this his work may be seen to correspond to that of Hezekiah, though the Chronicler in describing that ruler's reforms, is compelled to recognize that, in spite of the collapse of the north, only a small number of the people from the northern tribes did in fact come to unite themselves with the true people of God at Jerusalem. The point is implicit rather than explicit in the Ezra narrative, a mark of the Chronicler's hesitations about the contemporary situation.

3. *The Land*

The linking of Ezra with Exodus themes and his portrayal as giver of the law point the way to the final stage of the description. The proper sequel should lie in the renewed occupation of the land, the re-establishment in its proper form of the people of God.

It has been observed that a close link exists in Old Testament usage between the specific term for a nation (*gōy*) and the ideas of king and kingdom (so in Gen. 17.6, 16; 35.11; 1 Kgs 18.10; Ps. 105.13; Isa. 60.12; Jer. 18.7 [9]; 27.8, and of particular interest for our present purpose Exod. 19.6: *mamleket kōhᵃnîm, ṭōy qādôsh*) and the further link between nation (*gōy*) and the idea of the land (Gen. 12.2; [46.3]; Exod. 33.13;

1. On the possible failure of Ezra, cf. In der Smitten 1973: 141ff., though his comments are much tied in with what appears to be an anachronistic consideration of the 'Samaritan' problem. This cannot be discussed here, but cf. the material in Coggins 1975.

Josh. 3.17; 4.1; 5.8; 10.13; Ezek. 37.22 including also the royal theme).[1] It is the second aspect of this that is developed in the prayer in Nehemiah 9.[2] We may observe the apparent playing down of the theme of monarchy, referred to here only in the context of the general condemnations of the earlier life of the community in the pre-exilic period, most plainly in 9.35 where the period of the monarchy, a period of prosperity and blessing in the land which God had given, is typified as one of great disobedience.

Seen in the light of what precedes, Nehemiah 9—which would seem, like the prayer in Ezra 9, to owe much to earlier material and may be an earlier poem updated by precise reference especially in the last two verses—makes the point that the culminating moment of the new age has not yet been reached. The community has its temple, but it does not possess the land in any true sense; there is a further stage to be passed before the full promise of God is again realized.

The whole emphasis of Nehemiah 9 is upon the land. Its choice to occupy this position in the Chronicler's work leads us on from the moment of the reading of the law to the consideration of the community's contemporary situation. The new people of God occupies the land—and the rehearsal of the past underlines the nature of the divine promise from the beginning: from Abraham, through the vicissitudes of history which emphasize the consistency of divine promise and the repeated human failure; the deliverance from Egypt and its counter-

---

1. Cf. Rost 1934, Speiser 1960, Cody 1964, May 1968; and cf. also the important comments by W.L. Moran (Moran 1962) arguing convincingly, that *mamlākā* means 'king, royality' (accepted by G. Fohrer [1964]); cf. also Cody 1973: 324: 'If Exod. 19.6 dates from this (i.e. the early post-exilic) period, the expression *mamleket kōhănîm* in that text refers to the fact that the ruling power in the restored community was vested in the hands of priests.' Moran had argued for such a date; Fohrer, much less convincingly, for the late pre-exilic period. If we see this in the light of the comments here on Ezra, we may observe that such a political organization was not necessarily universally acceptable in the post-exilic community.

2. Cf. the paper by M. Gilbert, S.J., 'Comparaison entre les confessions des péchés de Néhémie 9 et Daniel 3 Théod.', read to the Oxford Biblical Congress, September 1973, for a number of valuable observations on this passage.

part in the bringing to the land, which is belied by the faith-lessness of Israel in its desire to return to Egypt (9.17); the blessings of protection in the wilderness which contrast with the refusal of Israel to enter the land (9.15f.); the giving of the land which was followed by rebellion, particularly in disobedi-ence to the law and in the killing of the prophets (cf. Steck 1967, esp. 65ff.); the repeated deliverance, and failure, and the ultimate disaster after many years of divine patience. It is a rehearsal which may be read now as if it were a summary of the reiterated sermons which the Chronicler offers by way of exposition of the whole period of the monarchy.[1] The conclud-ing verses summarize the theme: vv. 32-35 reiterate the theme of disobedience, underlining the theme of divine justice and faithfulness; and in the context of this confession, a con-fession of sin and a confession of faith, vv. 36-37 simply set out the current distress of the community: they are slaves in the land of divine promise, and its produce goes to the kings whom God has set over his people in their sins. They themselves in their own persons, and their cattle are at the free disposal of the rulers. The final word is of 'the great distress in which we are'.[2]

Much has been made by commentators of the discrepancy between this negative view of the Persian rulers and the posi-tive appraisal which we find elsewhere in the Chronicler. Yet we may question whether such a contrast is not fully intelligi-ble. The Chronicler here inherits the thought of earlier prophecy and sees the foreign power in two contrasting ways. Persia is, at one and the same time, the agent of the divine will, and also the evil, alien world, hostile to God and itself under judgment. As the Chronicler presents the restoration of Israel after the exile, he inherits the thought of Deutero-Isaiah in his understanding of Cyrus as the first agent of restoration, bringing about the first return and the initial stage of rebuild-ing. He subsequently sees Darius as the fulfiller of this promise; under the controlling divine hand, Darius is brought to sup-

1. Cf. my commentary (Ackroyd 1973a); and comments by R. Mosis (1973).
2. Isa. 62.8-9 offers a counter to such a position of distress, though we may not suppose any direct connection. There are no verbal links; the similarities lie in the thought.

port the rebuilding of the temple, and this, in the present chronologically disordered form of the text in Ezra 4–6, is set in contrast to the endeavours of opponents to bring about frustration and delay (so Ezra 4.8-24 and the opening of Ezra 5). The framework for the work of Ezra in 7.1-10 stresses, as we have noted, the action of Ezra which, because of the divine overruling of events, is totally accepted by the Persian ruler. The prayer of Ezra in 9.6-15 makes the same point, and provides a fitting counterpart to the prayer in Nehemiah 9. The repeated guilt of the community—exemplified in foreign marriages and religious contamination—has resulted in judgment and humiliation (Ezra 9.7), and 'such is the position of humiliation and shame even today'. Verses 8-9 stress the graciousness of God who has retained survivors for himself. 'Though we are slaves (i.e. under foreign rule), God has not forsaken us in our slavery.' The divine will has made the Persian rulers benevolent towards the rebuilding of the temple. The remainder of the prayer in Ezra 9 concentrates on the problem of the present situation, the risk of the loss yet again of the land which was lost to its previous inhabitants by reason of their abominable practices (cf. also Vogt 1966: 28ff.).

It is too easily overlooked that in this prayer the themes of divine protection through the agency of the alien rulers and of slavery under these rulers run together. Isaiah could describe Assyria as the rod of God's anger and also see her as under judgment (so Isa. 10); Jeremiah and Ezekiel could recognize the Babylonian ruler Nebuchadnezzar as the instrument of divine judgment, and yet at the same time recognize judgment upon Babylon (in the Jeremiah tradition, as in Jer. 25 and 50–51) or feel anguish at the disaster so brought about by alien power (so Ezekiel). So too the Chronicler is able to see in Persian rulers the agents of restoration, but also to recognize that the situation is one of distress. It is a theme which finds echoes in his narratives of the monarchy period too, when alien forces may be understood in judgment terms, and when it is even possible for the divine word to be mediated through Pharaoh Mecho to Josiah. The same point is brought out in the parallel prayer in Nehemiah 9.

It is in this passage that we may see the clearest evidence of the Chronicler's hesitations about the contemporary situation.[1] K.F. Pohlmann, building particularly upon the work of Rudolph in this respect, sees the conclusion of the Chronicler's work in the rejoicing of the festival of Nehemiah 8. 'We can hardly imagine (he writes) a better conclusion for this work, concerned as it is for the legitimation of the Jerusalem cult-community as the successor to that of ancient Israel' (Pohlmann 1970: 146). Perhaps not, provided we accept the supposition that the Chronicler sees in his contemporary community the fulfilment of the hopes of the past, a point strongly emphasized by W. Rudolph in his commentaries[2] and taken up by subsequent writers.[3]

It is to the credit of Mosis to have opened up a questioning of this too simple conclusion.[4] Not that W. Rudolph is entirely wrong, for the post-exilic community was deeply concerned about its continuity with what preceded it; the problem of bridging the gulf of the exilic period is a real one (Ackroyd 1972 [= Ackroyd 1987b, ch. 4]). To the Chronicler, the stress upon the ideal establishment of the Davidic and Solomonic period makes sense when we see his belief that the rebuilding

1. It is to these negative points that M. Noth (1957: 179-80) attaches his brief statement about the Chronicler's 'open question regarding the future', and links it to the continuing existence of a Davidic hope. That such a hope existed in the post-exilic period is not in doubt, but that the Chronicler shared it appears much less clear. Noth finds confirmation in the modified ending to the Solomonic prayer in 2 Chron. 6.40, 42, with its verbal allusions to Ps. 132.9f. and Isa. 55.3. (On this, cf. Ackroyd 1973a: 113-14.) But the stress in this passage is on the temple, and the parallel of *māšîaḥ* and David suggests an equating of priestly and royal figures. The absence of any Davidic element in the narratives of the post-exilic period—Sheshbazzar was not of Davidic descent (cf. P.R. Berger in *ZAW* 83 [1971], pp. 98-100), the Davidic descent of Zerubbabel is slurred over (contrast the mere naming of his father Shealtiel in Ezra 3.2 with the significant genealogy of Ezra in 7.1-5, and the relatively subordinate place given to Zerubbabel in the narrative), there is a member of the Davidic family mentioned in the list in 8.3, placed after the two priestly families—strongly suggests that for the Chronicler the true successor to the Davidic monarch was to be found in temple and priesthood.

2. See Rudolph 1955a: xxiv; Rudolph 1955b: xxx; also Rudolph 1954: 409.

3. So. e.g. Plöger 1968: 41-42; Steck 1968; Willi 1972; so also Hanson 1975.

4. Cf. esp. Mosis 1973: 226-27. So also Koch (1974).

of the temple after the exile and the centring of the community around this represents the re-embodiment of that earlier moment. But it is not yet the final age in its fulness. R. Mosis argues this in a relatively brief survey at the end of his study where he deals, quite clearly too sketchily, with the period of restoration. Accepting the supposition of K.E. Pohlmann (whose work he discusses and criticizes in some detail: cf. Mosis 1973: 215-20), that the Chronicler's work ends at Nehemiah 8, he nevertheless underlines the 'temporary' quality of the post-exilic temple, arguing that it does not yet mark the final age.[1] He sees rightly that the prayer in Ezra 9 (6-15, esp. vv. 8f.) describes the present situation as one of the continuing distress, with the rebuilding of the temple as a moment of relief, and rightly refutes the contention[2] that because the prayer points to a sense of unease, it must belong to some other interpretation of the post-exilic period than that offered by the Chronicler. He fails to see that the sequel to the moment of the reading of the law in Nehemiah 8 reaches its climax in an indication of the tentative and precarious nature of the situation in which the community is living. It is evident that the end is not yet.

Now this final hesitation may be interpreted in various ways. I have earlier quoted the view of W.T. In der Smitten to the effect that the Chronicler's question in Ezra 9.10, 'What should we say after all this?', has a somewhat forlorn quality. 'The situation of a salvation already present but not yet visible remains for the Chronicler an unresolved problem.'[3] He adds to this a footnote to the effect that the New Testament, and in particular Paul and the Johannine writings, was to be able to meet this hesitation (*Aporie*) with the dimension of faith

---

1. I think he offers a wrong interpretation of the 'weeping' of Ezra 3, failing to see that this is not a sign of distress that the new temple is not like the old, but rather part of an act of worship in which such ritual weeping is in place. To justify this view of the second temple, he quotes from Tobit to the effect that the new temple 'was not like the first' (Tob. 14.5). He might better have made use of the implicit negative view expressed in Zech. 4.8-9 and in Hag. 2.3. But a too simple correlation of Ezra 1–6 and the prophecies of Haggai and Zechariah is not satisfactory. Cf. Ackroyd 1968a: 138ff. (chs. IX–XI).

2. R. Mosis here quotes O.H. Steck (1968: 451).

3. See Part 1 above on In der Smitten (1973: 28).

(*pistis*). It is interesting to note how W.T. In der Smitten here provides a contrasting echo to the last words of W. Rudolph's summary; for where W.T. In der Smitten leaves the Chronicler in a state of indecision, unable to answer the radical problem of his time, W. Rudolph makes the Chronicler overconfident in the achievement of salvation, only to be proved wrong as 'the wheel of history' rolls onward (Rudolph 1955a: xxiv; Rudolph 1954: 409). Are we really in such a cleft stick? Is it not possible to recognize (as R. Mosis does in a footnote criticizing O.H. Steck), that while it is proper to see the Chronicler finding in the restored community after the exile the embodiment of the hopes of a day of salvation—it is the new age, and here the Chronicler owes much to the prophetic thought of Haggai and Zechariah, themselves heirs to that of Deutero- and Trito-Isaiah and Ezekiel—yet this has 'for the Chronicler only a temporary quality' (Mosis 1973: 228 n. 47). This temporary quality is nowhere more clearly expressed than in the sequel to the reading of the law. The temple is rebuilt; the new community gathers to hear and accept the law. But the status of people is denied to them, since, while they occupy the land, it is not theirs. They are slaves, and aliens take the produce of their land and dispose of them and their possessions.

The Chronicler has been thought to be non-political. He has been accused of complacency. In fact he goes much further than this. He makes his own political protest against the conditions imposed on the people of God, not yet enjoying its true status because of the alien occupation of the land. And if it is right, as I on the whole think most likely, that we should go on to read the essential part of Nehemiah 10—omitting the list in vv. 2-28—as the sequel to the prayer of distress, then the story of Ezra ends not in a word of distress and hesitation, but in a covenant renewal, a setting out of certain basic acts of obedience, culminating in the recognition that at the very centre of the community's life (so 10.40) there must be the worship of the temple. It is the application to the realities of the post-exilic situation of the teaching of the great exilic prophets. Restoration involves both a renewal of the promise and gift of the land (a theme which so deeply underlies the Deuteronomic presentation: Diepold 1972); it involves the re-establishment of the temple at Jerusalem as the centre of the people's life (so Haggai and Zechariah), with which there goes, as the Chronicler's narrative exemplifies it, the recognition that possession of the temple does not of itself guarantee the divine presence and blessing (so Hag. 2.10-14, and cf. also the critique in Isa. 66.1f.). It is a token of his willingness to be present and to bless. The tension of divine presence and temple building has not been fully resolved.

The theme of this chapter is: *God and People in the Chronicler's presentation of Ezra.* When I was asked for a title, I chose this rather than *The Idea of God* because it appears to me impossible to effect a satisfactory separation between the Chronicler's understanding of the nature and action of God and his understanding of the people. Throughout his writings, we look in vain for a coherently worded theological statement, though there are many points at which his understanding of God stands out, particularly in prayer and confession passages, which are so characteristic a part of his exposition. But for the most part, what concerns him is the way in which in particular situations there is an interaction between humanity and God, between people's response or failure to respond and the divine action in judgment and in deliverance. Out of the narratives of the kings he has made a series of expositions. It may be that in doing so he has less of a sense of history than his predecessors, but he has more of a sense of the ways in which the older traditions may be understood as exemplary.[1] The result is that his portrayals of the kings of Judah, while they have a certain sameness about them, nevertheless illustrate a variety of shades of human behaviour and its consequences. In the final part of the work—and we may rightly expect that it is here that we may see the writer's full intention—he portrays a reenactment of earlier experience, in which there is an integration of a variety of ideas. Restoration belongs to the God who is known best in his action towards his people in the Exodus events; the influence of the exile as a moment of judgment has made of Egypt a symbol of the place from which Israel is to be delivered as from a distress which is bound up in her own failure. (The supreme height of faithless-

1. Cf. Guthrie 1966 and comments by E. Jacob (1975: 112).

ness is in Neh. 9 the moment of choosing a leader to return to Egypt.) We may see in this understanding of Exodus and exile the influence of both D and P, as well as that of the exilic prophets and particularly Deutero-Isaiah and Ezekiel. There is much to be said for viewing the Chronicler as representing a harmonizing and development of a variety of theological trends.[1] In the sequel to restoration in the work of Ezra, we may find a further echo of this Exodus theme, linked both to the protection ideas of the wilderness and to the giving of the law. The law, which the Artaxerxes rescript regards as providing a basis for unifying the adherents of the people in the whole province, is here seen as an expression of divine promise and warning for the people of God. The acceptance of the law prompts the reminder that the true people occupies the land divinely given—again a theme of both D and P. The pointer to the future lies in the confidence of divine action set over against the present distresses of a community which does not properly own its own land.

Like his successors in the later Old Testament writings and in the intertestamental and New Testament works, the Chronicler is concerned with a basic problem of religious thought, that of the relationship between divine promise, understood in the context of the older traditions, and the realities of the contemporary situation. He is concerned at one and the same time with giving reassurance to his own people that they are truly the people of God, the inheritors of the promises of the past, and with pointing to the reality of that God who, just as he has acted in the past, will meet the present situation which belies their true status. In this concern for the people's identity, we may detect a link—one of the links—to the association of Ezra with the formation of the canon, 'the community rule'.

Like others before and after, the Chronicler is hesitant about the precise nature of the future. The Priestly writers leave open the question of the actual possession of the land, paving the way for it and laying down the mechanisms of obedience

---

1. Ackroyd 1967 (= Chapter 11 above).

and purity, but not describing the actual conquest.[1] The Deuteronomic writers see the reality of the past in the actual possession of the land and its consequences, but leave open the question as to how and when a re-entry will become a reality. For the Chronicler, both these are now in a measure part of past experience, for there has been a kind of re-entry into the land ('a token of renewal': Koch 1974), and there is a recognition of the degree to which obedience and purity are both achieved and not achieved. For him, the full reality lies ahead, and his confidence in that reality is expressed in his picture of the ideal age of David and Solomon, in his warnings of the ways in which rulers and people may go astray, in his consciousness of contemporary failure and of contemporary distress over against the reality of God. His successors—and here I would see the apocalyptic writers as being in a real sense in this succession (so too Welton 1973: 206)—are equally conscious of the contemporary situation as disastrous, of the reality of faith and obedience even in such a situation, confident that there is to be a future of divine deliverance, but equally hesitant when it comes to setting down the full nature of that moment to come. The sources of their thought are wider, not least because they make a different use of prophetic teaching. But they are not unrelated.

The God of the Chronicler is a God of past and of future; the assurance of his hopes rests in his knowledge of what Israel's story tells. But he is equally a God who makes himself known to the contemporary community in judgment and in hope, for it is this community which is, in however incomplete a manner, the people of God.

---

1. Plöger (1968: 40) offers too simplified a statement of the Priestly writing's aims.

Chapter 13

THE CHRONICLER AS EXEGETE[1]

The theme of this paper arose from repeated study of the writings of the Chronicler during the past few years, both in preparation for lectures on *The Age of the Chronicler*[2] and for a short commentary on *I and II Chronicles, Ezra, Nehemiah* (Ackroyd 1973a).[3] The rehandling of earlier material by the Chronicler, the relationship between him and his sources, the purpose or purposes for which this work was written, the nature of the readership or of the hearers, the strongly homiletical features of the work[4]—all these features raise the question of exegesis, of the Chronicler as exegete.

1. Reprinted from the author's article in *Journal for the Study of the Old Testament* 2 (1977): 2-32.
2. The Selwyn Lectures, 1970 (published as Ackroyd 1970 and reprinted in Chapter 1 above).
3. Torch Bible Commentary (London: SCM, 1973).
4. Reference may be made here to the study by M.D. Goulder, *Midrash and Lection in Matthew* (1974). The author kindly discussed with me an earlier form of some of his material on the Chronicler, as this was given in his Speaker's Lectures in Oxford (cf. Ackroyd 1970: 45). I saw and briefly discussed with him a chapter originally entitled 'The Development of the Histories Cycle', the essential of which now appears as ch. 10, 'The Chronicler and the Jewish New Year'. Here he argues for a liturgical origin of the structures to be found in the Pentateuch and the books of the so-called 'Deuteronomic History'. He views the writings of the Chronicler as representing a further extension of this liturgical process, and raises points which are of great interest both for the consideration of the nature and arrangement of these various works, and also for the possibility that lectionary cross-references may help in the explanation of modifications and allusions to be found in the Chronicler's writings. The questions raised are important, and must in due course be adequately discussed. They suggest alternative lines of approach to a number of points which are considered in this present discussion.

The intention to read the paper was underlined by the appearance, in the latter part of 1972, of an important study which contributes much to the whole area of discussion. This is the monograph by Thomas Willi, whose title *Die Chronik als Auslegung*[1] indicates its relevance to the present study. It was only after the acceptance of the paper for the Congress that a further substantial study appeared which had also to be taken into account. This is Rudolf Mosis, *Untersuchungen zur Theologie des chronistischen Geschichtswerkes* (1973), a discussion with which I find myself closely in sympathy since it presents a view of the Chronicler as theologian akin to that which I have sought to maintain in various articles as well as in my commentary, and since it also appreciates what had become very apparent to me, namely that there is a marked degree of patterning and stylizing in the Chronicler's writings which needs to be carefully appreciated.[2]

In view of the two major studies already mentioned, in which some themes which must properly be the concern of this paper are very fully developed in sharply divergent fashion, it may well seem an impertinence for me to offer such a brief contribution to so importnat and controversial a subject. It has therefore seemed proper to attempt no wide-ranging discussion and to make only very brief and tentative concluding comments. The subject, for all the space now devoted to it

1. Subtitled *Untersuchungen zur literarischen Gestaltung der historischen Überlieferung Israels* (Willi 1972). The monograph was originally a dissertation submitted at Tübingen in 1969 (cf. *TLZ* 97 [1972]: 236-37).
2. Mosis could not have made use of my commentary since this appeared only shortly before his own book. He makes no reference to my earlier studies, e.g. *The Age of the Chronicler* noted above, or my 'History and Theology in the Writings of the Chronicler' (1967; see Chapter 10 of the present volume), or the relevant section of *Israel under Babylon and Persia* (1970: 294-305); nor does he know R. Braun, 'The Message of Chronicles: Rally Round the Temple' based on his dissertation *The Significance of 1 Chronicles 22, 28 and 29 for the Structure and Theology of the Work of the Chronicler* (1971) in which much attention is given to the place of Solomon in the Chronicler's presentation. Cf. also his 'Solomonic Apologetic in Chronicles', *JBL* 92 (1973), pp. 503-16. Some further points to which some reference is made in the conclusion to this paper, are to be found in my 'The Theology of the Chronicler' (Ackroyd 1973 [= Chapter 11, present volume]).

in these recent studies, is by no means fully covered, and some parts of the works concerned with it are in reality concerned with much wider and important problems of intrepretation of biblical literature in the post-exilic period. What I propose to do here is to offer some comments on three passages in the Chronicler's work, by way of inviting attention to some aspects of his method and from this, not to generalize about either method or purpose, but simply to note a few pointers which will need fuller investigation.[1]

1. *Saul (1 Chronicles 10)*

It has for long been felt to be a curiosity in the Chronicler's presentation that one chapter is devoted to Saul, since it is so evident that his primary interest lies in David and the true royal dynasty which stems from him. It is not therefore surprising that it has sometimes been suggested that the passage is an insertion, though, quite apart from other difficulties, this suggestion faces the virtually insuperable one that it is not possible to see why, granted the overall outlook of the work, any later editor should have added something so apparently out of step.[2]

More appropriate are the endeavours to see a relationship between the placing of the Saul narrative and what follows,

1. Much has inevitably to be assumed for such a short discussion. I would still hold, in spite of the arguments of Willi and others, that the work—Chronicles–Ezra–Nehemiah—is to be treated as a whole, as Mosis does. I regard the Nehemiah narrative as essentially separate, as has now become a much more generally held view (cf. Mosis 1973: 215ff., in his comments on K.-F. Pohlmann, *Studien zum dritten Esra* [1970], a work curiously not mentioned by Willi). Furthermore, while it is clear that the original work—if indeed such a term is entirely appropriate—has been added to, I am both doubtful of the degree to which certainty can be established in regard to additions, and also doubtful of the supposition that the additions have radically altered the trend of the work (cf. Willi 1972: 203 and n. 58). The one exception which I would tentatively make in this is the degree to which the Nehemiah material has caused a shift in emphasis to a more exclusive way of thought, though here it is less the case that the work has in itself been altered and more that it has been interpreted in the light of this more exclusive line.
2. For reference cf. Willi 1972: 9ff.; Mosis 1973: 17ff.

and these have generally been in terms of the contrast between the dark and the light.[1] In *The Age of the Chronicler*, I suggested that we may trace in the writings of the Chronicler a recurrence of what I described as the 'exile and restoration' theme. This is to be seen first in 1 Chron. 9.1, where the conclusion of the genealogies is set out in terms of the exiling of Judah for unfaithfulness (*ma'al*),[2] and this is followed by the list of returned exiles, closely related to that of Nehemiah 11. This theme is then picked up in ch. 10:

> The theme of restoration, of the rebuilding of Jerusalem and its temple, of the establishment in security of the people of God, is presented... in terms of contrast. It is out of the moment of disaster, the consequence of the unfaithfulness of Saul, that David is brought to the throne. It is, of course, the first true kingship; yet it was by transfer from the failed Saul. It is only at this moment that Jerusalem is occupied; but it is the occupation of the city which now shows that a new age has begun. Only now can the true and full life begin for the people, but it can nevertheless be pictured as restoration, since it is in a sense the rehabilitation of the true people.[3]

This interpretation, which goes beyond the understanding of the Saul narrative as merely a foil to the David material, is related to the recognition of this same pattern throughout the chapters which follow, right up to the end of the narrative in the story of Ezra (and the Nehemiah narrative—rehabilitation out of disaster—may be seen to be related in style). What I suggested in rather generalized terms is more fully developed by Mosis in his substantial chapter on the Saul narrative (1973: 17-43). The full argument is worth examination, but I shall here simply select the main lines and incorporate one or two additional points and critical comments. There are, I believe, a number of points where an attempt at explaining every detail of 1 Chronicles 10 in comparison with 1 Samuel 31 breaks down, and it is better in these to recognize either that the modifications are of no immediate significance or that

---

1. Cf. Boecker 1969: 62 for references and citations; and Mosis 1973: 20.
2. On this word, cf. below.
3. Ackroyd 1970: 48 (= Chapter 1, p. 68 above); cf. also Ackroyd 1973a: 49-51.

they derive from other considerations. The very full and sometimes over-elaborate analysis by Willi in his consideration of the types of modification serves to point to the very wide range of possibilities which exist, though his discussion all too often tends to bypass the question of what exactly was the text before the Chronicler.[1]

Mosis rightly emphasizes (1973: esp. 22), as others have done, that the story of the battle leads up to the total destruction of the house of Saul (v. 6). The occurrence of personages from Saul's family elsewhere (the genealogy 8.33-40 largely = 9.39-44, and the reference in 12.2) does not fundamentally affect this total judgment. It is ratified in the entire absence in the Chronicler of any material relevant to the succession to Saul and the long struggle of 2 Samuel 2–4, and similarly the absence of the Mephibosheth narratives of 2 Sam. 9; 16.1-4; 19.24-30; as well as in the exclusion from 1 Chronicles 15 of any reference to the barrenness of Michal which in 2 Samuel 6 is quite evidently tied in with the problem of the succession to David that forms so important an element in the succeeding chapters. We may observe too that the Chronicler, who does not use the narrative of 2 Sam. 21.1-14, may nevertheless be seen to take over its motif of total obliteration of the house of Saul (2 Sam. 21.5).

10.7 describes the flight of all Israel who are in the Valley and the occupation of their cities by the Philistines. This represents a modification of the geographical description given in 1 Sam. 31.7 which speaks of those in the Valley (of Jezreel) and in the Jordan valley.[2] Mosis argues (1973: 23) that the changes here, and the avoidance of other geographical

---

1. An example from Mosis (1973: 18-19) may suffice: he considers that the replacement in v. 1 of the participle niph. *nilḥᵃmîm* by the perfect niph. *nilḥāmû* is a deliberate change designed to suggest that whereas 1 Samuel points to a long-drawn-out struggle, the Chronicler sees the battle as a single moment. But this overlooks the possibility of a very simple textual variant, since the word is followed by the preposition *bᵉ* and *beth* and *mem* in the old script may be readily confused; it is quite reasonable to think that the two text forms are simple variants due to one scribe reading a *mem* at the end of the verbal form while another did not. The point is a minor one, but suggests the danger of trying to prove too much.

2. On the problems of the text, cf. e.g. Stoebe 1973: 521, 527ff.

identifications in the chapter[1] mean that the Chronicler saw here the flight of the whole people—i.e. a denudation of the land and its taking over entire by the enemy. It may be doubted if so much should be read into the verse. The Chronicler appears rather to preserve here some of the elements of the older story without modifying them essentially. The point which Mosis wishes to make comes out subsequently and he is straining the evidence to get what he believes to be a consistent witness to the Chronicler's intention. It is more probable that uncertainty as to the precise meaning of the geographical terms underlies the textual difference.

It is in fact in vv. 8-10 that some hints of this total disaster may be detected, and these are further elaborated in vv. 13-14. Caution must again be exercised, since it is by no means impossible that more than one version of the death of Saul and the fate of his corpse had been preserved, so that the differences between Samuel and Chronicles must not be overpressed. We may recall that there is an alternative version of the death of Saul preserved in 2 Samuel 1 which does not entirely accord with that in 1 Samuel 31. Mosis rightly observes that some of the changes in the Chronicles text remove any reference to Beth-Shean and locate the head of Saul and his weapons in Philistia itself. The reference to the temple of Ashtoreth which, from its sequel, points probably, though not certainly, to Beth-Shean, is replaced by a general reference to 'the temple of their god(s)'. I had myself supposed (Ackroyd 1973: 50) that this was because the mention of the name of the goddess was unacceptable, but this leaves the puzzling reference to Dagon. Mosis provides a better explanation. By substituting the general term 'god(s)', the Chronicler invites the reader simply to think of the normal Philistine deity, and in parallel with this, he places a reference to the 'temple of Dagon'. It is there that the head of Saul is hung up. Mosis suggests (1973: 24-25) that the Chronicler is here making use of the ark narrative of 1 Sam. 5.1-6 and suggest-

---

1. The omission of Beth-Shean in vv. 10 and 12; the survival of the title 'Mount Gilboa' he thinks may be set aside, suggesting that 'the name of the mountain is not intended to specify a geographical interest on the part of the Chronicler in the historically precise location of the battle' though he does not explain why this should be so.

ing a parallel between the taking of the ark and the overthrow of Dagon in his shrine (his head and hands broken off) and the defeat of Israel, powerless to resist the Philistines, symbolized by the presence of the head of Saul which is within the power of the alien. This might be termed a reversal of the ark theme. In 2 Samuel 5–6, Yahweh, symbolized by his ark, is the real power in the land of the enemy. By contrast here, Israel, symbolized by Saul's head, is impotent. It is certainly noteworthy that the 'head' motif does not appear in 1 Samuel 31. Suggestions that the phrase which appears in 1 Chronicles was to be found in the original 1 Samuel text—and now lost—are without firm foundation, though they are not so unlikely as Mosis supposes.[1] The decision on this point is not in fact important. It is more important to acknowledge that Mosis is right in seeing a possible allusion to the ark theme. I would add the Chronicler found it or which he created may also have been influenced by that of 1 Samuel 17 in which (v. 54) the head of the Philistine giant is said to have been taken to Jerusalem and, by implication, exposed in the shrine there. There is a neat contrasting parallel between David's killing and beheading of the giant, with its sequel in the flight of the Philistines and the 'dedication' of the head, and the death and beheading of Saul, the flight of Israel and the 'dedication' of his head. And there is here a link with a further point underlined by Mosis (1973: 25), namely that the narrative of Israel and the Philistines has already in 1 Samuel 4–6 moved from being historical to being typical. He quotes H.W. Hertzberg (1960: 39-40 = ET 1964: 52-53) as commenting that the Philistines appear 'not so much as political opponents, but as heathen ... Israel always regarded her differences with the Philistines,

1. If we suppose a text which has the suspending of Saul's head (ראה נללהו תקעו בית רנון) side by side with the suspending of his body (ואת נייהו תקעו הומת בית שן)—the order appears immaterial—we may observe two points: (1) the phrases are so alike that they may readily be understood as variants; (2) the Samuel and Chronicles MT forms have each only one of these phrases. In this case, we could not argue that the Chronicler introduced the reference to the temple of Dagon; but we may still appropriately argue that his understanding of the reference is, as Mosis suggests, related to his knowledge of and understanding of the story of the ark in 1 Sam. 5. On the textual problems, cf. Stoebe 1973: 522, Mosis 1973: 24 n. 22.

the 'uncircumcised', as being in the realm of sacral theology rather than politics... the compiler (is) governed not by political and military, but by theological interests'. This point is stressed in the late narrative of 1 Samuel 7, but it is not new there; it has been developed from the already stylized presentation of the Philistine-Israelite conflict in 1 Samuel 4–6 and the other narratives of 1 Samuel, not least that of ch. 17. The Chronicler may thus be seen rather as the developer of an already existing theological tradition than as an innovator in this respect. But the allusion to the ark which Mosis finds here fits well with the further use of it in 1 Chron. 13.3, which stresses that the ark was not sought (*drš*) in the time of Saul,[1] and the modification of 1 Chronicles 15 where Michal becomes a despiser of the ark (cf. Ackroyd 1973: 63) rather than a despiser of David's dancing and self-exposure. Thus even with the discounting of Mosis's less than satisfactory interpretation of v. 7, we may see the propriety of his understanding of vv. 8-10 as pointing to a total overthrow of Israel, a placing of them within the power of the alien, an apparent defeat of God. The degree of parallel to the exilic situation becomes clear.[2]

The detailed comment of the Chronicler on the reign of Saul and its significance comes in vv. 13-14.[3] The recognition that this points up the total rejection of Saul and his house is readily made. Here again Mosis, by a detailed analysis of the phrases used, makes the meaning of the passage clearer.

(1) He points to the wide use of the word *ma'al*,[4] reveals its use especially of religious unfaithfulness, and its particular links to conquest and exile themes.[5] This usage, common in the Chronciler's own writing, is also to be found particularly in Ezekiel, in Deuteronomy (cf. esp. Deut. 32.51-52), and in Neh.

---

1. On the use of *drš*, cf. below.

2. It also becomes evident that 1 Sam. 4–6 is an 'exile-restoration' passage. Cf. my comments in *The First Book of Samuel* (Ackroyd 1971b: 63) and 'An Interpretation of the Babylonian Exile: A study of 2 Kings 20, Isaiah 38–39' (Ackroyd 1974 = Ackroyd 1979a: 152-71).

3. On these verses cf. Willi 1972: 9-12, and esp. 169-70; Boecker 1969: 61-63; Mosis 1973: 28-41; Ackroyd 1973a: 50-51.

4. Cf. also references on Mosis 1973: 29-30 and in his notes.

5. E.g. 1 Chron. 9.1; cf. above.

1.8. Its use in the Ezra narrative (Ezra 9 and 10) in relation to the apostasy involved in foreign marriages is of particular interest in that it virtually equates unfitness for being in the land (so Deut. 32.51-52 of Moses and Aaron) with unfitness to be the true people of God.

(2) Saul fails to keep the word of Yahweh; this has been thought to refer to either 1 Samuel 13 or 1 Samuel 15, the two disobedience and condemnation narratives concerning Saul. Mosis considers it to be unlikely that the Chronicler left the matter thus open, and observes that the Targum here makes a reference both to the Amalekite war of 1 Samuel 15 and to the massacre of the priests of Nob in 1 Samuel 22. Mosis himself shows the close connections of the phrase *šāmar dᵉbar Yahweh* with Deuteronomy and with Psalm 119; he shows how it is linked with the possession of the land and the theme of 'rest' (*mᵉnûḥāh*); he observes how such failure is linked to conquest by aliens, as in the case of Rehoboam and Shishak. He refers to 2 Chron. 34.21 which speaks of there being only a remnant of Judah because of their not keeping the word of Yahweh. Thus a similar range of ideas comes into play at this point, suggestive of the themes of the land and its occupation, of exile and judgment. Mosis's criticism of the endeavour to find allusion to a particular Saul narrative in the wording used is reasonable. We may allow that the Chronicler's allusions are not necessarily to be narrowly limited. What these last verses of 1 Chronicles 10 in fact do is invite the reader to contemplate the whole Saul tradition—familiar in its already strongly negative form in 1 Samuel—and to see it in the light of the comments. The result—and here the Targum may be said to be not merely an endeavour to make precise what seems indefinite, but an aligning of narratives with the comment in a homiletic fashion—is that for the reader now familiar with the Chronicler's judgment, it becomes even more difficult than with only 1 Samuel available to see the more positive side of Saul's achievement. Saul becomes even more clearly the symbol of the disobedient.[1] I would myself wish to draw

---

1. Cf. my comment in the commentary (Ackroyd 1973a) on the Michal material in 1 Chron. 15.29: '...the members of the house of Saul show themselves unable to recognize the true meaning of events;

attention to the poetic fragment in 1 Sam. 15.22-23 which so neatly equates improper religious practice and apostasy (cf. Ackroyd 1971: 51), and hence suggests a closer link than Mosis allows between this second expression and the third.

(3) Saul is guilty of not seeking (*drš*) Yahweh. The wider use of this expression again points to the theme of apostasy and so to inevitable rejection. The denial that Saul ever sought Yahweh (Mosis 1973: 41) represents in effect a repudiation of the account in 1 Samuel 28 to which the last phrase of v. 13 alludes; Saul is in fact there described as having sought Yahweh in vain by every known legitimate mechanism (so v. 6), and only then turning to forbidden necromantic practice. In his exposition, Mosis repudiates the alternative suggested by Willi (1972: 170) that v. 13*b* is the kernel around which the condemnatory phrases have been exegetically grouped. I think he is right in this critical remark, but it would seem more probable that we should go further and suggest that this last clause of v. 13 is a gloss—the exegetical comment of a later scribe, who identifies the particular moment and thereby sustains the Chronicler's negative judgment and at the same time clarifies the relationship between alien religious practice and apostasy to which I have referred above. In fact we may observe that in doing this he makes explicit an explanation of Saul's name which is negative. This is brought out by Willi when he observes the use in this phrase of the key-words of 1 Samuel 28: *šā'al bᵉYhwh*, v. 6; *drš*, v. 7; *šā'al*, v. 16 (Willi 1972: 70). The phrase *wᵉgam lišᵉ'ôl bā'ôb* may be seen to contain both allusion and pun. Saul (*šā'ûl*) does not *šā'al* of Yahweh, but of a medium.

If we may see a relic in the Samuel birth story of a Saul tradition—not an equating, but a motif[1]—then we may see

they are typical of unfaith'. Cf. also my comment on Saul in the commentary on 1 Samuel (Ackroyd 1971b): 'He is both the divinely chosen leader, picked at the moment of crisis to bring deliverance and hope, and one in whom the demand for absolute obedience to the divine will is expressed, his doom being sealed in his failure...and example of that pattern of obedience and blessing, disobedience and doom which is written also into the book of Judges and the books of Kings.'

1. Cf. my commentary on 1 Samuel (Ackroyd 1971b: 25-26), on other aspects of word-play in 1 Sam. 1. The problem of the naming of Samuel

the possibility that a positive appraisal of Saul—was he not the one asked (*šā'ûl*) of Yahweh?—has been lost to him; there remains only a negative tradition[1], utilized in some measure in 1 Samuel 28 and taken further in the addition to 1 Chron. 10.13. The occurrence of *lidrôš* as an alternative to *liš°'ôl* may be seen as a linking of this theme with what follows, so that we might paraphrase 'he even inquired of a medium, inquired in the sense in which he did not inquire of Yahweh'.

Mosis's analysis of this passage and the final summary (Mosis 1973: 41-47) in which he notes how many of the allusions are to be found paralleled more fully in narratives concerning post-Solomonic rulers, suggests to him, and very properly, that the Saul narrative is used skilfully to present a pattern which is to be seen more fully exemplified in subsequent parts of the Chronicler's work. But there is one further aspect of the discussion which needs consideration. In a comment on the final clause of 10.14 'and he (Yaweh) turned over the kingdom to David, the son of Jesse', in the context of his discussing the inadequacy of regarding the Saul narrative as merely a dark foil to the brightness of the account of David, he writes '[This expression] does not prove, any more than do the other transition formulae at the end of the accounts of later kings, that what precedes is merely introduction to what follows and has no significance of its own' (Mosis 1973: 20). It must be clear that the use—and modification—of the transition formulae is part of the mechanism the Chronicler inherited from his predecessors. He utilizes them to show judgment or approval on what has been related. Equally it is clear that the use of such a formula cannot be said (as Mosis rightly argues) to reduce the significance of what precedes. But what he does not take into account is the particular nature of the transition formula here. At a later point (1973: 28), commenting on vv. 11-12, he notes that the only element of the tradition of the affection of the men of Jabesh-Gilead for Saul which the

is widely discussed in the Commentaries, but without there being any clear consensus of opinion (cf. e.g. Stoebe 1973: 92, 97-98).

1. Cf. Stoebe's comment (1973: 98): 'At the most we may consider whether there is expressed here a criticism of Saul's kingship, entirely possible at the time at which we may suppose this narrative (i.e. 1 Sam. 1.1-20) to have come into being'.

Chronicler uses is the one of his burial in Jabesh. David's approving comment in 2 Sam. 2.4-7 and the reburial of Saul and his sons in the grave of Kish in 2 Sam. 21.11-14 are not used. Thus the only burial comment for Saul places him in a remote grave, not in a proper (royal) grave. Here is a negative counterpart to a common element of the transition formulae, namely the reference to proper burial or otherwise, according to the quality of the king in question. Thus Saul's burial is itself negatively stated. But the phrase in v. 14 *wayyassēb 'et-mᵉlûkāh* is not found in any other transition formula. The significant parallel to it is to be found in 2 Chron. 10.15 which describes as a *nᵉsibbāh* from God the refusal of Rehoboam to respond to the people's demand; this is taken over from the corresponding passage in 1 Kgs 12.15 which is identical, except that it employs the alternative word *sibbāh* from the same root *sbb*. This suggests that the Chronicler, familiar with and approving the description of the disruption as a 'turning about' by God then applies this same concept to the loss of the monarchy to the house of Saul.[1] In other words, for him the change from Saul to David is to be seen as being as momentous for Israel's history as the change from the age of David and Solomon, the age of the united kingdom, to that of the kings of the south alone. It is a moment of judgment of a kind which may be regarded as typical[2] rather than merely historical.[3]

1. Cf. also 2 Chron. 22.7 where תבוסה, 'down-treading', may be an error for חסובה, a divine directing of events to bring judgment upon Ahaziah of Judah.

2. We may see the same point in the absence of Saul's name from the Chronicler's version of the royal promise in 1 Chron. 17.13 (2 Sam. 7.15 refers to Saul). The theme of withdrawal of divine favour is generalized so that Saul becomes merely a type; at the same time the reapplication of the promise to later generations can be the more readily made. (Cf. on this Boecker 1969: 63).

3. It is of note that what appears to be another stage in the development of this kind of thinking—probably earlier than the Chronicler, perhaps even known to him—is to be found in Isa. 7.17: 'Yahweh will bring upon you and upon your people and upon your ancestral house days such as have not come since the day when Ephraim turned away from Judah' (omitting the last words as a gloss). Whether this is taken in a positive sense—a restoration of the time of the united kingdom—or, as seems more probable, in a negative sense—a judgment like that

This point provides yet further support for the contention that the Chronicler's presentation of Saul is significantly related to the whole pattern of his work.

2. *Hezekiah*

The whole range of the Hezekiah material, integrated as it is with the Ahaz section which precedes and the Manasseh section which follows, cannot be handled here.[1] I propose to examine only the limited group of verses at the end of the account in 2 Chron. 32.24-33 and some related points.

The note of the illness of Hezekiah in v. 24 follows abruptly on the glory of Hezekiah's triumph in faith over the Assyrian enemy; this itself, much modified by comparison with the long account in 2 Kings 18–19, stands in the context of the reform which marks out Hezekiah as the king of loyalty (cf. 32.1: 'after this display of loyalty' would be a possible paraphrase). Now at the moment of his greatest triumph, held in honour by all the nations (32.23), Hezekiah falls mortally ill. The allusive brevity of 32.24 can only be understood by a reader who already knows the full account of 2 Kgs 20.1-11 (Isa. 38).[2] Central to the allusion is the mention of the sign (*môpēt*) which God gives, an allusion to the second element in the 2 Kings narrative which has in fact become the sole motif in the Isaiah version where a scribal addition alone has provided a reference to the healing by means of a cake of figs.[3] The Chronicler preserves the 'sign' motif, but makes no further immediate use of it; it is in fact held in suspense until v. 31.

Meantime, in comment upon the illness and recovery of Hezekiah, the Chronicler introduces in vv. 25-26 a quite different theme, one which is in fact derived not from the illness

---

of the loss of the north—the momentous nature of that particular event and its typical character are brought out.

1. Cf. my commentary (1973a: 173-74) and Mosis 1973: 186-94.
2. For a fuller discussion of 2 Kgs 20, cf. Ackroyd 1974. The text of 2 Chron. 32.24 is in fact in all probability somewhat corrupted, but whether we should read (cf. LXX) 'and he implored his' for MT 'and he said to him', or, comparing 2 Kgs 20.5, add 'I will heal you', does not affect the real point.
3. For a note on this point, cf. Ackroyd 1974.

narrative but from the ambassador narrative which follows in
2 Kgs 20.12-19 (Isa. 39).[1] Whereas in 2 Kings the two are
simply placed side by side, linked only by a general chronological note and the indication that the ambassadors came
because Hezekiah had been ill and had recovered (so Isa. 39.1),
the Chronicler takes from the second narrative the theme of
judgment, repentance and deferment of judgment, and
utilises it in comment upon the recovery from illness. He thus
invites his readers, who must be assumed to know the earlier
narratives, to consider the effect upon the faithful king
Hezekiah of so signal a mark of divine favour. Just as in the
case of Josiah he depicts a good king, a reformer, who fails at
the end (2 Chron. 35.20-25), so too here he shows how
Hezekiah in this instance does not respond as he ought to
God's favour, but with pride; the result is divine wrath against
Judah and Jerusalem. This is followed by an act of self-abase-
ment on his own part and on that of the inhabitants of
Jerusalem, as a result of which the divine wrath does not come
upon them in the days of Hezekiah. The Chronicler has evidently understood Hezekiah's response to the divine wrath of
judgment as an acceptance of its rightness and as requiring
penitence from him (cf. 2 Kgs 20.19); so judgment is deferred
to the period of his descendants, that of the Babylonian exile.
The Chronicler does not in fact specify when the judgment
will take place, and we shall see that he offers a modified
interpretation of this point in due course. It is appropriate to
observe (so Mosis 1973: 109 n. 85; cf. Jones 1955: 239 n. 61)
that in the Chronicler's writings and elsewhere the expression
'Judah and Jerusalem' or 'Judah and the inhabitants of
Jerusalem' (v. 25—cf. also v. 33) consistently refers to the
post-exilic community. Thus in describing the miraculous act
of God and Hezekiah's and the people's wrong reception to it,
the Chronicler invites the attention of his contemporaries to
their own failure to apprehend the nature of divine favour to
them—in their miraculous restoration to life from the death
of exile—and the need for a response in humility which will at
the very least defer judgment.

---

1. So W. Rudolph 1955a: 313; Willi 1972: 173-74.

In vv. 27-29 a detailed description is offered of Hezekiah's wealth and prosperity; such a description (so Willi 1972: 141) belongs properly to the Solomon tradition (cf. 1 Kgs 3.13); it is utilized by the Chronicler in regard to David (1 Chron. 29.12, 28, but cf. also the preceding chapters) and Jehoshaphat (2 Chron. 17.5, 18.1).[1] The description may thus be seen as an aspect of the patterning of the accounts of the rulers of Judah.

Verse 30a contains a reference to the making of the water-conduit by which the water of the spring of Gihon was brought within the city. This represents a restatement of the corresponding archival note of 2 Kgs 20.20, but we must note that the Chronicler has in fact already utilized this theme in a different manner in his striking account of the defeat of the Assyrians. In 32.3-4 we read:

> He consulted with his officers and warriors about shutting off the waters of the springs which were outside the city. So they helped him by gathering together a great company who shut off all the springs and the stream flowing through the land, commenting: 'Why should the kings of Assyria come in here and find great waters?'

There are three points to note here. First, the containing of one spring becomes a total action directed against all springs outside the city; the archival record has been universalized. Second—universalizing again—it is directed not against the particular ruler of Assyria, but against 'kings' in the plural;[2] the Hezekiah–Sennacherib event becomes a type of the frustrating of the rulers of the nation who set themselves against Jerusalem.[3] Third, the reference to great waters (*maîm rabbîm*) may be seen as an interpretative extension of the claim of the Assyrian alluded to in the Isaianic taunt-song of 2 Kgs 19.21ff., where v. 24 refers to the drinking of strange waters and the drying up of the rivers of Egypt. The Chronicler has extended this to suggest the impotence of the alien powers in

1. The use of *misk^enôt* (v. 28) in particular provides a clear link: the word is used for Solomon (2 Chron. 8.4, 6: cf. 1 Kgs 9.19), and Jehoshaphat (2 Chron. 17.2). Otherwise it appears only in Exod. 1.11 and in 2 Chron. 16.4 in a reference to Naphtali.
2. Cf. Willi 1972: 164 n. 214, and also his comments on typological interpretation (160ff.).
3. Cf. e.g. Pss. 2; 46; Zech. 14.

the face of Hezekiah and his people who, acting in relation to the divine favour, can stop up all the waters. The 'great waters' belong in the mythological context, and it is in the light of this that we may also understand the curious expression 'the stream flowing through the land'. This is not a mistake for 'through the city', as the LXX suggests; the LXX rendering in fact merely takes it to be a literal reference to the underground conduit; nor is it, as some have supposed, to be understood as 'through the earth, i.e. ground', an underground tunnel. It should be taken to mean that stream of waters which flows out from Jerusalem, known to Ps. 46.5 and particularly to Ezekiel 47, waters which are not natural but cosmic. The contest between Hezekiah and Sennacherib has become a great confrontation between the people of God and the alien world.

The last phrase of v. 30 belongs with v. 31: 'So Hezekiah prospered in all that he did, including the instance of the Babylonian ambassadors who were sent to him[1] to inquire about the sign which had occurred in the land; God left him on his own, to test him so as to find out his true nature.' The implication of this remarkable use of the narrative of 2 Kgs 20.12-19 is that on this occasion Hezekiah shows himself entirely able to deal with the test and to find success even in this. The judgment element of the story has been used already; the Chronicler prefers here to draw out the interpretation that Hezekiah was able to respond rightly to what occurred— though we should be totally at a loss to understand the matter if we did not have the earlier narrative.[2]

Verse 32 summarizes the reign of Hezekiah, with the inclusion of the prophetic witness to that reign which is character-

---

1. On the text, cf. Rudolph 1955a: 312; but we may suppose more probably that MT contains a duplicate reading: *śārê bābel* is an alternative to *mᵉlîṣê bābel*.

2. This verse provides an example of the problems we should face if we only possessed Chronicles; it also serves to demonstrate how, by inference, we may assume that narratives have similarly been omitted in Samuel and Kings and elsewhere, but the readers are expected to be familiar with them. A good example is in fact found in 2 Sam. 21.2.

istic of a number of the Chronicler's archival statements.[1] We may follow Willi in seeing the significance of such prophetic references as pointing to the Chronicler's understanding of the authority of the records he claims to use. Later tradition was to understand the books from Joshua to Kings as 'former prophets'; the Chronicler provides a pointer to this view. But we must add that the Chronicler in fact introduces his prophetic references only in relation to 'good' kings, 'good' not in the sense that they are without fault, but in the sense that they are found faithful even though they fail at certain points. We may detect here also a further develpment of what is already observable in the earlier forms of the material. Whereas Hezekiah the good has a narrative in which the activity of Isaiah is largely integrated with the separate elements, his predecessor Ahaz, for whom a similar Isaianic tradition is known,[2] is described in 2 Kings 16 without any such references; and similarly, whereas a full and integrated account of Jeremiah and the last king of Judah is to be found in Jeremiah 37–44 (cf. Ackroyd 1968b: 43-50 = Ackroyd 1987b: 142-47), it is not this form which has survived in the narrative material of 2 Kgs 2.24-25. The move towards particularizing of prophetic comment is already to be found developing within the earlier forms of the material.[3]

The final element of the Chronicler's Hezekiah tradition in v. 33 adds to the normal pattern the statement that 'all Judah and the inhabitants of Jerusalem (again the post-exilic community is being alluded to) made a "glory" for him at his death'. The precise meaning of this is not known. Most naturally it may be related to the 'burning' undertaken for Asa (2 Chron. 16.14), said to have been deliberately omitted for

---

1. Such prophetic references appear also for David, Solomon, Rehoboam, Abijah, Jehoshaphat, Uzziah and Manasseh (anonymous); cf. Willi 1972: 234 n. 69.

2. Isaiah 7–8, and Ackroyd 1968b: 22-23 (= Ackroyd 1987b: 128-29).

3. This is a point which needs fuller investigation, especially in relation to the David, Jeroboam–Rehoboam, and Elijah–Elisha traditions. But the particular examples of Ahaz, Hezekiah and Zedekiah are striking. Cp. also my article, 'A Judgment Narrative between Kings and Chronicles? An Approach to Amos 7.9-17' (Ackroyd 1977 = Ackroyd 1987b, ch. 12).

Joram (2 Chron. 1.19), and described as normal for a king's death (Jer. 34.5) But whatever the precise meaning, the stress is here clearly laid upon the community's acknowledgment of the significance of Hezekiah's reign; by this final expression, the Chronicler underlines its significance for his contemporaries too.[1]

To these points concerning the Chronicler's treatment of Hezekiah there must be added two of wider import. First (cf. Ackroyd 1973; Mosis 1973: 186-94), the presentation of Hezekiah is to be seen in the light of the preceding picture of Ahaz in which the theme of exile is underlined; it appears repeatedly through ch. 28.[2] In contrast to this theme of exile, the story of Hezekiah represents the overthrow of the alien powers and the establishment of new life for the people of God. Second, the deferment of judgment which the Chronicler has used in 32.26 is not simply, as in 2 Kings, picked up in the exilic situation. In the following chapter, the narrative of Manasseh, the son of Hezekiah, includes his exiling to Babylon, his humble repentance, and his restoration; where 2 Kings 20 and Isaiah 39 point to the fate of the later descendants of Hezekiah's line, the Chronicler, while eventually using the theme of exile, makes use of this particular motif by presenting Manasseh as a type of the exile,[3] Here is yet another example of the subtle way in which the Chronicler, while apparently not making use of a particular narrative, in fact picks up a variety of themes from it and presents them in a new pattern.

1. On the progressive development of the Hezekiah theme, cf. Ackroyd 1974. The death of Hezekiah merits closer examination ('The Death of Hezekiah', in Ackroyd 1987b, ch. 10).

2. Cf. Mosis 1973: 186-88—cf. vv. 5, 8, 17 and more generally 23; the theme of restoration at the hands of the northern kingdom in 28.8-15 may be understood in various ways, but we may perhaps properly see here too an exemplification of that element in the prayer of Solomon, found in 1 Kgs 8.50 but not in the Chronicler's form of the text, which asks that God should 'put pity for them (i.e. the exiles) in their captors' hearts'.

3. Cf. Ackroyd 1973a: 198; Mosis 1973: 38, 193; Willi 1972: 160ff. on typology. The relationship of this to 2 Kings is more fully set out in Ackroyd 1974.

This passage—with its rich allusions and subtle cross-references—invites the reader both to see the true meaning of earlier narratives already known to him, and also to recognize the typical, the universal, in the particular account. It is a history even more dehistoricized than that of the Chronicler's predecessors.

3. *Ezra*

On the assumption that the work of the Chronicler is to be understood solely in terms of exegesis and that this is to be conceived within certain terms of limited description,[1] it is inevitable that Willi has excluded the books of Ezra and Nehemiah from his consideration, treating them as an independent, probably earlier work, by the same compiler (Willi 1972: 181). In fact the exclusion is based on a variety of other points which need not be discussed here, though clearly they must be examined fully if the argument for treating Chronicles–Ezra–Nehemiah as essentially a single work is to be properly maintained. An examination of those chapters (Ezra 7–10; Neh. 8–9[10]) which deal with the figure of Ezra himself may indicate in some degree whether or not the procedures adopted are similar to those found elsewhere in the Chronicler's work, and whether the same themes are taken up and handled as there.[2]

In fact, even if exegesis is conceived in precise and relatively narrow terms, it may still be argued that the exegetical procedure to be observed here is to be seen also in Ezra 1–6. It is only if we supposed that the Chronicler was here composing quite freely, writing his own account of Ezra and his work without reference to any previous material, that we could largely exclude the use of the term 'exegesis'. Largely, not entirely. For we must ask ourselves whether it is legitimate so to nar-

1. Cf. Willi 1972, e.g. pp. 55, 66, 193; Mosis comments on the narrowness of this view, e.g. 1973: 12-13 and n. 10.
2. Willi is, in fact, trying very hard to have his cake and eat it! By assuming the likelihood of the same author for the two works, Chronicles and Ezra-Nehemiah, he can account for the similarities; by assuming that they were produced for quite different purposes, he can account for differences and keep them separate.

row the term as to suppose that it is only appropriate when it involves the handling, the exposition and elucidation, of an already written and recognized text; or whether we may not at this relatively early stage in the evolution of the procedures, consider exegesis to be a not entirely inappropriate term for that selecting and arranging and interpretation of information, whether written or oral, which we may detect not only in the case of the Chronicler's work but also at an earlier stage in the books of Samuel and Kings. For the reader or hearer to whom the story is already familiar—and must not this be so in the case of earlier narratives as also in the case of the Ezra story?—the writer invites attention to a particular line of interpretation. By his selection and arrangement of what is at least in some measure already familiar, he tells us how he believes it is to be read. The fact that the interpretation of the person and work of Ezra has in more recent times been so very variably presented makes it clear both that the Chronicler has preserved some information which is open to more than one understanding and also that, for various reasons, some better than others, his particular presentation has been doubted. Of course, if it were right to believe that Ezra is a figment of the Chronicler's own imagination, then our appreciation of what he has done inevitably shifts somewhat. But even then we should—in our more sophisticated manner—be prompted to ask: how far does this flight of the imagination present, through a fictional character, an intelligible and acceptable view of that stage in the evolution of the post-exilic community? A historical novel may not make use of historical characters alone; we are not necessarily thereby offered a totally misleading picture of a historical situation. The traditional concept of the 'Great Synagogue' as the succession to Ezra cannot be regarded as historical,[1] yet our understanding of the period into which it is projected is not entirely misled by such a construction. As an attempt to clarify the nature of religious continuity in that period, it may well preserve elements of a proper appreciation of the problems which the people of the period actually faced.

1. For references, cf. e.g. Ryle 1909: 261ff.; Eissfeldt 1965: 564 and references in n. 9; Moore 1927: 29-36; Moore 1930: 7ff.

The precise detection of the materials available to the Chronicler in the Ezra section is very difficult. We may observe what we may describe as a 'commissioning and journey narrative' in Ezra 7–8, which incorporates the Aramaic 'document', the decree issued to Ezra in 7.12-26, introduced by a Hebrew sentence in 7.11. Within this section we already observe a change between third and first person forms which appears again in other parts of the Ezra material. In the light of comparable material elsewhere in such variant styles, it appears more satisfactory to view this change as a stylistic device rather than as an indication of separate sources, though the latter cannot necessarily be entirely ruled out. In this section we observe that 7.1-10 is third person; after the Aramaic passage, 7.27 is neutral, as a doxological expression, but 7.28 is in the first person and so too is the major part of ch. 8 and ch. 9. But in fact in the last verses of ch. 8, it appears likely that we should see a change to third person forms; the last actual first person form here is in v. 32, and vv. 33-34 are of such a nature that it is not surprising to find none in them. With v. 35, however, we get a transition to the third person (with its reference to 'those who had come from the captivity') where it would be more natural to have a plural 'we' if the first person narrative continued. 9.1 resumes the first person. This change-over may be of some importance in clarifying the relationship between the journey narrative and is sequels in the foreign marriage narratives of Ezra 9–10 and the law reading in Nehemiah 8.[1]

Ezra 9–10 contains the 'foreign marriage' narrative. Here, again without overstressing the change of person but simply observing it as a feature, we may note that there is a measure of parallel between 9.1-15 and 10.1-6. This is indicated by the part played in 10.2-4 not by Ezra but by a completely different character, Shecaniah. Has an Ezra reform narrative, perhaps

1. The original, that is to say, historical order of the Ezra narratives has been much discussed, and the issue is of importance in that rearrangement by the Chronicler would serve as a pointer to his interpretation. The point has been fully discussed by Pohlmann (1970: 127-32); he rejects the rearrangement Ezra 7–8; Neh. 8; Ezra 9–10; Neh. 9–10. But it is by no means certain that the issue is thereby resolved. Cf. also Mosis 1973: 218.

existing in more than one form (cf. 9.1-4 and 10.6), incorporated elements from a non-Ezra narrative, since Shecaniah's
address to the assembly in 10.2-4 overlaps substantially the
kind of appeal which is elsewhere attributed to Ezra? There
are numerous Old Testament parallels to the attributing to a
known and named hero elements of narratives which belong
to less significant or anonymous personages.

This possibility is strengthened by the recognition of a comparable pattern in Nehemiah 8–9, which contain the highly
stylized reading of the law in Nehemiah 8 together with the
further reading of the law and the long prayer in Nehemiah 9.
It is noteworthy here again that the figure of Ezra does not
appear in the Hebrew text of ch. 9, though the prayer is—
understandably enough—attributed to Ezra in the Greek text.
Have we here an alternative version of the reading and acceptance of the law, one in which Ezra was not named, which has
been identified and so dovetailed with the Ezra narrative by
the Chronicler?

We must further observe that the 'foreign marriage' theme,
so fully set out in Ezra 9–10, is also a part of the law-reading
section as this is now presented, for Neh. 9.2 makes it an element of the acceptance of the law, and it also appears as a
feature of the covenant document of Nehemiah 10 (cf. vv. 28,
30), though there remains uncertainty as to whether or not
this latter passage should be regarded as associated with the
Ezra material—as appears to me most likely—or whether it
belongs with Nehemiah, as the appearance of his name at 10.1
and certain overlaps with Nehemiah 13 have been held to
demonstrate.[1]

This very short survey of the Ezra material already indicates some of the very considerable problems of the literary
analysis, and also suggests that it can be no easy task to
describe the work of the Chronicler in bringing the material
together. Certain points emerge, however, which suggest the

---

1. This point cannot be discussed here, but cf. my brief observations
in my commentary (Ackroyd 1973a: 303-306).

way in which he has worked in this context, and these provide a basis for comparison with his methods elsewhere.[1]

First, we may observe that, as other Old Testament compilers have done, the Chronicler has integrated into what now appears as a continuous narrative, elements which do not originally belong together. The fact that we may detect non-Ezra traditions of the receiving and acceptance of the law and of the action on foreign marriages suggests that, viewing the moment of Ezra's action as the most significant, he has incorporated into this (and has thereby reinterpreted) other traditions which were similar in general purport.

Second, we may note that the theme of the law as it is presented in Nehemiah 8 and Nehemiah 9 is markedly stylized. It has long been observed that the procedures described point to an established practice which is being adapted by the narrator for the purpose of what he presents as a single historic moment. But the existence of the alternative in Neh. 9.1-5 and in the Nehemiah tradition in Neh. 13.1-3, as well as earlier comparable material such as is indicated in Deut. 31.10-13, make it seem proper to consider that a practice of periodic reading of the law is here being drawn upon. This suggests that we should be cautious of offering too literal an interpretation of certain features. The response of the people—weeping as they listened to the words of the law (Neh. 8.9)—is not to be held to suggest that the law was unfamiliar to them, any more than Josiah's response in 2 Kgs 22.11 necessarily suggests this; the weeping is a ritual response, an acknowledgment—here related to the mourning procedures described in Neh. 9.1—of the rightness of the law and the need for acceptance. The point is made even clearer by the description of the making of booths in Neh. 8.17, where it is claimed that this had not been done since the days of Joshua. It is clear that what is significant here is not some historical claim for innovation or revival, but the parallel drawn between the action in the time of Ezra and that in the time of Joshua (cf. the passover celebration in Josh. 5).

---

1. I am indebted for a number of points in the discussion of Ezra to the paper by Professor Klaus Koch, entitled 'Ezra and the Origins of Judaism' delivered to the Society for Old Testament Study in July, 1973, and published in *JSS* 19 (1974): 173-97.

The people at this moment are, like those of the past, at the
beginning of a new and this time a spiritual entry into the
land. Such an entry, as the Deuteronomic laws particularly
underline, cannot be undertaken without obedience to the
law.[1]

The suggestion that the Chronicler in Nehemiah 8–9 presents the reading and acceptance of the law in stylized form
invites the question whether there are other parts of the
material which are similarly handled. Here I would like to
take up a point made by Koch (1974: 184-90). He suggested
that the march from Babylonia to Jerusalem was a cultic procession, which Ezra himself understood as a second Exodus.
And in relation to this he stressed the position of Ezra as 'the
real high priest of Aaron's family'. I would myself wish to
qualify the first of these points by asking whether it was Ezra
who so saw the journey, or whether it was not rather the
Chronicler. In the discussion which followed Koch's paper, the
question was raised about the 'second Exodus' features of the
first return narrative in Ezra 1: these features are clear, both
in actual content—the theme of the 'spoiling of the Egyptians'
(Exod. 11.2; 12.33-34) finds its counterpart in Ezra 1.4 and 6—
and in cross-reference, for underlying the passage is the
theme of the fulfilment of prophecy, particularly that of the
Second Isaiah with his concerning the 'second Exodus' (so the
Cyrus prophecy of Isa. 41.25; 44.28–45.7) and the return of
the temple vessels (cf. Isa. 52.11).[2] Thus, while it seems proper
to see Ezra's return in such terms, noting parallels with the
first Exodus and observing, for example, the theme of divine
protection in Ezra 8, the description of the journey in Ezra 7.9
as *ma'ᵃleh* (the date given here is stated to be that of the *yᵉsûd
hamma'ᵃleh*—'the initiation of the procession'), it is better to

1. For this general view, cf. Mosis 1973: 218; Pohlmann 1970: 128-35
and esp. 136; Kellermann 1967: 29. Koch (1974: 182) argues—I believe
wrongly—that the distress of the people points to a new and unknown
law; the pointer to Joshua is rightly underlined by him.
2. On this theme, cf. my 'The Temple Vessels—A Continuity
Theme' in Ackroyd 1972: 166-81 = Ackroyd 1987b, ch. 4; and also, for
the much wider range of questions raised by this theme, Collins 1972.
For the more general points here, cf. my commentary (Ackroyd 1973a:
212-17).

regard this presentation of Ezra's work as being due to the Chronicler who thus, in a clear pattern, portrays the two stages of the return, that of Sheshbazzar-Zerubbabel and Jeshua and that of Ezra, as being equally expressions of the same theme of second Exodus, leading to climaxes in religious celebration, the temple-dedication and passover of Ezra 6 and the law reading and acceptance and tabernacles of Nehemiah 8–9 (10).

In regard to the status of Ezra, Koch has drawn attention to the remarkable genealogy of Ezra 7.1-5. This is remarkable both for what it contains and for what it omits. It draws clear attention to the legitimacy of Ezra's priestly descent by tracing it back in a few names to Aaron who is here significantly designated 'the chief priest'; it gives as immediate predecessor in the genealogical line the name of Seraiah which is that of the high priest taken into exile by the Babylonians in 587 BCE (2 Kgs 25.18). It is a proper inference that the Chronicler is here, as is often the case in genealogical information, not concerned with giving a complete line but with a significant line which establishes a contention (cf. Wilson 1972, 1976). For him, Ezra is in a real sense the immediate successor of the high priest taken into exile in 587. This is not a denial of the status of Jeshua of Ezra 3–4,[1] but an affirmation of the status of Ezra as successor. The Chronicler appears to be claiming a status and authority for Ezra (perhaps Ezra claimed this too) which other traditions do not admit. That there were problems regarding the high priesthood in the post-exilic period we know well from the later Maccabaean times and the struggles for power in the succeeding years. Josephus's account of this period (*Ant.* 11.7.1) has a story of murder and intrigue. If his chronology is right, and this must be open to question, Ezra could be seen as claiming, and the Chronicler as continuing his claim, that he was the true high priest. We may observe the non-mention of Ezra by ben Sira, which presents a prob-

---

1. Jeshua is also mentioned in Ezra 5.2, but it seems possible to me that the mention of Zerubbabel and Jeshua here is part of the harmonizing tendency of the Chronicler in the handling of the two disparate accounts of the rebuilding which he has utilized in Ezra 3–6.

lem, and we may speculate whether to some these claims were regarded as improper.

The apparent leaping of time in the abbreviated genealogy of Ezra 7.1-5 presents no real problem, since the list is not to be regarded as complete. It does, however, link with two further points. First, we may observe how, in 2 Esdras, Ezra actually appears to belong to the exilic age (so 3.1 dated to the thirtieth year after the fall of Jerusalem), just as we find Nehemiah in 2 Macc. 1.18ff. presented as sent by the Persian ruler to build the temple and altar—the intervening years are simply bypassed. Second, we may note that, without necessarily actually thinking that there was no chronological gap, the Chronicler invites the supposition of continuity between Ezra 6 and 7 by his placing of events of a sixth year (that of Darius) in ch. 6 and those of a seventh year (that of Artaxerxes) in ch. 7 (cf. Ackroyd 1973: 240). Significance is for the Chronicler greater than mere chronology.

It is similarly observable that the question of foreign marriages in Ezra 9–10 is presented in a stylized manner.[1] The list of nations in 9.1 is highly artificial.[2] The occasion is utilized for the incorporation of a homiletic prayer in 9.6-15 which (cf. Mosis 1973: 227-28) has links back with 2 Chron. 29.6-9; 30.6-7; 36.20, and provides also a summary of the accounts of Ezra 1–6. It is thus both integrated with other Chronicler material and designed to clarify the pattern of events.

Or again, we may observe in the relationship between the commissioning of Ezra as this is set out in the Aramaic of Ezra 7.12-26 and the actual description of his activity, discrepancies which suggest that the Chronicler, making use of existing material and traditions, has shifted the emphasis of Ezra's work from a more political to a more theological angle.[3]

A full and detailed discussion of the Chronicler's handling of the Ezra material is beyond the scope of this discussion.[4] But sufficient has been said to show that these chapters reveal a

1. Cf. above on *ma'al*.
2. Cf. Ackroyd 1973a: 252ff.; Ackroyd 1970a: 39 (= Chapter 1, 54-55 above); Mosis 1973: 239.
3. Cf. Ackroyd 1970a: 35-38 (= Chapter 1, 49-54); Ackroyd 1973a: 242-47.
4. A fuller study may be found in my 'God and People in the Chronicler's Presentation of Ezra' (Ackroyd 1976 = Chapter 12 above).

rehandling and reshaping of material similar to that which may be discovered in other parts of the work. Mosis, whose treatment of the Ezra section is very brief (1973: 226-32), nevertheless underlines this, seeing in these passages the same concern with the patterning of events—and seeing also, and rightly, that the Chronicler's concern is not simply (as has been argued by Rudolph[1]) in finding in his own age the embodiment of the promises of the past, important though this element in fact is; but it is also in pointing forward to a future in which the Davidic/Solomonic age will indeed come again. Mosis somewhat overstresses what he considers to be the provisional nature of the post-exilic temple (1973: 226-29)—arguing from the brevity of the descriptions and, rather too literally, from the weeping provoked at the rebuilding by those who remembered the earlier temple; such weeping is not necessarily to be understood as expressing the feelings of disappointment which may be detected in Hag. 2.3 and Zech. 4.10, (but like that in Neh. 8) as part of a ritual in which, in fact, weeping and rejoicing recombined.[2] But that the second temple is not to be regarded as final appears fully intelligible in the light of the sense of distress at being a subject people which comes out so fully in the prayers of both Ezra 9 and Nehemiah 9. Without any precision as to what kind of future there ought to be, both these passages point forward; there is a measure of hope in the Chronicler which is rooted in his appeal to his contemporaries to understand both their own tradition and their position aright.

4. *Some Conclusions*

The three passages which we have examined represent three very different modes of handling already existing material. It is perhaps therefore not surprising to find that Willi sets out nine categories for the discussion of the differences between

1. Rudolph 1955a: xxiii-xxiv; Rudolph 1954, esp. 408-409. This view is strongly approved by O. Plöger (Plöger 1968, e.g. 39ff.).
2. Mosis 1973: 221 and n. 32. The danger here is in conflating information from two entirely different types of source, without sufficiently examining the nature of their contributions.

Chronicles and its predecessors.[1] Of these, the first two are purely text-critical and are therefore held to fall outside the realm of exegesis; however, observe that the decision as to what differences are due to textual dislocation and the like is often very uncertain, and the dividing lines between textual modification and exegesis are unclear. Willi's next two categories are at the level of orthographic and grammatical alterations, and of small alterations and shortenings of the text; here the precise form of the text available to the Chronicler remains (inevitably) not fully ascertainable, and it may be doubted whether sufficient account is taken of the more general problems of the evolution of ancient texts.[2] Furthermore, as may been seen in one or two of the examples already cited, the distinction between larger and smaller changes is itself somewhat arbitrary it is always possible that by the change of a single word the whole tenor of a passage is altered. This fourth category therefore overlaps the fifth which comprises explanatory additions and alterations, often of a minimal kind; and this in its turn the remaining four—adaptation, theological modificaton, recension (particularly involving harmonization), and typology. While I would very happily concur in the use of such terminology in general, I find myself less certain whether it is possible to draw the clear lines which Willi does, though it may be observed that in the detailed discussion, the same passages may in fact appear under more than one heading. It is evident that the Chronicler was not aware of the categories, but was writing with a much more integrated belief in the significance of what he was handling. The analysis may be convenient, but it may do less than justice to the richness and fluidity of the Chronicler's style and method.

To judge the issues solely on the basis of the three passages discussed—and in none of these have anything like all the questions been raised which could assist a full study—must inevitably be less than adequate. Yet even the limited discussion of these passages shows quite widely diverging proce-

---

1. Willi 1972: 66-68, and his full discussion of the categories (68-175).

2. On this, cf. particularly the rather extreme position of Lemke (1965), and my comments in Ackroyd 1967: 507 n. 25 (= Chapter 10, 261 n. 1, above).

dures. It is possible (so the Saul passage) for the material of the earlier work to be quoted very nearly exactly—though some of the differences, small as they are, may point to particular motives—and then for a radical change in understanding to be brought about by the introduction of a very significant comment and link passage, as in 1 Chron. 10.13-14. It is possible—so the Hezekiah passage—for there to be allusion to material not appearing in the Chronicler's work but assumed to be known to the readers or hearers, and for such allusion to be so made that a radical difference in the understanding of the earlier material is enjoined. What these two methods have in common is clear. They invite the reader to consider the already known narratives, whether these are set out or not, in the light of some particular comment or pointer, and so, inevitably, to read them in a manner quite different from that enjoined by the earlier compilers.[1] There is here an extension of procedures which can already be observed in the earlier works, for editorial comment, whether of the brief introductory and concluding form as in Judges or more substantial as in such punctuating speeches as 1 Samuel 12 and 2 Kings 17, obliges the reader to consider the material, already in some measure familiar, in a new light. The degree to which subsequent readers—including ourselves—have been inescapably influenced by such editorial procedures may be detected in much of what is written about the Old Testament; and indeed not without the justice of observing that the compiler or editor nearer to the events may have a better understanding than we who stand further away. The observation of the radical changes brought about by the Chronicler's presentation is in itself a confirmation of this, though it does not remove the problems presented by the already very evident shifts of emphasis provided in the earlier presentations available to us. Even our original sources are nevertheless edited presentations.

The Ezra section—our third example—offers yet another style of presentation in which our verifying of the Chronicler's method must inevitably be more difficult since we do not have

---

1. On the effect of reading diverse passages together, cf. also my paper on 'The Theology of the Chronicler' (Chapter 11, above).

an alternative coherent account. But a consideration of the Chronicler's procedures elsewhere and an examination of the alternative presentations of 1 Esdras and Josephus provide us with some clues to the degree of shift which we may expect the Chronicler to have introduced here. If for him Ezra marks the climax of his presentation and this part of the work must have therefore a very special significance, we may see that in his portrayal of this his last hero there are indications of his own viewpoint and outlook which are of major importance.

It is at this point that we may usefully contrast the understanding of exegesis which is to be found in the two major studies which have been much referred to in this discussion, those of Willi and Mosis. Part of the problem here inevitably rests in the definition of terms. The categories set out by Willi point to relationships to the subsequent development of rabbinic exegetical method. The same kind of question arises here as is often asked in relation to the use of the technical term *midrash*. Its later, very precisely defined, use inevitably means that if it is used in relation to earlier stages, which may provide pointers to that full development, there is the danger of confusing those earlier stages with the more elaborate and precise form. Much the same may be said in regard to the particular categories of exegesis as these are developed by Willi. On the other hand, we must not forget that the term *midrash* is itself to be found in the Chronicler's writings (2 Chron. 13.22; 24.27), though its precise meaning is not altogether clear in these two passages.[1] Some terms are necessary for the description of earlier stages in the evolution of what eventually becomes more precisely defined. Probably it will be necessary always to qualify any use in reference to earlier material, and to avoid such terms as 'proto-midrash' since they may be held to prejudge the nature of the development. We may expect to find exegetical procedures which did not evolve towards the later fixed form; later exegesis is in any case not limited to formal *midrash*. In so far as Willi points to earlier stages in a

---

1. 'Story, commentary, book' are all possible renderings; literally a *midrash* is something 'sought out', but that piece of etymology does little to help our understanding. Cf. Willi 1972: 66 n. 81 with references, arguing for a relatively neutral meaning.

long process, he performs a useful service; further aspects of such an investigation may be seen in R.A. Mason's study, 'Examples of Inner Biblical Exegesis in Zech. 9–14'.[1]

It is, however, important also to recognize the limitation of Willi's own understanding of the Chronicler's exegesis, as this is stated, for example, in the following:

> It follows that Chronicles cannot be understood apart from the books of Samuel and Kings (and to a lesser extent but in the same manner, the Pentateuch and a few other older biblical writings) and in particular in relation to those parts which were not included; indeed one may go further and say that it was not intended to be understood without them. Its style of history-writing, exegesis in the best sense of the word, aims at clarifying the understanding of the source, at illuminating this primary underlying work in relation to a precise historical theological point, a *heilsgeschichtliche*, at bringing the text of the original to concentrate upon this theme and at clarifying its interconnections (Willi 1972: 66).

With the first part of this statement we may certainly agree, not least in that the material not handled in the Chronicler is seen to be of great significance for the reader's understanding and for our own. All is to be read now in the light of this style of exposition. The latter part of the statement is repeated at a number of points in different wordings[2] with an even greater emphasis on the backward look. The books of Chronicles are seen as explanatory, and it is felt to be dangerous or illusory to attempt to discover the writer's own period in his work.[3] This is surely to miss an important aspect of exegesis and its understanding. Exegetes, even if they consciously aim simply at

1. A paper also delivered at the Oxford Biblical Congress in 1973 and published in the proceedings. Cf. also his dissertation: 'The Use of Earlier Biblical Material in Zechariah IX-XIV: A Study in Inner Biblical Exegesis' (PhD, London, 1973—unpublished).
2. Cf. 55, 193 and Mosis's comment, p. 39 n. 65.
3. Willi very usefully relates his understanding of the work to the problem of the development of the canon and to his belief, surely right but over-simplified, that the Chronicler regarded the earlier works as 'canonical'. The question which remains here is how far he is right to use another later category and one which is very precisely defined, to describe its earlier but certainly important stages.

clarifying an older writing, cannot detach themselves from
their own positions in the history of exegesis.

It is here that Mosis makes a much more distinctive contribution, with his recognition that the Chronicler's interpretation of the past not only illuminates the earlier texts—in the
sense that they are now to be differently read—but that he also
sheds light on the needs of his own situation and furthermore
points to the future in his hope of a resolution of contemporary
problems. The pattern which is to be discerned in the Chronicler's writings has not come to its final fruition, however much
the ideals are concentrated in the presentation of Ezra. The
situation remains politically and economically unsatisfactory.[1]
The second temple has a temporary quality; it is not yet a full
re-establishment of the temple in its Solomonic glory. But it is
in continuity with that temple and is not to be despised because
it does embody the essentials that belong to the original temple
(cf. Ackroyd 1972, Collins 1972).

The Chronicler may also be considered as a conciliator, and
I would here wish to suggest two aspects of this which are
important for our understanding of his exegesis. He is a conciliator between different groups and interests in that he appeals
for a true adherence to the one right line. He portrays Ezra as
the conciliator, the one who is to establish the true community,
'the holy seed', by the exclusion of alien influence but also by
the drawing together of all who should belong to the people of
the law. He is also a conciliator between different lines of
thought, for we may see drawn together and in some degree
harmonized within his writings what appear in other works
as separate and even as diverse.[2] Willi, in the last section of his
work, concentrates on the Chronicler's appreciation of the
prophetic way of thought, and sees him presenting his history
in prophetic terms. Along with this we may observe also the
presence of strong Deuteronomic and strong Priestly elements
in his thinking, even if some of the latter may belong to later

1. Cf. Ackroyd 1970a: 13ff. (= Chapter 1 above, 17ff.); Ackroyd 1973a:
256, 303ff.

2. So Koch 1974, Ackroyd 1973a, Ackroyd 1973b (= Chapter 11,
present volume). So too R.L. Braun, *CTM* 42 (1971): 511ff.; *JBL* 92
(1973): 503ff. Other aspects of such an exegetical development are
brought out in Williamson 1976, 1977.

amplifications of the work. He may be seen—and this is a point I have endeavoured to present more fully in my paper on 'The Theology of the Chronicler'[1]—as the first Old Testament theologian, offering a unifying of strands and trends which may otherwise appear separate; his exegesis of the earlier material provides a harmonization, but it is one that is also an appreciation of the richness and diversity of the Old Testament religious tradition.

1. Ackroyd 1973b (= Chapter 11 above).

Chapter 14

CHRONICLES–EZRA–NEHEMIAH: THE CONCEPT OF UNITY[1]

1.

There are two certainties which underlie the discussion of the nature and unity or disunity of Chronicles–Ezra–Nehemiah. The first is the existence of the books of Samuel–Kings; the second that of the books of Chronicles, Ezra and Nehemiah. These platitudinous remarks provide the sole or effectively sole basis on which discussion proceeds.

In fact, both certainties have to be qualified, though the essential point remains.

(a) The text of Samuel–Kings (MT) exists. Variants within it are minimal, though three short sections exist in deviant form within the Hebrew Bible (other than in Chronicles): 2 Samuel 22/Psalm 18; 2 Kings 18–20/Isaiah 36–39; 2 Kgs 24.18–25.30/ Jeremiah 52. Of these variants, the second has some importance for our question; and the third perhaps also, at least minimally. Substantial variation exists in the LXX form of the Samuel–Kings texts; and the existence of Qumran fragments of Samuel which point to a variant text, in some respects supporting LXX, indicates the importance of taking seriously the evidence for alternative forms of those books which may or may not shed light on the relationship with Chronicles. (The Qumran evidence for Kings remains meagre, except in so far as the Isaiah manuscripts provide information in relation to 2 Kgs 18–20/Isa. 36–39). Any discussion of Chronicles and its congeners must wrestle with the problem of what text we may suppose to relate to the alternative form of materials found

---

1. Reprinted from the author's article in *Zeitschrift für die alttestamentliche Wissenschaft* 100 (1988): 189-201.

there and corresponding to Samuel–Kings in such a degree as to invite comparisons. Since it has been supposed that Samuel–Kings itself shows marks of editorial levels (and Isa. 36–39 at the very least provides an importantly variant text), consideration of hypothesized earlier forms of Samuel–Kings is also relevant.

(b) The text of Chronicles relates not simply to Samuel–Kings, but also to a variety of other texts, notably genealogies but also poetic and prophetic texts. Claims are also made for textual bases where the Chronicles text contains material unparalleled in Samuel–Kings, with various hypotheses as to what kinds of text—e.g. narratives, archives—might be in question. Extension of the point to Ezra–Nehemiah elicits the comment that it is evident there too that already existing texts have been utilized. This is clear for the Nehemiah memoir (however this is demarcated); it is probable also for the Ezra narrative, though this is less demonstrable; and the existence of Aramaic passages in Ezra 4–6 and 7, claiming to cite Achaemenid documents, also strongly suggests some kind of literary base. It is possible, perhaps probable, for the psalm-passages in Ezra 9 and Nehemiah 9.

(c) The relationship between the Samuel–Kings text on the one hand and the Chronicles text on the other offers a specific problem of interpretation in view of (i) the identity or virtual identity of the two texts in some sections, and (ii) the range of difference from the very close to the very divergent. Once the two texts stood side by side; i.e., from whatever date is assigned to the later of the two, there must also, on the analogy of other parallel or partly parallel texts (e.g. the Gospels), be the probability of some degree of mutual influence. There might be some analogy here to the endeavours at conforming the Greek translation to the Hebrew, such as may be detected in later Greek versions and in the work of Origen; or we may perhaps think simply in terms of textual reminiscence as a source of at least some measure of harmonization.

(d) The relationship between one text and another must allow for exegetical procedures such as those recently and admirably expounded by Fishbane (1985). We are not obliged to agree with any or every example which he discusses: but he has articulated the variety of possibilities with great acumen, and he offers a much more open and fruitful approach than the at times somewhat rigid procedures of Willi (1972).

(e) For completeness, it is desirable to recall the fact that the material covered in the two overlapping biblical works, Samuel–Kings, Chronicles–Ezra–Nehemiah, is partly re-handled in 3 Esdras (a much-discussed and still very problematic book); as also in Josephus's Antiquities, and in part in Pseudo-Philo's *Biblical Antiquities* and in various Samaritan writings. The relatively late dates of these latter works make their use in projecting back rather limited; but they illustrate the further development of procedures already thought to be in operation in the reshaping of earlier texts in Chronicles–Ezra–Nehemiah.

Everything else is hypothesis! Indeed the above cautious statements have already at several points moved over into the mention of some purely hypothetical alternatives. In the formulation of hypotheses, based on the actual available texts and on legitimate analogies from other texts which may assist in producing verisimilitude, there remains one fixed point: the hypothesis argued must contain somewhere within it a satisfying explanation of the existence of the actual texts. That does not, as I would understand it, mean that every detail has to be explained: the degree of adventitiousness in all texts must be kept in mind, and too many hypotheses depend upon an unrealistic degree of deliberation in the processes of textual formation. But it must in some measure indicate how and where the actual texts themselves are to be understood.

2.

The supposition that we are dealing with a 'Chronicler' or with 'the Chronicler'—or, alternatively, that we have a 'Chronistic work'—is based on literary, linguistic and ideological considerations: or, equally, is modified or rejected on the consideration of the same kind of evidence. With these we may also associate the evidence of the biblical canon in its various forms, as providing other indications of the possible ways in which the relationship between the books as we know them is to be described.

This canonical evidence may be set out briefly. In the tradition offered by LXX and Vulgate and supported by some other evidence, Chronicles, Ezra and Nehemiah stand in that order within the group of books viewed as 'histories'. If such an implication has done substantial damage to the proper understanding of these and the other books so viewed, the order has nevertheless presented an understanding of the books Chronicles, Ezra, Nehemiah as a series, and this must be given its due weight. In the Hebrew tradition, all three books appear in the Writings. Chronicles may there stand first in the series, before Psalms; or, more usually, it stands last. A small number of manuscripts place Chronicles before Ezra–Nehemiah. If Chronicles stands before Psalms, it may be seen to provide the context for understanding the Psalter as created under the authority of David, the divinely appointed orderer of every aspect of temple worship. The position of Ezra–Nehemiah after Daniel suggests an understanding of these books as concerned, as their biblical datings imply, with the destruction and restoration of the Solomonic temple and its cultus. The immediately preceding Five Scrolls, coming to be linked with specific festivals, include Lamentations, itself reflecting on that destruction. Daniel, though set in that context, in fact reflects on a later and comparable disaster. Ezra–Nehemiah, placed next, invite the hope, as they describe restoration under Achaemenid rule, that such restoration will be repeated at a yet later date. When Chronicles follows, it provides the guarantee of the restoration of the Davidic order, its final words stressing this and its full and detailed repeating of the building of the Solomonic temple emphasizing continuity with the past. Such considerations provide no answers to the literary questions: they do offer clues to stages of interpretation. Indeed, we may suspect that the ordering of the canon is in some measure related to the destruction of 70 CE, and perhaps even to later events, anticipating an ultimately hoped-for restoration. (On questions of order, see Beckwith 1985, especially 198ff.)

The MT itself treats these books as comprising two separate entities: 1 and 2 Chronicles are a single book, with the traditional colophon to such MT texts at the end. Here the position is identical to that for 1 and 2 Samuel, 1 and 2 Kings. Ezra–Nehemiah is also treated as a single unit for MT purposes. In all these cases, the division into the present smaller units, for whatever precise reason, is made at a convenient starting or stopping point. Thus 1 Chronicles ends with the final summary of the reign of David; 2 Chronicles begins with the reign of Solomon. In this respect the division is more satisfactory than that between the end of 2 Samuel and the beginning of 1 Kings. As in other such instances—and here the Joshua–Judges division is relevant—the new beginning in 2 Chronicles has already been anticipated in 1 Chron. 29.22b-25, which records Solomon's appointment, anointing and enthronement, before the death of David is recorded in 1 Chron. 29.26-30. The end of Joshua and the beginning of Judges overlap similarly. The division between 1 and 2 Chronicles was evidently not limited by the rigid MT separation between Samuel and Kings, though it does make the break at almost the same point. Since it has now for long been thought—perhaps without entirely adequate foundation—that 2 Samuel 9–20 and 1 Kings 1–2 form a single document (or the major part of it) interrupted by the appendices of 2 Samuel 21–24, it must be noted that those who hold that view do not consider the MT division to be absolute. We may indeed accept that those divisions represent one form of textual tradition, the one which ultimately prevailed: but the evidence for alternative divisions must be kept in mind. This point must also have relevance to the relationship between Chronicles and Ezra–Nehemiah: we cannot view this division as absolute on the grounds of the MT form.

3.

With these considerations in mind, we may now turn to the three main lines of approach: literary, linguistic and ideological.

(1) *Literary*. No implication regarding a stance on canonical criticism needs to be drawn from pointing out that, whatever the real relationship between Chronicles and Ezra–Nehemiah, we are now intended to read the two texts together. Where Chronicles in the canon is immediately followed by Ezra–Nehemiah, this is clear. The small overlap between the two, whatever explanation maybe given for it, provides an anticipatory glimpse at the end of Chronicles and a resump-

tive comment at the beginning of Ezra. Where Chronicles is
differently placed in relation to Ezra–Nehemiah—either
quite separate or in what we should regard as a false sequen-
tial position—that overlap provides a clear directive to the
reader to recognize that it is to Ezra–Nehemiah that one
should move after Chronicles. The problematic 1 Esdras text,
which knows no overlap but reads a continuous narrative,
represents another way of making the same point: if this is
simply a secondary product—and the alternatives are not
very realistic—it still supports the view which the MT itself
effectively presents. Either way, Ezra–Nehemiah is indicated
as sequel: at the very least, this represents an early view of
how the two are to be read. Early traditions of this kind have to
be evaluated: they are not to be accepted merely at face value.
We may weigh the evidence to mean simply that, with a separation, the reader is being reminded that they belong together;
or that Ezra–Nehemiah, intended as a sequel or believed to be
one even if not in reality so connected, is hereby designated as
such. We must be sensitive both to the realities of the literary
relationships and also to the ways in which authors or editors
or compilers wished their readers to understand them. What
is said or implied must be heard critically, but it cannot be
ignored.

Literary relationships, as has increasingly been recognized
in recent years, are linked to questions of structure. There are
problems here in the delimitation of units, and there is considerable risk of circular argument. In most instances, if a psalm
is examined for its structure, it may be accepted that we know
where the unit begins and ends: form-critical and structural
analysis can then start from a firm basis. In narrative works,
the only secure beginnings and endings are with final forms in
the books as we have them. In numerous instances these are
firm, as for example with Ruth or Judith. But in sequences of
books such as Joshua to Kings and Chronicles to Ezra–Nehemiah, the question may be begged if we assume that MT lines
of demarcation are absolute. If structural patterns are
detected and believed to demonstrate that there is a unity, of
whatever precise kind, marked off by the beginning and end of
a book, we may also need to consider whether we may not be
able equally to discover a convincing structural pattern which

covers a different section of material. Thus we may be able to detect a structure for 1 Chron. 1.1–9.34 which may help to explain its nature; one for 1 Chron. 9.35–29.30 which is coherent; a structure for 1 Chronicles 1–2 Chronicles 36. We might see two parallel structures for 1 Chron. 1.1–9.34 and 1 Chron. 9.35–Ezra 6. An imaginative coherence has lately been argued for Ezra–Nehemiah (Eskenazi 1986). Persuasive arguments may be produced for a multiplicity of such patterns.

The problem with this kind of approach, often marked by close insights into interconnections within a given body of material, is that there seems to be no limit to the possibilities. If, it would appear, we are once persuaded that a unit of material can be marked off, then our reading of the text will tend to pick up signals which suggest that it is a unit; vocabulary, ideas, assonances, and the rest of the structural undercarriage, point the way. But just how valid are the conclusions when we find that in some instances equally persuasive arguments can be found to support some alternative division? What I see as a clearly structured text the next reader may see as an incoherent over-edited mishmash. One scholar's hypothesis is another's flight of the imagination. We are at times tempted back to the form-critical dilemma: if only the biblical writers had been aware of the forms, how much more orderly their work would have been. If they had understood structuralism, they would have avoided the kind of inconclusiveness which we find in their evidence. That is not to deny the reality of structures: it is to suggest that, as in so much else, the texts as we have them are much more complex. And to create a hypothetical subtext on the basis of what the structures ought to be is a dangerous procedure.

(2) *Language*. The discussions of linguistic evidence for uniting or separating Chronicles and Ezra–Nehemiah have, on the whole, reached an inconclusive position. They have shown up the inadequacy of earlier listings of word usage, and made clear the greater complexity of using linguistic evidence. But they have still, in effect, reached their conclusions on the basis of alternative usages, without sufficient attention being given to some particular problems which attach to these texts. The attempts at a more precise description of what the

Hebrew of the later, post-exilic, period was actually like (Polzin 1976), have led in the end to the realization that the acceptance or non-acceptance of linguistic evidence for separation depends in reality on other factors: if the works are separated, then the linguistic evidence will support that view; if they are viewed as related more or less closely, the linguistic evidence will not really stand in the way. The arguments are not unlike those for the relative dating of Ezra and Nehemiah: if the answer is known or assumed to be known, then the arguments will support that answer. Thronveit (1982), who himself holds the separatist view, argues cogently for the inadequacy of the linguistic evidence.

Two areas of problem stand out. One is the relationship between the books of Chronicles, Ezra and Nehemiah and their sources; the other that of editing. In a recent discussion of the use of the forms 'A. the king' and 'The king A.', B.A. Mastin (Society for Old Testament Study, July 1986) examined the usage in Aramaic texts as part of a consideration of the arguments for dating Daniel by its Aramaic usage. In the course of the discussion, account was taken of the Hebrew usage in earlier and later texts. The evidence here shows that what may with all probability be regarded as earlier texts show a dominance of 'The king A.': the same form appears also in Esther, where it should perhaps be seen as one of its archaizing elements. Chronicles shows forty examples of this earlier style, of which twenty-three are in texts paralleled in Samuel–Kings and seventeen not paralleled; it shows twenty-one cases of the alternative 'A. the king', nineteen of which are not paralleled, one reverses the Kings form, one has an uncertain reading. So, in an almost equal number of cases, Chronicles uses both forms in texts without parallel. What weight do we then give to the strength of influence of the *Vorlage*, even where it is not available to us (or does not exist), and what weight to the pressure of what appears to be the more probable contemporary usage? On this particular point, for obvious reasons, the Ezra–Nehemiah evidence is very meagre: what exists is almost equally balanced, but too scanty to be of use.

If anything may be deduced from such limited evidence in Chronicles, the only conclusion would seem to be that where a writer is making use of sources—and this clearly applies here—there is no absolute means of determining just how far and at what points the author may be influenced by the vocabulary and usage of the sources or by the language which is in general use in that particular period. This is not to deny that overall both Chronicles and Ezra–Nehemiah will be likely to show evidence of the latter influence; even a conscious attempt at writing in an older style, however meticulous, is likely at some points to betray the writer's own context of use. But the degree of such betrayal, and the balancing forces of influence from older sources or patterns and from those of contemporary use, are likely to be insufficiently precise for viable conclusions to be drawn about diversity or unity of authorship between two such works as Chronicles and Ezra–Nehemiah.

The second problem, that of editing, belongs only partly here. It will be necessary subsequently to comment on theories of editorial levels in these works. But at this point it may be observed that any work which handles older material, whether or not we actually have that older material independently extant, is in some degree the product of an editorial process. The same observation applies here as has just been made on linguistic usage: there is no good reason to expect consistency of practice on the part of an editor; and again, however much we may properly expect editors to reflect the usage of their own times, this is no guarantee that they will necessarily make changes to conform the texts on which they are working to a specific standard. A general similarity of use is as much as we may legitimately expect.

(3) *Ideology / Theology*. The increasing interest in the Chronicles–Ezra–Nehemiah material in recent years has brought with it, as might be expected, considerable differences in expounding the nature and function of these writings, whether considered as a unity or as separable works. In the analysis of the books of Chronicles, there have long been sharply divergent views of integrity or disunity: in particular, major sections of 1 Chronicles 1–9 and 24–27 (for example) have been regarded as later additions to the work. Arguments for the separation of such passages are not without cogency; arguments for their original place in the work rely, and prop-

erly enough, on an understanding of the final or virtually final form of the work. Such questions underlie the basic problems of defining unity in biblical writings of many kinds.

The very diversity of theological and ideological interpretation is not in itself to be seen as disturbing. But there is always the danger that the recognition of one particular emphasis, one particular purpose, may lead to the assumption of a greater degree of uniformity than the work actually possesses.

If we begin from the end of the process—assuming on grounds of internal evidence (e.g. genealogies which extend to a roughly definable point in time) and of relationship to other biblical writings, a final date which almost certainly takes us down as far as the fourth century, perhaps even further into the third (the second century being less probable)—then there is some relevance in asking, on the basis of our knowledge or reasonable assumption about the life of the Jewish community under Achaemenid and early Greek rule, what kinds of purpose such a work or works might be directed to serve. Admittedly there is a risk again here of circularity of argument, but other writings, particularly prophetic texts, and non-biblical evidence, provide some check. One very broad element, too broad to give precision, would be the need for reinterpretation which results from the changed political and social position of the community as a small subject province, lacking during the sixth and fifth centuries anything much of control over its own life and perhaps only with the fourth century and beyond acquiring something more, if that is a proper deduction to make from the granting of coinage rights. The whole question of the relationship of such a subject community to the central imperial government during the Achaemenid period remains a difficult one to define in view of the lack of evidence—a problem which applies to the whole of the empire. It is also made more difficult by overready and unrealistic assumptions about a contrast between that rule and its predecessors. Our sources offer an interpretation: they also in some degree reveal a tension which belies the view that the Chronicler in particular was a quietist politically, and that the acceptance of Achaemenid rulers which appears more directly in Ezra–Nehemiah is evidence of satisfaction with the status quo.

More detailed examination of the material suggests the presence of a variety of views. In particular the presence within Ezra 1–6, dealing directly with the Achaemenid period, of unreconciled pictures of the recovery of the community's life, as well as the presence for a later period of confused and confusing accounts of Ezra and Nehemiah, suggests a considerable degree of disagreement under the surface. This is not to be defined simply in establishment and anti-establishment terms, an approach which relies too heavily on doubtful interpretation of difficult prophetic texts (cf. Hanson 1975); but rather of differences of view, both about the relationship between the present community and its past, and about the nature of the community itself and about its self-definition in relation to its context.

The theological and ideological questions here come up against the difficulty of assessing two different forms of presentation in Chronicles and Ezra–Nehemiah respectively. For the former, such deductions as may be made about the understanding of the contemporary situation have to be undertaken by assessing how far an account which purports to describe the past is in reality commenting on the present. This is in Chronicles assisted in some measure by the comparisons which can be made between its account and the parallels in Samuel–Kings; differences, however small, may reveal contemporary matters. But the arguments are always held somewhat in suspense by a measure of uncertainty about the precise form of the texts known to the Chronicler, even though an assumed different *Vorlage* may itself suggest a view of an intermediate stage of uncertain date and context. Inevitably, as with other biblical writings, deductions about what has come down from the past and what is the result of later reworking have to be made with caution. How much understanding of the period described and how much understanding of the writer's contemporary situation could we firmly extract from Chronicles if we had no alternative text at all? For Ezra–Nehemiah, the situation is different and similar: different because at least the narratives purport to describe the period after the exile, similar in that we may detect or assume the use of sources, and, where we may properly conclude that there is a time lapse—perhaps not inconsiderable—between what is being described and the date of the present form of the material, we have to reckon with the same uncertainty as to how we should set a balance between actuality and interpretation. For example, the Artaxerxes material in Ezra 4 is uncertain of dating and still more uncertain of interpretation: but it contributes an important element to our understanding of the differing ways in which the idea of a Davidic monarchy was viewed in the post-exilic period.

Such an example of theme highlights the problem. It is easy to draw a contrast between Chronicles, in which narratives and other material concerning the Davidic monarchy and the broader Davidic themes occupy so prominent a place, and Ezra–Nehemiah, in which these themes appear to be so played down. But it is much more difficult to detect how far the differences are to be understood in terms of a contrast between two sharply divergent attitudes, and these both in the same general period; or should we see not just two but more possible views, themselves eventually brought together within a more complex coming to terms with what now appears to be a permanent loss of the Davidic monarchy, but with various alternatives, political and religious, to be seen as legitimate successors?

4.

Aspects of Unity. A variety of developmental or editorial theories is now available for discussion. In this respect, the approaches to the Chronistic work have in many ways resembled those to the Deuteronomistic History: and indeed, similar ways of understanding the Tetrateuch or the Pentateuch (or the more fully extended series) have also been proposed. The possibility of tracing stages in the formation of the final form of the work in question has been considered in different ways. The assumption of originally separate sources eventually brought together, with the further refinement of supposing earlier 'complete' forms of it, has appeared in various ways in regard to all three of these large entities. One element in this has been the notion of parallel sources; the JEDP of the Pentateuch, continued by some into the following books, offered the possibility of postulating a several-stage editorial process. In general, such views have been abandoned so far as the Deuteronomistic History is concerned: editorial theories are there of a different kind. In the Chronistic work, there is the possibility that additional sources, in some measure parallel, may be postulated for those sections which do not depend on Samuel–Kings; and the opening chapters of Ezra may contain more than one account of the restoration, set partly in parallel in the present form of text, but with an attempt, only partially successful, at providing a consecutive chronology. In some measure, the Ezra and Nehemiah narratives may provide a rather different kind of parallelism in that there appears to be some degree of overlap, perhaps some degree of cross-influence; in the final shape, the two narratives have been interwoven to present a more unified picture of restoration.

Does Chronicles utilize coherent sources alongside Samuel–Kings, sources only reconstructable from the limited material which appears and which may be thought to be coherent? Or do these variations point to an already revised form of Samuel–Kings, in which case the question of provenance is merely pushed one stage further back? Or are they 'inventions' of the final author? The use of the term 'invention' is itself open to question, since it would appear most unlikely that such material is pure fiction, devised to fill a gap or to add to a narrative for some specific interpretative purpose. Much more probably, imaginative use has been made of familiar motifs, exegetical development of allusive phrases in the older material, explanatory comment in the form of narrative, thus building up the picture of a particular ruler or drawing out the meaning of particular stages of the work.

It is here that theories of editorial level also come in. It may be observed that older, and often very elaborate, editorial theories—for example, the multiplicity of editorial levels sometimes proposed for the book of Leviticus—have tended to be thought less acceptable for the Pentateuchal material, but have been developed for other parts of the Old Testament. Thus we have proposals for a multiplicity of editorial stages in the formation of the book of Isaiah (cf. the seven-stage proposals of Vermeylen 1977, 1978), and, more immediately relevant, theories of editorial stages for the Deuteronomistic History, as also for the Chronistic work.

It remains proper to observe that while contradictions or inconsistencies within a single work or in some part of it demand an explanation, not everything that a modern reader finds disconcerting would necessarily be so viewed by an ancient writer or reader. Yet the presence side by side of disparate elements is likely to point, if not to separate sources, at least to the incorporation into a particular narrative of motifs which derive from elsewhere. If the retelling of a story may be described as a 'new edition', then there is abundant evidence of such reworking. But such processes are not what is normally meant by editing. Editorial theories about both the Deuteronomistic History and the Chronistic work aim to show that modifications of an actual or hypothetical earlier form can be seen to be sufficiently consistent to provide evidence of an editorial level, and, if more than one such grouping of modifications can be traced, then of more than one such editorial level.

Both for the Deuteronomistic History and for the Chronistic work the evidence for such editorial levels, while of considerable interest as suggesting aspects of thought within the community at various stages, does not seem to provide a sufficient degree of coherence for it to be acceptable. No one of the alternative theories—single authorship (which clearly should never have been applied with any narrow rigidity, any more than this was possible for the similar view of the Deuteronomistic History); various ideas of stages and editions; the more thoroughgoing separation of two works, with disagreements on the order of their composition, and as to the same or different authorship, and with alternative views of how they are or have come to be related—none of these is really sufficiently demonstrable on the basis of the evidence available to us. This occasions no surprise: in view of the presence of the same kind of problems in regard to most Old Testament writings, we could hardly expect that a single, universally acceptable view could be discovered; or indeed, that the evidence really enables the demonstration of a single, clearly defined and coherent discussion of the work's formation. What recent discussion has demonstrated is such uncertainty.

5.

What kind of unity may we then consider? However strongly the division of the work is argued, we are in the end left with the reality of the biblical presentation: Chronicles–Ezra–Nehemiah is presented in such a way as to claim unity, but it is not a unity of uniformity.

We come back to basic questions of what we might expect or properly suppose about such a group of books. As indicated, the expectation of uniformity is a false one. If we may rightly ask of a modern author or editor that he presents a text which agrees completely with itself, and feel no surprise if a reviewer finds it proper to pick out from what we write those points at which we show inconsistency, it certainly does not follow from this that the formation of an ancient work such as Chronicles–Ezra–Nehemiah will offer such uniformity. Even if we consider that there is sufficient consistency to argue for a single author or final editor, it should occasion us no surprise that there will be differences from the main lines of thought. Indeed, in such delicate areas as theological or political view, we may doubt whether complete consistency is ever attainable or even desirable, granted the intangibility of some aspects of the area under discussion. This is not to argue that an ancient writer makes use of paradox in theological or ideological presentation; such a sophisticated method, which has both merits and demerits, hardly seems appropriate to postulate. But quite wide areas of divergence are to be expected. They may derive from sources, used but not slavishly subordinated or reworked. As often in biblical writings, such source material may be placed within a framework of interpretation which invites the reader to understand the story in a particular manner. The compilation of Chronicles was hardly directed to replacing the earlier form of the material, but constitutes rather an invitation to read that earlier form in a new manner.

Similarly, we may ask whether, in so far as our texts show evidence of exegetical procedures, we should expect the application of a single method, a single style of interpretation; or whether it is not more natural to suppose that, both in the process of formation and in the continuing use of the material, different slants have been introduced. If we may detect trends of interpretation, then it does not necessarily follow—though it may—that a single editorial hand has been at work; where similarities appear, both of thought and of language, we may see the impact of a particular style, itself reflecting some particular situation to which a response is being made.

The analogy of the book of Isaiah may help. No one sensitive to the realities of language and thought—let alone to the theological improprieties which arise from a simplistic reading—can fail to see the different levels and styles which appear within the book. But overready generalization from these has led to an artificial division of the book, for, with all the seriousness with which the differences must be taken, there is still a book of Isaiah with some kind of unity. Whether this unity is the result of a final editorial hand which, without overtidying, has drawn the material together and given it its final structure, or whether it results from the reading together of the various elements within their final form, it is still unmistakable that this is a single book.

The interrelationship between the component books of the 'Chronistic work' (as indeed also of the Deuteronomistic History) may be equally the result of one or other of these same causes. My own inclination is to the latter, though I should not thereby wish to exclude the possibility that there has been some impact of a guiding hand. But, in view of the complexity of the evidence, I should prefer not to attempt to quantify the relative weight to be given to each.

Chapter 15

RIGORISM AND OPENNESS IN THE THEOLOGY OF THE PERSIAN (ACHAEMENIAN) PERIOD[1]

1.

However proper it is to see the moment of the Babylonian conquest and the subsequent re-establishment of the Jewish community in Palestine as a watershed in the life and thought of that community, we must avoid over-simplified assumptions about the degree to which it necessarily marked changes of a radical kind. In part, the tendency to assume such radical change is conditioned by the convenience of the pre-exilic/post-exilic terminological divide; this in its turn is undergirded by the significant end of the monarchy and the destruction of the Jerusalem temple. In part, also, the assumption of difference is tied in with the degree to which, because of lack of information, the period of the Babylonian exile—itself a misleading expression—remains very largely a blank, filled only with what are largely conjectures based on too little evidence. Having myself used both 'Exile' and 'Restoration' in the title of a study of the period, I must acknowledge that these terms can and do mislead; and, for our purpose in this discussion, the assumptions which underlie the use of the word 'restoration' are particularly in need of scrutiny.

The title of this study refers to the 'Persian' period—better, though more technically, the 'Achaemenian' period (since the other term can be misleading)—thereby avoiding such a loaded term as 'post-exilic'; though a too precise historical attachment to the period which runs from Cyrus to Alexander

---

1. This essay was presented as a paper to the Society of Biblical Literature at its 1985 Annual Meeting in Amsterdam.

would assume a too exact knowledge of the chronology of the evidence available to us.

A context is needed for this discussion; and I therefore begin with some reference to the problems of definition for the earlier periods of religious history. For there too, we may apply such terms as 'rigorism' and 'openness' and I have used these terms as short-hand, recognizing that they can be loaded: 'openness' is thought to be a good quality, 'rigorism' a less satisfactory one. I would wish to avoid such pre-judgment. Equally we may think in terms of purity and syncretism, of Israelite and Canaanite, of a desert tradition and a settled one. The uncertainties about the earliest history—patriarchal, 'Mosaic', wilderness and conquest 'periods'—point to the unsatisfactory nature of such overgeneralized terms. Clearly, a more adequate understanding of the historical developments—for example, a resolution of the debates about the so-called conquest—could help in delineating and understanding religious change. Yet, even without such a picture, we may recognize the degree to which what is often said about the religious developments of that earlier period is in terms which imply, or indeed frequently actually state, a sharp contrast between (a) what is in one way or another assumed to be an ancient and coherent system, often thought to be pure and uncontaminated, and (b) other systems with which this comes into contact and which are, by assumption if not by descriptive definition, recognizably alien to it. Such an assumption of early purity in religion is historically unrealistic; it is evidently a critical statement about a later contemporary situation. Only a partial alleviation of this is offered when such a term as 'syncretism' is used. Not that I would wish to deny the propriety of such a term; but it does beg the question by assuming what is not necessarily demonstrable, namely that two distinct religious systems meet and partly merge. We may see the encounter between Greek and Jewish religion in the third and second centuries BCE as one in which questions of syncretism can emerge; but even there we have to take account of our now much greater awareness of earlier contacts between the Classical and Near Eastern worlds of thought. It is much less clear how far the term may be used for the 'Israelite/Canaanite', 'desert/settled' and other such contrasts, and how this

would bear upon the nature of religious change and development in Israel's early history.

We cannot expect to agree over the detailed appraisal of this
area of discussion. But however much or however little we
may believe it possible adequately to define those earlier stages,
we would, I suspect, be in agreement that our discovery of the
religion of the monarchical period too depends on whether or
not we can penetrate behind the idealized presentations which
the biblical text offers. And with that will go differences of view
as to how we are to treat the partially concealed indicators
within the biblical text and the often problematic evidence of
archaeological discovery. Of the latter, Kuntillet 'Ajrud stands
out as an example, though not an isolated one. How are we to
view the pointers in biblical and extra-biblical evidence to
other levels of religious thought and practice than those as it
were officially and ideally laid before us?' It remains an area
for difference of opinion as to whether we should describe such
'aberrations' as examples of alien influence, of divergent practice, of fringe activity, or whether, not treating them as aberrations at all but as part of a rich texture of religious belief and
practice, we should accept them as genuine elements of
Israelite religious life to be treated as such whether or not they
eventually survived and became part of the norm. For the
same way, like it or not, elements within the Christian tradition—the whole heaven and hell mythology of the mediaeval
period, for example—are equally real parts of the whole; however much we might incline to view them as theologically less
than satisfying, they still belong. So much of the biblical presentation of such elements tends to be at the level of carica-
ture—very vividly in the figures of Jezebel and Athaliah. The
emphasis on the idealistic presentation may easily produce a
view which does not make any adequate attempt at appreciating the ways in which we must endeavour to envisage the
realities of biblical religion, practice and belief. If our hope of
uncovering the ways in which the 'ordinary' Israelite of
Judaean thought is likely to be delusive, we may at least recognize that there is bound to be a gap between what pass for
the authorized norms of belief and the actuality. Nor is the gap
a simple one between what we might term the theologically
educated and articulate and the 'ordinary believer', since at

any level of sophistication there are disctinctions to be drawn
between intellectualized description and emotionally held
convictions. (The debate in Great Britain about the ordination
of women makes this abundantly clear.)

Part of the unreality of such discussions turns on the degree
to which areas of evidence tend to be treated in isolation from
one another, and in separation from attempts at understanding the realities of political life. I introduce that term too with
some measure of caution, since suspicions about politics and
assumptions that religion can somehow be separated from
politics still affect our judgments. It is easy, given the state of
the world, to be cynical about politics and politicians; and there
are good grounds for the suspicion that even in well regulated
societies what goes on under the surface of political life has its
considerable measure of at least what may be termed
'wheeling and dealing'. But the more positive appraisal
includes the recognition that—since religion in whatever
form is an element, and an important one, in human experience and thought—the handling of a community, its administration, demands that regard be paid to that element. Furthermore, there have always been those who have believed,
and sincerely, that a satisfactory political administration can
be built on a religious foundation. The millenarian experi-
ments of past and present constitute numerous examples of
this; and we can think readily of contemporary societies in
which there are either determined efforts at the top towards
imposing a rigid religious order, or minorities which would
like to see such a return to 'law and order', to moral standards,
to religious conformity. (So, very clearly, in some Christian,
Jewish and Muslim circles.)

It is therefore without cynicism that we may consider the
degree to which the understanding of the development of Old
Testament religion must be related to the moves of the politicians. It is a discussion which I do not need to elaborate in
regard to the monarchical period, since both the Judaean and
the Israelite monarchies testify to it. Eventually there was to
be an ambivalent attitude towards the Judaean monarchy: it
could be seen either as a divinely ordained institution which
continued to have its adherents among the idealists of a post-
monarchical age; or as a religious disaster of the first order to

those who saw kings as corrupters of both religion and social morality. Judgments on the kings are made in accordance with pre-formed views of what constitutes religious conformity. But the fact that, almost universally, kings are condemned for not removing the high places makes it clear that such institutions, whatever their precise nature, were a normal part of the religion of the monarchical period, though eventually to be discarded. (It is perhaps worthy of note that, among the kings who are praised for their reforming zeal, both Hezekiah and Josiah can be judged to have been less effective politically than some at least of their condemned associates.)

Centralization and uniformity are political as well as religious ideals. The notion that the religion of a community should be all of one piece is a political ideal, though this does not mean that it may not be shared by a considerable part of the religious as well as the political leadership. Since law and religion are closely bonded together, and the standards and indeed the detail of justice are regarded as having religious sanction, the unifying of religion and the unifying of law go together. The establishment of royal sanctuaries, whether in one or more administrative centres, helps to guarantee the stability of the administration. But it does not follow from this that religion is uniform; in reality, religion is always multi-formed. The contrast is not the simple one between a central truth which ought to be universally accepted and the variety of beliefs and practices which derive from alien influence, but between a state cult geared to the needs of the political community—itself incorporating a variety of elements, some eventually to be discarded—and the richness and variety of religious belief and practice which both continue to exist from the past and develop in the way in which religions do develop. (The prophets fit into this complex as reflecting various aspects of it, and not a uniform tradition; they have, of course, themselves been edited into a greater degree of conformity.)

2.

When we move from these brief reflections on the earlier stages to consider the position under Achaemenid rule, we may expect to find a degree of continuity. Changed political circumstances will have their effect. Clearly the politically subservient position of the Judaean community must be an important factor. A contrast should not, however, be too sharply drawn, since—apart from a brief period of what we may suppose to be political independence under Josiah (hardly more than a dozen years)—Judah was a subject state, albeit sometimes in rebellion, from the time of Ahaz onwards. By the time Cyrus conquered Babylon and took over the empire, Judah had already for nearly fifty years lacked both independence and monarchy. We may expect the political problems of subservience to continue to affect religious attitudes and practice. We may also legitimately suppose that the tradition of independent royal power in the remote past (cf. Ezra 4), and a more recent, if brief, period of actual independence, will have their effect on thinking. The fact that there were those who thought in terms of a revival under a renewed Davidic kingship occasions no surprise. But in view of the fact that political subservience was to remain a continuing experience for more than two centuries under the Achaemenids, we may expect there to have been a greater concern with what could constitute religious reality in such a political situation.

One part of our discussion must therefore involve the attempt at understanding that political situation; another must assess what evidence of more general attitudes may be extracted from biblical and non-biblical materials—here in particular considering the evidence of proper names.

We may observe a tendency in much discussion of this period to make sharp contrasts between two types of attitude: the terms 'openness' and 'rigorism' (used in the title of this study) represent one form of this contrast; others are universalism/particularism; assimilation/exclusivism. When we juxtapose these terms, we see their ambivalent quality. In discussions of the period, there is some viewing of the universalistic attitudes (often associated with Deutero-Isaiah) as being satisfying, a proper development natural from the once-achieved stress on monotheism. If no other god exists, the one and only god must of necessity control all nations and therefore may be expected to invite allegiance from them. By contrast, particularism, as found in Trito-Isaiah (in some passages), and in the Ezra–Nehemiah narratives, while intelligible as a necessary defence of the religious community and thus excusable, is often thought to be retrogressive. Exclusivity in religious belief may, however, be held to be commendable because it stresses the desirability of a strict adherence to the religious tradition, understood as being directed to a supposedly recognizable form of Yahwism; assimilation, of a kind suggested by the Elephantine texts and, in the next period, thought to be characteristic of the Hellenizers, is regarded as undesirable because weakening that central tradition.

A fully monotheistic and hence universalist attitude may be understood in ways which incorporate strongly nationalisatic and particularistic attitudes—as is indeed the case in some less often stressed elements in the Deutero-Isaianic tradition. To be particularist, and to exclude any religious relationship with the outside world, does not of itself preclude the possibility that the worship of the deity of the community incorporates what may be recognized as assimilationist elements (rigid and exclusive sects often hold doctrines which must be regarded as odd and ill-founded). It would seem more appropriate to view the situation as more complex, and to expect to find more shades of opinion than are expressed in the slogans which tend to characterize some of the discussions of the period.

a. *Politico-Religious Factors*

Religious attitudes and political realities go hand in hand. One effect of the reporting, both in Isaiah and in Ezra-Nehemiah, of the rise of Cyrus and his relationships with the Jewish community and of the various activities of subsequent Achaemenid 'rulers', has been to support a view of these rulers as religiously tolerant. It must be seriously doubted whether such concepts as 'tolerance' and 'intolerance' are appropriate; more properly we may see the Achaemenids as politicians, their actions much more dominated by political, military and economic considerations. Below the surface of the narratives, particularly perhaps in the case of Nehemiah, we may detect indications that Persian actions were not universally acceptable. If we may judge both from the Old Testament texts and from the extra-biblical sources, much of what was said and done by Cyrus, as also by Darius, was directed towards establishing the legitimacy of rule. This will have been the case for Cyrus, because as ruler taking over the former Babylonian empire, itself the successor to the Assyrians, a claim to be the true successor—and a more acceptable one than the last Babylonian ruler Nabonidus or than all Babylonians—is naturally to be expected; equally so for Darius, because as a rebel, whose precise relationship to the royal house remains problematic, the continuity of a dubious succession must be bolstered by comparable claims. When we look at the biblical record, making due allowance for the Jewish stance which that record naturally reveals, we may detect the claim that Cyrus, and in his footsteps Darius, is to be viewed as in succession to the Davidic monarchy, and that, as temple builders or restorers, they could be seen in parallel with the founders of that monarchy. Whatever the precise relationship between the books of Chronicles and Ezra–Nehemiah may be, it is evident that a succession from the David–Solomonic achievement is to be seen in the Cyrus–Darius story. Indeed a fuller succession is to be seen in the accounts of the various Davidide reformers and restorers and their post-exilic followers in Achaemenid rulers and Jewish agents. Again, whatever the precise nature of the 1 Esdras presentation, there would appear to be significance in seeing the succession on a more limited scale as comprehending Josiah—Cyrus/Sheshbazzar, Zerubbabel, Jeshua—Artaxerxes/Ezra (cf. also Ezra 6.14).

Granted such claims to status on the part of Achaemenid rulers, we may ask what kind of response we might expect to find in the Jewish community. In part this is related to questions about the kind of religious policy the rulers pursued, and here there is no single answer. Alongside claims, documented in various ways in addition to the biblical record, that they offered support and protection for religious institutions— temples and priesthoods—in various places, we may see that other elements in the accounts, both in the Greek sources and elsewhere, point to harsh treatment. In the case of rebellion, or suspicion of such, there are clear indications of firm, indeed ruthless, action being taken. There is no suggestion of a single, uniform policy of support for all religious institutions.

Equally we may recognize that there are no precise indications of the imposition of the rulers' own religious views on their subjects. This question as to whether ancient rulers imposed religious practice or belief on their subject peoples remains in general a debated one; if the older assumptions of such imposition by the Assyrians have given way to a much more cautious view, the question is not fully resolved. We may perhaps most naturally posit a degree of what we might call 'formal acknowlegment' of the deity or deities (particularly, we may assume, the chief deity as representative of the nation [Aššur in the case of the Assyrians, Marduk in the case of the Babylonians]). To pray for the Achaemenid ruler (as is laid down in Ezra 6.10), may be a somewhat ambivalent procedure. On the one hand, it may be understood (and the Cyrus cylinder gives support to this) as a recognition that the ruler is glad to have the protection and support, particularly no doubt within the relevant territory, of the deity of the specific subject people; on the other hand (and here there is a link with the royal claims of the Achaemenids), the position of the king in his more precise relation to the deity could easily tend to involve some degree of assimilation between the deity of the specific subject people, in the biblical instance Yahweh, and the deity recognized as supreme by the ruler and therefore related to his wider royal claims. The fact that the title 'God of heaven' is used in the biblical account—a title which may most probably be adjudged to be post-exilic, even if anticipated in some earlier material—makes possible a certain slurring over of the difficulty of deciding to which deity reference is actually being made. The fact, however, that no such problem arises in the Cyrus cylinder, where it is explicitly affirmed that Marduk chose Cyrus, suggests that the comparable document for Judah, whatever its precise relationship to the texts in Ezra 1 and 5–6, would name Yahweh (Yahweh appears with the title 'God of heaven' in 1.2-3, but not in 5–6); the Achaemenid ruler invites the protection of that deity.

The other side to this question concerns the attitudes of the Jewish community. Nothing directly in the texts suggests the acceptance of the Achaemenid deity or deities; but the recognition of the royal claims of the ruler to succession to the Davidic monarchy carries with it such religious elements as we may suppose that monarchy to have had. The community is involved in a relationship to a ruler whose position vis-à-vis the deity remains not fully clear, partly no doubt because of the way in which the documentary evidence has come down to us; but the fact that he has a specific and particular relationship, as ruler and as member of the dynasty, is clear enough. We may therefore ask how far the enforced acceptance of such an alien ruler affects the religious attitudes of the members of the community. Whatever the origin and basic meaning of the royal law in Deut. 17.14-20 may have been, we need to consider whether, under these political circumstances, it takes on a more specific reference. Does it now represent an element of protest against the position occupied by an alien as king in Jerusalem? It could be placed alongside the protests to be found elsewhere: for example, Hag. 2.21-23, with its evident claims for royal status for Zerubbabel; the last part of the prayer-psalm in Nehemiah 9 with its stress on the unacceptable rights of alien rulers in the control of the Judaean economy (so especially vv. 36-37); the possible undercurrents in the Nehemiah narratives, where, whatever Nehemiah himself may be supposed to have thought, there could have been those who saw in him a new monarch—not Davidic, but at least a genuine member of the Jewish community. To this we may add the wider issues raised by the reinterpretation of the Davidic theme in priestly terms, with the application of royal procedures and royal status to the priestly line and in particular to the High Priest; and alongside this, and perhaps overlapping it, the whittling away of the Davidic theme as a political one, and its replacement by that of David as cult-founder and his successors as cult-preservers or restorers, with their most condemned examples (especially Ahaz) as cult-repudiators. For some, it would appear, the Achaemenid rulers themselves stood in that succession—our sources providing essentially only positive assessments. Another aspect of this, which may be held to preserve different elements in balance, is the hope of a future Davidic ruler, conceived in political and/or religious terms; and the two-messiah hopes expressed in some of the post-biblical writings.

Now these examples do not quite fit into the rigorism/openness categories. We might suppose that any who accepted the Achaemenid royal and hence religious claims as valid and unquestioned could be held to stand at one end of a scale of atti-

tudes; at an extreme from this would be potential rebels looking for a straight restoration of Davidic monarchy, and here
we might include those who took this view of Zerubbabel
(though whether that includes Haggai or Zerubbabel himself
remains uncertain). Between the extremes, but not neatly to
be arranged on a scale, would be the alternative possibilities
which could involve realistic acceptance of where political
control lay, while still loooking to a non-alien expression of the
realities of what underlay the concept of Davidic monarchy.
At this politic religious level, there is scope for numerous attitudes co-existing within the community.

b. *Literary Stances*
The various writings which may be assigned to the Achaemenian period or which in some measure reflect it themselves
show differences of attitude. The description of these works
has often tended to be too simplified. Thus an older tendency
was to view Chronicles–Ezra–Nehemiah as a single work
whose views are expressed most clearly in its final stages, the
exclusive, anti-foreign attitudes of Ezra 9–10 and Nehemiah
13. More recently, distinction has been seen between the more
open attitude of Chronicles (even describing this as a protest
against a policy of isolationism) and the narrower views of
Ezra–Nehemiah. Neither seems adequate to the material.
Chronicles, re-presenting the earlier story of the monarchy,
clearly sees the true focus in the Jerusalem-centred Davidic
kingdom, itself pictured as the context for the restored community which is reached at the end of the genealogical
scheme of 1 Chronicles 1–9. To that centre, the loyal from all
the tribes of Israel can be restored; but realism, as expressed in
the Hezekiah narratives (2 Chron. 29–31) recognizes that
only few of the north will in fact express their adherence. That
same realism appears to be present when, in Ezra–Nehemiah, the true restored community is pictured as the faithful
returned exiles, to whom those who separate themselves from
the defilement of the outside world may be joined (Ezra 6.21).
Within the whole corpus, we may recognize that the Ezra
material and the Nehemiah material contain what may be
seen as a different emphasis on the purity of the community
by the extension of the older marriage laws and customs, to

insist, the one on the breaking of foreign marriages, and the other on the relinquishing of the practice. It is appropriate in this to see at least three levels of thought regarding the nature of the community and the degree to which its life must be more or less strictly kept separate from the outside world; within this, the central principle is clearly a religious one.

It has also been common, though less so in recent years, to see the books of Ruth and Jonah as presenting a less rigorous view. (If Ruth is dated much earlier—which still seems to me improbable—then it is not relevant or barely so to this discussion.) It must be doubted whether in fact there is here a narrow contrast to the Ezra material in particular, though a different shade of emphasis may be detected. Ruth stresses the full adherence to the community of a woman who as a foreigner has contracted a marriage with a Judaean, but who has repudiated her alien religion; Jonah is more evidently concerned with the universality of divine judgment and with offering what could be seen as an exposition of the theme of Israel's greater responsibility for obedience in view of its particular relationship to God. Further aspects of such thought may be seen in Judith, Tobit, Esther.

If we go logically a stage further and recognize the degree to which all the earlier biblical traditions have received their more definitive form in the post-exilic period, then we should, for completeness' sake, consider all that material and ask how far we can detect in the finalizing stages evidence of a single style of thought or, as seems more probable, a diversity of emphases.

c. *The Evidence of Personal Names*

In recent discussion of the period, the evidence of personal names in both biblical and non-biblical material has been invoked. Is it possible by a consideration of these names, to draw any clear conclusions about the strictness or laxity of religious belief and practice? Some discussions of the matter show considerable caution in handling the evidence; others are more confident that deductions can be made to show a greater degree of syncretistic or alien belief or a greater conformity to a normative Yahwistic view. Non-Yahwistic names have sometimes been held to show that their bearers or those who gave the names could not have been of Jewish descent; conversely such names have been thought to provide clear evidence of syncretistic attitudes, whereas Yahwistic names bear the impress of the orthodox, sometimes termed the 'Yahweh alone' party.

A qualifier must be inserted here. The biblical evidence inevitably presents considerable problems of chronology; names which appear in Ezra–Nehemiah may be assumed to be post-exilic, those in Chronicles are in some instances clearly so (for example in 1 Chronicles 9 and in genealogical lists which run over into the later period), others less certain, and these will be variously assessed. Within such material, a chronological sequence is not always available; thus comparisons between the list associated with Zerubbabel in Ezra 2/ Nehemiah 7 (which cannot be given a precise date) and the names associated with Ezra in Ezra 8–10 and elsewhere— such comparisons do not permit the assumption that the absence (largely or completely) of foreign theophoric names in the latter shows a shift in naming policy and hence in religious allegiance (cf. Bickermann 1984: 256). Names known from archaeological evidence are sometimes clearly fixed in time; others, such as the governors' names belonging to the period, remain debated because of the lack of evidence of their find-spot. Appropriate weight must be given to local differences, particularly in areas which must be seen as border or outside Judah proper; at the same time the evidence from such fringe areas (and this will include both Babylonia and Egypt) must not be discounted if it suggests what may be termed 'deviant' belief or practice.

We may note first—and this general observation provides a useful context for the consideration of names—that the great majority of personal names are in fact Yahwistic in form. This is true of the biblical and extra-biblical texts. This is, of course, what we might expect, whatever precise view we take of the development of Old Testament religion. If we take into account further the names which have no theophoric element, some or perhaps many of which may be assumed to be shortened forms of normal Yahwistic names—this is a reasonable assumption given the general picture—then the minority of strictly non-Yahwistic names is even more firmly held in proportion. We do not need to postulate a 'Yahweh-alone' party to explain the preponderance. The absence of a theophoric element—which is attested in names through the whole biblical period—does not imply indifference; it may more naturally be held to imply a Yahwistic assumption.

Non-Yahwistic names may be divided into two groups: those in which another divine name or title appears, and those which are clearly non-Jewish in all respects. (i) In regard to the first group, a distinction should perhaps further be made between names which use a deity name known to be non-Jewish/Israelite: such is Barqos (Ezra 2.53 = Neh. 7.55) where the Qos element clearly indicates the Edomite deity of that name. Since the name appears in a list which, as now presented, distinguishes some groups which could not show a proper genealogy and whose position in the community was questioned, we may observe that no question is raised about this particular group: the Qos element (and indeed what appears to be the Aramaic Bar element) does not call for notice. Where we might have expected doubt, it would appear that the non-Yahwistic element is either acceptable or ignored. I believe this indicates an important point in the discussion of other names where such a context is not provided. We may suppose that this particular group belongs to an area of Judaean–Edomite contact, a border area, where mixture of communities is likely (cf. the names with Qos from Arad); though we may also postulate the presence within the Jewish community of persons of Edomite extraction. The use of the deity name may represent the assumption that Qos *is* Yahweh: if we could take Kushaiah in 1 Chron. 15.17 as also derived from this divine name, the point would be explicit, but such an identification is uncertain. We may also ask how far in the giving of names the religious motive may be held to be consciously present, and how far custom, which may include the giving of names which belong within the family of the recipient, is to be regarded as more important. Biblical accounts of the giving and meaning of personal names often seem to suggest that parents were fully conscious of the nature of their choices. But it must be doubtful whether we should assume that the naming stories associated with notable personages really reflect normal practice.

(My own father was named Jabez by his parents: since he was born at a period of family trial, the strongly Bible-oriented religious adherence of his parents could have been influenced by 1 Chron. 4.9-10, but since the name was that of a contemporary evangelist of some note, the choice may have reflected the desire to make a link there.)

We are sometimes in danger of assuming that biblical personages were more consciously religious, not least because our documentation limits our view. (L. Köhler's picture of the community in his *Hebrew Man*, while still of value, makes the assumptions too simply.)

The appearance of Qos in a name of the post-exilic period is matched by others in Chronicles–Ezra–Nehemiah which raise similar but not identical questions. It is noteworthy that there are names with the theophoric title Ba'al (Baalhanan in 1 Chron. 27.28; Beeliada in 1 Chron. 14.7; Bealiah in 1 Chron. 12.6). The female divine name Anath appears in a plural form—what kind of plural is this? is it like Elohim?—in personal names such as Anathoth (1 Chron. 7.8; Neh. 10.19) and Anathothiyah (1 Chron. 8.24). These are particularly relevant because of the use of the divine name Anath in association with Yahweh at Elephantine. Both the Anath-Yahu and Ishum-bethel forms (and presumably also the Heree-bethel form) should probably be seen as titles or descriptions which point to the assimilation into the concept of the single deity of elements which elsewhere exist in separation. The Elephantine evidence is also significant at another level in that we observe that none of our information implies any thought that the religious practice or belief there was unacceptable to Jerusalem. The natural inference from this would be that the current forms of belief and practice in Judah would not, on a close analysis, conform to that kind of strictness and rigor which later thought would suppose them to have had.

Conclusions from such evidence are limited. It is clear that whatever the precise beliefs held, the recognition of Yahweh as the deity of the community can be seen as normal. The problem arises when we ask (1) how far the worship of the deity or recognition of him rigidly excluded elements which we would see to belong to a 'broader', less rigorous, view; and (2) where the dividing lines would be drawn between what we (with hindsight) would consider to be a genuine and concentrated Yahwistic belief, and what we would think made concessions to eventually unacceptable ideas. We may need to ask how far a concept such as that of Wisdom being present at creation or functioning as the agent of creation—as this is presented in a sophisticated manner in Proverbs 8—may conceal a degree of latitude of religious belief, incorporating a feminine element in relation to the belief in a single and male deity; and how far such a latitude expressed in relation to the concept of a consort for Yahweh has entered into the eventual shaping of Jewish belief.

(ii) The other type of personal name is one which can be seen to be foreign in all respects. Such are the Babylonian and Persian names which are actually used. If in some instances it may be debated whether a name is foreign or not, in most the position is clear.

The evidence is again limited. It presents considerable problems of interpretation. The list includes several evidently Babylonian names; of these, two at least probably involve members of the Davidic family, Zerubbabel and Shenazzar; another, Sheshbazzar (who is not equatable with Shenazzar) is unknown to us from any other information than that appearing in Ezra 1 and 5, and he has no family attachment. This strongly suggests the he was not of Davidic family; it is most probable that he was Jewish, and his description as *nasi'* suggests high status; in Ezra 5 he is *peḥāh*. Also significant is Sanballat of Samaria, another high-ranking official and presumably of local family. In his case, we find an example of a family which, like other families in non-biblical sources, uses in alternation a foreign name, in this case Sanballat, and Yahwistic names, as we know from the Elephantine and Wadi Daliyeh papyri. Sanballat thus appears as a family name, used in alternate generations. No such alternation appears in the Davidic family lists. But the parallel between the Sanballat family and others elsewhere suggests that the choice of names reveals both an association with Yahwistic tradition and a political element.

The use of such Babylonian names does not appear to be widespread, and the association with the royal family or officialdom suggests a political motivation. There is no indication that the Babylonian name is a second one alongside a 'native' Jewish name. There is no analogy to the throne name, since our evidence in almost the same period, under Egyptian and Babylonian dominance, shows the use as throne name (Jehoiakim for Eliakim, Zedekiah for Mattaniah) of an equally home-based form (so too Shallum/Jehoahaz). We can hardly use the evidence of Daniel, which purports to explain that Babylonian names were imposed on Jewish heroes, but which may in fact have a different basis. The use of Babylonian names would seem to indicate a political gesture to the ruling power; both Shenazzar and Zerubbabel must be assumed to have been born in the Babylonian period (so too Sheshbazzar). The case of Sanballat is more difficult for we know only a local attribution—'of Horon'—and have no family tree or earlier governor's name (none appears in the intrusive section of Ezra 4). If this case suggests a continuation of the use of Babylonian names for high officials under Achaemenid rule, we may ask whether the recognition of the king as king of Babylon and of Beyond the River belonging with Babylonia as one administrative unit—which is the case in the earlier part of the period at least—results in the continued practice. The lists also include Bilshan, another leader with a Babylonian home, and Mordecai (Ezra 2.2 = Neh. 7.7); this latter can, of course, be an otherwise unknown leader, but we might wonder whether, in making up this document, the name has been taken from the Esther story in whatever form it was by then in circulation. The use of the deity names Marduk and Bel is no more and no less significant than the appearance of the deity name Shamash (abbreviated to Shesh) in Sheshbazzar or Sin in Sanballat.

Curiously the only clearly Persian name in the lists is Bigvai, known to us also from Elephantine and Josephus. The name appears to be similar to the Bigtha, Bigthan of Esther 1.10, 2.21. Its chronological place, since it appears also in the Ezra 2.2–Neh. 7.7 context, remains unclear. It can hardly be argued that it shows an early use of Persian names: its further occurrences are late fifth and fourth century, and perhaps this is where it belongs. The appearance of the name then for an important official, the governor of Judah, would suggest the replacement of the political use of Babylonian names by Persian names. But the evidence is very meagre.

In the Ezra 2–Nehemiah 7 list, the only other clearly non-Jewish name is Asnah (Barqos we have already considered). If it is Egyptian, we might wonder whether its use is linked with familiarity with the Joseph story rather than evidence for Egyptian connections of a direct kind.

Conclusion

Such a relatively brief overview of some of the relevant evidence does not lead easily to firm conclusions. The imprecision, and the difficulty of giving clearly acceptable definitions, suggest that it is not possible to define particular groups within the Jewish community in any hard and fast manner. In the areas of evidence which have been considered there are indications of shades of view, stretching over a wide range, and not to be treated as if they were mutually exclusive. The tendency, both in earlier and in more recent discussion, has been to oversimplify and to label: in some degree this would seem to be a retrojection from what is known, and sometimes merely what is popularly believed, about later parties and groups or perhaps sects within the Judaism of the turn of the era. If it is proper to look back to try to discover the antecedents of such groups as we then find described or alluded to, this must be done with a due recognition of the degree to which we still do not really know enough about the later groups for this to be more than a very tentative exercise.

The problem under discussion appears in reality to be but one facet of a question which faces any developing religious tradition: how is it possible, when we consider the multi-form character of a religion, to know on what basis and by what criteria we recognize it as coherent with its earlier stages and with its origins. This brings us back to where we started, in the recognition that, however much or little we may be able to know about the earlier periods, we must accept the reality of change within the religious tradition, and the degree to which the adherents of a particular religion will be under pressure either to maintain that nothing has changed or to acknowledge change and to suppose that it is possible to reactivate the purity of the original and thereby to recover the genuine tradition once again. Studies of religions which are amply documented over centuries suggest that the degree of change is much more extensive than conservative believers would like to think, and that attempts at recovering pristine purity, dependent as they are on theories about the nature of that purity, inevitably involve yet further shifts.

We still search, and the endeavour is not the less valuable for attempting to reach the unattainable, for that which defines Old Testament religion and makes it cohere for all its diversity. Too wide a definition blurs the edges; too precise, and we are stating what never was.

BIBLIOGRAPHY

Ackroyd, P.R.
1953   'Criteria for the Maccabaean Dating of Old Testament Literature', *VT* 3: 113-32.
1967   'History and Theology in the Writings of the Chronicler', *Concordia Theological Monthly* 38: 501-15.
1968a   *Exile and Restoration* (London: SCM).
1968b   'Historians and Prophets', in *Svensk Exegetisk Årsbok*, 33: 18-54.
1968c   'The Interpretation of Exile and Restoration', *The Canadian Journal of Theology* 14: 3-12.
1968d   'A Judgment Narrative between Kings and Chronicles? An Approach to Amos 7.9-17', in *Canon and Authority: Essays in Old Testament Religion and Theology* (ed. G.W. Coats and B.O. Long; Philadelphia: Fortress), 71-87 (reprinted as Ackroyd 1987b, Chapter 12).
1970a   *The Age of the Chronicler*. Supplement to *Colloquium—The Australian and New Zealand Theological Review*, Auckland, New Zealand (reprinted as Chapter 1 of the present volume).
1970b   *Israel under Babylon and Persia* (New Clarendon Bible; Oxford: Clarendon).
1971a   'Aspects of the Jeremiah Tradition', *Indian Journal of Theology* 20: 1-12.
1971b   *The First Book of Samuel* (CBC; Cambridge: Cambridge University Press).
1972   'The Temple Vessels: A Continuity Theme', VTS 23: 166-81; reprinted as Ackroyd 1987b, Chapter 4.
1973a   *I and II Chronicles, Ezra, Nehemiah* (Torch Bible Commentary; London: SCM).
1973b   'The Theology of the Chronicler', *Lexington Theological Quarterly* 8: 101-16 (reprinted as Chapter 11 of the present volume).
1974   'An Interpretation of the Babylonian Exile: A Study of 2 Kings 20, Isaiah 38–39', *Scottish Journal of Theology* 27: 329-52 (reprinted as Ackroyd 1987b, Chapter 9).
1976   'God and People in the Chronicler's Presentation of Ezra', in *La notion biblique de Dieu* (ed. J. Coppens; Louvain), 45-162.
1977a   'The Chronicler as Exegete', *JSOT* 2: 2-32 (reprinted as Chapter 12 of the present volume).
1977b   'Continuity and Discontinuity: Rehabilitation and Authentication', in *Theology and Tradition* (ed. D.A. Knight; Philadelphia: Fortress), 215-34.
1979a   'Faith and its Reformulation in the Post-Exilic Period', *Theology Digest* 27: 323-46.

— 1979b   'The History of Israel in the Exilic and Post-exilic Periods', in
           Tradition and Interpretation (ed. G.W. Anderson; Oxford: Oxford
           University Press), 320-50.
   1981   'The Death of Hezekiah: A Pointer to the Future?' in *De la Torah
           au Messie* (H. Cazelles Festschrift), 219-26 (reprinted as Ackroyd
           1987b, Chapter 7).
— 1982a   'Archaeology, Politics and Religion in the Persian Period', *The
           Iliff Review* 39: 5-24.
   1982b   'Isaiah 36–39: Structure and Function', in *Von Kanaan bis Kerala*
           (J. van der Ploeg Festschrift), 3-21 (reprinted as Ackroyd 1987b,
           Chapter 10).
   1983   'The Jewish Community in Palestine in the Persian Period', in
           Cambridge History of Judaism, I (ed. W.D. Davies and L. Finkel-
           stein; Cambridge: Cambridge University Press), 130-61.
   1987a   'The Death of Hezekiah' in P.R. Ackroyd, *Studies in the Religious
           Tradition of the Old Testament*, Chapter 10.
   1987b   *Studies in the Religious Tradition of the Old Testament* (London:
           SCM).
Ahlström, G.W.
— 1982   *Royal Administration and National Religion in Ancient Palestine*
           (Studies in the History of the Ancient Near East, 1; Leiden: Brill).
Alt, A.
   1934   'Die Rolle Samariens bei der Entstehung des Judentums', in
           Festschrift O. Procksch, 5-28 = *Kleine Schriften*, II (Munich, 1953),
           316-37 = *Grundfragen der Geschichte des Volkes Israel* (Munich,
           1970), 418-39 (shortened version of the *Kleine Schriften* version).
Avigad, N.
   1976   *Bullae and Seals from a Post-Exilic Judean Archive* (Qedem, 4;
           Jerusalem).
Baltzer, K.
   1961   'Das Ende des Staates Juda und die Messiasfrage', in *Studien zur
           Theologie der alttestamentlichen Überlieferungen* (ed. R. Rend-
           torff and K. Koch; Neukirchen: Neukirchener Verlag), 33-43.
Barth, L.M.
   1976   'The Great Synagogue', *IDBSup*, 844-45.
Beckwith, R.
   1985   *The Old Testament Canon of the New Testament Church* (London:
           SPCK).
Beuken, W.A.M.
   1967   *Haggai–Sacharja 1–8* (Assen: van Gorcum).
Bevan, E.
— 1912   *Jerusalem under the High Priests* (London: Longmans).
Bickermann
   1984   *Cambridge History of Judaism*. (Cambridge: Cambridge Univer-
           sity Press) I.
Blenkinsopp, J.
   1981   'Tanakh and the New Testament: A Christian perspective', in L.
           Boadt, H. Croner, L. Klenicki (eds.), *Biblical Studies. Meeting
           Ground of Jews and Christians* (New York, 1980), 96-119.

Boecker, H.J.
1969   *Die Beurteilung der Anfänge des Königtums in den deuteronomistischen Abschnitten des I. Samuelbuches* (WMANT, 31; Neukirchen: Neukirchener Verlag).
Braun, R.
1971a   'The Message of Chronicles: Rally Round the Temple', *CTM* 42: 502-13.
1971b   *The Significance of 1 Chronicles 22, 28 and 29 for the Structure and Theology of the Work of the Chronicler* (St Louis: Concordia).
1973   'Solomonic Apologetic in Chronicles', *JBL* 92: 503-16.
1979   'Chronicles, Ezra, and Nehemiah: Theology and Literary History', *VTS* 30: 52-64.
Brueggemann, W.
1977   *The Land: Place as Gift, Promise and Challenge in Biblical Faith* (Overtures to Biblical Theology, I; Philadelphia).
Brunet, A.M.
1953   'Le Chroniste et ses Sources', *RB* 60: 483-508.
1954   'Le Chroniste et ses Sources', *RB* 61: 349-86.
Carroll, R.P.
1979   *When Prophecy Failed: Cognitive Dissonance in the Prophetic Tradition of the Old Testament* (London: SCM).
Cassuto, U.
1967   *A Commentary on the Book of Exodus* (ET I. Abrahams; Jerusalem).
Childs, B.S.
1967   *Isaiah and the Assyrian Crisis* (London: SCM).
Clements, R.E.
1965   *God and Temple* (Oxford: Blackwell, 1965).
Coats, G.W.
1968   *Rebellion in the Wilderness* (Nashville: Abingdon).
Cody, A.
1964   'When is the Chosen People called a Goy?' *VT* 14: 1-6.
1973   'Priesthood in the Old Testament', *Studia Missionalia* 22: 309-29.
Coggins, R.J.
1975   *Samaritans and Jews: The Origins of Samaritanism Reconsidered* (Oxford: Basil Blackwell).
Collins, M.F.
1972   'The Hidden Vessels in Samaritan Traditions', *JSJ* 3: 97-116.
Cowley, A.
1923   *Aramaic Papyri of the Fifth Century B.C.* (Oxford: Clarendon Press).
Cross, F.M.
1961   *The Ancient Library of Qumran and Modern Biblical Studies* (rev. edn; Garden City, NY: Doubleday).
1964   'The History of the Biblical Text in the Light of Discoveries in the Judaean Desert', *HTR* 57: 281-99.
1975   'A Reconstruction of the Judean Restoration', *JBL* 94: 4-18 = *Interpretation* 29: 187-204.
Davies, W.D.
1974   *The Gospel and the Land* (Los Angeles).
Diepold, P.
1972   *Israels Land* (BWANT, n.s. 15; Stuttgart).

Eissfeldt, O.
1962   'The Promises of Grace to David in Isaiah 55.1-5', in *Israel's Prophetic Heritage* (ed. B.W. Anderson and W. Harrelson; New York), 196-207.
1965   *The Old Testament: An Introduction* (trans. P.R. Ackroyd; Oxford:Basil Blackwell).
Emerton, J.A.
1966   'Did Ezra go to Jerusalem in 428 B.C.?', *JTS* ns 17: 1-19.
Eskenazi, T.C.
1986   'In an Age of Prose: A Literary Approach to Ezra–Nehemiah' (Diss., Denver).
Eyre, R.
1979   *Ronald Eyre on the Long Search* (London).
Fishbane, M.
1985   *Biblical Interpretation in Ancient Israel* (Oxford: Clarendon Press).
Fohrer, G.
1964   '"Priesterliches Königtum" Ex. XIX.6', *TZ* 19: 359-62.
1968   *Geschichte der israelitischen Religion* (Berlin; ET, Nashville, 1972, London, 1973).
1972   *Theologische Grundstrukturen des Alten Testaments* (Theologische Bibliothek, 24; Berlin).
Freedman, D.N.
1961   'The Chronicler's Purpose', *CBQ* 23: 436-42.
Frei, P. and K. Koch
1984   *Reichsidee und Reichsorganisation im Perserreich* (OBO, 55 Gottingen: Vandenhoeck & Ruprecht).
Frye, R.N.
1984   *The History of Iran*.
Galling, K.
1954   *Chronikbücher, Ezra, Nehemia* (ATD, 12; Göttingen).
Gerleman, G.
1948   *Synoptic Studies in the Old Testament* (Lund C.W.K. Gleerup).
Gilbert, M.
1973   'Comparaison entre les confessions des péchés de Néhémie 9 et Daniel 3 Théod.' (paper read to the Oxford Biblical Congress, September 1973).
Gottwald, N.K.
1964   *All the Kingdoms of the Earth* (New York: Harper & Row).
Goulder, M.
1974   *Midrash and Lection in Matthew* (London: SPCK).
Gunneweg, A.H.J.
1985, 1987   *Esra–Nehemia* (KAT, XIX 1, 2; Gütersloh: Mohn).
Guthrie, H.H.
1966   *Wisdom and Canon* (Evanston, IL: Seabury–Western Theological Seminary).
Hanson, P.D.
1975   The Dawn of Apocalyptic (Philadelphia: Fortress Press).
Hertzberg, H.W.
1960   *Die Samuelbücher* (ATD, 10; Göttingen, 1960; ET *1 and 2 Samuel*; OTL; London: SCM, 1964).

In der Smitten, W.T.
1973   *Ezra* (Studia Semitica Neerlandica, 15; Assen: van Gorcum).
Jacob, E.
1975   'Principe canonique et formation de l'Ancien Testament' (VTS 28; Leiden: Brill).
Johnson, M.D.
1969   *The Purpose of the Biblical Genealogies* (SNTS Monograph Series, 8; Cambridge: Cambridge University Press).
Jones, D.R.
1955   'The Tradition of the Oracles of Isaiah of Jerusalem', *ZAW* 67: 226-46.
Kellermann, U.
1967   *Nehemia: Quellen, Überlieferung und Geschichte* (BZAW 102; Berlin: de Gruyter).
Knight, D.A.
1973   *The Traditions of Israel* (SBL Diss. Series, 9).
Koch, K.
1974   'Ezra and the Origins of Judaism', *JSS* 19: 173-97.
Köhler, L.
        Hebrew Man (London: SCM Press).
Kuhrt, A.
1983   'The Cyrus Cylinder and Achaemenid Imperial Policy', *JSOT* 25: 83-97.
Lemke, W.E.
1965   'The Synoptic Problem in the Chronicler's History', *HTR* 58: 349-63.
Levenson, J.D.
1976   *Theology of the Program of Restoration of Ezekiel 40–48* (Harvard Semitic Monograph Series, 10; Missoula, MT: Scholars Press).
Mason, R.A.
1973   'The Use of Earlier Biblical Material in Zechariah IX–XIV: A Study in Inner Biblical Exegesis' (PhD diss., London, 1973).
1977   'The Purpose of the "Editorial Framework" of the Book of Haggai', *VT* 27: 413-21.
May, H.G.
1968   ' "This people" and "This nation" in Haggai', *VT* 18: 190-97.
Moore, G.F.
1927   *Judaism I* (Cambridge, MA: Harvard University Press).
1930   *Judaism III* (Cambridge, MA: Harvard University Press).
Moran, W.L.
1962   'A Kingdom of Priests', in *The Bible in Current Catholic Thought* (ed. J.L. McKenzie; New York: Herder & Herder), 7-20.
Moriarty, F.L.
1965   'The Chronicler's Account of Hezekiah's Reign', *CBQ* 27: 399-406.
Mosis, R.
1973   *Untersuchungen zur Theologie des chronistischen Geschichtswerks* (Freiburger Theologische Studien, 29; Freiburg: Herder).
Mowinckel, S.
1964a   *Studien zu dem Buche Ezra–Nehemia. I. Die nachchronische Redaktion des Buches. Die Listen* (Oslo).
1964b   *Studien zu dem Buche Ezra–Nehemia. II. Die Nehemia-Denkschrift* (Oslo).

1965 *He that Cometh* (Oxford: Basil Blackwell).
Noordtzij, A.
1940 'Les intentions du Chroniste', *RB* 49.
North, R.
1963 'The Theology of the Chronicler', *JBL* 82: 369-81.
Noth, M.
1957 *Überlieferungsgeschichtliche Studien* (Tübingen [Königsberg]).
[1943]
Olmstead, A.T.
1965 *History of Palestine and Syria* (Grand Rapids).
[1931]
Plöger, O.
1968 *Theocracy and Eschatology* (Oxford: Basil Blackwell) (translation of *Theokratie und Eschatologie* [WMANT, 2; Neukirchen; 2nd rev. edn, 1962]).
Pohlmann, K.-F.
1970 *Studien zum dritten Ezra* (FRLANT, 104; Göttingen: Vandenhoeck & Ruprecht).
1978 *Studien zum Jeremia-buch* (FRLANT, 118; Göttingen Vandenhoeck & Ruprecht).
Polzin, R.
1976 *Late Biblical Hebrew: Toward an Historical Typology of Biblical Hebrew Prose* (Missoula, MT: Scholars Press).
Rad, G. von
1957-60 *Theologie des Alten Testaments* (2 vols.; München: Chr. Kaiser Verlag).
1962 *Theology of the Old Testament*, I (ET; 2 vols.; Edinburgh Oliver & Boyd).
1966 'The Levitical Sermon in I and II Chronicles' (ET), in *The Problem of the Hexateuch and other Essays* (London), 267-80 (orig. pub. in *Festschrift für Otto Procksch* [Leipzig, 1934], 113-24).
Richardson, H.N.
1958 'The Historical Reliability of Chronicles', *JBR* 26: 9-12.
Rost, L.
1934 'Die Bezeichnungen für Land und Volk im Alten Testament', in *Festschrift Otto Procksch* (Leipzig), 125-44.
Rowley, H.H.
1962 'The Samaritan Schism in Legend and History' in *Israel's Prophetic Heritage* (ed. B.W. Anderson and W. Harrelson; London: SCM Press), 208-22.
1963 *Men of God* (London).
Rudolph, W.
1954 'Problems of the Books of Chronicles', *VT* 4: 401-409.
1955a *Chronikbücher* (HAT, 21; Tübingen: Mohr [Paul Siebeck]).
1955b *Esra und Nehemia* (HAT, 20; Tübingen: Mohr).
Ryle, H.E.
1909 *The Canon of the Old Testament* (London: Macmillan).
Sancisi-Weerdenburg, H.W.A.M.
1980 *Yauna en Persai, Grieken en Perzan in een ander perspectief* (Groningen).

Schultz, C.
1980   'The Political Tensions Reflected in Ezra–Nehemiah', in *Scripture in Context. Essays on the Comparative Method* (ed. C.D. Evans *et al.*; Pittsburgh: Pickwick Press), 221-44.
Schürer, E.
1979   *The History of the Jewish People in the Age of Jesus Christ* II (rev. edn by F. Vermes, F. Millar and M. Black; Edinburgh: T. & T. Clark).
Smart, J.D.
1965   *History and Theology in Second Isaiah* (Philadelphia: Fortress Press).
Smith, M.
1971   *Palestinian Parties and Politics that Shaped the Old Testament* (New York).
Speiser, E.A.
1960   'People and Nation of Israel', *JBL* 79: 159-63.
Spek, R.J. van der
1983   'Cyrus de Pers in assyrisch perspectief', *Tijdschrift voor Geschiedenis* 96: 1-27.
Steck, O.H.
1967   *Israel und das gewaltsame Geschick der Propheten* (WMANT, 32; Neukirchen: Neukirchener Verlag).
1968   'Das Problem theologischer Strömungen in nachexilischer Zeit', *Evangelische Theologie* 28: 445-58.
Stern, E.
1971   'Seal Impressions in the Achaemenian Style in the Province of Judah', *BASOR* 202: 6-16.
1981   'The Province of Yehud: The Vision and the Reality', *The Jerusalem Cathedra–1981*, 9-21.
1982   *The Material Culture of the Land of the Bible in the Persian Period* (Warminster: Aris and Phillips).
Stinespring, W.F.
1961   'Eschatology in Chronicles', *JBL* 80: 209-19.
Stoebe, H.J.
1973   *Das erste Buch Samuelis* (KAT, VIII, I; Gütersloh: Mohn).
Swart, J.
1911   *De Theologie van Kronieken* (Groningen).
Talmon, S.
1976   'Ezra and Nehemiah', in *IDBSup*, 317-28.
Throntveit, M.A.
1982   'Linguistic Analogies and the Question of Authorship in Chronicles, Ezra and Nehemiah', *VT* 32: 201-16.
Tunyogi, A.C.
1969   *The Rebellions of Israel* (Richmond, VA).
Vaux, R. de
1961   *Ancient Israel* (ET; London).
Vermeylen, J.
1977, 1978 *Du prophète Isaïe à l'apocalyptique*, I, II (Études Bibliques; Paris: Gabalda).
Vink, J.G.
1969   *The Priestly Code* (*Oudestamentische Studiën*, 15; Leiden: Brill).

Vogt, H.C.M.
1966   *Studie zur nachexilischen Gemeinde in Esra–Nehemia* (Werl).
Welch, A.C.
1939   *The Work of the Chronicler* (London).
Wellhausen, J.
1883 [1878] *Prolegomena* (Berlin; ET, Edinburgh, 1885 [1957]).
Welten, P.
1973   *Geschichte und Geschichtsdarstellung in den Chronikbüchern* (WMANT, 42; Neukirchen: Neukirchener Verlag).
Werner, W.
1982   *Eschatologische Texte in Jesaja 1–39: Messias, heiliger Rest, Völker* (Forschung zur Bibel, 46; Würzburg: Echter Verlag).
Widengren, G.
1977   'The Persian Period', in *Israelite and Judaean History* (ed. J.H. Hayes and J.M. Miller; OTL; London: SCM Press), 489-538.
Willi, T.
1972   *Die Chronik als Auslegung* (FRLANT, 106; Göttingen: Vandenhoeck & Ruprecht).
Williamson, H.G.M.
1976   'The Accession of Solomon in the Books of Chronicles', *VT* 26: 351-61.
1977   *Israel in the Books of Chronicles* (Cambridge: Cambridge University Press).
1982   *1 and 2 Chronicles* (New Century Bible Commentary; Grand Rapids: Eerdmans).
1983   'The Composition of Ezra i–vi', *JTS* ns 4: 1-30.
Wilson, R.R.
1972   'Genealogy and History in the Old Testament. Form and Function of Old Testament Genealogies in their Near Eastern Context' (Diss. Yale).
1976   *Genealogy and History in the Biblical World* (New Haven: Yale University Press) (a revision of Wilson 1972).
Zimmerli, W.
1972   *Grundriss der alttestamentlichen Theologie* (Theologische Wissenschaft, 3; Stuttgart: Kohlhammer).

INDEXES

INDEX OF BIBLICAL REFERENCES

OLD TESTAMENT

INDEX OF AUTHORS

JOURNAL FOR THE STUDY OF THE OLD TESTAMENT

Supplement Series